COMMENTARIES
on ISAIAH *in the*
BOOK *of* MORMON

compiled by

K. DOUGLAS BASSETT

Covenant Communications, Inc.

Covenant

OTHER BOOKS COMPILED BY K. DOUGLAS BASSETT:

Latter-day Commentary on the Book of Mormon

Cover image *Christ Blesses the Nephite Children* © Robert T. Barrett

Published by Covenant Communications, Inc.
American Fork, Utah

Printed in Canada
First Printing: October 2003

09 08 07 06 05 04 03   10 9 8 7 6 5 4 3 2 1

ISBN 1-59156-292-9

Introduction

When I first read the Book of Mormon I found the Isaiah sections of the text most intimidating. From that moment I mentally sectioned off Isaiah's message, so that each time I traveled through the Nephite record I could glide over his words without the risk of being overwhelmed. In the process, I picked up just enough understanding that I could go into a seminary or Gospel Doctrine class and survive the experience.

However, a number of years ago I decided it was time to end the charade and honestly tackle the text of Isaiah. The result has been a wonderful journey of understanding. In my attempt to digest Isaiah's words, it seems that he has digested me. The Savior said to the Nephites, "Great are the words of Isaiah" (3 Ne. 23:1–3). Over the years I interpreted the word "great" as meaning "large like a mountain, almost insurmountable." Now that I have come to love the Isaiah text, I see this word as being an adjective of quality rather than quantity. Great, in this context, speaks of great worth and beauty, like a precious treasure that can only be mined through study and revelation.

This book is meant to be a companion volume to *The Latter-day Commentary on the Book of Mormon.* Like my first book, this commentary is designed to travel chronologically through the Isaiah chapters of the Book of Mormon. I have tried to rely on the Brethren in areas of doctrine, while leaning on the scholars in the arena of culture, language, history, and setting.

The purpose of this commentary is to aid gospel teachers as well as serious students in their studies. I did not compile this commentary in order to replace or overshadow the scriptures in any way! In fact, it is to be used as a companion to the scriptures.

I have come to love Isaiah as his words have brought me closer to the Lord. My hope is that this book will aid the reader on the same journey.

Dedication

I have dedicated this book to my wife Arlene. Her support and love have cradled me through nearly thirty years of marriage. Her efforts in this book have been such that its completion would have been impossible without her input.

Acknowledgments

I am especially grateful to my friend and fellow teacher Dr. Paul Hyde for his research in Conference Reports. Through his efforts this book has a flow of input from the Brethren which is the foundation of the text.

Finally, I give heartfelt thanks to Kris Swinson, Shauna Humphreys, and all those at Covenant who have given of themselves in order to strengthen this book.

Preface

If our eternal salvation depends upon our ability to understand the writings of Isaiah as fully and truly as Nephi understood them—and who shall say such is not the case!—how shall we fare in that great day when with Nephi we shall stand before the pleasing bar of Him who said: "Great are the words of Isaiah"? (3 Ne. 23:1). . . . It just may be that my salvation (and yours also!) does in fact depend upon our ability to understand the writings of Isaiah as fully and truly as Nephi understood them.

(Bruce R. McConkie, *Ensign*, Oct. 1973, 78.)

Isaiah is by every standard *the* messianic prophet of the Old Testament and as such is the most penetrating prophetic voice in that record. He, more than any other witness in the Old World, saw and wrote and prophesied of the Savior's coming both in the meridian of time and again in the latter days. . . .

Some 433 verses of Isaiah—roughly a third of the entire book—are quoted in the Book of Mormon. (When accounting for several of the same verses quoted more than once and a few verses clearly drawn from Isaiah but not identified as such in the text, the total number of Book of Mormon verses from Isaiah may run as high as 446. See Monte C. Nyman, *Great Are the Words of Isaiah* (Salt Lake City: Bookcraft, 1980), 283–87.) One student of Isaiah documents that no less than 391 of those verses refer to the attributes, appearance, majesty, and mission of Jesus Christ. (See Nyman, *Great Are the Words of Isaiah*, 7.) Another scholar [Donald Parry] has pointed out that Isaiah provided at least sixty-one names and titles of the Father and of the Son in his writings, most of those referring to some aspect of the mission of Christ. Those sixty-one titles are found 708 times in the Book of Isaiah, making an average appearance of once every 1.9 verses.

(Jeffrey R. Holland, *Christ and the New Covenant* [Salt Lake City: Deseret Book Co., 1997], 75–76.)

Regretfully I find that in some of our theological classes, and in our seminaries, not only pupils but teachers are . . . segregating the words of the Book of Isaiah, part as being his and other portions as the works of another. Could there be a grosser inconsistency than that of proclaiming a belief in the authenticity of the Book of Mormon while teaching or believing that the Book of Isaiah is other than what it purports to be—the writings of Isaiah the son of Amoz throughout?

(James E. Talmage, *Conference Report*, Apr. 1929, 47.)

1 Ne. 20–21

Toward the close of his book, Nephi quotes two chapters of Isaiah (48 and 49) in full. This would indeed be a daring thing for a forger to do—to include whole pages of the Bible in a work designed to fool the Bible-reading public. Still worse, the language is, without any attempt at disguise, that of the King James version. If the author of the Book of Mormon were an impostor, his attempts to deceive are prodigiously artless.

But the Book of Mormon follows the language of the King James Bible only as far as the latter conveys the correct meaning of the original. . . .

If we underline in red every word in the Book of Mormon text of Isaiah 48 and 49 that is not found in the King James Bible and vice versa, we get a surprising display of color, especially in the Book of Mormon. Most of the differences are quite minor ones, such as an extra "nevertheless," "yea," "but," "behold," etc., but there are four passages that stand out spectacularly in almost solid red. They are 48:1, 14, and 49:1, 13. Now one of the important results of recent Dead Sea Scrolls investigations is the recognition that the text of the Septuagint (the Greek translation of the Old Testament done in the third century B.C.) opens the door to very old and valuable texts of the Old Testament that differ quite markedly from the Masoretic text on which our King James translation is based. . . .

We do find significant variations when we compare chapters 48 and 49 of Isaiah in the King James (Masorete) Bible and the Septuagint. Again we compare the red markings, and again just four passages stand out, to wit, 48:1, 14, and 49:1, 13, that is, the Book of Mormon conflicts with the King James Bible in the *same* verses in which the Septuagint and the Masorete texts conflict!

(Hugh W. Nibley, *Since Cumorah,* 2nd ed. [Salt Lake City: Deseret Book Co., 1988], 113–14.
For further explanation, refer to 114–18.)

1 Ne. 20:1   **WATERS OF JUDAH—WATERS OF BAPTISM**
(Isa. 48:1)

This clause first appeared in the 1840 and 1842 editions of the Book of Mormon. It did not appear again until the 1920 edition, and it has been in all editions since that time. It appears to be a prophetic commentary by Joseph Smith to explain the meaning of the phrase "out of the waters of Judah." . . . If this phrase were a restoration of the original text, as found in the more pure version on the brass plates from which it comes, it would have appeared in the 1830 edition of the Book of Mormon. . . . Through the use of this phrase, Joseph Smith is calling our attention to the fact that the ordinance of baptism was as common to the people of the Old Testament as it was to the people of the Book of Mormon.

(Joseph Fielding McConkie and Robert L. Millet, *Doctrinal Commentary on the Book of Mormon,* 4 vols.
[Salt Lake City: Bookcraft, 1987–1992], 1:151–52.)

The second edition of the Book of Mormon contains an addition not found in the first: "out of the waters of Judah, *or out of the waters of baptism.*" It is said that Parley P. Pratt suggested the phrase, and certainly Joseph Smith approved it, for it stands in all the early editions after the first. Those added words are not only permissible—they are necessary. . . . Isaiah did not have to tell his ancient hearers that he had the waters of baptism in mind, but it is necessary to tell it to the modern reader, who without such an explanation would miss the point—for him the translation would be a misleading one without that specification. Where continued revelation is accepted and where all the prophets are speaking the same piece, this sort of thing makes no difficulty at all.

(Hugh W. Nibley, *Since Cumorah*, 2nd ed. [Salt Lake City: Deseret Book Co., 1988], 133.)

It is interesting that the excavations around the temple site in Jerusalem have revealed numerous baptismal fonts which archaeologists refer to as "ceremonial baths." Today, the Jewish people have virtually abandoned the rite of baptism, although they have carefully preserved the ritual of circumcision. Significantly, circumcision was given to God's people in the days of Abraham to remind them of baptism! The Lord said:

"My people have gone astray from my precepts, and have not kept mine ordinances, which I gave unto their fathers;

"And they have not observed mine anointing, and the burial, OR BAPTISM wherewith I commanded them;

"But have turned from the commandment, and taken unto themselves the washing of children, and the blood of sprinkling" (JST, Gen. 17:4–6; emphasis added).

This would suggest that the people were participating in infant baptism and sprinkling their children with blood after the manner of the heathens. The Lord said the ordinance of circumcision was being introduced so that when male children were circumcised on the eighth day, it would remind them that their children were to be baptized in their eighth YEAR. The Lord said that "children are not accountable before me [or eligible for baptism] until they are eight years old" (JST, Gen. 17:11).

(W. Cleon Skousen, *Isaiah Speaks to Modern Times* [Salt Lake City: The Ensign Publishing Company, 1984], 602.)

1 Ne. 20:2   NOT STAY THEMSELVES
(Isa. 48:2)

Isaiah points out that the tribes of Israel, including the Jews, take pride in identifying themselves with the holy city of Jerusalem. However, the Book of Mormon version then goes on to say, "but they do NOT stay themselves upon the God of Israel, who is the Lord of Hosts" (1 Nephi 20:2; emphasis added). Notice that the absence of the word "not" in the King James translation almost makes the verse meaningless. The Book of Mormon corrects this error.

(W. Cleon Skousen, *Isaiah Speaks to Modern Times* [Salt Lake City: The Ensign Publishing Company, 1984], 603.)

1 Ne. 20:3   **SUDDENLY**
(Isa. 48:3)

The Lord revealed it "suddenly," long before anyone would have guessed it. (Examples of this would be the translation of the City of Enoch; the cleansing of the earth by a universal flood; the escape of Israel from slavery in Egypt; the captivity and transmigration of the northern Ten Tribes to Assyria, etc. God often revealed these events to his prophets centuries before they occurred.)

(W. Cleon Skousen, *Isaiah Speaks to Modern Times* [Salt Lake City: The Ensign Publishing Company, 1984], 604.)

1 Ne. 20:4   **THY BROW BRASS**
(Isa. 48:4)

These introductory words of Isaiah apply so well to Laman and Lemuel, who often act wickedly but consider themselves righteous. Indeed, Isaiah's opening comments in chapter 48, though addressed to all Israel, seem to speak directly to the rebellious and stubborn members of Nephi's family. Isaiah's description of Israel—"thou art obstinate, and thy neck is an iron sinew, and thy brow brass" (Isaiah 48:4, parallel to 1 Nephi 20:4)—fits Nephi's older brothers Laman and Lemuel perfectly.

(Andrew C. Skinner, *Isaiah in the Book of Mormon,* ed. Donald W. Parry and John W. Welch
[Provo, Utah: Foundation for Ancient Research and Mormon Studies, 1998], 100.)

1 Ne. 20:10   **THE FURNACE OF AFFLICTION**
(Isa. 48:10; D&C 121:7–8; 122:5, 7; 101:2, 4, 127:2; 2 Cor. 12:9; 2 Ne. 2:2,11; Matt. 11:28–30; refer in *Latter-day Commentary on the Book of Mormon,* Bassett, to Eth. 12:26–27)

Our needed conversions are often achieved more readily by suffering and adversity than by comfort and tranquillity. . . . Most of us experience some measure of what the scriptures call "the furnace of affliction" (Isa. 48:10; 1 Ne. 20:10). Some are submerged in service to a disadvantaged family member. Others suffer the death of a loved one or the loss or postponement of a righteous goal like marriage or childbearing. Still others struggle with personal impairments or with feelings of rejection, inadequacy, or depression. Through the justice and mercy of a loving Father in Heaven, the refinement and sanctification possible through such experiences can help us achieve what God desires us to become.

We are challenged to move through a process of conversion toward that status and condition called eternal life. This is achieved not just by doing what is right, but by doing it for the right reason—for the pure love of Christ.

(Dallin H. Oaks, *Ensign,* Nov. 2000, 33–34.)

The terrain over which we have traveled is a grim reminder that struggle, persecution, and sorrow have been the lot of our forebears. Kirtland, Jackson County, Clay County, Haun's Mill, and Nauvoo seem synonymous with suffering—a part of the tribulation the Lord promised that his people would have to endure (see D&C 58:3).

As we look back in retrospect, we see that it was because of the opposition encountered in our early history that our progress today has been made possible.

(Howard W. Hunter, *Ensign,* May 1980, 25.)

Being human, we would expel from our lives physical pain and mental anguish and assure ourselves of continual ease and comfort, but if we were to close the doors upon sorrow and distress, we might be excluding our greatest friends and benefactors. Suffering can make saints of people as they learn patience, long-suffering, and self-mastery. The sufferings of our Savior were part of his education.

(Spencer W. Kimball, *Faith Precedes the Miracle* [Salt Lake City: Deseret Book Co., 1972], 98.)

Let us alone, and we will send Elders to the uttermost parts of the earth, and gather out Israel, wherever they are; and if you persecute us, we will do it the quicker, because we are naturally dull when let alone, and are disposed to take a little sleep, a little slumber, and a little rest. If you let us alone, we will do it a little more leisurely; but if you persecute us, we will sit up nights to preach the Gospel.

(Brigham Young, *Discourses of Brigham Young,* ed. John A. Widtsoe
[Salt Lake City: Deseret Book Co., 1925], 351–52.)

Let any people enjoy peace and quietness, unmolested, undisturbed,—never be persecuted for their religion, and they are very likely to neglect their duty, to become cold and indifferent, and lose their faith.

(Brigham Young, *Journal of Discourses,* 7:42.)

Repeated assurances have been given regarding the benefits and blessings of positive responses to adversity, however undeserved. . . . Spiritual refinement may be realized in the furnace of affliction. (See 1 Ne. 20:10.) Thereby we may be prepared to experience personal and direct contact with God.

In modern revelation we are instructed, "Sanctify yourselves that your minds become single to God, and the days will come that you shall see him . . ." (D&C 88:68). Ancient prophets teach us that "when he shall appear, . . . we shall see him as he is . . . [and] be purified even as he is pure" (Moro. 7:48; see also 1 Jn. 3:2).

The Lord's own way of preparing us to see him as he is may well include the refining furnace of affliction. . . . Without adversity, we may tend to forget the divine purpose of mortality and live our lives focused on the transitory things of the world.

Should we therefore desire or seek to experience adversity and suffering? No! May we appropriately try to avoid it? Yes! Is it proper to ask for relief? Yes, always adding, in accordance with the Savior's example, "nevertheless not as I will, but as thou wilt" (Matt. 26:39).

There are encouragement and comfort in knowing that we will not be tested beyond our capacity to endure, that we will benefit from our adversities, and that the resources and circumstances necessary for us to do so will be provided. (See 1 Cor. 10:13.)

(Ronald E. Poelman, *Ensign,* May 1989, 24.)

1 Ne. 20:11   I WILL NOT SUFFER MY NAME TO BE POLLUTED
(Isa. 48:11; Ex. 20:7; Mosiah 13:15; D&C 136:21; 63:61–62)

Recently our family was viewing what was supposed to be a wholesome movie on videotape. Suddenly, one of the actors used a vulgar expression. Embarrassed, we began to smooth this over for our ten-year-old daughter. She quickly assured us that we needn't worry because she heard worse than that every day from the boys and girls at her school. . . . The nature and extent of profanity and vulgarity in our society is a measure of its deterioration.

I cannot remember when I first heard profane and vulgar expressions in common use around me. I suppose it was from adults in the barnyard or the barracks. Today, our young people hear such expressions from boys and girls in their grade schools, from actors on stage and in the movies, from popular novels, and even from public officials and sports heroes. Television and videotapes bring profanity and vulgarity into our homes.

For many in our day, the profane has become commonplace and the vulgar has become acceptable. Surely this is one fulfillment of the Book of Mormon prophecy that in the last days "there shall be great pollutions upon the face of the earth" (Morm. 8:31).

The names of God the Father and his Son, Jesus Christ, are sacred. The prophet Isaiah taught that the Lord will not suffer these names to be dishonored—"polluted" as the scriptures say. (See 1 Ne. 20:11; Isa. 48:11.)

(Dallin H. Oaks, *Ensign,* May 1986, 49.)

The Lord implies that Israel will suffer even more because he will not allow his "name to be polluted" by his chosen people (1 Ne. 20:11), and this greater affliction will include Judah's deportation at the hands of the king of Babylon. At the same time, however, Jehovah will not "give [his] glory unto another" (1 Ne. 20:11, parallel to Isa. 48:11). In other words, regardless of Israel's transgressions, God will not select another group to be his "chosen" people.

(Andrew C. Skinner, *Isaiah in the Book of Mormon,* ed. Donald W. Parry and John W. Welch
[Provo, Utah: Foundation for Ancient Research and Mormon Studies, 1998], 101.)

The history of the house of Israel is the history of a martyred nation, suffering for the welfare of other nations—whatever may be said of the immediate cause of their woes, the transgressions that justified the Shepherd in bringing upon His sheep troubles that were doubtless among the "offenses" that "must needs come.". . . The chosen people were scattered over the world, in order that Gospel truth, following the red track of their martyrdom, might make its way more readily among the peoples with whom they were mingled.

(Orson F. Whitney, *Saturday Night Thoughts* [Salt Lake City: The Deseret News, 1921], 138.)

1 Ne. 20:12   MY CALLED
(Isa. 48:12; Abr. 2:9–11; Deut. 32:7–9)

Called to what? Chosen for what? . . . Called into the Church, but chosen to be sealed up unto eternal life and to have one's calling and election made sure.

(Bruce R. McConkie, *Doctrinal New Testament Commentary*, 3 vols. [Salt Lake City: Bookcraft, 1966–1973], 3:349.)

The phrase "my called" has reference to the foreordination given those born into the house of Israel to be the ministers of salvation to all other peoples of the earth (see Abraham 2:9–11; Deuteronomy 32:7–9).

(Joseph Fielding McConkie and Robert L. Millet, *Doctrinal Commentary on the Book of Mormon*, 4 vols. [Salt Lake City: Bookcraft, 1987–1992], 155.)

Isaiah decrees that Israel is God's chosen people because they were called and foreordained by him in premortality to be such (see 1 Ne. 20:12, parallel to Isa. 48:12)—a doctrine reminiscent of instruction given to Israel through Moses in an earlier day (see, for example, Ex. 4:22).

(Andrew C. Skinner, *Isaiah in the Book of Mormon*, ed. Donald W. Parry and John W. Welch [Provo, Utah: Foundation for Ancient Research and Mormon Studies, 1998], 101.)

1 Ne. 20:12   FIRST AND LAST
(Isa. 48:12; 41:4; 44:6; Rev. 22:13; Alma 11:39; D&C 110:4; Heb. 12:2)

These words express the eternal nature of the Lord Jesus Christ . . . Jesus was the first to be born in the spirit. He is the first in position and dominion. He is the last in that he will continue as God, preeminent over all, through all eternity. Jesus is also the first and the last in that he is both the "author and finisher of our faith" (Heb. 12:2).

(Donald W. Parry, Jay A. Parry, and Tina M. Peterson,
Understanding Isaiah [Salt Lake City: Deseret Book Co., 1998], 418.)

1 Ne. 20:13   **RIGHT HAND**
(Isa. 48:13; Ps. 110:1; Matt. 22:44; 25:31–46; 26:63–64; Acts 7:55)

The showing favor to the right hand or side is not something invented by man but was revealed from the heavens in the beginning. . . . There are numerous passages in the scriptures referring to the right hand, indicating that it is a symbol of righteousness and was used in the making of covenants. . . . The right hand or side is called the dexter and the left the sinister. Dexter connotes something favorable; sinister, something unfavorable or unfortunate. It is a well-established practice in the Church to partake of the sacrament with the right hand and also to anoint with the right hand, according to the custom which the scriptures indicate is, and always was, approved by divine injunction.

(Joseph Fielding Smith, *Answers to Gospel Questions,* 5 vols.
[Salt Lake City: Deseret Book Co., 1957–1966], 1:156–58.)

Two domains of imagery emerge. The first is one of prominence or favored position. Aaron and his sons were to be sprinkled with blood on their right ear, thumb and big toe (Ex. 29:19–20; cf. Lev. 8:23–26; 14:14–28). To be seated at the right hand is to occupy a position of recognition and prestige. Solomon's mother was given a throne at the right hand of the king (1 Kings 2:19). The messianic king is ordered to be seated at the right hand of the Lord, a position of conquest and rule (Ps. 110:1; cf. Matt. 22:44). Jesus announced his destiny to be seated at the right hand of God (Mark 14:62; Luke 22:69). Finally, to have extended the right hand was an indication of specification and favor (Gal. 2:9; Rev. 1:17). . . .

The second domain of "right hand" portrays an image of intense power and strength. Most frequently it is used by the psalmists of the Lord as a God who rescues and sustains by means of his mighty "right hand" (Ps. 17:7; 18:35; 21:8; 118:15b–16; 138:7; cf. Ex. 15:6, 12). . . . The conquering Jesus is portrayed as holding the seven stars in his "right hand" (Rev. 1:16; cf. 1:20; 2:1). . . .

The symbolic significance of the right and left hands are evidenced in Joseph's attempt to change his father's deliberate crossing of his hands in the blessing of Ephraim and Manasseh (Gen. 48:13–18).

(*Dictionary of Biblical Imagery*, ed. Leland Ryken, James C. Wilhoit, and
Tremper Longman III [Downers Grove, Illinois: InterVarsity Press, 1998], 361.)

1 Ne. 20:14–15   THE LORD HATH LOVED HIM
(Isa. 48:14–15)

Sidney Sperry suggests the servant is Cyrus, king of Persia, through whom the Lord will accomplish His work. . . . This is consistent with the footnote reference in the LDS edition of the Bible. Monte Nyman believes the referent of "him" is Israel . . . while Victor Ludlow believes the description best fits the Lord Jesus Christ Himself . . . In the latter instance, Jesus could be delivering a prophecy about Himself as a Spokesman for the Father. In any event, the work to be done by this servant, whoever he may be, has the divine approbation of Deity.

(Hoyt W. Brewster, Jr., *Isaiah Plain and Simple* [Salt Lake City: Deseret Book Co., 1995], 181–82.)

Isaiah seems to be alluding to a specific historical episode when he proclaims that one will come along who will "do his pleasure on Babylon," and whose "arm [will] come upon the Chaldeans" (1 Ne. 20:14, parallel to Isa. 48:14). Surely this is a prophetic reference to Cyrus the Great, king of Persia, whom the Lord raised up to conquer the very kingdom responsible for the fall of Jerusalem in 586 B.C.—Babylon. History shows that Cyrus was indeed a redeemer to Israel who did "his pleasure on Babylon" and afterwards sponsored the return of Israel's remnant to their homeland. He even financially supported the reconstruction of Jerusalem and the holy temple. But this prophecy also points to the Lord himself, who, as scripture teaches, stands behind those whom he raises up and who guides the destinies of nations (see, for example, 2 Kgs. 17).

(Andrew C. Skinner, *Isaiah in the Book of Mormon,* ed. Donald W. Parry and John W. Welch [Provo, Utah: Foundation for Ancient Research and Mormon Studies, 1998], 102.)

1 Ne. 20:14, 20   BABYLON
(Isa. 48:14, 20; D&C 133:5, 7, 14; refer in this text to 2 Ne. 23:1.)

1 Ne. 20:20   GO YE FORTH OF BABYLON . . . THE CHALDEANS
(Isa. 48:20; Jer. 25:11; 29:10)

The Lord promised ancient Israel that after seventy years of Babylonian captivity, Israel would be blessed to return to the land of her inheritance (Jer. 25:11; 29:10). A second meaning is to leave the carnal world for the spiritual.

(Donald W. Parry, Jay A. Parry, and Tina M. Peterson, *Understanding Isaiah* [Salt Lake City: Deseret Book Co., 1998], 421.)

Verse 20 also seems to hold a double meaning. Israel was commanded to go forth from Babylon in a literal sense, and this they did when they returned to Jerusalem in 538 B.C. Through Cyrus, the Lord redeemed his people and brought them out of Babylon after they had endured fifty years of captivity. But Israel was also commanded to go forth or flee from Babylon in a spiritual sense. In a revelation given to the Prophet Joseph Smith in 1831, when the Church was still young, the Lord issued a similar command, adding a few words of clarification: "Go ye out from among the nations, even from Babylon, from the midst of wickedness, which is spiritual Babylon" (D&C 133:14). Thus ancient Israel was to go forth from the literal place called Babylon as well as to flee from the wickedness and spiritual corruption that existed in their world—just as modern Israel has been commanded to do.

(Andrew C. Skinner, *Isaiah in the Book of Mormon*, ed. Donald W. Parry and John W. Welch
[Provo, Utah: Foundation for Ancient Research and Mormon Studies, 1998], 103.)

1 Ne. 20:21–22   NO PEACE UNTO THE WICKED
(Isa. 48:21–22)

Isaiah reinforces the idea of God's power to save and redeem Israel by reminding his audience of the great miracles Jehovah performed during an earlier but defining moment in Israel's redemptive history—the time when they were brought forth out of Egypt . . . Yet, despite all that the Lord has done and will continue to do in behalf of his people, they will enjoy no lasting peace or geographical redemption while they remain wicked. . . .

These verses are especially well suited to Nephi's family, particularly to the rebellious and spiritually impoverished brothers. Though Isaiah's words seem to have made little sense to many in Nephi's audience (see 2 Ne. 25:1–2), there were some gathered in the group to whom the Spirit of the Lord testified of the truthfulness of Isaiah's words. Father Lehi and his younger son Jacob seem to have been forcefully affected by Isaiah's message of hope and redemption for a broken-off branch of Israel (see 2 Ne. 1:1 and 10:7–9, respectively), even if Laman and Lemuel and their followers continued to waver. It would be but a few short years before Lehi's family learned that Jerusalem's destruction had occurred according to the promise of the Lord (see 2 Ne. 1:4).

(Andrew C. Skinner, *Isaiah in the Book of Mormon*, ed. Donald W. Parry and John W. Welch
[Provo, Utah: Foundation for Ancient Research and Mormon Studies, 1998], 103–104.)

1 Ne. 21
Chapter 21 Foretells the Mission of Latter-day Saints & the Destiny of the Land of America in Connection with the House of Israel.

The patriarchs and prophets who saw by vision and revelation the last dispensation and fulness of times plainly tell us what is to come to pass. The 49th chapter of Isaiah [1 Ne. 21] is having its fulfillment.

(Wilford Woodruff, Joseph Fielding Smith, *The Signs of the Times*
[Independence, Missouri: Press of Zion's Printing & Publishing Co., 1943], 96.)

1 Ne. 21:1–6   SERVANT SONG
(Isa. 48:1–6; 42:1–4; 50:4–9; 52:13–53; Jer. 23:1–2; refer in this text to 2 Ne. 7:4–9.)

Jewish theology maintains that this prophecy of the "suffering servant" depicts the Jewish nation, but, taken together, the words Isaiah uses to describe this helper of Israel in the latter days apply only to two beings: the Messiah and the Prophet Joseph Smith. Nephi and Lehi seem to know not only that Isaiah intended to prophesy of Jesus *and* Joseph Smith (see 2 Ne. 3), but also that the latter-day restoration of the gospel would help bring about the final redemption of Israel.

That these characteristics refer primarily to the Savior is probably obvious to many Christians, but Joseph Smith also fits many of the qualifications of that special servant. After all, every true prophet is a type, a foreshadowing, or a symbol of the Lord Jesus Christ.

(Andrew C. Skinner, *Isaiah in the Book of Mormon,* ed. Donald W. Parry and John W. Welch
[Provo, Utah: Foundation for Ancient Research and Mormon Studies, 1998], 107.)

1 Ne. 21:1, 8   ISLES
(Isa. 49:1, 8)

Sir Isaac Newton observes that to the Hebrews the continents of Asia and Africa were "the earth," because they had access to them by land, while the parts of the earth to which they sailed over the sea were "the isles of the sea."

(George Reynolds and Janne M. Sjodahl, *Commentary on the Book of Mormon,*
ed. Philip C. Reynolds, 7 vols. [Salt Lake City: Deseret Book Co., 1955–1961], 1:214.)

Can refer to islands proper or . . . lands accessible by sea. . . . Although Solomon and then Jehoshaphat engaged in some seafaring expeditions (cf. 1 Kgs. 9:26–28; 22:48), the Israelites were not a seafaring people and their first port city, Joppa, did not come into their possession until the time of the Maccabbees. . . . For Israel, knowledge of the islands and coastlands of the Mediterranean was based on hearsay, the best source being the Phoenecians, their seafaring neighbors. . . .

Most of the OT's references to islands occur in Isaiah. . . . The islands are an image of the far-flung and little-known nations across the Mediterranean world. . . . For Isaiah the islands are images of the ends of the earth, borders of the . . . world that nevertheless fall under the sovereignty of Yahweh.

(*Dictionary of Biblical Imagery*, ed. Leland Ryken, James C. Wilhoit, and
Tremper Longman III, [Downers Grove, Illinois: InterVarsity Press, 1998], 429.)

1 Ne. 21:2   HID ME
(Isa. 49:2; D&C 86:9; Col. 3:3)

The Prophet Joseph Smith gave an interpretation to this phrase. Placing his hands upon one of the faithful members of the Church, he said: "Your life is hid with Christ in God, and so are many others. Nothing but the unpardonable sin can prevent you from inheriting eternal life for you are sealed up by the power of the priesthood unto eternal life, having taken the step necessary for that purpose."

(Hoyt W. Brewster, Jr., *Doctrine and Covenants Encyclopedia*, [Salt Lake City: Bookcraft, 1988], 241–42.)

1 Ne. 21:2   A POLISHED SHAFT
(Isa. 49:2)

I am like a huge, rough stone rolling down from a high mountain; and the only polishing I get is when some corner gets rubbed off by coming in contact with something else, striking with accelerated force against religious bigotry, priestcraft, lawyer-craft, doctor-craft, lying editors, suborned judges and jurors, and the authority of perjured executives, backed by mobs, blasphemers, licentious and corrupt men and women—all hell knocking off a corner here and a corner there. Thus I will become a smooth and polished shaft in the quiver of the Almighty.

(Joseph Smith, *Teachings of the Prophet Joseph Smith*,
comp. Joseph Fielding Smith [Salt Lake City: Deseret Book Co., 1976], 304.)

1 Ne. 21:3   MY SERVANT
(Isa. 49:3; D&C 90:3–4; 133:30–34; Isa. 42:1–4; 49:1–6; 50:4–9;
52:13–53:12)

The one called is God's servant, Israel, as we learn in 49:3 (43:1; 48:12). The name *Israel*, however, may be symbolic for another servant (Jesus Christ, Isaiah, Joseph Smith, another prophet, the tribe of Ephraim, or each of these in turn).

(Donald W. Parry, Jay A. Parry, and Tina M. Peterson,
Understanding Isaiah [Salt Lake City: Deseret Book Co., 1998], 425.)

The servant represented in this verse is the corporate personality of the covenant people. The Church is the servant of the Lord.

(Joseph Fielding McConkie and Robert L. Millet, *Doctrinal Commentary on the Book of Mormon*, 4 vols. [Salt Lake
City: Bookcraft, 1987–1992], 1:159.)

I believe that the servant Isaiah speaks of is none other than the Messiah or Savior. . . .

Other commentaries have suggested that the servant could be Israel, Isaiah, or the prophet of the Restoration—Joseph Smith. . . . Each such conclusion has logical support. Undoubtedly, as is often the case in prophecy, there are multiple applications. . . . The case for Joseph Smith as the promised servant is particularly strong. However, . . . I believe the major focus of *the Servant* should be our Lord and Redeemer, Jesus Christ.
S   piritual darkness will be dispelled by this Servant-Messiah, and prisoners (on both sides of the veil) will be freed from the bondage of sin through their repentance.

(Hoyt W. Brewster, Jr., *Isaiah Plain and Simple* [Salt Lake City: Deseret Book Co., 1995], 186.)

The servant spoken of here is actually Ephraim, who holds the birthright of the twelve tribes (see D&C 133:30–34; Jeremiah 31:9), but specifically it is the Prophet Joseph Smith, who heads the dispensation of the fulness of times (see D&C 90:3–4).

(Monte S. Nyman, *Great Are the Words of Isaiah* [Salt Lake City: Bookcraft, 1980], 177.)

This servant is not named, so readers and scholars often disagree about the servant's identity. Generally, the Jewish scholars believe the servant is either the prophet Isaiah or a representation of the people of Israel in their chosen rule as the Lord's servants to the world. Christian scholars usually believe Jesus Christ is the servant prophesied by Isaiah. Latter-day Saint readers often recognize that the covenant members of the restored gospel serve as the Lord's servants. They as a people, and the prophet of the restoration, Joseph Smith, may be identified as Isaiah's promised servant. . . .

Rather than categorically stating that Isaiah's servant songs apply only to one servant, we might be wise in recognizing that the characteristics of God's servant are best exemplified in Christ and are also demonstrated through the lives of all of God's righteous children. In short, the precise identity of the servant is not as important as studying his characteristics and seeking to develop them in our own lives.

(Victor L. Ludlow, *Isaiah: Prophet, Seer, and Poet* [Salt Lake City: Deseret Book Co., 1982], 358–360.)

1 Ne. 21:4   **LABORED IN VAIN**
(Isa. 49:4)

The servant laments that the people will not listen to him, but he acknowledges that God is his judge and ultimately it is He whom the servant must seek to please.

(Donald W. Parry, Jay A. Parry, and Tina M. Peterson,
Understanding Isaiah [Salt Lake City: Deseret Book Co., 1998], 426.)

1 Ne. 21:6   **SALVATION UNTO THE ENDS OF THE EARTH**
(Isa. 49:6)

In other words, the Lord has a much greater work for the servant than to simply bless Israel—the servant is destined to bless the whole earth.

(Donald W. Parry, Jay A. Parry, and Tina M. Peterson,
Understanding Isaiah [Salt Lake City: Deseret Book Co., 1998], 427.)

1 Ne. 21:6   **A LIGHT TO THE GENTILES**
(Isa. 49:6; 42:6; D&C 86:11; Luke 2:25–32)

How could the Holy One of Israel—who is sinless and perfect, and who is the same everlastingly—come into mortality without remaining as the Sinless One and therefore being a light and an example to all men? If the Great Jehovah . . . was destined to make flesh his tabernacle, how could he do other than bring with him the effulgent light and glory which dwelt in his person? . . .

The prophetic word abounds in such statements as: "The Lord is my light and my salvation." (Ps. 27:1.) "O send out thy light and thy truth: let them lead me." (Ps. 43:3.) "God is the Lord, which hath shewed us light." (Ps. 118:27.) "Thy word is a lamp unto my feet, and a light unto my path." (Ps. 119:105.) None can doubt that the Jewish Jehovah who led their fathers was himself the source of light and truth for all.

With reference to his future Messianic ministry, his ministry among mortals as the Son of God, it is written: "I will also give thee for a light to the Gentiles, that thou mayest be my salvation unto the end of the earth." (Isa. 49:6.)

(Bruce R. McConkie, *The Mortal Messiah*, 4 vols. [Salt Lake City: Deseret Book Co., 1979–1981], 3:147.)

His hearers well knew that their Messiah should stand as a light to all men; that is, they knew that he as the very source of light and truth, would stand forth as a light, an example, a dispenser of truth. . . . Messianic prophecies given to their fathers promised that he would be "a light to the Gentiles."

(Bruce R. McConkie, *Doctrinal New Testament Commentary*, 3 vols.
[Salt Lake City: Bookcraft, 1966–1973], 452–53.)

God's servant not only will gather and restore the descendants of Abraham but will also reach out to the Gentiles. Thus salvation will reach "unto the end of the earth." The *light to the Gentiles* is variously defined in the scriptures as Jesus Christ (Isa. 42:6–7; Luke 2:32), the priesthood

(D&C 86:11), and Zion (60:3). If the servant referred to in this section is not the Messiah himself, he certainly will shine with the light of the Messiah.

(Donald W. Parry, Jay A. Parry, and Tina M. Peterson,
Understanding Isaiah [Salt Lake City: Deseret Book Co., 1998], 427.)

1 Ne. 21:7   SERVANT OF RULERS

The Promised Messiah shall be one "whom man despiseth, . . . whom the nation abhoreth, . . . a servant of rulers." (Isa. 49:7.)

(Bruce R. McConkie, *The Promised Messiah* [Salt Lake City: Deseret Book Co., 1978], 493.)

1 Ne. 21:7   HOLY ONE
(Isa. 49:7)

Christ is the *Holy One*, a designation signifying that he is a holy, pure, sanctified Person, One who was and is without sin, who had no need for repentance, and who stands perfect in all things. . . . (Isa. 43:15; 49:7; Ps. 16:10; Acts 2:27; 3:14; 13:35; 2 Ne. 9:20, 41; 3 Ne. 26:5; Morm. 9:5, 14; D&C 78:16.) . . . (Isa. 6:3). "Holiness unto the Lord" will be emblazoned on useful items of every sort in that millennial day when the Holy One reigns personally upon the earth (Zech. 14:20–21).

(Bruce R. McConkie, *Mormon Doctrine*, 2nd ed. [Salt Lake City: Bookcraft, 1966] 360.)

1 Ne. 21:9   PRISONERS GO FORTH
(Isa. 49:9; 1 Pet. 3:19–20; D&C 138; Isa. 61:1–3; D&C 45:28; 128:22)

Christ brought freedom to mortal beings imprisoned by ignorance, sin, apostasy, and death. He also brought deliverance to those on the other side of the veil who had not heard the gospel but would receive it in their spirit prison. . . . On both sides of the veil, the captives rejoice and praise their God as Christ throws wide the prison doors.

(Jeffrey R. Holland, *Christ and the New Covenant* [Salt Lake City: Deseret Book Co., 1997], 82–83.)

The phrase has a double meaning. It extends the teaching of the restored gospel to both sides of the veil. The promise to those who are in the prison of apostate doctrines and the bondage of false traditions is that they shall be brought out of "captivity." . . . The phrase also refers to the teaching of the gospel to those in the world of the spirits.

(Joseph Fielding McConkie and Robert L. Millet,
Doctrinal Commentary on the Book of Mormon, 4 vols. [Salt Lake City: Bookcraft, 1987–1992], 162.)

Peter, also, in speaking concerning our Savior, says that "He went and preached unto the spirits in prison, which sometimes were disobedient, when once the long-suffering of God waited in the days of Noah" (1 Pet. 3:19, 20). Here then we have an account of our Savior preaching to the spirits in prison, to spirits that had been imprisoned from the days of Noah; and what did He preach to them? That they were to stay there? Certainly not! Let His own declaration testify. "He hath sent me to heal the broken-hearted, to preach deliverance to the captives, and recovering of sight to the blind, to set at liberty them that are bruised." (Luke 4:18.) Isaiah has it—"To bring out the prisoners from the prison, and them that sit in darkness from the prison house" (Isaiah 42:7). It is very evident from this that He not only went to preach to them, but to deliver, or bring them out of the prison house.

(Joseph Smith, *Teachings of the Prophet Joseph Smith*,
comp. by Joseph Fielding Smith [Salt Lake City: Deseret Book Co., 1976], 219.)

1 Ne. 21:10   SPRINGS OF WATER
(Isa. 49:10; Ether 8:26; 12:28; Num. 20:1–13; Jer. 2:13; 17:13; Alma 5:34; 42:27; John 4:7–14; Rev. 7:17; 21:6; 22:17)

This passage refers to the Lord's blessings for those who are returning from exile, as well as for those returning from spiritual bondage. In physical captivity, exiles suffer from hunger and thirst. The heat of the sun threatens them. Spiritual exiles thirst for gospel truth and peace. The Lord protects and nourishes them. In all circumstances, it is only through Christ that spiritual hunger can be satisfied (John 6:35; Alma 31:38; 32:42; 3 Ne. 12:6; 20:8). The expression "springs of water" symbolizes living water (Isa. 35:6–7; 41:17–18; 43:19–20), or Jesus Christ.

(Donald W. Parry, *Visualizing Isaiah*
[Provo, Utah: The Foundation for Ancient Research and Mormon Studies, 2001], 67.)

Without water man dies—temporally and spiritually. Bread and breath and water, these three, they are the essentials of existence. If any one of them is withdrawn, life ceases—temporally and spiritually. . . .

Even the Son of God—pierced, bleeding, in pain beyond recording, hanging at death's door on the cross of Calvary—had but one plea pertaining to his physical suffering, and that was the agonizing cry, "I thirst." (John 19:28.) How vital it is that men have water. A dearth of drink deals death to those so deprived. Those who dwell in deserts and pitch their tents on arid plains, as ancient Israel often did, have the need and desire for drink ever before them. . . .

We might well expect to find Messianic prophecies saying that King-Messiah, during his mortal ministry, would be the source of living waters. . . . One of the greatest of these is Isaiah's proclamation that "a king shall reign in righteousness," and that among other things, he shall be "as rivers of water in a dry place" (Isa. 32:1–4). Most of the Messianic utterances of this nature, however, were destined to have only partial fulfillment in the meridian of time and were to come to a glorious consummation in the dispensation of restoration when the promised King would reign personally upon the earth.

Speaking of the latter-day gathering of Israel, Jehovah's promise is: "I will open rivers in high places, and fountains in the midst of the valleys: I will make the wilderness a pool of water, and the dry land springs of water" (Isa. 41:18). This has reference to more than climatic changes (D&C 133:29).

Another great Messianic utterance says: "I will pour water upon him that is thirsty, and floods upon the dry ground: I will pour my spirit upon thy seed, and my blessing upon thine offspring" (Isa. 44:3). Similar truths are found in Isaiah 41:10–20; 48:20–21; and 49:9–12. Isaiah 12 tells of a millennial day when men shall "draw water out of the wells of salvation"; and Zechariah, speaking of that same day of peace and righteousness, tells how "living waters shall go out from Jerusalem" (Zech. 14:8). . . .

Before his mortal birth our Lord's call was: "Ho, every one that thirsteth, come ye to the waters, . . . and I will make an everlasting covenant with you" (Isa. 55:1–3; 2 Ne. 9:50). . . .

During his mortal sojourn it was the same. On the eighth day of the Feast of Tabernacles, while the priest poured water upon the altar and the words of Isaiah were sung, "With joy shall ye draw water out of the wells of salvation" (Isa. 12:3), our Lord stepped forth and proclaimed: "If any man thirst, let him come unto me, and drink" (John 7:37). . . .

Those who do come to quench their thirst, and who are true and faithful, shall drink forever from the pure fountain. As Isaiah expressed it, their "waters shall be sure" (Isa. 33:16), meaning they shall be as their Lord, enjoying and possessing the same eternal life which he lives. As he said in our day: "Unto him that keepeth my commandments I will give the mysteries of my kingdom, and the same shall be in him a well of living water, springing up unto everlasting life" (D&C 63:23).

(Bruce R. McConkie, *The Promised Messiah* [Salt Lake City: Deseret Book Co., 1978], 204–207.)

As used by Isaiah, . . . this . . . language applies to the latter-day gathering of Israel. . . . Isaiah's clear meaning is that the spiritual famine of centuries shall cease; Israel shall now have the gospel; they shall feast again upon the good word of God; once again shall they drink from the fountains of living waters; and in their new found joy, all their sufferings of the past (even the heat of the sun!) shall be forgotten.

(Bruce R. McConkie, *Doctrinal New Testament Commentary*, 3 vols.
[Salt Lake City: Bookcraft, Inc., 1966–1973], 3:496.)

1 Ne. 21:12   LAND OF SINIM
(Isa. 49:12)

This phrase may refer to Syene, in southern Egypt, also known as Aswan, where there was a large Jewish colony after the Exile. Or it may refer to the desert of Sin, which is in the peninsula of Sinai. The point is that the Lord will gather his people from wherever they have been scattered. The same is true spiritually. The Lord will find us wherever we are and bring us back to our inheritance, if we will hearken to him and do our part.

(Donald W. Parry, Jay A. Parry, and Tina M. Peterson,
Understanding Isaiah [Salt Lake City: Deseret Book Co., 1998], 430.)

Sinim stands for distant lands generally; in the opinion of most scholars it strictly signifies China.

(J. R. Dummelow, *The One Volume Bible Commentary* [New York: Macmillan, 1936], 445.)

1 Ne. 21:13–16   I WILL NOT FORGET ISRAEL
(Isa. 49:13–16)

This poetic passage provides yet another reminder of Christ's saving role, that of protective, redeeming parent to Zion's children. He comforts his people and shows mercy when they are afflicted, as any loving father or mother would toward a child, but, as Nephi here reminds us through Isaiah, much more than any mortal father and mother could do. Although a mother may forget her sucking child (as unlikely as any parent might think that could be), Christ will not forget the children he has redeemed or the covenant he has made with them for salvation in Zion. The painful reminders of that watch care and covenant are the marks of the Roman nails graven upon the palms of his hands.

(Jeffrey R. Holland, *Christ and the New Covenant* [Salt Lake City: Deseret Book Co., 1997], 84.)

A young woman approached me in a city far from my home and came under some pressure from her husband. She admitted to me that she had committed adultery. She was a bit hard and unyielding, and finally said: "I know what I have done. I have read the scriptures, and I know the consequences. I know that I am damned and can never be forgiven, and therefore why should I try now to repent?"

My reply to her was: "My dear sister, you do not know the scriptures. You do not know the power of God nor his goodness. You *can* be forgiven for this heinous sin, but it will take much sincere repentance to accomplish it."

Then I quoted to her the cry of her Lord:

Can a woman forget her sucking child, that she should not have compassion of the son of her womb? yea, they may forget, yet I will not forget thee (Isa. 49:15).

I reminded her of the Lord's words in our own dispensation to the effect that whoever repents and obeys God's commandments will be forgiven (D&C 1:32). My visitor looked bewildered but seemed to be yearning as though she wanted to believe it. I continued: "Eventually forgiveness will come for all but the unpardonable sins to that transgressor who repents sorely enough, long enough, sincerely enough.". . .

She wanted so much to believe it. She said she had known all her life that adultery was unforgivable. And I turned again to the scriptures and read to her the oft-repeated statement of Jesus: Wherefore I say unto you, All manner of sin and blasphemy shall be forgiven unto men: but the blasphemy against the Holy Ghost shall not be forgiven unto men . . . (Matt. 12:31–32).

She had forgotten that scripture. Her eyes lighted up. She reacted joyously to it, and asked, "Is that really true? Can I really be forgiven?" . . .

How great the joy to feel and know that God will forgive sinners! . . . This woman, who was basically good, straightened up and looked me in the eye, and in her voice was a new power and resoluteness as she said: "Thank you, thank you! I believe you. I shall really repent and wash my filthy garments in the blood of the Lamb and obtain that forgiveness."

Not long ago, she returned to my office a new person—bright of eye, light of step, full of hope as she declared to me that, since that memorable day when hope had seen a star and had clung to it, she had never reverted to adultery nor any approaches to it.

(Spencer W. Kimball, *The Miracle of Forgiveness* [Salt Lake City: Bookcraft, 1969] 340–42.)

1 Ne. 21:14   ZION
(Isa. 49:14; refer in this text to 2 Ne. 12:3 & 2 Ne. 14:5–6)

The whole of America is Zion itself from north to south, and is described by the Prophets, who declare that it is the Zion where the mountain of the Lord should be, and that it should be in the center of the land.

(Joseph Smith, *Teachings of the Prophet Joseph Smith*,
comp. by Joseph Fielding Smith [Salt Lake City: Deseret Book Co., 1976], 362.)

1 Ne. 21:14   THE LORD HATH FORSAKEN ME
(Isa. 49:14)

The shepherd is so constantly with his sheep that sometimes his life with them becomes monotonous. Therefore he will occasionally play with them. He does this by pretending to run away from his sheep, and they will soon overtake him, and completely surround him, gamboling with great delight. Sometimes God's people think He forsakes them when trouble comes their way. They say: "The Lord hath forsaken me" (Isa. 49:14). But actually their divine Shepherd says to them: "I will never leave thee, nor forsake thee" (Heb. 13:5).

(Fred H. Wight, *Manners and Customs of Bible Lands* [Chicago: Moody Press, 1953], 158.)

1 Ne. 21:16   GRAVEN UPON THE PALMS
(Isa. 49:16; Zech. 13:6; Luke 24:39–40; 3 Ne. 11:14–15; D&C 45:51–52)

The clause is an allusion to the ancient practice of tattooing the palm with a symbol of the temple or some other sacred emblem to show devotion so that it might serve as a reminder of one's commitment. This is an idiomatic and graphic way for the Lord to say: "You are constantly before me; I have not forgotten my covenant with you."

(Joseph Fielding McConkie and Robert L. Millet,
Doctrinal Commentary on the Book of Mormon, 4 vols. [Salt Lake City: Bookcraft, 1987–1992], 1:165.)

This is a figurative way of expressing that Jehovah will never forget Zion. . . . It is thought that the Jews of that day were in the habit of tattooing on their hands or arms representations of the city or temple in order to keep before them something to remind them of the sacred places.

(James M. Freeman, *Manners and Customs of the Bible* [Plainfield, New Jersey: Logos International, 1972], 272.)

The phrase "graven thee upon the palms of my hands" refers to the marks of the nails in Christ's hands. These marks remained after his resurrection (Luke 24:38–40; 3 Ne. 11:13–14). The nail marks are a sign to Israel—and to the world—that Christ fulfilled his mission as Savior (Isa. 22:23, 25; John 20:25; 3 Ne. 11:14–15; D&C 6:37; 45:48–53).

The words "thy walls are continually before me" likely refer to the walls of Jerusalem. These walls are ever present in the consciousness of those who dwell in the city. In the same way, an awareness of the people of Israel is ever present with the Lord.

(Donald W. Parry, *Visualizing Isaiah*
[Provo, Utah: The Foundation for Ancient Research and Mormon Studies, 2001], 88.)

"For the mountains shall depart and the hills be removed," He said, "but my kindness shall not depart from thee, neither shall the covenant of my peace be removed [from thee]" (3 Ne. 22:10; see vv.13–14). I love that. The hills and the mountains may disappear. The seas and oceans may dry up completely. The least likely things in the world may happen, but "my kindness shall not depart from thee, neither shall the covenant of my peace be removed [from thee]." After all, He has, He reminds us, "graven thee upon the palms of my hands" (1 Ne. 21:16). Considering the incomprehensible cost of the Crucifixion, Christ is not going to turn His back on us now.

(Jeffrey R. Holland, *Trusting Jesus* [Salt Lake City: Deseret Book Co., 2003], 67.)

1 Ne. 21:17   MAKE HASTE AGAINST THY DESTROYERS
(Isa. 49:17; 3 Ne. 21:11–13; Morm. 5:22–24; 3 Ne. 20:15–16;
refer also in this text to 2 Ne. 27:1–2)

Consider the role played by Great Britain and the United Nations in Palestine following the end of World War I. The British were made responsible by the allied nations for seeing to the peace of the Holy Land, and almost at once Lord Balfour, the British Prime Minister, announced that "his majesty's government" viewed with favor the establishment in Palestine of a permanent homeland for the Jews. After serving as the land's protectorate for about 29 years, Britain relinquished control to the United Nations in 1946. These same Gentile nations helped create the modern State of Israel in 1947–48. Since that time, the world has witnessed a reversal of power from that which existed in ancient times. Isaiah prophesied of such a reversal: "Thy children [in the latter days] shall make haste [gain strength] against thy [ancient] destroyers; and they that laid thee waste [anciently] shall [in the latter days] go forth of thee" (49:17; also in 1 Ne. 21:17).

Even a limited understanding of modern history and the present situation in the Middle East shows the literal fulfillment of this promise. Descendants of ancient powers which surround Israel today—Syria, Lebanon, Jordan, Egypt, Iran and Iraq (to name but a few)—respect Israel's military might, even though they find it difficult to accept. And from whence has Israel's might and power come? From a mighty Gentile father, even that nation among whom Isaiah prophesied the Lord would set up his "standard."

(Leland Gentry, *Second Nephi, The Doctrinal Structure*,
ed. Monte S. Nyman and Charles D. Tate, Jr. [Provo, Utah: Religious Studies Center, BYU, 1989], 163.)

In the full and true sense, Israel shall triumph over her foes only when the Millennium is ushered in, only when her Messiah comes to deliver them from the aliens, only when the wicked are destroyed and the Lord reigns gloriously among his saints.

(Bruce R. McConkie, *The Millennial Messiah* [Salt Lake City: Deseret Book Co., 1982], 242.)

It is not a war that a few Lamanites or any remnant of Israel shall wage against Gentile oppressors; the Lord does not operate in that manner. When he comes the wicked shall be destroyed and the righteous preserved; those who have not hearkened to the prophets shall be cut off from among the people; thus, the 'enemies' of Israel 'shall be cut off.' And it shall be with power, as though a young lion went forth rending and tearing in pieces a helpless flock of sheep. And so, if the Gentiles do not repent and believe in Christ after the gospel is restored among them, then, when the Lord comes, they will be destroyed and the triumph of Israel—because they kept the commandments and did receive the gospel—that triumph will be complete.

(Bruce R. McConkie, *The Mortal Messiah*, Book 4 [Salt Lake City: Deseret Book Co., 1981], 334–35.)

1 Ne. 21:18   **GATHERING OF ISRAEL**
(Isa. 49:18; refer in this text to 2 Ne. 21:10–12)

The essence of the gathering is the gathering to the covenants of the gospel of Jesus Christ, as Nephi taught (1 Ne. 10:14)—the same covenants that God made with Israel's great ancestors, Abraham, Isaac, and Jacob. Because such phrases as "the gathering of Israel" usually refer to joining the Church, the idea of a physical return in the scriptures may often be a metaphor for returning to the covenants, accepting the gospel, and joining Christ's church. Geographical relocation plays a lesser role. Today the gathering of Israel is taking place as individuals from all over the earth are gathering to the Church in their own lands. And Gentiles—those who are not of literal Israelite descent—are equally welcome.

(Kent P. Jackson, *Studies in Scripture, Vol. 4,* ed. Kent P. Jackson
[Salt Lake City: Deseret Book Co., 1993], 142–43.)

The gathering of Israel consists of joining the true church and their coming to a knowledge of the true God. . . . Any person, therefore, who has accepted the restored gospel, and who now seeks to worship the Lord in his own tongue and with the Saints in the nations where he lives, has complied with the law of the gathering of Israel and is heir to all of the blessings promised the Saints in these last days.

(Spencer W. Kimball, *The Teachings of Spencer W. Kimball,*
ed. Edward L. Kimball [Salt Lake City: Bookcraft, 1982], 439.)

In the scriptures there are set forth three phases of the gathering of Israel. One, the gathering of Israel to the land of Zion which is America, this land. That is under way and has been under way since the Church was established and our missions abroad were inaugurated. Then two, the return of the lost tribes, the ten lost tribes, from the land of the north (see D&C 133). And the third phase is the reestablishment of the Jews of Palestine as one of the events to precede the second coming of the Master.

(Ezra Taft Benson, *The Teachings of Ezra Taft Benson* [Salt Lake City: Bookcraft, 1988], 91.)

One of the most important points in the faith of the Church of the Latter-day Saints, through the fullness of the everlasting Gospel, is the gathering of Israel (of whom the Lamanites constitute a part) . . . when . . . there will be none to molest or make afraid; when He will turn to them a pure language, and the earth will be filled with sacred knowledge, as the waters cover the great deep; when it shall no longer be said, the Lord lives that brought up the children of Israel out of the land of Egypt, but the Lord lives that brought up the children of Israel from the land of the north, and from all the lands whither He has driven them. That day is one, all important to all.

(Joseph Smith, *History of the Church of Jesus Christ*, 2:357.)

Not many of the Jews, I take it from my reading of the scriptures, will believe in Christ before he comes. The *Book of Mormon* tells us that they shall *begin* to believe in him. . . .

But in the main they will gather to Jerusalem in their unbelief; the gospel will be preached to them; some of them will believe. Not all of the Gentiles have believed when the gospel has been proclaimed to them, but the great body of the Jews who are there assembled will not receive Christ as their Redeemer until he comes himself and makes himself manifest unto them.

(Joseph Fielding Smith, *Doctrines of Salvation: Sermons and Writings of Joseph Fielding Smith,*
ed. Bruce R. McConkie, 3 vols. [Salt Lake City: Bookcraft, 1954–1956], 3:9.)

And thus shall Israel come: not a dark corner of the earth shall remain unexplored, nor an island of the seas be left without being visited; for as the Lord has removed them into all corners of the earth, he will cause his mercy to be as abundantly manifested in their gathering. . . . He will, as he said by the prophet, (Jer. 16:16) send for many fishers and they shall fish them; and after send for many hunters, who shall hunt them; . . . with glad tidings of great joy, with a message of peace, and a call for their return. . . .

Though the house of Israel has forsaken the Lord, and bowed down and worshipping other gods, . . . they will know the voice of the Shepherd when he calls upon them this time; . . . God is preparing the way for their return. . . .

What is to be fulfilled in the last days, is not only for the benefit of Israel, but the Gentiles, if they will repent and embrace the gospel, for they are to be remembered also in the same covenant, and are to be fellow heirs with the seed of Abraham. . . .

In consequence of the transgression of the Jews at the coming of the Lord, the Gentiles were called into the kingdom, and for this obedience, are to be favored with the gospel in its fulness first, in the last days; for it is written. The first shall be last, and the last first. Therefore, when the fulness of the gospel, as was preached by the righteous, upon this land, shall come forth, it shall be declared to the Gentiles first.

(Oliver Cowdery, *Messenger and Advocate*, Apr. 1835, 111.)

1 Ne. 21:20   **THIS PLACE IS TOO STRAIT**
(Isa. 49:20)

If the work rolls forth with the same rapidity it has heretofore done, we may soon expect to see flocking to this place [Nauvoo], people from every land and from every nation . . . persons of all languages, and of every tongue, and of every color; who shall with us worship the Lord of Hosts in His holy temple and offer up their orisons in His sanctuary.

It was in consideration of these things . . . that induced us to purchase the present city for a place of gathering for the Saints, and the extensive tract of land on the opposite side of the Mississippi. Although the purchase at the time, and under the peculiar circumstances of the Church, appeared to many to be large and uncalled for; yet from what we now see, it is apparent to all that we shall soon have to say, "This place is too straight, give us room that we may dwell." We therefore hope that the brethren who feel interested in the cause of truth, and desire to see the work of the gathering of Israel roll forth with power, will aid us in liquidating the debts which are now owing, so that the inheritances may be secured to the Church, and which eventually will be of great value.

(Joseph Smith, *History of the Church,* 4:213–14.)

1 Ne. 21:22   SONS IN THEIR ARMS, DAUGHTERS UPON THEIR SHOULDERS
(Isa. 49:20)

"In their arms" may also be rendered in their *bosom.* . . . The large lap or pocket made by the folds of the outer garment . . . was a convenient and comfortable place for carrying a child. . . . It was customary for fathers to carry their infants in this manner when going on a journey.

Another Oriental mode of carrying children is on the shoulders. This is sometimes done by placing them astride the neck. . . . At other times the child is placed astride one shoulder, usually the left, with one leg hanging down on the back and the other on the breast. In either case the child steadies itself by putting its arms around the parent's head, and by clinging with its feet. In Egypt women are often seen carrying a child on one shoulder and a jar of water on the other.

(James M. Freeman, *Manners and Customs of the Bible* [Plainfield, New Jersey: Logos International, 1972], 730.)

1 Ne. 21:22;   SET UP MY STANDARD
22:6–9   (Isa. 49:22; D&C 45:9; 115:3–5; 2 Ne. 6:6; 29:2)

A standard is a measure by which a judgment is made. The Book of Mormon is the standard by which the children of men will be measured and judged.

(Monte S. Nyman, *Isaiah: Prophecies of the Restoration* [Salt Lake City: Millennial Press, 1998], 29.)

"Behold, I will lift up mine hand to the Gentiles, and set up my standard to the people: and they shall bring thy sons in their arms, and thy daughters shall be carried upon their shoulders. And kings shall be thy nursing fathers, and their queens thy nursing mothers" (Isa. 49:22–23). This is one of several prophecies that show the nations no longer oppressing the Lord's people but serving them. The Book of Mormon provides important interpretations. Nephi, who recognized that Isaiah's prophecies are fulfilled in "temporal and spiritual" ways (1 Ne. 22:3), foresaw the Gentiles contributing to the temporal blessing of his descendants and others of the house of Israel (1 Ne. 22:6). He also saw them contributing in an even more important spiritual way. According to Nephi, the fulfillment of this prophecy will be "the making known of the covenants of the Father," "in bringing about his covenants and his gospel unto those who are of the house of Israel." The bringing of the gospel of Jesus Christ to the house of Israel is the great blessing from the Gentiles and the great fulfillment of this prophecy. It began with the restoration of the gospel and continues as missionaries from Gentile nations take the gospel to Lehi's descendants and others of the house of Israel. Being "brought out of obscurity and out of darkness," the covenant people are thus learning "that the Lord is their Savior and their Redeemer, the Mighty One of Israel" (1 Ne. 22:9, 11–12). The Lord revealed to Jacob a yet-future temporal fulfillment of Isaiah 49:23. When the Jews believe in him, that he is Christ, then he will fulfill the covenant to their fathers that they will be restored "unto the lands of their inheritance" and will be "gathered in from their long dispersion. . . . And the nations of the Gentiles shall be great in the eyes of me, saith God, in carrying them forth to the lands of their inheritance. Yea, the kings of the Gentiles shall be nursing fathers unto them, and their queens shall become nursing mothers" (2 Ne. 10:7–9).

(Kent P. Jackson, *Studies in Scripture, Vol. 4*, ed. Kent P. Jackson, [Salt Lake City: Deseret Book Co., 1993], 144.)

The Constitution of the United States is a glorious standard; it is founded in the wisdom of God. It is a heavenly banner; it is to all those who are privileged with the sweets of liberty, like the cooling shades and refreshing waters of a great rock in a thirsty and weary land. It is like a great tree under whose branches men from every clime can be shielded from the burning rays of the sun.

We, brethren, are deprived of the protection of its glorious principles, by the cruelty of the cruel. . . . But notwithstanding, . . . we cannot be weaned from the milk, neither can we be driven from the breast; neither will we deny our religion because of the hand of oppression; but we will hold on until death.

We say that God is true; that the Constitution of the United States is true; that the Bible is true; that the Book of Mormon is true; that the Book of [Doctrine and] Covenants is true; that Christ is true; that the ministering angels sent forth from God are true.

(Joseph Smith, *Teachings of the Prophet Joseph Smith*,
comp. by Joseph Fielding Smith [Salt Lake City: Deseret Book Co., 1976], 147–48.)

And who are these modern Gentiles? *We are!*

We are they to whom the gospel was restored. . . . We are also of Israel, however—mostly of Ephraim—but we are Gentiles too, inasmuch as Ephraim was widely scattered among the Gentiles in ancient times and intermarried with them.

Ephraim now is the first of the scattered tribes to be gathered, since Ephraim holds the birthright in Israel.

We are referred to . . . as Gentiles, but we are the "believing Gentiles." . . . In the revealed dedicatory prayer for the Kirtland Temple, the Prophet used this expression: ". . . concerning the revelations and commandments which thou hast given unto us, who are identified with the Gentiles." (D&C 109:60.)

It is inspiring indeed to realize that we who live now and have received this restored gospel are the very ones to whom Nephi and the Christ [3 Ne. 21:2–4] referred some two thousand years ago. We have lived in prophecy!

(Mark E. Petersen, *The Great Prologue* [Salt Lake City: Deseret Book Co., 1975], 5–6.)

1 Ne. 21:23;   **KINGS AND QUEENS: NURSING PARENTS**
22:6   (Isa. 49:23; 2 Ne. 10:7–9; Ezra 1:1–4; Isa. 49:23)

From Nephi we learn that kings and queens are representative of the Gentiles among whom the house of Israel was scattered. . . . The role the "Gentile nations," particularly the United States and Great Britain, have played in that gathering [of the Jewish people] is significant.

(Monte Nyman, *Ensign*, Aug. 1994, 61–62.)

Only through us, the "nursing fathers and mothers," may they [the Lamanites] eventually enjoy a fulfillment of the many promises made to them.

(Spencer W. Kimball, *Teachings of Spencer W. Kimball*,
ed. Edward L. Kimball [Salt Lake City: Bookcraft, 1982], 606.)

Since the Church was restored in 1830, the Jewish population in the Holy Land has grown from seven thousand to over three million people. Whereas in 1830 only one out of five hundred Jews resided in Palestine, one out of five now live in the modern state of Israel. . . . Britain assisted in the establishment of a Jewish homeland in Palestine after World War I; Holland and Denmark helped protect many Jews from the holocaust; the United States, Russia, and others in the United Nations voted for the creation of a Jewish free state in 1947; the United States and France assisted Israel with military equipment in the first decades of her existence after 1948; and German reparation payments and large contributions from the United States and other nations have helped Israel financially.

(Victor L. Ludlow, *Isaiah: Prophet, Seer, and Poet* [Salt Lake City: Deseret Book Co., 1982], 414.)

This day of the Lamanite brings opportunity. . . . They must have the emancipating gospel. . . . They must hear the compelling truths of the gospel. Millions are tied to reservations, deprived, untrained, and less than they could be. They must have the enlightening gospel. It will break their fetters, stir their ambition, increase their vision, and open new worlds of opportunity to them. Their captivity will be at an end—captivity from misconceptions, illiteracy, superstition, fear. . . .

The brighter day has dawned. The scattering has been accomplished; the gathering is in process. May the Lord bless us all as we become nursing fathers and mothers (see Isa. 49:23 and 1 Ne. 21:23) unto our Lamanite brethren and hasten the fulfillment of the great promises made to them.

(Spencer W. Kimball, *Conference Report*, Oct. 1965, 72.)

The Lamanites will blossom as the rose on the mountains. I am willing to say here that . . . when I see the power of the nation destroying them from the face of the earth, the fulfillment of that prophecy is perhaps harder for me to believe than any revelation of God that I ever read. It looks as though there would not be enough left to receive the gospel; but notwithstanding this dark picture, every word that God has ever said of them will have its fulfillment, and they, by and by, will receive the gospel. . . . Their chiefs will be filled with the power of God and receive the gospel, and they will go forth and build the new Jerusalem, and we shall help them.

(Wilford Woodruff, *The Discourses of Wilford Woodruff,* ed. G. Homer Durham, [Salt Lake City: Bookcraft, 1946], 121.)

1 Ne. 21:23   **LICK UP THE DUST**
(Isa. 49:23; Gen. 42:6; 1 Sam. 24:8, Ps. 72:8–11; 2 Ne. 6:13;
Mosiah 4:1–2; refer in this text to 2 Ne. 8:23)

In the ancient Near East, these actions were signs of submission to a king or ruler (Gen. 42:6; 1 Sam. 24:8; Ps. 72:8–11; 2 Ne. 6:13). In times past, Israel was repeatedly conquered and forced to submit to the kings of the earth. But in the last days kings and queens will bow in obeisance and submission to the children of Israel.

(Donald W. Parry, Jay A. Parry, and Tina M. Peterson,
Understanding Isaiah [Salt lake City: Deseret Book Co., 1998], 436.)

Proskynesis was the falling to the earth, literally, 'kissing the ground,' in the presence of the king. . . . A flat prostration upon the earth was the proper act of obeisance in the presence of the ruler.

(Hugh Nibley, *An Approach to the Book of Mormon* [Salt Lake City: Deseret News Press, 1957], 264.)

1 Ne. 21:23   **THEY SHALL NOT BE ASHAMED THAT WAIT FOR ME**
(Isa. 49:23; 40:31; 41:10; 2 Ne. 6:7, 13; 2 Ne. 8:5; Mosiah 21:34;
D&C 98:2; 133:45; 1 Jn. 2:28)

The word *wait* in Hebrew means hope for or anticipate. Thus, one who waits upon the Lord places his trust in Him and lives in accordance with His will as he or she anticipates His coming. Such persons will have their "confidence wax strong in the presence of God" (D&C 121:45), for they will have no unresolved sins to cause them to be ashamed.

(Hoyt W. Brewster, Jr., *Isaiah Plain and Simple* [Salt Lake City: Deseret Book Co., 1995], 204.)

Closely associated with our willingness to trust in the Lord is our patience amid adversity. It is difficult to "wait upon the Lord" (Isaiah 40:31), yet numerous scriptural passages admonish us to be patient in tribulation (see D&C 31:9; 54:10; 66:9; 122:5–7; Alma 26:27). It is a natural inclination to be impatient and to think that no matter how long our "small moments" of adversity may last, they are too long (see D&C 122:4). This natural tendency can be characterized by a saying I first saw on a plaque on the kitchen wall of my parents' home: "God grant me patience—RIGHT NOW!"

Impatience and a lack of trust in God are twin traits found in the natural man. Just as the natural man is an "enemy to God" (Mosiah 3:19), impatience and an unwillingness to trust in God's designs for us can become enemies to our spiritual development and faithful endurance. "When we are unduly impatient," Elder Neal A. Maxwell observed, "we are suggesting that we know what is best—better than does God. Or, at least, we are asserting that our timetable is better than His. . . ." ("Patience," In *1979 Devotional Speeches of the Year* [Provo, Utah: Brigham Young University Press, 1980], 215.)

Patient endurance requires waiting—not passive waiting, foolish fretting, or idle twiddling of our thumbs, but waiting upon the Lord. "Wait on the Lord: be of good courage, and he shall strengthen thine heart: wait, I say, on the Lord" (Ps. 27:14). Waiting on the Lord implies not only trust but also active submissiveness to his ultimate purposes for our lives. This kind of faithful submission to the Lord's will means humbly accepting not only the "what" but also the "when" and the "how long." Tribulations and trials bring us to our knees until we, like Job, stop resisting and surrender our lives to the Lord. Only through such liberating surrender can we find, amid our own suffering, the peace and comfort that Job ultimately found.

(Brent L. Top, *A Peculiar Treasure* [Salt Lake City: Bookcraft, 1997], 139–140.)

1 Ne. 21:26;   **FED WITH THEIR OWN FLESH . . .**
22:13–14   (Isa. 49:26; 2 Ne. 6:18)

Perhaps the depraved condition of the ancient Nephites is descriptive of those wicked ones of the future who will "be drunken with their own blood": "They have lost their love, one towards another; and they thirst after blood and revenge continually." (Moroni 9:5). The carnage among the wicked may be such that they resort to cannibalism both to satisfy their physical hunger and to demonstrate their depravity. Once again we look to the past for a prototype of this abominable behavior: "They did murder them in a most cruel manner . . . and after they have done this, they devour their flesh like unto wild beasts, because of the hardness of their hearts; and they do it for a token of bravery" (Moro. 9:10).

(Hoyt W. Brewster, Jr., *Isaiah Plain and Simple* [Salt Lake City: Deseret Book Co., 1995], 204–205.)

Nephi gave this verse [Isa. 49:26] two interpretations: the great and abominable church would war among themselves and become drunken with their own blood, and the nations who would fight against the house of Israel or against Zion would "fall into the pit which they digged to ensnare the people of the Lord."

(Monte S. Nyman, *Great Are the Words of Isaiah* [Salt Lake City: Bookcraft, 1980], 185.)

What is the crowning evil on earth, the one that spreads the greatest suffering, the one that spawns all other evils? Surely it is war. Murder is the most wicked of all sins, and war is mass murder. Millions among men have suffered untimely deaths in the wars of the past; and before the coming desolations are ended, the number will be in the billions. . . .

Surely war is the greatest evil that has or can spread its soul-destroying power over all the earth. . . . The great and dreadful wars have been reserved for the last days, the days after the invention of the machine, the days when the number of wicked persons would swell into the billions. This is the day when a new order of war would be instituted, and that new order began with the Civil War in America. It was then that modern armaments had their birth. Already they have grown into a hideous monster, and the end is nowhere to be seen. . . .

These wars and plagues and desolations shall continue—and increase—until the kingdoms of this world are destroyed and He reigns whose right it is. . . . This coming will not be ushered in by righteousness, but by wickedness. . . . Indeed, the great battle of Armageddon itself will be in progress when the Lord comes. . . .

Truly, in the last days men "shall be drunken with their own blood, as with sweet wine" (Isa. 49:26). All these things have begun; they are now underway, and they shall increase in intensity and in horror until that dreadful day when the God of battles himself shall descend from heaven with a shout and with the trump of the archangel.

(Bruce R. McConkie, *The Millennial Messiah* [Salt Lake City: Deseret Book Co., 1982], 370–74.)

RESULTS OF NEPHI'S USE OF ISAIAH 48 & 49

What were the results of Nephi's efforts to teach his brethren by reciting Isaiah 48 and 49? Nephi's brothers were too spiritually immature to understand the teachings of Isaiah; they asked Nephi what it all meant. In response to this query, Nephi gave the profound interpretations found in 1 Nephi 22. . . . Father Lehi was apparently present to hear Nephi's instruction, for Nephi says, "After I, Nephi, had made an end of teaching my brethren, our father, Lehi, also spake many things unto them, and rehearsed unto them, how great things the Lord had done for them in bringing them out of the land of Jerusalem" (2 Ne. 1:1). Lehi clearly understood the message of Isaiah, as did Nephi's brother Jacob, who was profoundly affected by Nephi's and Isaiah's message. . . . That Jacob was in perfect harmony with Nephi's interpretation of Isaiah is evident in Jacob 6:4, which explains that it was Nephi who "desired" that Jacob speak to the people of Nephi. In fact, Jacob added some significant details to Nephi's interpretation of Isaiah 49 that indicate that Lehi's, Nephi's, and Jacob's appreciation for and understanding of Isaiah 48 and 49 was without parallel in all Israel.

(Andrew C. Skinner, *Isaiah in the Book of Mormon,* ed. Donald W. Parry and John W. Welch
[Provo, Utah: Foundation for Ancient Research and Mormon Studies 1998], 118.)

1 Ne. 22:4	Interprets	1 Ne. 21:1
1 Ne. 22:6–9	Interprets	1 Ne. 21:22–23
1 Ne. 22:12	Interprets	1 Ne. 21:12–13
1 Ne. 22:13–16	Interprets	1 Ne. 21:17, 25–26

1 Ne. 22:15–17	MALACHI

These verses, or part of them, may also have been a part of Isaiah's writings at one time. Although we recognize the similarity between verse 15 and Malachi 4:1, Nephi's words could not have come from this book. Malachi had not written his work at the time Lehi left Jerusalem, so it could not have been included on the plates of brass. It might very well be that Malachi, living several hundred years after Isaiah, was quoting from the original Isaiah text.

(Monte S. Nyman, *Great Are the Words of Isaiah* [Salt Lake City: Bookcraft, 1980], 185.)

2 Ne. 6:6–7	(Isa. 49:22–23; refer in this text to all sections under 1 Ne. 21:22–23.)

2 Ne. 6:15

(Isa. 29:6; refer in this text to 2 Ne. 27:1–2.)

2 Ne. 6:16–18

(Isa. 49:24–26; refer in this text to 1 Ne. 21:26.)

2 Ne. 7:1–2   **BILL OF DIVORCEMENT—TO WHOM HAVE I SOLD YOU?**
(Isa. 50:1; Deut. 24:1–4; D&C 133:66–69; refer to *Latter-day Commentary on the Book of Mormon,* Bassett, under 3 Ne. 12:31–32)

The question posed to Israel about her divorced status is a metaphorical reference to the law of divorce given in Deuteronomy 24:1–4. Under this law, if a wife was found unfaithful (unclean) her husband could dissolve the marriage by giving her a "bill of divorcement." Even though Israel had been unfaithful to her husband—the Lord—He had never given her such a document; she was never officially divorced. . . . The Lord further states that neither has Israel been sold into bondage to relieve a debt, for He has no creditors. (At that time, one in debt could sell his children into servitude to pay the debt. See Ex. 21:7; Neh. 5:1–5. . . . In speaking to latter-day Israel, who is to be redeemed, reference is made to her "mother" who was "put away" (separated) because of her "transgressions." Some have suggested this implies ancient Israel (the mother) was divorced (put away) but that the bill of divorcement does not apply to modern Israel. However, it appears that ancient "mother Israel" left her Husband (put herself away).

(Hoyt W. Brewster, Jr., *Isaiah Plain and Simple* [Salt Lake City: Deseret Book Co., 1995], 206, 208.)

In the time of Isaiah, if a man was pressed by his creditors, he had the possibility of relieving his debt by selling his children as slaves (Ex. 21:7; Neh. 1–5; Matt. 18:25). And if he died, a creditor might take his children as payment (2 Kgs. 4:1). This slavery was not permanent; the person was indentured to work for a fixed number of years. In answer to the question "To whom has the Lord ever been in debt?" Isaiah answers that the Lord is indebted to no one and therefore has not been forced to sell Israel; Israel's separation and captivity is her own fault.

(Victor L. Ludlow, *Isaiah: Prophet, Seer, and Poet* [Salt Lake City: Deseret Book Co., 1982], 420.)

These children will have a happy home and sealed parents yet. In the last days that bill of divorcement against their mother will be set aside, and so will the demands of any creditors. The Lord is in debt to no one, so neither will his children be. He alone can pay the price for the salvation of Israel and the establishment of Zion. His wrath is turned away, and he will not cast off his bride or allow her children to be sold into slavery.

As for the shortening of his hands, the scriptures repeatedly testify that the reach of God's arm is more than adequate, the extent of his grace entirely sufficient. He can always claim and embrace the Israel that he loves. In spite of their unfaithfulness, his hand remains constant, not shortened or slackened or withheld.

(Jeffrey R. Holland, *Christ and the New Covenant* [Salt Lake City: Deseret Book Co., 1997], 84–85.)

This passage employs several well-known images from the Old Testament to make its points: (1) a husband (Jehovah), (2) a wife (Israel), (3) a bill of divorce, and (4) the sale of personal property, in this case a member of one's own family, to satisfy a debt. Both the divorcing and paying a debt by selling a family member for domestic service have Old Testament relevance (see Deut. 24:1–2; 2 Kgs. 4:1). The picture given here, then, is of a wife who felt she had been divorced by her husband or sold into service as described. The husband, however, rightly asks, "Where is the bill of your mother's divorcement? Or to which of my creditors have I sold you?"

The Lord, of course, had not set Israel aside permanently but only until she repented of her wrong doings. Most certainly, the Lord has no creditors since all men are in debt to him. The perceived divorce or sale was merely supposition of Israel's part. Besides, the breach between the husband and his wife was clearly the result of her doings and not his. . . .

When the Savior appeared on earth among the nation of Judah, she rejected him. That is the apparent meaning of Isaiah's words, that "there was none to answer" or "no man" to respond. The Lord insists that in spite of this rejection by his chosen one—Judah—his power or arm is not curtailed.

(Leland Gentry, *Second Nephi, The Doctrinal Structure*,
ed. Monte S. Nyman and Charles D. Tate, Jr. [Provo, Utah: Religious Studies Center, BYU, 1989], 167–68.)

2 Ne. 7:3   BLACKNESS
(Isa. 50:3; Matt. 24:29–30; D&C 29:11–14; 45:39–44)

"I clothe the heavens with blackness" (Isa.50:3), and there is no more revelation. . . . Thus saith our God. Such is his promise, spoken prophetically of our day. And here, given in modern times, is his announcement that as he spake, so has it come to pass: "Verily, verily, I say unto you, darkness covereth the earth, and gross darkness the minds of the people, and all flesh has become corrupt before my face" (D&C 112:23).

(Bruce R. McConkie, *The Millennial Messiah* [Salt Lake City: Deseret Book Co., 1995], 209.)

2 Ne. 7:3   **SACKCLOTH THEIR COVERING**
                       (Isa. 50:3; Ex. 10:21)

In describing the darkness as a covering of "sackcloth" . . . Isaiah presents a double picture. At the second coming of Christ, the heavens will be darkened, and the wicked will mourn in sackcloth. By closing with this symbol, Isaiah reminds Israel both of merciful redemption and the consequences of refusing his invitation."

(Victor L. Ludlow, *Isaiah: Prophet, Seer, and Poet* [Salt Lake City: Deseret Book Co., 1982], 421.)

2 Ne. 7:4–9   **SERVANT'S SONG**
                       (Isa. 50:4–9; refer in this text to 1 Ne. 21:1–6)

These verses are known among biblical scholars as a "servant's song." This is a major poetic passage wherein a servant of the Lord is described, although not specifically identified. . . . There are differences of opinion among commentaries regarding the identity of this Servant. While there may be dual meaning to these verses, the author believes the song in Isaiah 50 refers primarily to the Messiah. He will be treated despicably, but the power of God will be manifest in Him. Those who oppose Him will be destroyed.

(Hoyt W. Brewster, Jr., *Isaiah Plain and Simple* [Salt Lake City: Deseret Book Co., 1995], 209.)

As with the other servant songs, controversy surrounds the interpretation of these verses. The servant could be any number of people or peoples. Perhaps it is the prophet Isaiah himself telling how he has been insulted, or perhaps it is the nation of Israel that has suffered persecutions throughout the long centuries of their dispersal from the land of Palestine. However, as far as the Bible records, Isaiah was not persecuted during his ministry. Also, the verses do not seem to apply to Israel as a nation, since they suffered a just punishment for their disobedience, whereas the servant suffers undeservedly for others. The most acceptable identification is Christ, because these verses describe events in the life of Jesus. In reading this servant song, however, we should not limit these references to the life of Christ, but should try to apply them to many of God's chosen servants.

(Victor L. Ludlow, *Isaiah: Prophet, Seer, and Poet*, [Salt Lake City: Deseret Book Co., 1982], 422.)

2 Ne. 7:5   **OPENED MINE EAR**
                       (Isa. 50:5)

Part of the ceremony of consecration of Aaron, in the Mosaic dispensation, was the application of a drop of sacrificial blood to the right ear, to signify his willingness to hear and obey the laws of

God (Ex. 29:20). A similar ceremony, with the same import, was part of the healing of a leper. (Lev. 14:14). The "servant" in this paragraph, therefore, says that the Lord had healed him, giving him the Priesthood, and made him willing to obey. This is particularly true in our day when the restored Gospel is received chiefly by those in whose veins the blood of Israel is flowing.

(George Reynolds and Janne M. Sjodahl, *Commentary on the Book of Mormon*, 7 vols., ed. Philip C. Reynolds [Salt Lake City: Deseret book Co., 1955–1961], 1:286.)

2 Ne. 7:6   **CHEEKS . . . PLUCK OFF HAIR**
                       (Isa. 50:6; Matt. 5:39; 26:67; 27:26; John 19:1)

"The Oriental regarded the beard as a sign of freedom and respect, and to pluck out the hair of the beard (for *cheek* in effect would refer to a beard) is to show utter contempt" (Neh. 13:25; 2 Sam. 10:5.).

(Donald W. Parry, Jay A. Parry, and Tina M. Peterson, *Understanding Isaiah* [Salt Lake City: Deseret Book Co., 1998], 443.)

The strikers or smiters would be those who have the public duty of beating a criminal. . . . The Oriental regarded the beard as a sign of freedom and respect, and to pluck out the hair of the beard (for *cheek* in effect would refer to a beard) is to show utter contempt (Young, *The Book of Isaiah*, 3:300).

(Victor L. Ludlow, *Isaiah: Prophet, Seer, and Poet* [Salt Lake City: Deseret Book Co., 1982], 422.)

2 Ne. 7:7   **FACE LIKE FLINT**
                       (Isa. 50:7)

The course of his life was toward the cross, and he was steadfast and immovable in his determination to follow this very course, one laid out for him by his Father. He had said of himself through the mouth of Isaiah, "I set my face like a flint, and I know that I shall not be ashamed." (Isa. 50:7) Clearly, there was to be no turning back.

(Bruce R. McConkie, *Doctrinal New Testament Commentary*, 3 vols. [Salt Lake City: Bookcraft, 1965–1973], 1:439.)

2 Ne. 7:8   **STAND TOGETHER**
                     (Isa. 50:8)

In an ancient Middle Eastern civil court, the two opponents stood together to hear the judge's decision. In a criminal court, the accuser made the charge personally to the defendant. Here, the servant is persecuted from all sides, but "the Lord is near, and he justifieth me."

(Donald W. Parry, Jay A. Parry, and Tina M. Peterson,
Understanding Isaiah [Salt Lake City: Deseret Book Co., 1998], 444.)

2 Ne. 7:11   **WALK IN THE LIGHT OF YOUR FIRE**
                     (Isa. 50:11; D&C 1:16)

People who kindle and walk in the light of their own fire are those who walk in their own way. They act according to their own will, rather than according to the will and direction of the Lord. They seek to be spiritually self-sufficient, relying on themselves instead of on God. They attempt to create their own light, but their efforts produce no more than short-lived sparks compared to the everlasting bright light that comes from God. Sadly, they deny themselves his greater light. Such will eventually be judged by the Lord, resulting in sorrow.

(Donald W. Parry, *Visualizing Isaiah*
[Provo, Utah: The Foundation for Ancient Research and Mormon Studies, 2001], 53.)

Thus they are their own revelators. Such was the folly of ancient Israel! Such is the folly of many today as we prepare for his Second Coming.

(Leland Gentry, *Second Nephi, The Doctrinal Structure*,
ed. Monte S. Nyman and Charles D. Tate, Jr. [Provo, Utah: Religious Studies Center, BYU, 1989], 168.)

2 Ne. 8:1–2   **LOOK UNTO THE ROCK**
                     (Isa. 51:1–7)

Isaiah 51 is a call to those who "follow after righteousness." The call is repeated again and again: "hearken," "look," "hearken," "lift up your eyes," and again "hearken" (vv. 1–7). The call reminds the righteous that they are descendants of Abraham and Sarah and heirs to the blessings of the Abrahamic covenant. Their rock and quarry are Abraham and Sarah, from whom they descend. Even as Abraham and Sarah received promises when fulfillment seemed beyond hope, so will the Lord fulfill his promises to comfort Zion (v. 3).

Ultimately, of course, the rock from which the righteous come is God the Father, and Christ, who is called the Rock at least thirty-four times in the scriptures. For example, the Lord informed Enoch, "I am Messiah, the King of Zion, the Rock of Heaven, which is broad as eternity" (Moses 7:53).

(Donald W. Parry, *Visualizing Isaiah*
[Provo, Utah: The Foundation for Ancient Research and Mormon Studies, 2001], 69.)

2 Ne. 8:3	**THE LORD SHALL COMFORT ZION** (Isa. 51:3)

If there are disappointments, let us not turn away. . . . Let all of us be filled with . . . quiet determination concerning the marvelous things we have been called to do in such stress-filled times, "for the Lord shall comfort Zion. . . . Joy and gladness shall be found therein, thanksgiving and the voice of melody" (2 Ne. 8:3).

With Paul, we can say, "We are troubled on every side, yet not distressed; we are perplexed, but not in despair; persecuted, but not forsaken; cast down, but not destroyed" (2 Cor. 4:8–9)—perhaps adding, "We are confronted, but not surprised; we are falsely accused, but pray for our accusers; we are reviled, but respond with Christian service." Brothers and sisters, we can be walking witnesses and standing sermons to which objective onlookers can say a quiet amen.

(Neal A. Maxwell, *Ensign,* Nov. 1980, 15.)

The restoration of the Gospel is a process, and Isaiah had seen that there would be times when the modern Israelites would wonder whether or not they would ever make it. This verse was a great comfort to the Saints when they were driven out of Missouri and later out of Illinois. The Lord assured the Saints that eventually he would pour out comfort and blessings upon his people in America. He said her wilderness areas would become as the Garden of Eden. Her deserts and barren regions would become like a "garden of the Lord." There would be a time of joy and gladness, and the thanksgiving of the Saints would pour forth in "the voice of melody." The moment the Gospel began to be restored in these latter days, the Lord commanded the people to gather their hymns and sing their praises to the Lord (see D&C 25:11–12; 136:28). Later their choirs became famous worldwide.

(W. Cleon Skousen, *Isaiah Speaks to Modern Times* [Salt Lake City: Ensign Publishing Co., 1984], 633–34.)

2 Ne. 8:4–6	**HEAVENS VANISH . . . EARTH WAX OLD** (Isa. 51:4–6)

We hear a divine voice acclaim: "Hearken unto me, my people," and the Latter-day Saints are the Lord's people, "and give ear unto me. O my nation: for a law shall proceed from me, and I will make my judgement to rest for a light of the people." Thanks be to God, that law now has come; it is the fulness of his everlasting gospel; by it he will judge the world. . . . "My righteousness is near." The millennial day is almost upon us. "My salvation is gone forth." The gospel is being preached to prepare a people for the coming day. . . Hence, "Lift up your eyes to the heavens, . . . and look upon the earth beneath." Read the signs of the times, the signs now being shown forth in the heavens above and in the earth beneath. "For the heavens shall vanish away like smoke, and the earth shall wax old like a garment, and they that dwell therein shall die in like manner." This old world shall die; there shall be a new heaven and a new earth; it will be a millennial earth. . . . (Isa. 51:4–6).

(Bruce R. McConkie, *The Millennial Messiah* [Salt Lake City: Deseret Book Co., 1985], 514–15.)

In LDS theology, "the earth will be renewed and receive its paradisiacal glory" (A of F 10). That renewal will include restoration of its former components—for example, the return of the city of Enoch—and also its former purity and Edenic state. . . .

Book of Mormon prophets likewise speak of a new heaven and a new earth (Ether 13:9) and of "all things" becoming new (3 Ne. 15:2). The Doctrine and Covenants contains prophecies that every corruptible "element shall melt with fervent heat; and all things shall become new, that [God's] knowledge and glory may dwell upon all the earth" (D&C 101:23; cf. 29:23–24; 42:35, 62, 67, 45:66; 84:2–4; 133:56).

The Hebrew root for "new" (*chadash*) points to a time of refreshing rather than replacement. Consistent with this understanding, Mormons expect that the earth will not be destroyed but glorified, not transcended but transformed, and that ultimately the polarization of earth and heaven will be overcome. Faithful Saints are promised the "fulness of the earth" (D&C 59:16) and "an inheritance upon the earth when the day of transfiguration shall come, when the earth shall be transfigured" (D&C 63:20–21).

"This earth will be Christ's" (D&C 130:9). It will have a one-thousand-year sabbatical and then become a veritable Urim AND Thumim in fulfillment of John's vision of its appearance as a "sea of glass" (D&C 130:7–9; Rev. 2:17), a habitation worthy of God. "It will be rolled back into the presence of God," and "crowned with celestial glory" (*TPJS*, 181; cf. *WJS*, 60)."

(Thomas J. Riskas, Jr., *Encyclopedia of Mormonism*, ed. Daniel H. Ludlow, 4 vols.,
[New York: Macmillan Publishing Co., 1992], 3:1009.)

2 Ne. 8:7   FEAR NOT . . . NEITHER BE YE AFRAID
(Isa. 51:7; refer in this text to 3 Ne. 22:17.)

Most fears . . . do not, as a rule, just happen. We nurse them and feed them until, from as inconsequential trifle, they have grown to monstrous proportions. . . .

A young man told me that he could not sleep. He gave me a long psychological explanation of how this had come about, "Can you help me get rid of this obsession?" he asked. "No," was my reply. "Then what can I do?" he implored. "Run around the block at night until you are ready to drop. What you need is exertion. You have put too much of your physical energies into imagining things. If you run hard enough, you will automatically relax and go to sleep. You have thought yourself into this fear with your mind, you can run yourself out of it with your legs"—and he did. . . . It is . . . true that many people who are obsessed by nagging fears might find a new interest in life if they became concerned *about other people* through participation in community activities. . . .

Every step in the conquest of fear requires, at the outset, an act of will. . . . As Emerson said, do the thing you fear and the death of fear is certain. Actually our fears are the forces that make us, when dealt with by decisive action, or that break us if dealt with by indecision, [or] procrastination . . . at the bottom of most fears, both mild and severe, will be found an overactive mind and an underactive body. Hence, I have advised many people, in their quest for happiness, to use their heads less and their arms and legs more—in useful work or play. We generate fears while we sit; we overcome them by action. Fear is nature's warning signal to get busy.

In its mild and initial stages, fear takes the form of . . . criticism of, certain activities and people. . . . The world is full of malcontents . . . who, because they will not change themselves, talk about changing the entire system. . . . Through conversation they rationalize their anger with the world, instead of becoming enraged with themselves and flying into worthwhile action.

(Henry C. Link, Ph.D., *Getting The Most Out Of Life, An Anthology from The Reader's Digest* [Pleasantville, New York: The Reader's Digest Association, Inc., 1946], 85–88.)

You were not born with the worry habit. You acquired it. . . .

Worry . . . is derived from an old Anglo-Saxon word meaning "to choke." If someone were to put his fingers around your throat and press hard, cutting off the flow of vital power, it would be a dramatic demonstration of what you do to yourself by long-held and habitual worry. . . .

Fear is the most powerful of all thoughts with one exception, and the one exception is faith. Faith can always overcome fear. Faith is the one power against which fear cannot stand. . . . Master faith and you will automatically master fear. . . .

Fear something over a long period of time and there is a real possibility that by fearing you may actually help bring it to pass. The Bible contains a line which is . . . terrible in its truth: "For the thing which I greatly feared is come upon me . . ." (Job 3:25) Of course it will, for if you fear something continuously you tend to create conditions in your mind propitious to the development of that which you fear. An atmosphere is encouraged in which it can take root and grow. You tend to draw it to yourself.

(Norman Vincent Peale, *The Power of Positive Thinking* [New York: Fawcett Crest Book, 1952], 122–26.)

Let us recognize that fear comes not of God, but rather that this gnawing, destructive element comes from the adversary of truth and righteousness. Fear is the antithesis of faith. It is corrosive in its effects, even deadly.

(*Teachings of Gordon B. Hinckley* [Salt Lake City: Deseret Book Co., 1997], 220.)

Fear . . . is a principal weapon in the arsenal that Satan uses to make mankind unhappy. He who fears loses strength for the combat of life in the fight against evil. Therefore, the power of the evil one always tries to generate fear in human hearts. In every age and in every era fear has faced mankind.

(Howard W. Hunter, *The Teachings of Howard W. Hunter*, ed. Clyde J. Williams [Salt Lake City: Bookcraft, 1997], 83.)

When I went on a mission, my father gave me a little card with a verse from the New Testament, the words of the Lord to the centurion servant who brought news concerning the little daughter of the centurion. Those words, "be not afraid, only believe." I commend those words to each of us, my brothers and sisters. You do not need to fear if you are on the side of right.

(*Teachings of Gordon B. Hinckley*, [Salt Lake City: Deseret Book Co., 1997], 221.)

So many of us are fearful of what our peers will say, that we will be looked upon with disdain and criticized if we stand for what is right. . . .

We need not be [afraid]. We need not slink off in a corner, as it were. We need not be ashamed. We have the greatest thing in the world, the gospel of the risen Lord. Paul gives us a mandate: "Be not thou therefore ashamed of the testimony of our Lord" (2 Tim. 1:8).

(*Teachings of Gordon B. Hinckley* [Salt Lake City: Deseret Book Co., 1997], 222.)

Dr. Joseph F. Montague, . . . says: "You do not get stomach ulcers from what you eat. You get ulcers from what is eating you."

More than half of our hospital beds are occupied by people with nervous troubles. Yet, when the nerves of these people are studied under a high-powered microscope in a post-mortem examination, their nerves in most cases are apparently . . . healthy. . . . Their "nervous troubles" are caused not by a physical deterioration of the nerves, but by emotions of futility, frustration, anxiety, worry, fear, defeat, despair. Plato said that "the greatest mistake physicians make is that they attempt to cure the body without attempting to cure the mind; yet the mind and body are one and should not be treated separately!"

Worry can make even the most stolid person ill. General Grant discovered that during the closing days of the Civil War. . . . Grant had been besieging Richmond for nine months. General Lee's troops, ragged and hungry, were beaten. Entire regiments were deserting at a time. . . . Grant was in hot pursuit, banging away at the Confederates from both sides and the rear. . . . Grant, half blind with a violent sick headache, fell behind his army and stopped at a farmhouse. "I spent the night," he records in his *Memoirs*, "in bathing my feet in hot water and mustard, and putting mustard plasters on my wrists and back part of my neck, hoping to be cured by morning."

The next morning, he was cured instantaneously. And the thing that cured him was not a mustard plaster, but a horseman galloping down the road with a letter from Lee, saying he wanted to surrender.

"When the officer [bearing the message] reached me," Grant wrote, "I was still suffering with the sick headache, but the instant I saw the contents of the note, I was cured."

Obviously it was Grant's worries, tensions, and emotions that made him ill. He was cured instantly the moment his emotions took on the hue of confidence, achievement, and victory.

(Dale Carnegie, *How to Stop Worrying and Start Living* [New York: Simon and Schuster, 1950], 19–22.)

We live in a day when the moral and spiritual values of the world are pretty tough. We can look forward with great yearning, and hope things get better. Well, they are not going to get better! The trend that is happening all around us—in society and government and education and all else—is a continuous trend.

And yet with all of that, I stand with great hope and great optimism. I have no fear. Fear is the antithesis of faith. With all that is happening and with all the impossible challenges that we face, we have that supernal gift of the Holy Ghost conferred upon us. And yet, for the most part, we know it not. It's interesting how in our lives we are operating, to an extent, as though we had not received it.

We have so much that is available, and we shouldn't fear! . . .

I remember sending some elders over to Harvard University to meet with someone—the home of a professor who was going to entertain himself at the expense of a couple of our missionaries. They begged me to go with them. I didn't want to go. I didn't want to face Harvard professors! If I had gone, I would have robbed them. I knew that.

I said, "You just go. I know they will belittle you and ridicule your beliefs. Just remember, bear your testimony; just bear your testimony."

Well, interesting! One young man particularly—who was from a little town in southern Utah, hardly old enough in maturity to be a missionary—went there with great fear.

The next morning they came into my office. They were walking on air above the floor, speaking figuratively.

I said, 'What happened?'

He said, 'We confounded them! We confounded them!'

You do not need to fear. Be a Latter-day Saint.

When I was in the military, I was put together up at Washington State University with a group of young men. There were about ten of us in an apartment in Stimpson Hall. We were there for some special pilot training. They began to introduce themselves. I was at the end of the row. As they went around the circle, I began to shrink. They had all been to college except me. I had barely escaped from high school. One of them mentioned that each summer his family had gone on "the Continent." I didn't know that meant they had gone to Europe. Another one was a son of a man who had been governor of Ohio and at that time was one of the cabinet members in the federal government. And all of them, it seemed to me, had everything to recommend them, and I had nothing.

It came to me, and I said, "I come from a little town in northern Utah that you have never heard of. My dad runs a garage. I come from a big family, and we have the blessings of the Church." I said another thing or two.

To my great surprise, I was accepted. They didn't care that my father wasn't a member of the president's cabinet or that our family hadn't gone on "the Continent." I learned something. Since that time I have had no fear of meeting people of high station or any people, and I have felt the confidence that comes when you have the gift of the Holy Ghost. . . .

Go forward without fear. Do not fear the future. Do not fear whatever is ahead of you. . . . And the Spirit of the Lord will attend you, and you will be blessed as it was intended that we should all be blessed by this supernal gift of the Holy Ghost.

(Boyd K. Packer, "'And They Knew It Not'", Satellite Broadcast: 5 March 2000,
Utah Valley State College, [Salt Lake City: The Church of Jesus Christ of Latter-day Saints, 2000], 4–7.)

Don't ever try to frighten anyone into the celestial glory. Joy is the pathway to the celestial glory—joy and happiness. . . . I have in my office every day good and faithful members of this Church who are depressed, who are frustrated, who think they are not being saved, and most of those people whom I see are just as worthy as I and some more worthy. Why they are frustrated, I don't know, unless someone is trying to scare them into the celestial glory.

(Matthew Cowley, *Matthew Cowley Speaks* [Salt Lake City: Deseret Book Co., 1954], 133.)

2 Ne. 8:9   RAHAB—DRAGON
(Isa. 51:9)

The Sea has several aliases: the Deep, the Abyss. It does not rage alone in its rebellion against God; it also has allies: Storm (Rahab) and Sea-serpent (Dragon, Leviathan). The sea is almost inseparable from the storms it brews. The poetic personifications of God's enemies blur the identities of Sea, Storm and Serpent, which are frequently paired or even substituted for each other. . . .

In a hymn of praise to the Creator, the psalmist says, "Thou dost rule the raging of the sea; when its waves rise, thou stillest them. Thou didst crush Rahab like a carcass, thou didst scatter thy enemies with thy mighty arm" (Ps. 89:9–10). "By his power he stilled the sea; by his understanding he smote Rahab" (Job 26:12 RSV). "Was it not thou that didst cut Rahab in pieces?" (Isa. 51:9 RSV). "God will not turn back his anger; beneath him bowed the helpers of Rahab" (Job 9:13 RSV). Who are these helpers of Rahab? The Sea as Abyss is the prison of rebellious spirits and the keeper of the dead (Job 26:5). It parallels Abaddon as keeper of shades and evil powers (cf. Ps. 88:11; Rev. 9:11). . . .

The primordial sea serpent goes by several names (Dragon, Leviathan, Tannin) and is sometimes difficult to distinguish from Rahab, with whom it appears in parallel. . . . (Isa. 51:9–1; Job 26:12–13; Ps. 74:13–15).

Occasionally the imagery applies to present enemies. Among various other mythical animals, Egypt is a subdued sea-monster, a "Rahab who sits still" in contrast to the trashing, twisting serpent (Isa. 30:7; cf. Ps. 87:4).

(*Dictionary of Biblical Imagery*, ed. Leland Ryken, James C. Wilhoit, and
Tremper Longman III, [Downers Grove, Illinois: InterVarsity Press, 1998], 171.)

2 Ne. 8:12   GRASS
(Isa. 51:12)

Isaiah saw the transient appearance of grass, herbs, and flowers as an image for the destruction of the wicked. Much of the Holy Land is arid and can support an abundance of vegetation only during the rainy seasons from about November to April. Many plants begin to grow during the colder, winter months, but most do not mature and flower until the warmer weeks of spring from February to April. During those few short weeks, land that is usually barren can be covered with grasses, herbs, and flowers; but with the end of the rains, most of the vegetation withers and dies. By June the land that was once verdant is bleak and bare. Moreover, occasionally an east wind, heated by the desert sand of Arabia, will sweep across the country, withering the vegetation as if in a furnace. In Isaiah this phenomenon is used as a type of the brief existence of mortality.

(Terry Ball, *Thy People Shall Be My People and Thy God My God:*
The 22nd Annual Sidney B. Sperry Symposium [Salt Lake City: Deseret Book Co., 1994], 26.)

2 Ne. 8:12   I AM HE THAT COMFORTETH YOU
(Isa. 51:12; refer in this text to 2 Ne. 8:3)

With many of you there is the gnawing pain of bereavement and fear. To you the Lord has said, "Blessed are they that mourn: for they shall be comforted" (Matt. 5:4).

We know there are many days of loneliness and nights of longing. But there is also that which comes from Him who said, "I, even I, am he that comforteth you" (Isa. 51:12).

The Lord is your strength. He is available to you, and when invited, by His Spirit He will come to you. . . .

You will find comfort and strength as you lose yourself in . . . service. Your own troubles will be forgotten as you help others with theirs. Your burdens will become lighter as you lift the burdens of the downtrodden and the oppressed.

(*Teachings of Gordon B. Hinckley* [Salt Lake City: Deseret Book Co., 1997], 688–89.)

2 Ne. 8:12–16   THE LORD ASKS THREE QUESTIONS
(Isa. 51:12–16)

The Lord asks Israel three questions: Why do you fear mortal man? Have you forgotten your creator? Why fear your oppressors? He then answers them (in reverse order): You will be freed from your oppressors. I am the great creator. You are my people; I will teach and protect you.

Although these promises seem to be extended to all types of Israelites, they apply more particularly to those who become a part of covenant Israel, members of The Church of Jesus Christ of Latter-day Saints. Joseph Smith foretells that one group of Israelites, the remnants of the Ten Tribes, will come to Ephraim at "the boundaries of the everlasting hills." (See D&C 133:32–35.)

The parallels between these three verses and Isaiah 51:9–16 are evident. They help us to understand Isaiah's words and to see their fulfillment in those who join the Church in this dispensation.

(Victor L. Ludlow, *Isaiah: Prophet, Seer, and Poet* [Salt Lake City: Deseret Book Co., 1982], 429.)

2 Ne. 8:17   CUP
(Isa. 51:17)

Our Lord's frequent mention of His foreseen sufferings as the cup of which the Father would have Him drink (Matt. 26:39, 42; Mark 14:36; Luke 22:42; John 18:11; compare Matt. 20:22; Mark 10:38; 1 Cor. 10:21) is in line with Old Testament usage of the term "cup" as a symbolic expression for a bitter or poisonous potion typifying experiences of suffering. See Ps. 11:6; 75:8; Isa. 51:17, 22; Jer. 25:15, 17; 49:12.

(James E. Talmage *Jesus the Christ: A Study of the Messiah and His Mission According to Holy Scriptures both Ancient and Modern* [Salt Lake City: The Church of Jesus Christ of Latter-day Saints, 1981], 620.)

2 Ne. 8:17   DREGS . . . WRUNG OUT
(Isa. 51:17; Mosiah 3:24–27)

The last drops of the cup of wrath will be wrung out for Israel to drink, including the sediment in the bottom of the cup which may symbolize the bitterest trials.

(Donald W. Parry, Jay A. Parry, and Tina M. Peterson,
Understanding Isaiah [Salt lake City: Deseret Book Co., 1998], 459.)

2 Ne. 8:17   STAND UP O JERUSALEM
(Isa. 51:17)

Because of wickedness, the ancient Jews were scattered and taken captive to Babylon. Later, some Jews returned to Jerusalem and rebuilt the temple. Unfortunately, this Jewish community also became wicked, and most of their descendants rejected Christ when he lived on earth. Because of their iniquities, they suffered great destruction, another scattering, and the hatred of men. (See 2 Ne. 6:10–11; 10:3–6.) But punishment, dispersion, and persecution are not to be their permanent condition. The Lord will bless, gather, and protect them as they return to the Lord, especially after they accept him as their Messiah (2 Ne. 6:11; 10:7–9). . . . In these verses, Isaiah speaks of the time when the covenants of the Lord are fulfilled and the Jews are brought back home again through their righteousness.

(Victor L. Ludlow, *Isaiah: Prophet, Seer, and Poet* [Salt Lake City: Deseret Book Co., 1982], 429–30.)

2 Ne. 8:19–20   TWO SONS
(JST, Isa. 51:19–20; Zech. 4:11–14; D&C 77:15; Rev. 11:1–14)

These two prophets were also spoken of by John the Revelator (Rev. 11:1–14), Zechariah (Zech. 4:11–14), and Joseph Smith (D&C 77:15). The two will "have power to shut heaven, that it rain not in the days of their prophecy: and have power over waters to turn them to blood, and to smite the earth with all plagues, as often as they will" (Rev. 11:6). . . . At the end of their designated ministry, the two prophets will be slain. Their dead bodies will lie in the streets of Jerusalem for three and one-half days while the wicked of the world rejoice. However, their victory will be short-lived, for the two martyrs will arise as resurrected beings. A great earthquake, of a magnitude never before known, will follow and the Savior will shortly appear. The wicked will be destroyed and the earth prepared for the millennial reign.

(Hoyt W. Brewster, Jr., *Isaiah Plain and Simple* [Salt Lake City: Deseret Book Co., 1995], 225–26.)

These two shall be followers of that humble man, Joseph Smith. . . . No doubt they will be members of the Council of the Twelve or of the First Presidency of the Church. Their prophetic ministry to rebellious Jewry shall be the same in length as was our Lord's personal ministry among their rebellious forebears.

(Bruce R. McConkie, *Doctrinal New Testament Commentary*, 3 vols. [Salt Lake City: Bookcraft, 1965–1973], 3:509–10.)

Revelation 11:1–12 further expands and clarifies the event alluded to in Isaiah 51. According to the passage in Revelation, the Lord will give to two of his witnesses in the last days power over their enemies, as well as over the elements—accounting for destruction and famine. They will have power to withstand the enemy for a period of twelve hundred and sixty days, until "they shall have finished their testimony" (Rev. 11:7), at which point they will be killed by the forces of evil. Their bodies will lie in the street for three and one-half days while their enemies rejoice. Then they will be resurrected and will ascend to heaven in glory. The book of Revelation further associates these two witnesses with the symbolism of two olive trees and two candlesticks mentioned in Zechariah 4:11–14 (Rev. 11:4). In the Doctrine and Covenants the Lord identified these two witnesses as "two prophets that are to be raised up to the Jewish nation in the last days, at the time of the restoration, and to prophesy to the Jews after they are gathered and have built the city of Jerusalem in the land of their fathers" (D&C 77:15).

(David Rolph Seely, *Studies in Scripture, Vol. 4*, ed. Kent P. Jackson [Salt Lake City: Deseret Book Co., 1993], 148.)

At the end of their designated ministry—"when they shall have finished their testimony," the Revelator tells us—"the beast . . . shall overcome them, and kill them." For three and one-half days, their dead bodies will lie in the streets of Jerusalem while the wicked of the world "shall rejoice over them, and make merry, and shall send gifts one to another; because these two prophets tormented them that dwelt on the earth" (Rev. 11:7–10). Jerusalem will then be overrun and ravished: "For I will gather all nations against Jerusalem to battle; and the city shall be taken, and the houses rifled, and the women ravished; and half of the city shall go forth into captivity, and the residue of the people shall not be cut off from the city" (Zech. 14:2). "Every one that is found shall be thrust through; and every one that is joined unto them shall fall by the sword. Their children also shall be dashed to pieces before their eyes; their houses shall be spoiled, and their wives ravished" (Isa. 13:15–16).

Just when it seems that the wicked have won this final battle, their victory celebration will be cut short with the resurrection of the two slain prophets: "And after three days and an half the Spirit of life from God entered into them, and they stood upon their feet; and great fear fell upon them which saw them. And they heard a great voice from heaven saying unto them, Come up hither. And they ascended up to heaven in a cloud; and their enemies beheld them. And the same hour was there a great earthquake, and the tenth part of the city fell, and in the earthquake were slain of men seven thousand; and the remnant were afrighted, and gave glory to the God of heaven" (Rev. 11:11–13).

(Hoyt W. Brewster Jr., *Behold, I Come Quickly: The Last Days and Beyond*
[Salt Lake City: Deseret Book Co., 1994], 101–02.)

John, in the eleventh chapter of Revelation, gives us many more particulars concerning this same event. He informs us that after the city and temple are rebuilt by the Jews, the Gentiles will tread it under foot forty and two months, during which time there will be two prophets continually prophesying and working mighty miracles. And it seems that the Gentile army shall be hindered from utterly destroying and overthrowing the city, while these two prophets continue.

(Parley P. Pratt, *A Voice of Warning*, p. 33, as quoted in *Old Testament Student Manual, 1 Kings –Malachi,* Religion
302 Student Manual, 2d. ed. [Salt Lake City: The Church of Jesus Christ of Latter-day Saints, 1982], 293–94.)

The description of these two sons calls to mind the two witnesses who will be the major factor in keeping enemy armies from totally defeating the Jews (Rev. 11:1–6). John the Revelator describes two great servants of God who will stand and fight for Jerusalem against the armies of the world. For three and one-half years they will have power over the heavens, earth, and their enemies. Then they will be killed (Rev. 11:3–13; see Zech. 4:11–14). The two sons in Isaiah's prophecy wield similar power and are depicted as a wild bull in a net; while the bull may be captive, it is still dangerous until it is worn down. In a few words, Isaiah describes the ministry of these two great sons. While they can not stop the eventual overthrow of Jerusalem, they keep away the destruction until they are finally subdued and killed.

(Victor L. Ludlow, *Isaiah: Prophet, Seer, and Poet* [Salt Lake City: Deseret Book Co., 1982], 431.)

2 Ne. 8:23   **BOW DOWN, THAT WE MAY GO OVER**

(Isa. 51:23; Josh. 10:24; Ps. 110:1; refer to this text to 1 Ne. 21:23)

In some ancient societies, the vanquished were forced to lie on the ground while the victor walked over them (Josh. 10:24; Ps. 110:1).

(Donald W. Parry, Jay A. Parry, and Tina M. Peterson,
Understanding Isaiah [Salt Lake City: Deseret Book Co., 1998], 460.)

2 Ne. 8:24   **BEAUTIFUL GARMENTS**

(Isa. 52:1)

What comes about as a result of exercising the Priesthood is equivalent to putting on "her beautiful garments."

(Hyrum M. Smith, as quoted in Hoyt W. Brewster, Jr., *Doctrine & Covenants Encyclopedia*
[Salt Lake City: Bookcraft, 1988], 40.)

According to the Lord's instruction in Leviticus concerning the Day of Atonement, the high priest was to "wash his flesh in water" and then to "put on the holy linen coat," "linen breeches," "a linen girdle," and a "linen mitre" (Lev. 16:4). While wearing these garments, the high priest was to make atonement for himself, the temple, and the people by sacrifice (see Lev. 16:33). During this ceremony, the high priest and priests were instructed on numerous occasions to remove their garments, wash themselves, and wash their clothes (see Lev. 16:23–24, 26, 28).

Such emphasis on garments being kept clean (for example, from the blood of the sacrifices) in connection with the temple and the Day of Atonement may have inspired Jacob to take off his garments and display them before the Nephites, saying, "I pray the God of my salvation that he view me with his all-searching eye; . . . that the God of Israel did witness that I shook your iniquities from my soul, and that I stand with brightness before him, and am rid of your blood" (2 Ne. 9:44). This theme is further supported by Jacob's reference to "being clothed with purity, yea, even with the robe of righteousness" (2 Ne. 9:14) and by an Isaiah passage Jacob quotes: "Awake, awake, put on they strength, O Zion; put on thy beautiful garments, O Jerusalem, the holy city; for henceforth there shall no more come into thee the uncircumcised and the unclean" (2 Ne. 8:24, parallel to Isa. 52:1).

(John S. Thompson, *Isaiah In The Book of Mormon*, ed. Donald W. Parry and John W. Welch
[Provo, Utah: Foundation for Ancient Research and Mormon Studies, 1998], 131–32.)

2 Ne. 8:24–25   PUT ON THY STRENGTH, O ZION
(Isa. 52:1–2; D&C 113:8; 2 Ne. 9:1–3;
refer in this text to 3 Ne. 20:36 & 3 Ne. 22:2)

The Book of Mormon, in 2 Nephi 8, combines the first two verses of Isaiah 52 with the entirety of Isaiah 51. Isaiah 52:1–2 is quoted or paraphrased in three places in the Book of Mormon: by Jacob in 2 Nephi 8:24–25, by the Savior in 3 Nephi 20:36–37, and by Moroni in Moroni 10:31. Jesus explained that the fulfillment of these verses would come after the Jews were gathered to Jerusalem in the last days.

(Donald W. Parry, Jay A. Parry, and Tina M. Peterson,
Understanding Isaiah [Salt Lake City: Deseret Book Co., 1998], 457.)

Never has the Church had the opportunity and the challenge which it faces today. Now is the time for us to arise and shine as a people (D&C 115:5), to put on our beautiful garments (2 Ne. 8:24), to demonstrate to the world the fruits of the gospel, and to proclaim the standards which the Lord has revealed for the blessings of His children.

(Ezra Taft Benson, *The Teachings of Ezra Taft Benson* [Salt Lake City: Bookcraft, 1988], 461.)

2 Ne. 9:50–51   FEAST UPON THAT WHICH PERISHETH NOT
(Isa. 55:1–2; 2 Ne. 26:25; 32:3)

The Day of Atonement was the only fast prescribed by the law of Moses (Lev. 16:29, 31; 23:27, 32—the word "afflict" parallels the word "fast" in Isaiah 58:3 and is typically understood to mean to "deny oneself"). Louis Jacobs describes this day as "a day of feasting without eating or drinking; the nourishment provided is for the soul." Isaiah promises that those who fast properly by dealing "thy bread to the hungry" and bringing the "poor that are cast out to thy house" will be blessed, for the Lord will "satisfy thy soul in drought, and make fat thy bones" (Isa. 58:7, 11; see also Isa. 58:3–12). A similar allusion to fasting can be seen in the prophet Jacob's words . . . (2 Ne. 9:50–51; parallel to Isa. 55:1–2).

(John S. Thompson, *Isaiah In The Book of Mormon*: Edited by Donald W. Parry and John W. Welch
[Provo, Utah: Foundation for Ancient Research and Mormon Studies, 1998], 133–34.)

Far too many individuals and families have incurred too much debt. Be careful of the many attractive offers to borrow money. It is much easier to borrow money than it is to pay it back. There are no shortcuts to financial security. There are no get-rich-quick schemes that work. Perhaps none need the principle of balance in their lives more than those who are driven toward accumulating "things" in this world.

Do not trust your money to others without a thorough evaluation of any proposed investment. Our people have lost far too much money by trusting their assets to others. In my judgment, we never will have balance in our lives unless our finances are securely under control.

The prophet Jacob said to his people: . . . (2 Ne. 9:51).

Brothers and sisters, remember to always pay a full tithing.

(M. Russell Ballard, *Ensign,* May 1987, 14–15.)

We may build a beautiful, spacious home that is far larger than we need. We may spend far too much to decorate, furnish, and landscape it. And even if we are blessed enough to afford such luxury, we may be misdirecting resources that could be better used to build the kingdom of God or to feed and clothe our needy brothers and sisters.

Jacob, the Book of Mormon prophet, warned us, "Do not spend money for that which is of no worth, nor your labor for that which cannot satisfy" (2 Ne. 9:51). And in even stronger words, he said:

> "Because some of you have obtained more abundantly than . . . your brethren ye are lifted up in the pride of your hearts, and wear stiff necks and high heads because of the costliness of your apparel, and persecute your brethren because ye suppose that ye are better than they.
>
> "And now, my brethren, do ye suppose that God justifieth you in this thing? Behold, I say unto you, Nay. But he condemneth you. . . .
>
> "Do ye not suppose that such things are abominable unto him who created all flesh? And the one being is as precious in his sight as the other" (Jacob 2:13–14; 21).

Pride and vanity, the opposites of humility, can destroy our spiritual health as surely as a debilitating disease can destroy our physical health.

The Savior taught clearly the proper value of worldly possessions in his conversation with the rich young ruler who asked what more was required to have eternal life; he had kept all the commandments from his youth. He asked the Master what he still lacked. Jesus told him to sell all that he had and give to the poor, and come and follow Him. But the man went away sorrowing, for he loved his possessions. (See Matt. 19:16–22.) How many of us would pass this test?

Many of us have made sacred covenants to live the laws of sacrifice and consecration. But when the Lord blesses us with riches and affluence, we may give little thought to how we should use these blessings to help build up his church.

(Joseph B. Wirthlin, *Ensign,* Nov. 1990, 65.)

2 Ne. 11:2–8   NEPHI, JACOB, AND ISAIAH

There were three . . . witnesses—special witnesses—not only of the divine origins of the Book of Mormon but also of Divinity himself. These early witnesses were Nephi, Jacob, and Isaiah, and it is not by coincidence that their testimonies appear so conspicuously at the beginning of this ancient record. . . .

The "greater views" of the gospel found in the teachings of the small plates of Nephi come from the personal declarations of these three great prophetic witnesses of the premortal Jesus Christ—Nephi, Jacob, and Isaiah. These three doctrinal and visionary voices make clear at the very outset of the Book of Mormon why it is "another testament of Jesus Christ."

In declaring the special preparation these three had for receiving and teaching such "greater views" of the gospel, Nephi revealed the most persuasive qualification of all: They had seen the premortal Jesus Christ (2 Ne. 11:2–3).

One could argue convincingly that the primary purpose for recording, preserving, and then translating the small plates of Nephi was to bring forth to the dispensation of the fulness of times the testimony of these three witnesses. Their writings constitute a full 135 of the 145 pages from the small plates. . . . After reading these three witnesses from the small plates of Nephi, the reader knows two things in bold relief: that Jesus is the Christ, the Son of the Living God, and that God will keep his covenants and promises with the remnants of the house of Israel. Those two themes constitute the two principal purposes of the Book of Mormon, and they are precisely the introductory themes addressed by Nephi, Jacob, and Isaiah.

(Jeffrey R. Holland, *Christ and the New Covenant* [Salt Lake City: Deseret Book Co., 1997], 34–35.)

2 Ne. 11:2   DELIGHT IN ISAIAH

In order to delight in Isaiah's words we need to understand the spiritual and cultural and geographical barriers that separate us. This is not an overwhelming task. Nephi was telling us that Isaiah can be comprehended if we (1) seek the Holy Ghost as we study the words of Isaiah (2 Ne. 24:4), (2) understand the manner of prophesying among the Jews (2 Ne. 25:5), (3) become acquainted with the geography of the Holy Land (2 Ne. 25:6), and (4) know the judgments of God (specifically the blessing versus cursing relationship as outlined in the law of Moses) (2 Ne. 25:6).

(John Lewis Lund, *Religious Educators' Symposium: on the Old Testament*
[Salt Lake City: The Church of Jesus Christ of Latter-day Saints, 1979], 194.)

2 Ne. 12:1   WORD, SAW
                         (Isa. 2:1)

The Hebrew word *davar,* translated here as *word,* can also be translated *message.* The Hebrew word *khazah,* translated here as *saw,* indicates that Isaiah received this message also from the Lord in a vision (cf. Isa. 1:1).

(Ellis T. Rasmussen, *A Latter-day Saint Commentary on the Old Testament*
[Salt Lake City: Deseret Book Co., 1993], 504.)

2 Ne. 12:1–4   MOUNTAIN OF THE LORD'S HOUSE
                           (Isa. 2:1–4; Ps. 65:4; D&C 133:10–13;
                           2 Ne. 30:15; Micah 4:1–2; Zech.6:12–15)

The expression "the mountain of the Lord's house," as here indicated, was undoubtedly to be referred to as a place as well as a definition of a righteous people. . . . And then the ancient prophet said, "And many nations shall come, and say, Come, and let us go up to the mountain of the Lord, to the house of the God of Jacob; and he will teach us of his ways, and we will walk in his paths; for the law shall go forth of Zion, and the word of the Lord from Jerusalem." (Mic. 4:2.) With the coming of the pioneers to establish the Church in the tops of the mountains, our early leaders declared this to be the beginning of the fulfillment of that prophecy. . . . Years ago I went with the brethren to the Idaho Falls Temple [dedication], and I heard in that inspired prayer of the First Presidency a definition of the meaning of that term "out of Zion shall go forth the law." Note what they said: "We thank thee that thou hast revealed to us that those who gave us our constitutional form of government were men wise in thy sight and that thou didst raise them up for the very purpose of putting forth that sacred document. . . . We pray that kings and rulers and the peoples of all nations under heaven may be persuaded of the blessings enjoyed by the people of this land by reason of their freedom and under thy guidance be constrained to adopt similar governmental systems, thus to fulfill the ancient prophecy of Isaiah and Micah that '. . . out of Zion shall go forth the law and the word of the Lord from Jerusalem'" (*Improvement Era,* October 1945, 564).

(Harold B. Lee, *Ensign,* Nov. 1971, 15.)

The test lies in our capacity to live the gospel rather than adopt the ways of the world.

I do not advocate a retreat from society. On the contrary, we have a responsibility and a challenge to take our places in the world of business, science, government, medicine, education, and every other worthwhile and constructive vocation. . . . In so doing we must work with others. But this does not require a surrender of standards. . . .

We can maintain the integrity of our families. . . . We can oppose the tide of pornography and lasciviousness. . . . We can refrain from buying on the Sabbath day. . . . As we observe these and other standards taught by the Church, many in the world will respect us and find strength to follow that which they too know is right.

And, in the words of Isaiah, "Many people shall go and say, Come ye, and let us go up to the mountain of the Lord, to the house of the God of Jacob; and he will teach us of his ways, and we will walk in his paths" (Isa. 2:3).

We need not compromise. We must not compromise.

The candle which the Lord has lighted in this dispensation can become as a light unto the whole world, and others seeing our good works may be led to glorify our Father in heaven and emulate in their own lives the examples they may have observed in ours.

(Gordon B. Hinckley, *Ensign,* Nov. 1974, 100.)

All of the holy temples of our God in the latter days shall be built in the mountains of the Lord, for his mountains—whether the land itself is a hill, a valley, or a plain—are the places where he comes, personally and by the power of his Spirit, to commune with his people. . . .

Isaiah names the building of latter-day temples as a sign both of the gathering of Israel and of the second coming of Christ. Israel, as we are aware, is to gather to places where there are temples so her municipals may gain the blessings made available in these holy houses, and these blessings prepare their recipients to meet the Lord, who will suddenly come to his temple. . . .

The building of a temple in both the mountain of the Lord and the tops of the mountains, unto which the elect of the Lord shall come out of all nations, is the promised sign. This is first and foremost the temple, capped with six spires and crowned with an angelic ministrant sounding the trump of God, that now stands in Salt Lake City in the tops of the mountains of America. All of the temples now built or that may be built in the high mountains of America also do or will fulfill this prophetic word.

(Bruce R. McConkie, *The Millennial Messiah* [Salt Lake City: Deseret Book Co., 1982], 275–76.)

This has specific reference to the Salt Lake Temple and to the other temples built in the top of the Rocky Mountains, and it has a general reference to the temple yet to be built in the New Jerusalem in Jackson County, Missouri. Those in all nations, be it noted, shall flow to the houses of the Lord in the tops of the mountains, there to make the covenants out of which eternal life comes.

(Bruce R. McConkie, *A New Witness for the Articles of Faith* [Salt Lake City: Deseret Book Co., 1985], 539.)

The word mountain is used in the scriptures in different allegorical or figurative senses. In 2 Nephi 12:1–4 the word mountain refers to a high place of God, a place of revelation, even the temple of the Lord.

(George Reynolds and Janne M. Sjodahl, *Commentary on the Book of Mormon,* ed. Philip C. Reynolds, 7 vols. [Salt Lake City: Deseret Book Co., 1955–1961], 1:214.)

It will be noted that the words of the above verses from the Book of Mormon are identical with the King James translation of Isaiah 2:1–4 except for the change of one word. In the second verse the word "that" (an italicized word) in the King James translation is changed to "when." . . . If the word "when" is used, time is indicated and not place. Thus the Book of Mormon supplies a key to understanding these passages by saying that *when* the mountain of the Lord's house is established in the top of the mountains, then certain events will follow.

(Ross Warner, *The Fulfillment of Book of Mormon Prophecies*
[Salt Lake City: Hawkes Publishing, Inc., 1975], 175.)

[The dedicatory prayer of the Salt Lake Temple, Apr. 6, 1893:] In past ages thou didst inspire with thy Holy Spirit thy servants, the prophets, to speak of the time in the latter days when the mountain of the Lord's house should be established in the tops of the mountains, and should be exalted above the hills. We thank thee that we have had the glorious opportunity of contributing to the fulfillment of these visions of Thine ancient seers. . . .

(Wilford Wooddruff, *Discourses of Wilford Woodruff*, ed. G. Homer Durham
[Salt Lake City: Bookcraft, 1946], 337.)

While many Latter-day Saints believe that the establishment of "the mountain of the Lord's house" in the tops of the mountains represents the Salt Lake Temple, verse 2 has a broader application. The Zion of North and South America was labeled by some Old Testament prophets as the "everlasting hills" or the "ancient mountains" (see Gen. 49:26; Deut. 33:15). This would suggest that Isaiah's prophecy relates to the whole continent, not just Salt Lake City. The first temple built in the "everlasting hills" in this dispensation was the Kirtland Temple in 1836, and the Lord appeared to the Prophet Joseph Smith and Oliver Cowdery in that temple on 3 April 1836 (see D&C 110).

(Monte S. Nyman, *Great Are the Words of Isaiah* [Salt Lake City: Bookcraft, 1980], 26.)

I believe that prophecy applies to the historic and wonderful Salt Lake Temple. But I believe also that it is related to this magnificent [Conference Center] hall. For it is from this pulpit that the law of God shall go forth, together with the word and testimony of the Lord.

(Gordon B. Hinckley, *Ensign,* Nov. 2000, 69.)

For a gathering of people to "flow," as a river up a mountain, a power greater than gravity must be at work. This power is the power of God and of the temple.

(Donald W. Parry, *Visualizing Isaiah*,
[Provo, Utah: The Foundation for Ancient Research and Mormon Studies, 2001], 98.)

This great prophecy, as is often the case, is subject to the law of multiple fulfilment. 1. In Salt Lake City and other mountain locations temples, in the full and true sense of the word, have been erected, and representatives of all nations are flowing unto them to learn of God and his ways. In this connection and as part of the general fulfilment of Isaiah's prophecy, is the fact that one of the world's greatest genealogical societies has been established in Salt Lake City—a society to which people of all nations come to do the ancestral research which must precede the performance of vicarious temple ordinances. 2. But the day is yet future when the Lord's house is to be built on that "Mount Zion" which is "the city of New Jerusalem" in Jackson County, Missouri (D&C 84:2–4). Mount Zion, itself, will be the mountain of the Lord's house in the day when that glorious temple is erected. 3. When the Jews flee unto Jerusalem, it will be "unto the mountains of the Lord's house" (D&C 133:13), for a holy temple is to be built there also as part of the work of the great era of restoration (Ezek. 37:24–28).

The law cannot go forth from Zion and the word of the Lord from Jerusalem, in the full millennial sense that Isaiah foresaw and specified, until these two great future temples are constructed in the old and new Jerusalems (Isa. 2; Mic. 4; 2 Ne. 12).

(Bruce R. McConkie, *Mormon Doctrine*, 2d ed. [Salt Lake City: Bookcraft, 1966], 518.)

"The prophecy of Joseph Smith that the Saints would be driven to the Rocky Mountains, there to become a mighty people, was in confirmation of an earlier prophecy of Isaiah 'that the mountain of the Lord's house shall be established in the top of the mountains' (Isa. 2:2). This prophecy was fulfilled and further confirmed by Brigham Young, who, when entering the valley, rose from his sick bed in Wilford Woodruff's carriage and said, 'This is the right place!'"

(S. Dilworth Young, *Conference Report*, April 1974
[Salt Lake City: The Church of Jesus Christ of Latter-day Saints, 1974], 88–89.)

We are commanded by God to take this gospel to all the world. That is the cause that must unite us today. Only the gospel will save the world from the calamity of its own self-destruction. Only the gospel will unite men of all races and nationalities in peace. Only the gospel will bring joy, happiness, and salvation to the human family.

Isaiah said that many in latter times would say: "Come . . . let us go up . . . to the house of the God of Jacob; and he will teach us of his ways, and we will walk in his paths" (Isa. 2:3; 2 Ne. 12:3).

Is there any greater cause than to teach others the gospel so that they may be united in walking in the ways of the God of Israel? Will we so live His commandments that others will see that the ways of the God of Jacob are distinctive from the world? That is our challenge. Let us then make His cause our cause.

(Ezra Taft Benson, *The Teachings of Ezra Taft Benson* [Salt Lake City: Bookcraft, 1988], 188.)

2 Ne. 12:2–4   ISAIAH—MICAH
(Isa. 2:2–4)

Interestingly, the first words Isaiah records in verses 2–4 of chapter 2 are also found with only slight variations in Micah 4:1–4. It may be that Isaiah "saw" the words of Micah or that he "saw" his own vision and Micah borrowed his words. Or, both prophets may have read the prophecy of some earlier prophet. Scholars differ in their opinions on which of these possibilities best explains the textual similarities. There is yet a fourth possibility, however, that seems plausible, particularly to Latter-day Saints: Isaiah and Micah, by virtue of their prophetic callings, each "saw" the same heavenly vision and were inspired to record it in essentially the same words. Since Isaiah and Micah were contemporaries dealing with the same people and problems, it seems likely that they would share similar spiritual manifestations. Precedents for this explanation exist elsewhere in the scriptures, because several prophets far distant from each other have recorded the same inspired messages: compare the "charity" sermon in 1 Corinthians 13 with Moroni 7, and the discourse on gifts of the Spirit in 1 Corinthians 12 with Moroni 10 and Doctrine and Covenants section 46. Certainly it is possible for two prophets to use the same vocabulary in recording revelations if, as the Lord said, "these words are not of men, nor of man, but of me" (D&C 18:34).

The important point here is that these verses have authority, regardless of their authorship. They are authentic and prophetic, and carry a beautiful message concerning the Lord's kingdom in the last days.

(Victor L. Ludlow, *Isaiah: Prophet, Seer, and Poet* [Salt Lake City: Deseret Book Co., 1982], 85–86.)

2 Ne. 12:3   THE LAW FROM ZION—THE WORD FROM JERUSALEM
(Isa. 2:3; refer in this text to 2 Ne. 20:24–25)

He [God] will assemble the Natives, the remnants of Joseph in America; and make of them a great, and strong, and powerful nation: and he will civilize and enlighten them, and will establish a holy city, and temple, and seat of government among them, which shall be called Zion.

And there shall be his tabernacle, his sanctuary, his throne, and seat of government for the whole continent of North and South America for ever.

In short, it will be to the western hemisphere what Jerusalem will be to the eastern.

And there the Messiah will visit them in person; and the old Saints, who will then have been raised from the dead, will be with him. And he will establish his kingdom and laws over all the land. . . .

The city of Zion, with its sanctuary and priesthood, and the glorious fulness of the gospel, will constitute a *standard* which will put an end to jarring creeds and political wranglings, by uniting the republics, states, provinces, territories, nations, tribes, kindred, tongues, people, and sects of North and South America in one great and common bond of brotherhood. . . .

Americans! This mighty and strange work has been commenced in your midst, and must roll on in fulfillment.

("Proclamation of the Twelve Apostles of the Church of Jesus Christ
of Latter-day Saints to all the Kings of the World," April 6, 1845, as quoted in James R. Clark,
comp., *Messages of the First Presidency,* 5 vols. [Salt Lake City: Bookcraft, 1955–1975], 1:259–61.)

Moses received the word of the Lord from God Himself; he was the mouth of God to Aaron, and Aaron taught the people, in both civil and ecclesiastical affairs; they were both one; . . . so will it be when the purposes of God shall be accomplished: when "the Lord shall be King over the whole earth" and "Jerusalem His throne." "The law shall go forth from Zion, and the word of the Lord from Jerusalem."

(Joseph Smith, *Teachings of the Prophet Joseph Smith,*
comp. Jospeh Fielding Smith [Salt Lake City: Deseret Book Co., 1976], 252.)

These will be the two religious "capitals for the kingdom of God during the millennium." (Smith, *Doctrines of Salvation,* 3:71.) One will be located in Independence, Missouri (D&C 57:3; 84:2–4); the other will be found in old Jerusalem (Ether 13:2–11). Both centers will be called Zion and Jerusalem, and they will possess great temples.

(Donald W. Parry, Jay A. Parry, and Tina M. Peterson,
Understanding Isaiah [Salt lake City: Deseret Book Co., 1998], 27.)

The statement about the law going forth from Zion and the word of the Lord from Jerusalem will come to pass during the Millennium. . . .

We expect to see the day when temples will dot the earth. . . . Perhaps they will number in the hundreds, or even in the thousands, before the Lord returns. During the Millennium their presence will be everywhere, for the billions of church members will all be entitled to the fulness of the ordinances and blessings of the Lord's holy houses. But there are two great temples in particular, two glorious houses of the Great Jehovah, that must be built by his people before he comes—one in Jerusalem of old, the other in the New Jerusalem. . . .

Solomon built a majestic mansion for the Lord in the day of Israel's glory. Zerubbabel built it anew when the remnant returned from bondage in Babylon. And Herod—a wretched, evil man whose every act bore Satan's stamp—built it for the final time in the day our Lord made flesh his tabernacle. . . . This is the temple that was torn apart, stone by stone, by Titus and his minions. And thus ended temple work in Jerusalem. . . . And thus was it to be in Jerusalem until the promised day when a new temple should arise—perhaps on the very site of the old one—in which the gospel ordinances of the new kingdom shall be performed. . . .

And then shall the Millennium be ushered in. . . . Who shall build this temple? The Lord himself shall do it by the hands of his servants the prophets. . . . There is only one people who know how to build temples and what to do in them when they are completed. That people is the Latter-day Saints. The temple in Jerusalem will not be built by Jews who have assembled there for political purposes as at present. . . . But it will be built by Jews who have come unto Christ, who once again are in the true fold of their ancient Shepherd. . . .

All of this brings us to that inspired statement of the Prophet Joseph Smith relative to the temple in Jerusalem and the Second Coming: "Judah must return," he said, "Jerusalem must be rebuilt, and the temple, and water come out from under the temple, and the waters of the Dead Sea be healed. It will take some time to rebuild the walls of the city and the temple, etc.; and all this must be done before the Son of Man will make His appearance" (*Teachings*, 286).

We now turn to a consideration of the temple in the New Jerusalem. . . . In July 1831 the Prophet Joseph Smith, then in Jackson County, Missouri, importuned the Lord in these words: "When will the wilderness blossom as the rose? When will Zion be built up in her glory, and where will thy Temple stand, unto which all nations shall come in the last days?" (Introductory heading, D&C 57). In answer the Lord said: "This is the land of promise, and the place for the city of Zion. . . . Behold, the place which is now called Independence is the center place; and a spot for the temple is lying westward, upon a lot which is not far from the court-house" (D&C 57:1–3).

It is in this city, the New Jerusalem in Jackson County, that the house of the Lord unto which all nations shall come in the last days shall be built. . . . When the appointed time comes, the Lord will reveal it to his servants who preside over his kingdom from Salt Lake City, and then the great work will go forward. . . . Some Lamanites may assist and some Gentiles may bring their wealth to adorn the buildings, but the keys are with Ephraim.

(Bruce R. McConkie, *The Millennial Messiah* [Salt Lake City: Deseret Book Co., 1982], 276–81.)

It would be foolish to say that these references [Isa. 2:2–5; Mic. 4:1–7; 2 Ne. 12:2–5] to Zion were to the hill in Jerusalem where David dwelt. Through modern revelation the Lord has made it known that the *American continent is Zion*. It is to be on this land that the city Zion, the New Jerusalem, shall be built. These predictions are clearly stated in the *Book of Mormon* and are in perfect accord with the writings of the Bible. (*Era*, vol. 26, 960; 3 Ne. 20:22; 21:20–29; Ether 13:2–11.)

This western continent is known *as the land of Joseph* and is also designated as the *land of Zion*. The holy city which is to be built upon this land is sometimes called the *City of Zion*. We should keep in mind that these terms (City of Zion, and New Jerusalem) have reference to the same sanctified place from whence shall go forth the law, with the word of the Lord from Jerusalem.

(Joseph Fielding Smith, *Doctrines of Salvation: Sermons and Writings of Joseph Fielding Smith*, ed. Bruce R. McConkie, 3 vols. [Salt Lake City: Bookcraft, 1954–1956], 67.)

Traditionally the world has supposed that Isaiah's reference to the law going forth from Zion and the word of the Lord going forth from Jerusalem was a Hebrew parallelism and that both references pointed to the Old World. That such was not Isaiah's intent is illustrated in a revelation given to Joseph Smith wherein it was announced that the Gentiles (meaning non-Jewish nations) were to flee to the Zion of the New World while those who are of Judah were to flee to Jerusalem, "unto the mountains of the Lord's house" (D&C 133:12–13).

(Joseph Fielding McConkie and Robert L. Millet,
Doctrinal Commentary on the Book of Mormon, 4 vols. [Salt Lake City: Bookcraft, 1987–1992], 278.)

We believe the people of the United States, moving forward under the provisions of this inspired Constitution, have a manifest destiny—not a destiny of territorial expansion and worldly aggression, but the destiny of promoting, upholding, and defending the ideals of free institutions in government and righteousness in human relations. . . .

To proclaim these truths—free government, free institutions, free men—to live them, to encourage their observance by example—this is the destiny of America. . . .

Then America will take her true place as a leader among the nations, and her principles, her ideals, her laws, shall fill the earth.

Thus would be realized the prophecy of Isaiah of old, "for out of Zion shall go forth the law, and the word of the Lord from Jerusalem."

(J. Reuben Clark, Jr., *Liahona: the Elders' Journal*, 31:461–62.)

2 Ne. 12:4, 11   HE SHALL JUDGE AMONG THE NATIONS—NEITHER SHALL THEY LEARN WAR
(Isa. 2:4, 11; D&C 43:29–30; refer in this text to 2 Ne. 21)

"Rebuke" . . . like the term "judge," also carries with it a positive and a negative aspect. It can mean either to justify or to convict. However, the root of the word means "to be in the front, the forepart," and hence, figuratively "to be in the sunshine, to be clear, manifest, or to appear." It has a very strong positive meaning associated with justice and arbitration. Yet, it also means "to put down, force back, reprimand, or humble."

When Isaiah said that God would "judge among nations and rebuke many people" he apparently meant that God would select from among the nations those willing to follow His word. . . . At the same time they would be rebuked, humbled, or made lower. Although to humble or rebuke a person, and at the same time set them up in the forefront, may seem to be a contradiction, that same thought has been expressed in similar words in modern times. The Lord stated that the people of the church must be chastened, chastised, and stand rebuked before Him that their sins may be forgiven (D&C 95).

(Loren D. Martin, *Isaiah: An Ensign to the Nations* [Salt Lake City: Valiant Publications, 1982], 55–56.)

Obviously Isaiah is describing a condition in the world that shall come at or after the Second Advent of the Lord.

(Sidney B. Sperry, *Book of Mormon Compendium* [Salt Lake City: Bookcraft, 1968], 175.)

Egypt, Babylon, Greece, Persia, Carthage, Rome—each was raised to dignity amidst the clash of arms and the din of war. . . . Before them the earth was a paradise, and behind them a desolate wilderness; their kingdoms were founded in carnage and bloodshed. . . . The designs of God, on the other hand, have been to promote the universal good of the universal world; to establish peace and good will among men; . . . to bring about a state of things that shall unite man to his fellow man; cause the world to "beat their swords into plowshares, and their spears into pruning hooks," make the nations of the earth dwell in peace, and to bring about the millennial glory.

(Joseph Smith, *Teachings of the Prophet Joseph Smith*, comp. by Joseph Fielding Smith [Salt Lake City: Deseret Book Co., 1976], 248.)

[Isaiah] further declared that the natural fears and enmities within the animal kingdom will cease, that "the wolf also shall dwell with the lamb, and the leopard shall lie down with the kid" (Isa. 11:6–9; cf. D&C 101:26). Ezekiel prophesied that the earth, which lost its pristine character as a result of the fall of Adam (cf. Gen. 3:17–19), will return to its paradisiacal state once again (Ezek. 36:35; cf. A of F 10). For the duration of the Millennium, Satan will be bound (Rev. 20:1–3). In place of the diabolical regime of the "prince of this world" (John 12:31; 14:30; D&C 1:35), the Lord Jesus Christ will dwell personally among the inhabitants of earth, ruling over the kingdom of God with the aid of righteous mortals and resurrected Saints from all ages (Isa. 35:2; Dan. 7:14, 27). . . .

During the Millennium, members of the Church of Jesus Christ from any era of time will help in the government of the earth under Christ's direction (Dan. 7:27; D&C 103:7; cf. Matt. 5:5).

John the Revelator saw that at the commencement of the Millennium a New Jerusalem would descend to earth from heaven. . . . Revelations given to the Prophet Joseph Smith show that the new Jerusalem in the Western Hemisphere will coexist with the old Jerusalem, each as a hemispheric capital. . . .

Life will go on for those on earth: "And they shall build houses, and inhabit them; and they shall plant vineyards, and eat the fruit of them, . . . and mine elect shall long enjoy the work of their hands" (Isa. 65:21–22). Righteous mortal men and women who die after the beginning of the Millennium "shall not sleep . . . in the earth, but shall be changed in the twinkling of an eye" (D&C 101:31), and children born in this era "shall grow up until they become old" (D&C 63:51; Isa. 65:20). The devil will have no "power to tempt any man," being bound because of the righteousness of the earth's inhabitants, and children will grow up without sin (1 Ne. 22:26; D&C 43:30–31; 45:58; 101:28–31). However, those who are wicked will not be resurrected or returned to the earth until after the millennium of righteousness (D&C 76:81, 85).

Whereas numerous temples will already dot the earth prior to the Millennium, their number and distribution will increase during this time. . . . The work of preaching the gospel of Jesus Christ to all the inhabitants of the earth will continue under his direction. Meanwhile, a similar teaching program will continue among the spirits of those who have departed this life and are waiting the day of their resurrection (D&C 138). While such spirits may hear the gospel of salvation and accept or reject it in the spirit world, mortals on earth will perform saving ordinances such as baptism on their behalf.

(Paul B. Pixton, *Encyclopedia of Mormonism*,
ed. by Daniel H. Ludlow, 4 vols. [New York: Macmillan Publishing Co., 1992], 906–908.)

This is the word of the Lord: "*All flesh is corrupted before me*" (D&C 38:11). Now, the world has not improved since the Lord uttered those words in 1831. This earth is groaning today under the violence of corruption and sin. Wickedness is in the hearts of the children of men; and so it will continue according to the revelations of the Lord *until* that day when Christ shall come. . . . *We speak of the time when the earth shall be cleansed from sin as the millennium.* We look forward to it; the prophets have spoken of it.

In our own day messengers have come from the presence of the Lord declaring that it is even now at our doors, and yet many, even among the Latter-day Saints, go about their affairs as though this coming of the Lord Jesus Christ and the ushering in of this reign of peace had been indefinitely postponed for many generations. I say to you that *it is at our doors.* I say this will all confidence because the Lord has said it. His messengers have said it as they have come from his presence bearing witness of him.

(Joseph Fielding Smith, *Doctrines of Salvation: Sermons and Writings of Joseph Fielding Smith*,
ed. Bruce R. McConkie, 3 vols. [Salt Lake City: Bookcraft, 1954–1956], 3:55.)

Every gun made, every warship launched, every rocket fired signifies, in the final sense, a theft from those who hunger and are not fed, those who are cold and are not clothed.

This world in arms in not spending money alone: It is spending the sweat of its laborers, the genius of its scientists, the hopes of its children. . . . This is not a way of life at all, in any true sense. Under the cloud of threatening war, it is humanity hanging from a cross of iron.

(Dwight D. Eisenhower, *Peace With Justice:*
Selected Addresses of Dwight D. Eisenhower [New York: Columbia University Press, 1961], 37–38.)

Give me the money that has been spent on war, and I will clothe every man, woman, and child in an attire of which kings and queens would be proud. I will build a schoolhouse in every valley over the whole earth. I will crown every hillside with a place of worship, consecrated to the gospel of peace.

(Charles Sumner, as quoted by Gordon B. Hinckley, *Ensign*, Mar. 1971, 20.)

Nicholas Murray Butler has figured that money spent for the World War could have built a $2,500.00 house, placed in it $1,000.00 worth of furniture, put it on five acres of land worth $100.00 an acre, and have given this to every family in the United States, Canada, Australia, England, Wales, Ireland, Scotland, France, Belgium, Germany, and Russia; could have given to each city of 20,000 or over in each of these countries a five-million dollar library and a ten-million dollar university; and could still with what was left set aside a sum at 5 per cent that would provide a $1,000.00 yearly salary for over 125,000 teachers and a like number of nurses.

(Author unknown, *Improvement Era*, 41:160.)

We have grasped the mystery of the atom and rejected the Sermon on the Mount . . . Ours is a world of nuclear giants and ethical infants. We know more about war than we know about peace, more about killing than we know about living.

(General Omar Bradley, as quoted in Hugh B. Brown, *Continuing the Quest* [Salt lake City: Deseret Book Co., 1961], 255.)

"To judge" . . . carries with it the primary meaning of "to set up or to erect," "to establish the righteous in judgment." Although, the term also carries with it a meaning of condemnation or punishment, the primary meaning is positive. Therefore, to "judge among the nations" means to select the righteous from the unrighteous, the saint from the sinner.

2 Ne. 12:5 THE LIGHT OF THE LORD
(Isa. 2:5)

Gospel *light* is the mental and spiritual enlightenment from God which enables men to receive truth and knowledge and gain salvation. Light is an attribute of Deity and shines forth from him; in him it is found in its fulness and perfection. . . .

Christ is the light of the world, and the gospel is his message of light and salvation to all men. . . . Where the gospel is there is light; where the gospel is not darkness prevails.

(Bruce R. McConkie, *Mormon Doctrine*, 2d ed. [Salt Lake City: Bookcraft, 1966], 444.)

2 Ne. 12:6 FORSAKEN
(Isa. 2:6)

Forsake means "to desert or abandon." The original Hebrew is more clear in meaning. The word translated forsaken . . . does mean "to send away, to let go, to leave or desert;" but it also carries the meanings of "to disperse or to spread abroad." The entire meaning of the word taken as a whole is exactly what happened to the house of Jacob. God withdrew and they were spread to all quarters of the earth.

(Loren D. Martin, *Isaiah: An Ensign to the Nations* [Salt Lake City: Valiant Publications, 1982], 61.)

2 Ne. 12:6   REPLENISHED FROM THE EAST
(Isa. 2:6; Ps. 106:35)

To the Israelites, "east is the sacred direction. Holy temples are oriented eastward, . . . Jesus Christ enters his temples from the east (Ezek. 43:1–2; see Ezek. 10:19); and at the time of the Second Coming, the Lord will come from the east (JS–M 1:26; Matt. 24:27; *Teachings*, 287)," In 2:5, the prophet Isaiah commands the house of Israel to "walk in the light of the Lord," which comes from the east. Yet the house of Israel attempted to be spiritually revitalized (*replenished*) through apostate, spurious sources from the east (such as the deities and religious systems of the heathen countries), which constituted mockery unto God.

(Donald W. Parry, Jay A. Parry, and Tina M. Peterson,
Understanding Isaiah [Salt lake City: Deseret Book Co., 1998], 29.)

2 Ne. 12:6   SOOTHSAYERS LIKE THE PHILISTINES
(Isa. 2:6; 2 Kgs. 1; Lev. 18:26; Deut. 18:10–12)

2 Ne. 12:6   PLEASE THEMSELVES IN THE CHILDREN OF STRANGERS
(Isa. 2:6; Ex. 23:32; Deut. 7:1–9)

Hebrew *sepiyqu* means to "clasp hands" rather than the KJV "please themselves."

(Donald W. Parry, Jay A. Parry, and Tina M. Peterson,
Understanding Isaiah [Salt lake City: Deseret Book Co., 1998], 29.)

The tenderness of the bond which united Jewish parents to their children appears even in the multiplicity and pictorialness of the expressions by which the various stages of child-life are designated in the Hebrew. Besides such general words as "ben" and "bath"—"son" and "daughter"—we find no fewer than nine different terms, each depicting a fresh stage of life. The first of these simply designates the babe as the newly-"born"—the "jeled," or, in the feminine, "jaldah"—as in Ex. 2:3, 6, 8. But the use of this term throws a fresh light on the meaning of some passages of Scripture. Thus we remember that it is applied to our Lord in the prophecy of His birth (Isa. 9:6): "For a babe ('jeled') is born unto us, a son ('ben') is given to us;" while in Isa. 2:6 its employment adds a new meaning to the charge: "They please themselves (or strike hands) with the 'jaldé'—the 'babes'—of strangers"—marking them, so to speak, as not only the children of strangers, but as unholy.

(Alfred Edersheim, *Sketches of Jewish Social Life* [Peabody, Massachusetts: Hendrickson Publishers, 1994], 99.)

The term . . . translated strangers, means foreign as in opposition to the son or lawful heir. In Ecclesiastes 6:2, the feminine form of the word is used to refer to a strange woman as in opposition to one's own wife, especially with regard to illicit intercourse; hence an adulteress. . . . The people had become strangers to the House of the Lord. Therefore, the term also was used to signify the worship of idols or strange gods. Yet, a most interesting term is the word "please." . . . The Jerusalem Bible translates the phrase, "they clap foreigners by the hand." That interpretation is footnoted by the comment, "by the hand"; signifies, "a gesture of friendship, or else a magic rite: the text is obscure." The whole phrase may be taken several ways and has multiple meaning. It may be taken as a condemnation of association with harlots, foreign gods, persons who worship idols, or marrying or being in league with followers of idols. Yet, even further, Isaiah may have also been condemning those who clap hands with strangers in secret rites, delivering sacred things to those not worthy to receive them. The Hebrew term translated "please" means to strike, to clap the hands, or to make an agreement concluded with the striking of the hands or handshake. They left God, turned unto soothsayers and "strangers". They served the gods of this earth. Silver and gold became gods. Collecting treasure became the objective of life.

(Loren D. Martin, *Isaiah: An Ensign to the Nations* [Salt Lake City: Valiant Publications, 1982], 62–63.)

2 Ne. 12:7–18 SYMBOLS OF PRIDE BROUGHT DOWN BY THE SAVIOR'S COMING
(Isa. 2:7–18; Deut. 17:17; Doctrines of the Book of Mormon, ed. Bruce A. Van Orden and Brent L. Top [Salt Lake City: Deseret Book Co., 1992], 16–28; refer in this text to 2 Ne. 15:14–15, 21)

Taken too literally, one might wonder what the Lord has against trees, ships, and so on; but the underlying principle appears in verses 11–12, 17. The Lord is speaking of haughty men who are lifted up in pride. Not only shall they be brought low, but so shall their "lofty looks." Contributing to their lofty looks are the status symbols of the day—the splendor, glory, and strength of the cedars used in major buildings; the often rare commodity of oaks from Palestine, acquired by the most wealthy; the high mountains and hills of false worship and apostate religion; the man-made defenses of towers and walls; the wonder of the ships of Tarshish (ancient Spain), noted for distance, capacity, and strength as war vessels; and the pleasant pictures, or perhaps beautiful crafts or pleasure ships of the day. In other words, the haughty and proud will fall, and their materialistic castles, which were built with wealth, pride, and power, shall crumble away in the presence of the Lord's coming (S. Brent Farley, CES Symposium, Aug. 1983, 63).

As surprising as the traits Isaiah despises are those which he prizes. Not drive, initiative, industry, enterprise, hard work, thrift, piety—none of the Zoramite virtues, though they are truly virtues when they are not . . . [initiated by] selfish motives or a morbid obsession with routine. And let me observe in passing that work is after all not a busy running back and forth in established grooves, though that is the essence of our modern business and academic life, but the supreme energy and disciplined curiosity required to cut *new* grooves. In Isaiah's book the quality which God demands of men are such as our society looks down on with mildly patronizing contempt. Isaiah promises the greatest blessings and glory to the meek, the lowly, the poor, the oppressed, the afflicted, and the needy. . . . In Zion, we are promised there will be no poor. That is because Satan will not be present there with his clever arrangement of things. . . .

If we believe Isaiah, the son of Man himself was "despised and r ejected . . ." From which one concludes that to be highly successful in this life is hardly the ultimate stamp of virtue. For Satan's golden question "Have you any money?" has a paralyzing and intriguing effect that enlists all but the noblest spirits in the great conspiracy. . . . Whoever refuses to put up with this sort of thing . . . must expect to take a beating. . . . Everybody is cheating and God does not like it at all. "Behold the world lieth in sin at this time, and none doeth good, no not one. . . and mine anger is kindling against the inhabitants of the earth to visit them according to this ungodliness." Such were the opening words of the Lord in this dispensation spoken to the Prophet Joseph in the grove (*BYU Studies* 9, spring 1969, 280f). The words "the world lieth in sin," call for a more particular statement in the manner of Isaiah, and we find the same expression explained in D&C 49:20: ". . . it is not given that one man should possess that which is above another, WHEREFORE the world lieth in sin." Mammon is a jealous God; you cannot serve him and any other master. To escape the powerful appeal of the things of this world and the deadly threat that hangs over all who do not possess them takes a meek and humble soul indeed—and a courageous one.

(Hugh W. Nibley, "Great Are the Words of Isaiah," in *Sidney B. Sperry Symposium* [Provo, Utah: Religious Instruction, BYU, January 28, 1978], 204–205.)

The majority are discontented with their lot, . . . being preoccupied with their material needs, and under the obsession of cares for the morrow. . . . One must [only] go to the homes of those who have begun to enjoy a little prosperity, to learn how much the satisfaction with what they have is troubled by regret for that which they lack. . . . *The more goods a man has the more he thinks he needs.* . . .

All this has resulted, [in] . . . a state of mind . . . which can . . . be compared to the humor [of] spoiled children, . . . overwhelmed with gifts and still discontented. . . .

The man who gives himself up entirely to the service of his appetites makes them grow and multiply so rapidly that they become stronger than he. . . . Moral life consists in the government of one's self. Immorality consists in the government of ourselves by our . . . [wants] and our passions. . . . [The world declares the worth of a man is] estimated . . .[by his] selling price, . . . [which is measured by] the profit [he has]. . . made. . . . [He who] brings nothing is worth nothing, and he who has nothing is nothing.

What is a good lamp? It is not the one most ornamented, the best carved or that which is made of the most precious metal. A good lamp is the one that gives good light. And so, also, we are . . . [valued] not by the number of goods or pleasures that we procure for ourselves, . . . but by the solidity of our moral fibre.

(Charles Wagner, *The Simple Life* [New York: Grosset & Dunlap, 1904], 13–21.)

2 Ne. 12:10, 19   ENTER INTO THE ROCK AND HIDE
(Isa. 2:10, 19; Rev. 6:16)

Concerning the prayer that mountains fall to crush and hide, Farrar (*Life of Christ*, 645, note), says: "These words of Christ met with a painfully literal illustration when hundreds of the unhappy Jews at the siege of Jerusalem hid themselves in the darkest and vilest subterranean recesses, and when, besides those who were hunted out, no less than two thousand were killed by being buried under the ruins of their hiding places. A further fulfilment may be yet future."

(James E. Talmage, *Jesus The Christ: A Study of the Messiah and His Mission According to Holy Scriputres Both Ancient and Modern* [Salt Lake City: The Church of Jesus Christ of Latter-day Saints, 1981] 667.)

To say that men shall go into the holes of the rocks and into the caves of the earth is very descriptive of some areas of the Middle East. Many poor, then and now, live amid the caves and rocks. Often in history, men would flee to the mountains to hide in the rocks when threatened by destruction or war. The Qumran community hid the Dead Sea Scrolls in caves.

(Loren D. Martin, *Isaiah: An Ensign to the Nations* [Salt Lake City: Valiant Publications, 1982], 67.)

2 Ne. 12:11   IN THAT DAY
(Isa. 2:11)

Isaiah almost always uses this phrase to refer to the last days or the dispensation of the fullness of times.

(Victor L. Ludlow, *Unlocking the Old Testament* [Salt Lake City: Deseret Book Co., 1981], 149.)

2 Ne. 12:12   DAY OF THE LORD
(Isa. 2:12; refer in this text to 2 Ne. 23:6–9)

The phrase "day of the Lord" is used frequently by Isaiah and seems to refer to any day of retribution or reward. For example, the day when Judah fell to the Babylonians was a day of the

Lord, as will be the day of his second coming. It is both a great and dreadful day, great for the righteous and dreadful for the wicked (Mal. 4:5).

(Terry B. Ball, *Voices of Old Testament Prophets:*
The 26th Annual Sidney B. Sperry Symposium [Salt Lake City: Deseret Book Co., 1997], 59.)

A day of the Lord is a period fixed by him to execute judgment upon the nations of the earth. There have been many such days. Such days are a foretaste of the coming great and dreadful day of the Lord. Before the destruction of Babylon, Isaiah thus prophesied to the people of that wicked city: "Howl ye: for the day of the Lord is at hand." Babylon's pride was humbled in utter desolation. It was a day of the Lord unto that corrupt city: His judgments were executed upon her. When the Savior was crucified the Western Hemisphere was visited by terrible tempests, thunder, earthquakes, whirlwinds and fire, resulting in a great and terrible destruction. This awful disaster killed many people. The survivors in one place cried: "Oh, that we had repented before this great and terrible day." It was a day of the Lord unto the Nephite people.

I believe that the Civil War was a day of the Lord; so also was World War and the epidemic of influenza. This worldwide depression is a day of the Lord, but no one of these days is that great and dreadful day of the Lord which is to come at the end of the world.

(Charles A. Callis, *Conference Report,* Apr. 1935, 17.)

2 Ne. 12:13   CEDARS OF LEBANON AND OAKS OF BASHAN
(Isa. 2:13; refer in this text to 2 Ne. 24:8)

One of the ways in which the proud will "be brought low" (vs. 12) is the destruction of, or the taking away of, those material possessions they hold so dear. Among these are the "cedars of Lebanon," which provided beautiful, fragrant wood for buildings of status. . . . Bashan was the area east of Jordan and the Sea of Galilee and north of Gilead. Its wooded areas provided highly prized but scarce hardwood. It too will be taken from the proud.

(Hoyt W. Brewster, Jr., *Isaiah Plain and Simple* [Salt Lake City: Deseret Book Co., 1995], 19.)

The cedars of Lebanon, *Cedrus libani,* were an especially appropriate species to liken to pride and worldliness. These were the noblest, tallest, and most massive trees the Israelites knew. Unlike the small and shrubby junipers called "cedars" in the Rocky Mountain West, these true cedars were monarchs of the forest, reaching heights of 120 feet and diameters of up to eight feet. They were once common in the mountains of Lebanon and parts of Cilicia and can still be found there in reduced numbers today. They were esteemed for the fragrance and durability of their wood, which was fit for palaces and temples, thrones and altars. Likewise the oaks of Bashan, most likely *Quercus aegilops*, were impressive trees. Bashan is a fertile region east of Galilee and today is called the Golan Heights. In Bashan the oaks reached heights of up to fifty feet. In biblical times they were prized as a source of food, dye, and tanning agents.

(Terry Ball, *Thy People Shall Be My People and Thy God My God:*
The 22nd Annual Sidney B. Sperry Symposium [Salt Lake City: Deseret Book Co., 1994], 24.)

Lebanon is the source of fire wood for Israel and a paradise in the Hebrew imagination. Yet it is home to idol worship and so is judged by God. . . .

Lebanon is a region made up of two mountain chains, the coast fringing Mount Lebanon range and the lesser easterly Anti-Lebanon range, separated by the Bekaa Valley. The biblical references are probably only to Mount Lebanon itself. . . .

The cedars of Lebanon represent the finest of earthly materials. Solomon studied the lightness and strength of cedars (1 Kgs. 4:33), bargained with Hiram, who ruled the area, and created a conscript labor force thirty thousand strong to log the Lebanon cedars for the temple in Jerusalem (1 Kgs. 5). Using cedar, these men, working one month out of three, built a magnificent palace out of the forests of Lebanon. The famous cedar also provided the main supports of the temple. In Song of Songs the bridegroom's carriage is made of wood from Lebanon (Song 3:9), and in Ezekiel a fine ship is built whose mast is a cedar of Lebanon (Ezek. 27:5). . . .

The prophets predict a day of humbling for the proud whom Isaiah calls "the cedars of Lebanon, tall and lofty" (Isa. 2:13). . . . Because her beauty breeds pride, the last image of Lebanon is one of judgment: "Open your doors, O Lebanon, so that fire may devour your cedars!" (Zech. 11:1 NTV).

(*Dictionary of Biblical Imagery*, ed. Leland Ryken, James C. Wilhoit, and
Tremper Longman III [Downers Grove: InterVarsity Press, 1998], 499.)

2 Ne. 12:16   SHIPS OF THE SEA . . . SHIPS OF TARSHISH . . . PLEASANT PICTURES
(Isa. 2:16)

[The ships of the sea] The added phrase from the Book of Mormon is also found in the ancient Greek (Septuagint) text. "All the ships of the sea," represent the commercial enterprises of the proud and lofty. Tarshish is believed to be a location in Spain. Her ships were renowned for their strength, size, and ability to successfully complete long voyages. These too will be stripped from the wicked when the Lord returns.

(Hoyt W. Brewster, Jr., *Isaiah Plain and Simple* [Salt Lake City: Deseret Book Co., 1995], 20.)

Tarshish, whose precise location is unknown, was probably a prosperous and bustling Mediterranean seaport. For instance, it was through Tarshish that Solomon imported such luxury items as gold, silver, ivory, apes, and peacocks (1 Kgs. 10:22). Perhaps because of the city's connection with wealth and affluence, the destruction of Tarshish and its ships symbolizes the Lord's judgment on the proud and arrogant (Ps. 48:7).

(Donald W. Parry, Jay A. Parry, and Tina M. Peterson,
Understanding Isaiah [Salt Lake City: Deseret Book Co., 1998], 34.)

In 2 Nephi 12:16 (cf. Isa. 2:16) the Book of Mormon has a reading of remarkable interest. It prefixes a phrase of eight words not found in the Hebrew or King James versions. Since the ancient Septuagint (Greek) Version concurs with the added phrase in the Book of Mormon, let us exhibit the readings of the Book of Mormon (B.M.), the King James Version (K.J.), and the Septuagint (LXX) as follows:

B.M.	And upon all the ships of the sea,
K.J.	
LXX	And upon every ship of the sea,
	and upon all the ships of Tarshish
	And upon all the ships of Tarshish
	And upon all pleasant pictures.
	And upon all pleasant pictures.
	And upon every display of fine ships.

The Book of Mormon suggests that the original text of this verse contained three phrases, all of which commenced with the same opening words, "and upon all." By a common accident, the original Hebrew (and hence the King James) text lost the first phrase, which was, however, preserved by the Septuagint. The latter lost the second phrase and seems to have corrupted the third phrase. The Book of Mormon preserved all three phrases. Scholars may suggest that Joseph Smith took the first phrase from the Septuagint. The prophet did not know Greek, and there is no evidence that he had access to a copy of the Septuagint in 1829–30 when he translated the Book of Mormon.

(Sidney B. Sperry, *The Voice of Israel's Prophets* [Salt Lake City: Deseret Book Co., 1965], 90–91.)

The "ships of the sea" . . . represent the people's commercial enterprises, especially the "ships of Tarshish," which were noted for their ability to travel long distances, their strength as war vessels, and their large storage capacity as commercial carriers. . . . The . . . "pleasant pictures" . . . were apparently the pleasure crafts or ships in which the wealthy traveled throughout the Mediterranean. Isaiah prophesies that the Lord will abase all these superficial symbols of wealth and power.

(Victor L. Ludlow, *Isaiah: Prophet, Seer, and Poet* [Salt Lake City: Deseret Book Co., 1982], 91.)

"Pleasant Pictures" refers to the standard or figure heads of the ships. . . . In Acts 28:11 the student will find an illustration of the meaning of the expression, "pleasant pictures." There we are informed that the ship in which Paul traveled from Malta to Rome had Castor and Pollux for a "sign." Those mythical twin sons of Zeus were the supposed protectors of the ship, and their images were painted, or sculptured in a prominent place on the ship. Others had different protectors and therefore different images and standards. But idols, whether on land or sea will be utterly destroyed in the wrath of the day of the Lord.

(George Reynolds and Janne M. Sjodahl, *Commentary on the Book of Mormon*,
ed. Philip C. Reynolds, 7 vols. [Salt Lake City: Deseret Book Co., 1955–1961], 325–26.)

Footnote *a* to 2 Nephi 12:16 notes that the Hebrew Mosoretic text of Isaiah 2:16 reads "upon all the ships of Tarshish," while the Greek Septuagint reads "upon all the ships of the sea." The Book of Mormon text reads "upon all the ships of the sea, and upon all the ships of Tarshish." One can offer several speculations about why both phrases appear in the Book of Mormon: (1) Perhaps Joseph Smith fabricated the Book of Mormon and somehow had access to the Septuagint. Discovering there was a discrepancy between the Septuagint and the Masoretic texts of this passage, he decided to include both text versions in the Book of Mormon to deceive readers into thinking he was actually translating a more complete ancient record, that is, the gold plates; or (2) Maybe while Joseph Smith was fabricating the Book of Mormon he accidentally, by chance, inserted into the Book of Mormon the very phrase left out of the Masoretic text; or (3) while the Prophet Joseph Smith was translating the Book of Mormon from the gold plates by the gift and power of God, he translated the phrase "upon all the ships of the sea, and upon all the ships of Tarshish" because that is exactly what the record said. Both phrases were on the gold plates Joseph Smith was translating because the brass plates of pre-600 B.C. origin, from which the gold plates text was taken, were a more ancient and complete text than either the Masoretic text (ca. A.D. 500–1000) or the Septuagint (ca. 250 B.C.). Apparently the Septuagint had lost the phrase "the ships of Tarshish" and the Masoretic text had lost the phrase "the ships of the sea." The Book of Mormon restores both.

From a purely logical point of view, the last option, option 3, is the only tenable one. From personal conviction, I testify that option 3 is the truth.

(Terry B. Ball, *Voices of Old Testament Prophets*:
The 26th Annual Sidney B. Sperry Symposium [Salt Lake City: Deseret Book Co., 1997], 59.)

2 Ne. 12:20   CAST IDOLS TO THE MOLES AND BATS
(Isa. 2:20; refer in *Latter-day Commentary on
the Book of Mormon*, Bassett, to 3 Ne. 13:19–24, 33)

The Lord says we would throw our idols of gold and silver which men worship in these days, to the moles and the bats, and we have nearly done this, have we not? You do not have much gold and did not the Government take it and bury it? This is close to giving it to bats and moles.

(Joseph Fielding Smith, *The Signs of the Times* [Salt Lake City: Deseret News Press, 1952], 56.)

The imagery of verse 20 is striking: the people will throw their gold and silver idols to moles and bats, animals who are blind from living so long in darkness. The irony of this is that people who understood the material value of the precious metals, and should also have seen the spiritual impotence of the idols, will throw these precious items to animals who will not be able to see them at all.

(Victor L. Ludlow, *Isaiah: Prophet, Seer, and Poet* [Salt Lake City: Deseret Book Co., 1982], 92.)

2 Ne. 12:21   HE ARISETH TO SHAKE TERRIBLY THE EARTH
(Isa. 2:21; Rev. 11:11–13; 16:18, 20; Ezek. 38:20;
Isa. 62:4; Haggai 2:6–7; D&C 45:48; 133:23)

This great earthquake, of a magnitude never before recorded on the Richter Scale, will be "such as was not since men were upon the earth," (Rev. 16:18.) "The mountains shall be thrown down, and the steep places shall fall" (Ezek. 38:20). "Every island [shall flee] away" (Rev. 16:20) as the earth's land masses join together (see D&C 133:23; Isa. 62:4). "All nations shall be shaken" (Hag. 2:6–7).

The Savior will make His appearance during this earthquake: "And then shall the Lord set his foot upon this mount [of Olives], and it shall cleave in twain, and the earth shall tremble, and reel to and fro, and the heavens also shall shake" (D&C 45:48). "And his feet shall stand in that day upon the mount of Olives, which is before Jerusalem on the east, and the mount of Olives shall cleave in the midst thereof toward the east and toward the west, and there shall be a very great valley; and half of the mountain shall remove toward the north, and half of it toward the south" (Zech. 14:4).

The besieged people of Judah will escape through the valley created by the earthquake and will recognize the resurrected Lord as their long-awaited Messiah, yet they will sorrow at seeing the wounds of the crucifixion in His body. (See Zech. 14:5; 12:10; 13:6; D&C 45:51–53.)

(Hoyt W. Brewster Jr., *Behold, I Come Quickly* [Salt Lake City: Deseret Book Co., 1994], 102–103.)

2 Ne. 12:22   CEASE YE FROM MAN
(Isa. 2:22)

The wicked have always entered into compacts and alliances designed to protect them in their frauds, crimes, or secret machinations. Isaiah warns that such man-made citadels of security will mean nothing in the hour of God's judgment. . . . Mankind is never more than a breath away from death, and therefore any institution of security which depends upon man can also disappear in an instant. The only sound security is living so that we can enjoy the eternal blessings and security of a loving Heavenly Father.

(W. Cleon Skousen, *Isaiah Speaks to Modern Times* [Salt Lake City: Ensign Publishing Co., 1984], 160.)

2 Ne. 13

Isaiah's vision of the effects of wickedness continued from the preceding chapter. For Nephi and his people this would have been a prophetic confirmation of the suffering and degradation they were spared by fleeing Jerusalem. . . . Given that Nephi included these chapters of Isaiah in his record for the benefit of those of our day, we properly see in this description of Judah's haughtiness, pride, and intoxication with fashion a pattern and warning for the last days.

(Joseph Fielding McConkie and Robert L. Millet,
Doctrinal Commentary on the Book of Mormon, 4 vols. [Salt Lake City: Bookcraft, 1987–1992], 1:278–279.)

These pitiful circumstances describe well the condition of Jerusalem's citizens after the city's destruction in 587 B.C. The prophet Jeremiah, an eyewitness to Judah's fall, recorded it vividly (Jer. 40–42).

(Keith A Meservy, *Studies in Scripture, Vol. 4*, ed. Kent P. Jackson [Salt Lake City: Deseret Book Co., 1993], 93.)

2 Ne. 13:1   **STAY AND THE STAFF**
                        (Isa. 3:1)

"Stay" and "staff". . . are the masculine and feminine forms of the same root, *masen* and *masenah*. By using both forms, Isaiah seems to suggest complete destruction. . . .
Removing the staff . . . from a nation is analogous to suddenly taking away the props or stakes of a tent—the tent collapses shapeless on the ground. "The whole supply of bread and the whole supply of water" might be taken literally, since at both the first and second desolations of Jerusalem, the city was besieged and was at the mercy of a devastating famine. Jeremiah records in the seventh century B.C. that "the famine was sore in the city, so that there was no bread for the people of the land" (Jer. 52:6). The famine was probably even worse during a second siege in 70 A.D., for the ancient historian Josephus records the story of one woman, gone berserk from the ravages of war and famine, who roasted and ate her own child (*Wars of the Jews*, 6:3).

(Victor L. Ludlow, *Isaiah: Prophet, Seer, and Poet* [Salt Lake City: Deseret Book Co., 1982], 101.)

The idea of eating, as a metaphor for receiving spiritual benefit, was familiar to Christ's hearers, and was as readily understood as our expressions—"devouring a book," or "drinking in" instruction. In Isaiah 3:1, the words "the whole stay of bread," were explained by the rabbis as referring to their own teaching, and they laid it down as a rule, that wherever, in Ecclesiastes, allusion was made to food or drink, it meant study of the law, and the practice of good works. . . . Nothing was more common in the schools and synagogs than the phrases of eating and drinking, in a metaphorical sense.

(Geikie, *Life and Words of Christ*, vol.1, 184, as found in James E. Talmage
Jesus the Christ: A Study of the Messiah and His Mission According to Holy Scriptures
both Ancient and Modern [Salt Lake City: The Church of Jesus Christ of Latter-day Saints, 1981], 247–348.)

2 Ne. 13:2–8   JERUSALEM IS RUINED
(Isa. 3:2–8; Amos 3:7; Matt. 15:14.)

Everyone is after a career, . . . aspiring to be a VIP: "The mighty man of war, the judge, the prophet, the prudent, the elder, the captain, the honorable man, the counsellor, the cunning craftsman, the eloquent orator . . . (3:2–3). What about them? "I will give children to be their princes, and babes shall rule over them." (3:5). So much for their authority—and why? Because everyone is out for himself in this game of one-upmanship: "And the people shall be oppressed every one by another, every one by his neighbor (there's competition for you!): the child shall behave himself proudly against the ancient (what else can you expect?) And the base against the honorable" (3:5). Everything will get out of control. A man will take hold of his brother saying, you have clothes, so you be our ruler; you be responsible for this mess! But he will refuse the great honor, saying, "Don't try to make me a ruler—I'm flat broke! (3:6–7) Because everybody will be broke, Isaiah continues 3:8: "For Jerusalem is ruined . . ." All because they stubbornly think they can go it alone.

(Hugh W. Nibley, "Great Are the Words of Isaiah" in *Sidney B. Sperry Symposium*
[Provo, Utah: Religious Instruction, BYU, January 28, 1978], 200.)

2 Ne. 13:4   BABES SHALL RULE OVER THEM
(Isa. 3:4)

The fulfillment of this prophecy can be seen in the following tabulation of the reign of the seven kings who ruled from the death of Isaiah to the destruction of Jerusalem by Babylon in 589 B.C. (Book of Mormon dating):

King	Age When Appointed	Years of Reign	Biblical Label of Character
Manasseh	12	55	Evil (2 Kgs. 21:1–2)
Amon	22	2	Evil (2 Kgs. 21:19–20)
Josiah	8	31	Right (2 Kgs. 22:1–2)
Jehoahaz	23	3 mos.	Evil (2 Kgs. 23:31–32)
Jehoiakim	25	11 (3 yrs. as puppet king in Babylon)	Evil (2 Kgs. 23:36–37)
Jehoiachin	18 (2 Chr. 36:9 says 8 yrs)	3 mos. (under Babylon)	Evil (2 Kgs. 24:8–9)
Zedekiah	21	11	Evil (2 Kgs. 24:17–19)

Note that these kings were appointed between the ages of eight and twenty-five, and all but one were labeled "evil" in the Bible.

(Monte S. Nyman, *Great Are the Words of Isaiah* [Salt Lake City: Bookcraft, 1980], 35.)

In the time of Isaiah, the Lord was about to allow the invading Assyrians to destroy Israel's material security. The northern ten tribes were indeed conquered and taken away in the middle period of Isaiah's ministry (ca. 722 B.C.); however, one king of Judah hearkened to the Lord's warnings through the prophet Isaiah. As a result, though the people of Jerusalem suffered considerably during an Assyrian siege, the city was spared for another century, until it fell to the Babylonians.

When all capable leaders are decimated in a crisis, inept leaders take over; and then such moral and political problems develop that potentially capable people are reluctant to take office. Wicked leaders, who oppress their people and fail to defend them, will be held responsible by the Lord.

(Ellis T. Rasmussen, *A Latter-day Saint Commentary of the Old Testament* [Salt Lake City: Deseret Book Co., 1993], 505–506.)

With the leaders of society killed or taken into captivity, only the poor, weak masses remained. Therefore, the warning in verse 4 that "capricious children" or "babes" (KJV) shall rule over Israel most likely refers to people with childish understanding who will unsuccessfully face the challenge of bringing order to anarchy.

The warning can also be understood literally, though, since many of the Jewish kings before the Babylonian captivity came to rule at a very early age. Ahaz, Hezekiah, Amon, and Jehoiakim were all in their early twenties. Manasseh was only twelve, Josiah a mere eight years old, and Jehoiachim either eighteen or eight, depending upon whether the age recorded in 2 Kings or 2 Chronicles is correct. (See 2 Kgs. 24:8; 2 Chr. 36:9.)

Still another interpretation of verse 4 is possible. The children mentioned might represent those outside the house of Israel who came to rule over the Jews. Jesus said that the Father was able "of these stones to raise up children unto Abraham" (Luke 3:8); Joseph Smith later identified the "stones" as the Gentiles who subjugated the ancient Jews (*Words of Joseph Smith*, 234–36, 294–95). In the midst of ruin and "childish" rule, Isaiah prophesies that the people will accept any sort of credentials as a prerequisite for leadership.

(Victor L. Ludlow, *Isaiah: Prophet, Seer, and Poet* [Salt Lake City: Deseret Book Co., 1982], 103.)

A child prince would be one of little experience. The Hebrew term translated "babes" . . . has reference to an uncontrollable, ill-tempered, childish person. The root term . . . means "to drink again deeply." It is figuratively applied to gratification of lust. It describes petulant, wanton, lascivious, immodest and rude behavior.

(Loren D. Martin, *Isaiah: An Ensign to the Nations* [Salt Lake City: Valiant Publications, 1982], 77.)

2 Ne. 13:5   CHILD . . . PROUDLY AGAINST THE ANCIENT
(Isa. 3:5)

I urge you young people to develop the habit of always showing respect, courtesy, and deference to your parents and others, especially those who are older than you. My father taught me that every person in and out of the Church has a title, such as Mr., Mrs., Brother, Sister, Bishop, Elder, or President, and that they should be addressed with respect. When I was six years old, my father reinforced this principle when I made the horrid mistake of calling our local grocer by his first name. Upon leaving the grocery store, my father taught me with firmness that I had shown a lack of respect by being so casual to an older person. I have never forgotten that experience, nor have I after 60 years forgotten the name of the grocer. I even remember his first name.

(Harold G. Hillam, *Ensign*, May 2000, 10.)

I wish to say, with regard to the rising generation—the sons and daughters of the Latter-day Saints—that they should take the counsel of their fathers; they should honor their parents, and honor God, and receive such counsel as is given unto them by wise men. I think many times that our children do not comprehend what lies before them. . . . This work has got to . . . rest upon the sons and daughters of Zion.

(Wilford Woodruff, *The Discourses of Wilford Woodruff*, ed. G. Homer Durham [Salt Lake City: Bookcraft, 1946], 265.)

2 Ne. 13:6   **BROTHER . . . CLOTHING**
(Isa. 3:6)

These verses . . . reemphasize both the social breakdown of the patriarchal order and the extreme physical poverty of the state. That the man mentioned here should "lay hold of his brother in his father's house" indicates, first of all, that the father has disappeared and left the family in upheaval, for the son (by custom, the eldest) refuses to fulfill the duty that is his by lineage. The cloak [clothing], or *simlah*, which is the brother's so-called claim to power, is not a rich robe but is itself a sign of extreme poverty. In other words, the petitioner is saying, "You have at least some sort of cloak and the provisions necessary for physical sustenance, food and clothing." Without either physical or social "stays," it is no wonder that the brother declines a position for which he might otherwise be ambitious."

(Victor L. Ludlow, *Isaiah: Prophet, Seer, and Poet* [Salt Lake City: Deseret Book Co., 1982], 103–104.)

2 Ne. 13:9   **SODOM**
(Isa. 3:9; Lev. 20:13, 15–16; 1 Cor. 11:11;
refer in this text to the Boyd K. Packer quote under 2 Ne. 15:20)

What is the reason for Judah's destruction? She had sinned openly and flagrantly before the eyes of God, just as the Sodomites did when they proclaimed their unnatural lust directly and unabashedly to Lot's face. (Gen. 19:5.) Also, Judah had degenerated to a condition of sin not unlike Sodom's (though not as depraved), in that she had perverted sexuality through misusing it in the idolatrous fertility rituals of the Canaanites. Though this was done to insure productivity in the land, Isaiah warns that the wicked participants will reap only destruction.

(Victor L. Ludlow, *Isaiah: Prophet, Seer, and Poet* [Salt Lake City: Deseret Book Co., 1982], 105–106.)

There is a plague of fearsome dimensions moving across the world. . . .

The Surgeon General of the United States has forecast an AIDS death toll of 170,000 Americans in just four years. The situation is even more serious in some other areas of the world. . . .

Unfortunately, as in any epidemic, innocent people also become victims. . . . The observance of one clearly understandable and divinely given rule would do more than all else to check this epidemic. That is chastity before marriage and total fidelity after marriage.

Prophets of God have repeatedly taught through the ages that practices of homosexual relations, fornication, and adultery are grievous sins. . . . We reaffirm those teachings. . . .

Each of us has a choice between right and wrong. But with that choice there inevitably will follow consequences. Those who choose to violate the commandments of God put themselves at great spiritual and physical jeopardy.

(Gordon B. Hinckley, *Ensign*, May 1987, 46–47.)

[Practicing] homosexuality is an ugly sin. . . . It was present in Israel's wandering days as well as after and before. It was tolerated by the Greeks. It was prevalent in decaying Rome. The ancient cities of Sodom and Gomorrah are symbols of wretched wickedness more especially related to this perversion, as the incident of Lot's visitors indicates. (See Gen. 19:5.) So degenerate had Sodom become that not ten righteous people could be found (see Gen. 18:23–32), and the Lord had to destroy it. But the revolting practice has persisted. . . .

Those who would claim that the homosexual is a third sex and that there is nothing wrong in such associations can hardly believe in God or in his scriptures. . . . Of the adverse social effects of homosexuality none is more significant than the effect on marriage and home. . . . The seriousness of the sin of homosexuality is equal to or greater than that of fornication or adultery; and . . . *the Lord's Church will as readily take action to disfellowship or excommunicate the unrepentant practicing homosexual as it will the unrepentant fornicator or adulterer.* . . .

Next in seriousness to nonrecognition of the sin is the attempt to justify oneself in this perversion. Many have been misinformed that they are powerless in the matter, not responsible for the tendency, and that "God made them that way." This is as untrue as any other of the diabolical lies Satan has concocted. It is blasphemy. Man is made in the image of God. Does the pervert think God to be "that way"?

(Spencer W. Kimball, *The Miracle of Forgiveness* [Salt Lake City: Bookcraft, 1969], 78–85.)

The Savior . . . made reference to the wickedness "in the days of Lot." (See Luke 17:26–30.) Lot was warned to flee the gross perversion of Sodom and Gomorrah, where immorality, including homosexuality, was the accepted way of life. (See Gen. 19; see also JST, Gen. 19.) The Apostle Paul foresaw these same conditions in the last days: "In the last days perilous times shall come. For men shall be lovers of their own selves, . . . *without natural affection,* . . . lovers of pleasures more than lovers of God." (See 2 Tim. 3:1–4; italics added.) . . .

In order to give homosexuality a semblance of legitimacy, this violation of God's laws is depicted as an "alternative lifestyle" with no moral or legal consequences. Great effort has gone into portraying one's so-called sexual preference as a civil right, and those who oppose this lifestyle are branded as "homophobic" or "prejudiced."

In essence, the rights of moral people are trampled upon to accommodate the lifestyles of the immoral minority. Even the Boy Scouts of America, who have long required members to pledge that they will be "morally straight," have been denied funding, harassed, and sued because the organization has refused to alter its membership and oath requirements.

(Hoyt W. Brewster Jr., *Behold, I Come Quickly: The Last Days and Beyond*
[Salt Lake City: Deseret Book Co., 1994], 39–41.)

2 Ne. 13:9, 11 THEY HAVE REWARDED EVIL UNTO THEMSELVES
(Isa. 3:9, 11; Hel. 14:29–30)

Isaiah foresaw that Judah and Jerusalem would be punished by the Lord as a result of their wickedness. In 587 B.C. the city of Jerusalem was destroyed, and Judah was taken into captivity by Nebuchadnezzar, king of Babylon. In A.D. 70, 657 years later, the Romans destroyed Jerusalem and scattered the Jews to various portions of the world. Surely they had, as Isaiah said, "rewarded evil unto themselves" (2 Ne. 13:9).

(*Book of Mormon Student Manual, Religion 121 and 122*
[Salt Lake City: The Church of Jesus Christ of Latter-day Saints, 1989], 31.)

In Isaiah it is written: ". . . your iniquities have separated between you and your God . . ." (Isa. 59:2). Again, ". . . they have rewarded evil unto themselves" (Isa. 3:9).

Envy, arrogance, unrighteous dominion—these canker the soul of one who is guilty of them. . . .

There are two courses of action to follow when one is bitten by a rattlesnake. One may, in anger, fear or vengefulness, pursue the creature and kill it. Or he may make full haste to get the venom out of his system. If we pursue the latter course we will likely survive, but if we attempt to follow the former, we may not be around long enough to finish it.

(Marion D. Hanks, *Ensign,* Jan. 1974, 21.)

Because of this widespread tolerance toward promiscuity, this world is in grave danger. When evil is decried and forbidden and punished, the world still has a chance. But when toleration for sin increases, the outlook is bleak and Sodom and Gomorrah days are certain to return.

We were in Los Angeles years ago when the news broke of the illicit affair of a certain movie actress, from which she became pregnant. Because of her popularity, it was big news in heavy headlines in every paper in the land. We were not so surprised at her adultery—it was reported to be common in Hollywood as well as in the world generally. But that such dissoluteness should be approved and accepted by society shocked me. The Los Angeles papers took a poll of the people . . . and almost without exception, . . . these community members found little fault with her and criticized as "puritanical" and "victorian" those who disapproved. "Let her live her own life," they said. "And why should we interfere with people's personal liberties?" In state and nation and across the seas, such toleration for sin is terrifying.

There is no shame. Isaiah again strikes at the sin: . . . (Isa. 3:9).

That the Church's stand on morality may be understood, we declare firmly and unalterably it is not an outworn garment, faded, old-fashioned, and threadbare. . . . When the sun grows cold and the stars no longer shine, the law of chastity will still be basic in God's world and in the Lord's church. Old values are upheld by the Church not because they are old, but rather because they are right.

(Spencer W. Kimball, *Faith Precedes the Miracle* [Salt Lake City: Deseret Book Co., 1972], 154–155.)

2 Ne. 13:12   **CHILDREN OPPRESS, WOMEN RULE, THEY WHO LEAD THEE CAUSE THEE TO ERR**
(Isa. 3:12; Mosiah 25:12)

Put the father back at the head of the home. . . . The easiest, simplest way to reduce delinquency among the young [is] to put the father back as head of the family.

Far too many families have been denied the leadership and stabilizing influence of a good and devoted father who stands at the side of an able and caring mother in quietly training, gently disciplining, and prayerfully helping the children for whom they are both responsible.

I do not believe that women resent the strong leadership of a man in the home. He becomes the provider, the defender, the counselor, the friend who will listen and give support when needed. Who better than an exemplary father to effectively teach children the value of education, the dead-end nature of street gangs, and the miracle of self-esteem that can change their lives for good? . . .

I plead with fathers to resume their role as the head of their homes. . . . That does not carry with it any implication of dictatorship or unrighteous dominion. It confers the mandate to provide for the needs of their families. Those needs are more than food, clothing, and shelter. Those needs include righteous direction and the teaching, by example as well as precept, of basic principles of honesty, integrity, service, respect for the rights of others, and an understanding that we are accountable, not only to one another but also to God, for that which we do in this life. One writer observed, "It is not impossible that the true revolutionaries of the twenty-first century will be the fathers of decent and civilized children."

(Gordon B. Hinckley, *Standing for Something* [New York: Random House, 2000], 148–150.)

And so today, the undermining of the home and family is on the increase, with the devil anxiously working to displace the father as the head of the home and create rebellion among the children. The Book of Mormon describes this condition when it states, "And my people, children are their oppressors, and women rule over them." And then these words follow—and consider these words seriously when you think of those political leaders who are promoting birth control and abortion: "O my people, they who lead thee cause thee to err and destroy the way of thy paths" (2 Ne. 13:12).

(Ezra Taft Benson, *Conference Report*, Oct. 1970, 21.)

The Book of Mormon points out how . . . ancient conspirators were able to fill the judgment seats, usurp power, destroy justice, condemn the righteous, and let the guilty and the wicked go unpunished. Do you see any parallel between this and the present-day decisions of our Supreme Court?

President McKay has stated that the Supreme Court is leading this Christian nation down the road to atheism.

(Ezra Taft Benson, "The Book of Mormon Warns America," *BYU Speeches of the Year,* 21 May 1968, 5.)

Never before . . . have the forces of evil been so blatant, so brazen, so aggressive as they are today. Things we dared not speak about in earlier times are now constantly projected into our living rooms. . . .

Some to whom we have looked as leaders have betrayed us. . . . And their activity is only the tip of the iceberg. In successive layers beneath that tip is a great mass of sleaze and filth, of dissolute and dishonest behavior. . . .

I believe our problems, almost every one, arise out of the homes of the people. If there is to be reformation, if there is to be a change, if there is to be a return to old and sacred values, it must begin in the home. It is here that truth is learned, that integrity is cultivated, that self-discipline is instilled, and that love is nurtured.

The home is under siege. So many families are being destroyed. Where are the fathers who should be presiding in love in those homes?

(Gordon B. Hinckley, *Ensign*, Nov. 1998, 98–99.)

The term translated "women" . . . in this context is used as an accusation. Figuratively speaking, as a man is praised for valor, consistency, and intrepid mind, so, the term woman was used as a term of reproach to a cowardly man, "one timid, undecided, or fearful. As used here it refers to one timid, undecided, or fearful of righteous doing."

(Loren D. Martin, *Isaiah: An Ensign to the Nations* [Salt Lake City: Valiant Publications, 1982], 80.)

2 Ne. 13:15   GRIND THE FACES OF THE POOR
(Isa. 3:15)

The demand everywhere is for a church that is holding fast to the basic ideals of Christianity, as the apostle James has defined it: "Pure religion and undefiled before God and the Father is this, to visit the fatherless and widows in their affliction, and to keep himself unspotted from the world" (James 1:27).

There we have found a strong central authority . . . where emergency needs can be met in a way that fosters brotherhood, instead of a deadening process that is described, scripturally, as to "grind the faces of the poor" (Isa. 3:15).

(Harold B. Lee, *Ensign*, Dec. 1971, 29.)

There is so much of civil strife and conflict in our society that could be ameliorated by a small touch of mercy. Much of it has reached a point where the Mosaic law of an eye for an eye and a tooth for a tooth has been enlarged to require three eyes for one eye and three teeth for one tooth. Many victims, badgered and broken, cry in vain for a touch of kindness.

We see labor strife fraught with violence and untamed accusations. Were there a greater willingness on the part of each side to look with some element of mercy on the problems of the other, most of this could be avoided.

We have recently been reminded that in this land there still persists, notwithstanding the protection of the law, a merciless exploitation of children in certain industries.

And there are still those, not a few, who without compassion "grind the faces of the poor" (Isa. 3:15).

(Gordon B. Hinckley, *Ensign*, May 1990, 69.)

One cannot ask God to help a neighbor in distress without feeling motivated to do something oneself toward helping that neighbor. . . . I heard a man of prominence say the other day, "I have amended the language of my prayers. Instead of saying, 'Bless the poor and the sick and the needy,' I now say, Father, show me how to help the poor and the sick and the needy, and give me resolution to do so. . . .

We must take care of the poor. Said the Lord, "The poor ye have with you always." (See Mark 14:7; John 12:8). There have always been poor and I guess there always will be poor until the Millennium. We must take care of them. . . . We must not shift the burden that we ought to carry in our own hearts of spreading kindness and love and help to others, to the institution, which at best, is impersonal.

I do not want you to get any idea that I am saying we should not have the welfare program. . . . But I think there is a tendency among us to say, "Oh, the Church will take care of that. I pay my fast offering. Let the Church take care of that." We need as individuals, I think, to reach down and extend a helping hand without notice, without thanks, without expectation of anything in return.

(*Teachings of Gordon B. Hinckley* [Salt Lake City: Deseret Book Co., 1997], 457–59.)

2 Ne. 13:16   HAUGHTY, WANTON, MINCING—TINKLING WITH THEIR FEET
(Isa. 3:16)

The haughty are defined as those who are proud of self and scornful of others. Wanton is defined as undisciplined, unmanageable, lewd. Mincing is defined as short, feminine steps or as plain speech.

(Monte S. Nyman, *Great Are the Words of Isaiah* [Salt Lake City: Bookcraft, 1980], 37.)

Sandals consisted merely of soles strapped to the feet; but ladies wore also costly slippers, sometimes embroidered, or adorned with gems, and so arranged that the pressure of the foot emitted a delicate perfume.

(Alfred Edersheim, *Sketches of Jewish Social Life* [Peabody, Massachusetts: Hendrickson Publishers, 1994], 199.)

The "tinkling with their feet" may have been made simply by the striking of anklets one upon another, or by bells or other small ornaments attached to the anklets. These anklets were of gold, silver, or iron, according to the taste or means of the wearer, and are still worn by Oriental women. They are sometimes quite heavy, and special pains are taken to strike them together, in order to make a jingle. When they are hollow, as is often the case, the sharp sound is increased. In Egypt and in India some of the anklets have small round bells attached to them, and these bells sometimes have little pebbles in them, which strike like tiny clappers.

(James M. Freeman, *Manners and Customs of the Bible* [Plainfield, New Jersey: Logos International, 1972], 250.)

The anklets were generally so wrought as in walking to make a sound like little bells. Sometimes the two ankle-rings were fastened together, which would oblige the fair wearer to walk with small, mincing steps.

(Alfred Edersheim, *Sketches of Jewish Social Life* [Peabody, Massachusetts: Hendrickson Publishers, 1994], 201.)

2 Ne. 13:16–24 DAUGHTERS OF ZION
(Isa. 3:16–24; 2 Ne. 8:25; Amos 4:1–4; Isa. 4:4; Song 3:11; D&C 124:11)

If, indeed, Isaiah's words refer to the last days, we must look for a time when even some of the "daughters of Zion [or the children of Israel] are haughty, and walk with stretched-forth necks and wanton eyes." . . . Sometimes the phrase "daughters of Zion" . . . refers to the cities of Judah.

(*Book of Mormon Student Manual, Religion 121 and 122*
[Salt Lake City: The Church of Jesus Christ of Latter-day Saints, 1981], 91.)

Isaiah, one of the great prophets of early times, saw our day, and he described the conditions that would prevail among the "daughters of Zion" in these latter days. . . . As I sit on the stand in a stake conference and look down over the congregation, I see some of the conditions existing of which Isaiah spoke. . . . The standards expressed by the General Authorities of the Church are that women, as well as men, should dress modestly. They are taught proper deportment and modesty at all times.

It is, in my judgment, a sad reflection on the "daughters of Zion" when they dress immodestly. Moreover, this remark pertains to the men as well as to the women.

(Joseph Fielding Smith, *Answers to Gospel Questions*, 5 vols.
[Salt Lake City: Deseret book Co., 1957–1966], 5:172–74.)

The plural form *daughters of Zion* is infrequently used in the scriptures (Isa. 3:16–17; 4:4; Song. 3:11; D&C 124:11). Scholars generally agree that the singular expression *daughter of Zion* refers to the inhabitants of Jerusalem and Judah (Lam. 1:6–8; 2:8–11; Zech. 9:9; 2 Ne. 8:25). What then is the meaning of plural *daughters of Zion*? There are several possible interpretations. If the phrase *daughter of Zion* represents Jerusalem, then perhaps the plural *daughters* refers to Jerusalem at the time of Isaiah as well as Jerusalem in the last days. The plural *daughters of Zion* may also refer to ancient Jerusalem (and the Southern Kingdom of Judah) and to Samaria (and the Northern Kingdom of Israel). The phrase may be literal, referring to actual women, or it may point to women as symbols of pride and sin in the last days. Note the women's clothing described in 3:18–24 and the actual women that seem to be identified in 4:1. This interpretation parallels Isaiah's condemnation of male pride (2:10–22) and the sick nature of the inhabitants of Jerusalem (1:5–6, 21–23).

(Donald W. Parry, Jay A. Parry, and Tina M. Peterson, *Understanding Isaiah*
[Salt Lake City: Deseret Book Co., 1998], 43.)

President Young has been calling upon the daughters of Zion day after day, now, for years, to lay aside these Babylonish fashions. . . . I have been hoping . . . that the sayings contained in that chapter [Isa. 3] would never apply to the daughters of Zion in our day; but I believe they will. . . . I hope they will hasten the lengthening out of their skirts . . . that they will increase their round tires like the moon, increase their hoops, and their headbands, increase their Grecian bends at once and carry it out until they get through with it, so that we can turn to the Lord as a people. Some of the daughters of Zion do not seem willing to forsake the fashions of Babylon. I to such would say hasten it, and let the woe that is threatened on this account come, that we may get through with it, then we can go on and build up the Zion of God on the earth. . . . Think not, ye elders of Israel, ye sons and daughters of Zion, that we are going to live after the order of Babylon always. We are not. We shall be chastised and afflicted, and shall feel the chastening rod of the Almighty, unless we serve the Lord our God, and build up his kingdom.

(Wilford Woodruff, *The Discourses of Wilford Woodruff*, ed. G. Homer Durham
[Salt Lake City: Bookcraft, 1946, 1990], 226–27.)

The "daughters of Zion," representing Israel, strut proudly in their fine clothes and jewels, but the Lord will smite them with disease and exhibit their shame (vv. 16, 17). . . .

18. In that day the Lord will take away the bravery [glory, finery] of their tinkling ornaments [their anklets, bangles], and cauls [headbands], and round tires like the moon [crescents]; 19. the chains [pendants] and the bracelets, and the mufflers [veils]; 20. the bonnets [headdresses], and the ornaments of the legs [armlets], and the headbands [sashes], and the tablets [perfume boxes], and the ear-rings [amulets]; 21. the rings [signet-rings], and nose jewels [nose rings]; 22. the changeable suits of apparel [festal robes], and the mantles, and the wimples [cloaks], and the crisping pins [purses]; 23. the glasses [polished metal mirrors], and the fine linen, and hoods [women's turbans], and the veils [wraps]. . . .

Zion (so means Isaiah) will now adopt the garb of mourning, sackcloth. She will receive branding, the mark of slavery, instead of beauty. . . .

24. . . . And instead of a girdle, a rent [a rope, i.e., of captives]. . . .

And instead of a stomacher [fine robe], a girding of sackcloth;

Burning [Brand-mark] instead of beauty.

(Sidney B. Sperry, *Book of Mormon Compendium* [Salt Lake City: Bookcraft, 1968], 182–83.)

The prophet referred to the covenant people of this time as the "daughters of Zion." Like all good daughters of his day, they should have been keeping themselves pure and virtuous, awaiting the day when they would meet their bridegroom, or Christ. Instead, these worldly people were doing just the contrary. . . .

Isaiah described further how all the temporal, vain, and worldly adornments with which the promiscuous "daughters of Zion" had hoped to beautify themselves in an effort to attract adulterous (idolatrous) lovers would be taken away, leaving them disgusting and repulsive rather than tempting and alluring (Isa. 3:18–24): "And it shall come to pass, that instead of sweet smell there shall be stink; and instead of a girdle a rent; and instead of well set hair baldness; and instead of a stomacher a girding of sackcloth; and burning instead of beauty" (Isa. 3:24). In their humbled and contemptible state, they would sit at the gates of the city and wail, but to no avail, for the lovers they sought would have fallen "by the sword," and those remaining would not take these foul and filthy daughters regardless of what they offered (Isa. 3:25–4:1). Every evil thing in which they trusted and hoped to find pleasure would be lost or turned against them. Instead of finding happiness, they could expect to find abandonment, captivity, desolation, and humiliation.

(Terry B. Ball, *Voices of Old Testament Prophets:
The 26th Annual Sidney B. Sperry Symposium,* [Salt Lake City: Deseret Book Co., 1997], 50, 55.)

The description does not really refer to "women." The phrase "daughters of Zion" is an idiom, a "Hebraism of scripture." It is symbolic. It refers to those who are or ought to be building Zion. It refers to the people as a whole.

(Loren D. Martin, *Isaiah: An Ensign to the Nations* [Salt Lake City: Valiant Publications, 1982], 162.)

With respect to the women, and more particularly with regard to the manner in which they dress.
Never . . . have I seen such obscene, uncleanly, impure, and suggestive fashions of women's dress
as I see today. Some of them are abominable. I lift my voice against . . . these infamous fashions,
and I pray that you who have daughters in Zion will save them, if you can, from following these
obscene fashions, that if followed, will destroy the last vestige of true womanly modesty. . . .

While crossing the street the other day, I saw a woman dressed to the height of this ridiculous
fashion, and she was trotting along with little, short steps, she couldn't go any other way, hurry-
ing across the street to catch the car. She got hold of the rail of the car and tried to lift herself up,
but her foot would not go up to the step. By this time there was a crowd of men looking on. All
of a sudden she stooped down, caught the bottom of her dress and raised it high enough to climb
up. . . . Would you like your daughters to expose themselves in such a manner? To do so they must
of necessity part with their sense of womanly modesty. . . . God have mercy on our girls, and help
them to dress decently!

I suppose I shall incur the censure and displeasure of many in saying these things, but I do not
care. . . . In my sight the present day fashions are abominable, suggestive of evil, calculated to arouse
base passion and lust, and to engender lasciviousness, in the hearts of those who follow the fashions,
and of those who tolerate them. . . . It is infamous, and I hope the daughters of Zion will not descend
to these pernicious ways, customs and fashions, for they are demoralizing and damnable in their effect.

(Joseph F. Smith, *Conference Report*, Oct. 1913, 7–8.)

2 Ne. 13:17   CROWN OF HEAD, SECRET PARTS
(Isa. 3:17)

The phrase, "to smite with a scab the crown of the head" refers to the hair of the head and means
"to cause a disease or scab of the scalp," hence "to make bald." The removal of a woman's hair usually
is not considered an honor, but one of disgrace. "Make bare their secret parts" comes from the phrase
. . . meaning "to spread out or to open up" and has reference to making the intimacy of the naked female
exposed to the whole world. Though some people today may do that on the movie screen for money,
to anyone of honor and dignity it would be considered a most singular, ultimate disgrace. To cause
baldness and reveal intimate nakedness means "to inflict great shame and disrepute."

(Loren D. Martin *Isaiah: An Ensign to the Nations* [Salt Lake City: Valiant Publications, 1982], 164–65.)

2 Ne. 13:18   IN THAT DAY
(Isa. 3:18; refer in this text to 2 Ne. 12:11)

Since Jerusalem has been invaded so many times, it is difficult to identify which destruction best
fulfills Isaiah's prophecy. Since the warning of destruction is prefaced in verse 18 with the phrase "in
that day," Isaiah could be pointing to a fulfillment in the last days. Some students of Jewish history

observe parallels in the Nazi Holocaust. Also, it seems that the last verses of Isaiah 3 might even describe the effects of a nuclear holocaust. (Recent statements by the First Presidency indicate an inspired concern about the dangers of nuclear proliferation; see Bruce R. McConkie, *CR,* Apr. 1979, 133.) Of course, other disasters, such as disease, plague, or famine, could fulfill these conditions in the last days.

(Victor L. Ludlow, *Isaiah: Prophet, Seer, and Poet* [Salt Lake City: Deseret Book Co., 1982], 108.)

2 Ne. 13:18–24   FEMININE FASHION
(Isa. 3:18–24; refer in *Latter-day Commentary on the Book of Mormon,* Bassett, to Alma 1:6 & Alma 31:28)

In this section a very complete list of feminine jewelry and ornaments is furnished by the prophet. We notice "tinkling ornaments," probably rings worn on the feet; "cauls," nets, or perhaps diadems; "round tires," necklaces (v. 18); "chains, bracelets and mufflers;" probably, earrings, bracelets and veils (v. 19); "ornaments of the legs," chains connecting the legs, to prevent the wearer from taking too long steps when walking; "headbands, tablets and ear-rings," (v. 20), also translated, "girdles, perfume bottles and amulets, or charms;" "glasses," (v. 20) means "mirrors." The Lord would cause all these to be removed. Instead of finery there would be the misery of women in slavery, even "burning instead of beauty" (v. 24), which evidently refers to the mark of the cruel brand-iron on slaves.

(George Reynolds and Janne M. Sjodahl, *Commentary on the Book of Mormon,* ed. Philip C. Reynolds, 7 vols. [Salt Lake City: Deseret Book Co., 1955–1961], 328–29.)

He describes the party-people, the fast set: . . . Stupefied by the endless beat of the Oriental music which has become part of our scene: . . . And of course the total subservience to fashion: "Because the daughters of Zion are haughty and walk with stretched forth necks and wanton eyes, walking and mincing as they go"—in the immemorial manner of fashion models. An instructive list of words from the boutiques that only the fashion-wise will know. . . . (3:18–21) and of course clothes . . . (3:22) their beauty-aids will defeat their purpose as hair falls out and perfumes are overpowered (3:24).

The costly fashions reflect a world in which people are out to impress and impose themselves on others.

(Hugh W. Nibley, "Great Are the Words of Isaiah," *Sidney B. Sperry Symposium* [Provo, Utah: Religious Instruction, BYU, January 28, 1978], 199–200.)

Definitely a conservative society, the Hebrews resisted change in clothing styles—at least among the lower classes. They chose wool as their fabric, which they could produce from the backs of the sheep that they raised. . . . Men, women and children wore long tunics, extending from the neck almost to the ankles. Women and older girls also had long capes that covered their heads and reached to the bottom of their tunics. . . . We know they often wore [girdles or belts] if for no other reason than to provide a place to tuck the bottom of their tunics when working, or to keep their clothing from billowing in a breeze. . . . Much of the time they were [barefoot] both inside and out of their houses. Sometimes they did wear sandals. . . .

Isaiah severely criticized the well-to-do women of Jerusalem for their ostentation. . . . (Isa. 3:18–24).

Here we see, among other things, that like the Assyrians the Judeans wore gold or silver bands around their ankles, bracelets for the wrist, armlets for the upper arm, earrings (crescents), turbans or head bands, veils, fabric of linen, pendants of precious or semi-precious stones, amulets (to ward off evil or as good luck charms), and had their hair elaborately dressed. In addition, they even wore nose rings.

(Howard F. Vos, *Nelson's New Illustrated Bible Manners and Customs* [Nashville: Thomas Nelson, 1999], 295.)

Bravery of Tinkling Ornaments. . . . Bravery means "display, show, ostentation, and splendour." . . . The Hebrew word used by Isaiah has nothing to do with a modern day reference to a "brave" person. . . . The Hebrew term . . . translated tinkling ornaments has reference to "a band circling the flesh, particularly, an ornament of women loving display." . . .

Cauls. . . . A covering of the head worn by women like a net or fine mesh of parallel threads intersecting at right angles worn on the head and probably secured by a headband. . . .

Round Tires Like The Moon. . . . Ornaments worn on the necks of men, women, and even camels. See Judges 8:21, 26. . . . The reason for the King James use of the word "tires" comes from the fact that originally that word "tyre" meant "an ornamentation, dress or apparel." The word "attire" comes of the same origin and the modern reference to an automobile tire, etc., comes from the original sense that the tire was the "attire", "clothing", or covering of the wheel.

Chains. . . . The usual English understanding of this word describes a type of earring, especially when made with pearls or drops. . . .

Bracelets. . . . This term comes from the root word "to twist or to twine," from the idea of "turning, twisting, or going in a circle or being wreathed." This particular word is the feminine plural form and, hence, bracelets. . . .

Mufflers. . . . "A woman's veil." . . .

Bonnets. . . . An ornamental head covering and the term was used in Exodus 39:28 to describe the linen cap worn by the sons of Aaron as part of the priestly robes worn in the Temple.

Ornaments of The Legs. . . . This may refer to a stepping chain which was worn by women fastened to the ankle band of each leg so that the wearer was forced to walk elegantly with short steps. Bells were often attached to this chain to make a sound. . . .

Head-bands. . . . It has nothing to do with a band or anything else worn about the head. It is a good example of how reading an ancient language translated into old English may be misleading. The term in Hebrew meant "a band or sash worn around the waist." . . .

As to the meaning of the term "head-band" in English, in 1611 when the King James translation was made one definition meant "a sash at the top of or head of the trousers."

Tablets. . . . As to the origin of the English word "tablet" the King James translators may have used that word to designate "an ornament of precious metal or jewelry of a flat form, worn about the person." . . .

Other translators have interpreted the terms to refer to "receptacles or places for intimate things." Some have thought that the term meant "smelling bottles or perfume bottles." . . . The phrase translated "tablets" may be a reference to amulets or special small boxes containing items, "tablets" or scrolls, upon which sacred or intimate things were written. This conclusion would also be consistent with the fact that there developed a practice among the Jews of wearing small boxes or containers usually on the left arm and forehead secured to the body by connected leather ties. . . . Some Jews used this as a manner of exhibiting their own greatness, wisdom, piety and devotion; while at the same time demeaning others. The practice was condemned in Matthew 23:5. . . .

Ear-rings. . . . This term . . . stands for amulets, or superstitious ornaments, commonly gems and precious stones, or plates of gold and silver, on which magical formula were inscribed. . . . A mention of the earrings having religious significance related to the worship of idols is made in Genesis 35:4, in which all the household of Jacob were commanded to give up all their idols. . . .

Rings. . . . A signet ring or seal ring which is pressed into a soft substance to affix a seal or signet. . . .

Nose-jewels. . . . This was an item similar to an earring except that it was worn in the nose. . . .

Changeable Suits of Apparel. . . . "Splendid or costly garments which at home are put off or not worn." . . .

Mantels. . . . A spreading garment or cloak worn over other clothing. It was like a large tunic reaching to hands and feet. . . .

Wimples. . . . A spreading garment of a woman. . . .

Crisping-pins. . . . "Something turned or curved, especially a conical pouch or purse." . . .

Glasses. . . . Mirrors or thin plates made of polished metal. . . .

Fine Linen. . . . A wide garment made of linen, worn on a naked body, under the outer clothes.

Hoods. . . . "A head-piece or band wound around the head of a man." . . .

[Veils]. The word **veil**, spelled with an "**e**" denotes a piece of linen or other material forming part of a head-dress and worn so as to fall over the head and shoulders and down each side of the face."

(Loren D. Martin, *Isaiah: An Ensign to the Nations* [Salt Lake City: Valiant Publications, 1982], 165–74.)

2 Ne. 13:19–20   CHAINS, BONNETS
(Isa. 3:19–20)

Two kinds of necklaces were worn—one close-fitting, the other often consisting of precious stones or pearls, and hanging down over the chest, often as low as the girdle. The fashionable lady would wear two or three such chains, to which smelling-bottles and various ornaments, even heathen "charms," were attached. Gold pendants descended from the head-ornament, which sometimes rose like a tower, or was wreathed in graceful snake-like coils.

(Alfred Edersheim, *Sketches of Jewish Social Life* [Peabody, Massachusetts: Hendrickson Publishers, 1994], 201.)

2 Ne. 13:20–21   EAR-RINGS AND NOSE JEWELS
(Isa. 3:20–21)

The earring was either plain, or had a drop, a pendant, or a little bell inserted. The nose-ring, which the traditional law ordered to be put aside on the Sabbath, hung gracefully over the upper lip, yet so as not to interfere with the salute of the privileged friend.

(Alfred Edersheim, *Sketches of Jewish Social Life* [Peabody, Massachusetts: Hendrickson Publishers, 1994], 201.)

2 Ne. 13:22   APPAREL
(Isa. 3:22)

"Changeable suits of apparel," were costly garments of any kind which were used only on festival occasions, and put off when at home. . . . "Wimples," were wide upper garments. . . . "Crisping-pins," are . . . richly ornamented purses of gold or embroidered work, long and round in form, perhaps like an inverted cone, and suspended from the girdle. We have the idea more correctly expressed in 2 Kings 23, where the same word is translated "bags."

(James M. Freeman, *Manners and Customs of the Bible* [Plainfield, New Jersey: Logos International, 1972], 252–53.)

2 Ne. 13:23   GLASSES
(Isa. 3:23)

"Glasses," are probably the small metallic mirrors. . . . The Septuagint, however, and a number of eminent commentators, understand the word to mean "transparent garments," referring to the garments of thin gauze or other material so delicately made as to reveal the form of the wearer.

(James M. Freeman, *Manners and Customs of the Bible* [Plainfield, New Jersey: Logos International, 1972], 253.)

2 Ne. 13:23   VEILS
(Isa. 3:23)

We read of three kinds of veils. The Arabian hung down from the head, leaving the wearer free to see all around; the veil-dress was a kind of mantilla, thrown gracefully about the whole person, and covering the head; while the Egyptian resembled the veil of modern Orientals, covering breast, neck, chin, and face, and leaving only the eyes free.

(Alfred Edersheim, *Sketches of Jewish Social Life* [Peabody, Massachusetts: Hendrickson Publishers, 1994], 199.)

2 Ne. 13:24   INSTEAD OF WELL SET HAIR, BALDNESS
        (Isa. 3:24)

The hair, which was considered a chief point of beauty, was the object of special care. Young people wore it long; but in men this would have been regarded as a token of effeminacy (1 Cor. 11:14). . . . Peasant girls tied their hair in a simple knot; but the fashionable Jewesses curled and plaited theirs, adorning the tresses with gold ornaments and pearls. The favourite colour was a kind of auburn, to produce which the hair was either dyed or sprinkled with gold-dust.

(Alfred Edersheim, *Sketches of Jewish Social Life* [Peabody, Massachusetts: Hendrickson Publishers, 1994], 200.)

The absence of hair was a cause for shame. . . . The Bible views the shaving of the head as a mark of mourning (e.g., Jer 16:6) and as evidence of God's judgment, both on his own people (e.g., Isa. 3:17, 24; 7:20; 22:12; Ezek. 7:18; Amos 8:10; Micah 1:16) and on their enemies (e.g., Isa. 15:2; Jer. 47:5; 48:37; Ezek. 27:31; 29:18). . . .

To shave the head as a sign of mourning is forbidden for priests on the grounds that it would compromise their holy calling and "profane the name of their God" (Lev. 21:5; Ezek. 44:20).

(*Dictionary of Biblical Imagery*, ed. Leland Ryken, James C. Wilhoit, and Tremper Longman III [Downers Grove, Illinios: InterVarsity Press, 1998], 70.)

2 Ne. 13:24   SACKCLOTH
        (Isa. 3:24)

The often repeated phrase "in sackcloth and ashes" paints a vivid picture of mourning women and men in torn clothing, lying or kneeling on the ground as they heap ashes and dust upon themselves (2 Sam. 13:19; Esther 4:1, 3; Isa. 58:5, 61:3; Jer. 6:26, 25:34; Ezek. 27:30).

(*Dictionary of Biblical Imagery*, ed. Leland Ryken, James C. Wilhoit, and Tremper Longman III [Downers Grove, Illinios: InterVarsity Press, 1998], 50.)

2 Ne. 13:25   MEN SHALL FALL BY THE SWORD
(Isa. 3:25)

What makes a nation great? Power and gain is the answer we give today, the thing is to be number one in military and economic clout. They thought so in Isaiah's day too. . . . Where does security lie? In digging the defenses of Jerusalem you are merely digging your graves! The only true defense is the calling of the priesthood in the Temple. If you play the game of realistic power politics you can't expect any but the usual reward.

(Hugh W. Nibley, "Great Are the Words of Isaiah,"
Sidney B. Sperry Symposium [Provo, Utah: Religious Instruction, BYU, January 28, 1978], 204.)

2 Ne. 13:26   SIT UPON THE GROUND
(Isa. 3:26)

Sitting on the ground was a posture which denoted deep distress. When Job's friends came to sympathize with him, "they sat down with him upon the ground seven days and seven nights, and none spake a word unto him: for they saw that his grief was very great" (Job 2:13). When the Jews were in captivity, it is said, "By the rivers of Babylon, there we sat down, yea, we wept, when we remembered Zion." (Ps. 137:1). Jeremiah also alludes to the same custom in Lam. 2:10; 3:28. The same idea is represented in a more intensified form in the expressions, "wallow thyself in ashes" (Jer. 6:26), and "roll thyself in the dust" (Micah 1:10).

Most of the Roman coins which were struck in commemoration of the capture of Jerusalem have on one side the figure of a woman sitting on the ground. . . . The figure is generally represented with one hand to the head, which rests upon it inclining forward, and the other hanging over the knee, thus presenting a picture of great grief. In one instance, however, the hands are tied behind the back.

(James M. Freeman, *Manners and Customs of the Bible* [Plainfield, New Jersey: Logos International, 1972], 254–55.)

2 Ne. 14   ZION CLEANSED AND REDEEMED
(Isa. 4)

In the preceding chapter we read of the bitter winter seasons of apostate darkness. Now we read of darkness and wickedness giving way to light and righteousness; we read of the glorious spring of restoration with its heaven-sent cleansing rains, followed in turn by the pleasant summer of millennial splendor. It is a day when Zion's daughters have abandoned worldly fashions and have adorned themselves with robes of righteousness, while Jacob's faithful sons have, in the language of Isaiah, put on their beautiful garments—the authority and power of the holy priesthood (see Isa. 52:1; D&C 113:7–8).

(Joseph Fielding McConkie and Robert L. Millet,
Doctrinal Commentary on the Book of Mormon, 4 vols. [Salt Lake City: Bookcraft, 1987–1992], 1:279.)

2 Ne. 14:1   **SEVEN WOMEN SHALL TAKE HOLD OF ONE MAN**
                      (Isa. 4:1)

"In that day," (14:1) when the judgments will have removed so many men that there is a great scarcity of them, "seven women" (meaning simply a lot of women) will request a man's hand in marriage. Economic problems will be such that these women will be willing to provide their own food and clothing, contrary to the usual marriage customs. According to the Hebrew scriptures (Ex. 21:10), a man was required to provide a wife with food and clothing; but in this case Isaiah observes that the women are willing to waive that right. Having a good knowledge of the importance of marriage, they request a man to take away their reproach. In Isaiah's day and, indeed, in many parts of the Near East today, it was and is a disgrace to remain unmarried.

(Sidney B. Sperry, *Book of Mormon Compendium* [Salt Lake City: Bookcraft, 1968], 183–84.)

In a Semitic society, the greatest disgrace for a woman was to be barren. Isaiah describes a time when women will support themselves financially, but seek a husband who will make it possible for them to achieve the honor of motherhood.

(Victor L. Ludlow, *Unlocking the Old Testament* [Salt Lake City: Deseret Book Co., 1981], 149.)

Many years ago I attended a large gathering of Church members in the city of Berlin, Germany. . . . The majority of those who sat on crowded benches were women about middle age— and alone. Suddenly it dawned on me that perhaps these were widows, having lost their husbands during World War II. . . . So I asked the conducting officer to take a sort of standing roll call. When he asked all those who were widows to please arise, it seemed that half the vast throng stood. Their faces reflected the grim effect of war's cruelty. Their hopes had been shattered, their lives altered, and their future had in a way been taken from them.

(Thomas S. Monson, *Ensign*, Nov. 1994, 68.)

The JST and the Hebrew Bible place this verse in the previous chapter, where it fits the context much better. This condition will result from the war described in Isaiah 3:25–26. While this verse has been interpreted by some as a prophecy of plural marriage in the Church, a close examination will show that it refers to the world, not the Church. The offer of marriage as described by Isaiah is not in keeping with the law of plural marriage as revealed in the Doctrine and Covenants. The proposal to marry (or merely live together) is made here by the woman. Under the Lord's law, the man would initiate the marriage (see D&C 132:58–61). The women described by Isaiah volunteer to remain economically independent rather than make the man responsible for their care while they multiply and replenish the earth, as under the Lord's law (see D&C 132:63 and Jacob 2:30). The innate desire of the woman to be a wife and a mother is noted in the phrase to take away our reproach. To be childless was considered a reproach in ancient Israel (see Luke 1:25 and Gen. 30:23).

(Monte S. Nyman, *Great Are the Words of Isaiah* [Salt Lake City: Bookcraft, 1980], 37.)

Seven women. The headnote to the chapter in the LDS edition of the Bible places this prophecy in the Millennium. Because war has claimed the lives of many of the men of Jerusalem (identified in Isa. 3:25), the ratio of men to women is unequal. Thus *seven women* will take hold of one man. The number *seven* may be literal or symbolic.

Eat our own bread/wear our own apparel. It is the husband's duty to provide for his bride (Ex. 21:10–11), but in this prophecy Isaiah indicates that the seven women will provide for themselves. *reproach.* This word means disgrace caused by the barrenness of the womb (Gen. 30:23; Luke 1:25), a result of not having a husband.

(Donald W. Parry, Jay A. Parry, and Tina M. Peterson,
Understanding Isaiah [Salt Lake City: Deseret Book Co., 1998], 44–45.)

When a large part of the male population shall have been exterminated by war and its concomitants, seven women shall offer themselves to one man. . . . In the old times a woman, as a rule, considered it unfortunate not to have the privilege of motherhood. See the story of Rachel in the Old Testament, Gen. 30:33; or, in the New Testament, Elisabeth the mother of John the Baptist, Luke, 1:25. The misfortune must have been felt more keenly at a time when the population had been practically decimated. A plurality of wives in one household, under the protection of one man may, according to this prophetic utterance, be a more desirable arrangement than one by which six women of every seven are excluded from the joys and responsibilities of a mother. It is no defense of lawlessness to say that under similar circumstances the same remedy might be applied again. But only by divine revelation through the Prophet authorized to speak for the Lord. (See Jacob 2:27–30; D&C 43:2–6.)

(George Reynolds and Janne M. Sjodahl, *Commentary on the Book of Mormon*,
ed. Philip C. Reynolds, 7 vols. [Salt Lake City: Deseret book Co., 1955–1961], 330.)

I had been reading the revelations . . . [when] a strange stupor came over me and I recognized that I was in the Tabernacle at Ogden. I arose to speak and said . . . I will answer you right here what is coming to pass shortly. . . . I then looked in all directions . . . and I found the same mourning in every place throughout the Land. It seemed as though I was above the earth, looking down to it as I passed along on my way east and I saw the roads full of people principally women with just what they could carry in bundles on their backs . . . It was remarkable to me that there were so few men among them. . . . Wherever I went I saw . . . scenes of horror and desolation rapine and death . . . death and destruction everywhere. I cannot paint in words the horror that seemed to encompass me around. It was beyond description or thought of man to conceive. I supposed that this was the End but I was here given to understand, that the same horrors were being enacted all over the country. . . . Then a voice said "Now shall come to pass that which was spoken by Isaiah the Prophet 'That seven women shall take hold of one man saying . . .'" (*Journal of Wilford Woodruff*, June 15, 1878, Historical Department, The Church of Jesus Christ of Latter-day Saints, Salt Lake City.)

(Wilford Woodruff, as quoted in Victor L. Ludlow, *Isaiah: Prophet, Seer, and Poet* [Salt Lake City: Deseret Book Co., 1982], 109.)

2 Ne. 14:2   BRANCH
(Isa. 4:2; Jer. 33:15–17; Zech. 3:8–10; 16:12–15; 1 Ne. 15:12)

The word "branch" in Hebrew was symbolic of the Messiah. *The* Branch is the Messiah even Jesus Christ, He whose "glory def[ies] all description." (JS–H 1:17; see also Jer. 23:5–6). In another sense, the "branch" could represent dispersed remnants of the house of Israel who have been redeemed and brought back to the glory of the Lord. (See Isa. 60:21; 61:3; 2 Ne. 3:5; Jacob 2:25.)

(Hoyt W. Brewster, Jr., *Isaiah Plain and Simple* [Salt Lake City: Deseret Book Co., 1995], 37.)

2 Ne. 14:4   FILTH
(Isa. 4:4)

In its root sense, the Hebrew word for *filth* has reference to human excrement. The term is used symbolically to emphasize the terrible nature of the sins of Israel and the impurities found within the daughters of Zion.

(Donald W. Parry, Jay A. Parry, and Tina M. Peterson, *Understanding Isaiah* [Salt Lake City: Deseret Book Co., 1998], 49.)

2 Ne. 14:4   WASHED AWAY . . . PURGED
(Isa. 4:4)

"Washing away the filth of the daughters of Zion" and "purging the blood of Jerusalem" recalls the ancient sacrifices in which the burnt offerings were rinsed to remove impurities, the cleansing atonement of Christ, and washings and anointings.

(Victor L. Ludlow, *Isaiah: Prophet, Seer, and Poet* [Salt Lake City: Deseret Book Co., 1982], 110.)

2 Ne. 14:5–6   ZION—A PLACE OF REFUGE
(Isa. 4:5–6; D&C 45:64–75; 97:21; 115:6; 124:36;
refer in this text to 2 Ne. 12:32; 2 Ne. 20:24–25)

The time is soon coming, when no man will have any peace but in Zion and her stakes. I saw men hunting the lives of their own sons, and brother murdering brother, women killing their own daughters, and daughters seeking the lives of their mothers. I saw armies arrayed against armies. I saw blood, desolation, fires. The Son of Man has said that the mother shall be against the daughter, and the daughter against the mother. These things are at our doors. They will follow the Saints of God from city to city. Satan will rage, and the spirit of the devil is now enraged.

(Joseph Smith, *Teachings of the Prophet Joseph Smith*, comp. by Joseph Fielding Smith
[Salt Lake City: Deseret Book Co., 1976], 161.)

The time is to come when God will meet with all the congregation of his Saints, and to show his approval, and that he does love them, he will work a miracle by covering them in the cloud of his glory. I do not mean something that is invisible, but I mean that same order of things which once existed on the earth so far as the tabernacle of Moses was concerned, which was carried in the midst of the children of Israel as they journeyed in the wilderness. . . .

The Lord intended his people to be covered with the cloud continually, and he intended to reveal himself unto them, and to show forth his glory more fully amongst them; but they sinned. . . . Because of their wickedness he withdrew his presence, and his glory in a great measure was taken from them; but still Moses was permitted to enter the tabernacle, and to behold the glory of God, and it is said that he talked with the Lord face to face—a blessing which God did intend to bestow upon all Israel had they kept his law and had not hardened their hearts against him. But in the latter days there will be a people so pure in Mount Zion, with a house established upon the tops of the mountains, that God will manifest himself, not only in their Temple and upon all their assemblies, with a visible cloud during the day, but when the night shall come, if they shall be assembled for worship, God will meet with them by his pillar of fire; and when they retire to their habitations, behold each habitation will be lighted up by the glory of God,—a pillar of flaming fire by night.

Did you ever hear of any city that was thus favored and blessed since the day that Isaiah delivered this prophecy? No, it is a latter-day work, one that God must consummate in the latter times when he begins to reveal himself, and show forth his power among the nations.

(Orson Pratt, *Journal of Discourses*, 16:82.)

It [2 Ne. 14:5] suggests the protection of Zion and her stakes in a day when the world is in turmoil. For a fuller description of that time, see Doctrine and Covenants 45:63–75 and 84:2–5; the latter of these passages identifies the cloud as "the glory of the Lord." Note that there is more than one place for the assembly or gathering of the Saints. This is consistent with the Lord's admonition to stand in "holy places" when bloodshed, famine, plague, and other calamities sweep the earth (see D&C 87:6–8). . . .

According to Oliver Cowdery, when the angel Moroni appeared to the Prophet Joseph Smith in September 1823, he quoted Isaiah 4:5–6 as one of the prophecies which was soon to be fulfilled (MA, Apr. 1835, 110). President Harold B. Lee quoted Doctrine and Covenants 115:4–6 as a prophecy of the time when members of the Church would gather to the stakes of Zion (rather than a specific place in the land of Zion) as a refuge from the storm and wrath which would be poured out upon the whole earth (see *Conference Report,* Apr. 1973, 5).

(Monte S. Nyman, *Great Are the Words of Isaiah* [Salt Lake City: Bookcraft, 1980], 38–39.)

In that glorious day when literally the whole earth will be Zion ("for this is Zion—THE PURE IN HEART" [D&C 97:21]), the Lord will shield the people from heat and storm. His protective pavilion will encompass the pure in heart in all places.

(Hoyt W. Brewster, Jr., *Isaiah Plain and Simple* [Salt Lake City: Deseret Book Co., 1995], 39.)

In Bible times men did not build houses with the idea in mind that most of their daily living would be spent inside them. Their first interest was in spending as much time as possible in God's out-of-doors. The house served as a place of retirement. For this reason the outside walls of the humble house were not inviting. There was no effort to attract attention to this place of retirement. The purpose of these dwellings is borne out by the meaning of the Hebrew and Arabic words for "house." Rev. Abraham Rihbany, who was born in Syria and spent his early life there, has made a very illuminative statement about the meaning and purpose of the Palestinian house:

The Hebrew word *bavith* and the Arabic word *bait* mean primarily a "shelter." The English equivalent is the word "house." The richer term, "home," has never been invented by the son of Palestine because he has always considered himself "a sojourner in the earth." His tent and his little house, therefore, were sufficient for a shelter for him and his dear ones during the earthly pilgrimage.

Because the Palestinians lived out-of-doors so much, the sacred writers were fond of referring to God as a "shelter" or as a "refuge," rather than as a "home."

(Fred H. Wight, *Manners and Customs of Bible Lands* [Chicago: Moody Press, 1953], 20–21.)

The salvation of the Saints one and all depends on the building up of Zion, for without this there is no salvation, for deliverance in the last days is found in Zion and in Jerusalem, and in the remnant whom the Lord our God shall call, or in other words, in the stakes which He shall appoint . . . It is in Zion where the Lord is to create upon every dwelling place and upon her assemblies a cloud of smoke by day and the shining of a flaming fire by night. It is upon the glory of Zion that there will be a defense.

It is in Zion that there shall be a tabernacle for a shadow in the day time from the heat, and for a place of refuge and for a covert from storm and from rain (Isa. 4:5, 6). . . . The day of calamity draweth nigh, and unless the Saints hasten the building of the city they will not escape. . . .

And let not covetousness, which is idolatry, nor worldly ambition hinder you . . . that there may be a place of refuge for you and for your children in the day of God's vengeance, when He shall come down on Idumea, or the world, . . . and none shall escape but the inhabitants of Zion. . . . With all the power that the Saints have, and with all the diligence they can use they will scarcely escape.

The time is not far distant when some of those who now deride and mock the Saints for devoting their all to build up the Zion of God, will bless their name for having provided a city of refuge for them and their children.

(Newel K. Whitney, Reynolds Cahoon, Vinson Knight, *History of the Church*, 2:516–18.)

The First Presidency has called on the parents of the Church to hold family home evening and family prayer, to study the gospel in the home, and to spend time with children in wholesome activities. . . .

When I was growing up, my father often led our family in gospel discussions around the dinner table. Only with the perspective of years do I understand today the contribution those family hours made to my own testimony. I rejoice in the prophecy of Isaiah that the time will come when "upon every dwelling place of mount Zion" there shall be "a cloud . . . by day, and . . . a flaming fire by night" (Isa. 4:5), when the Spirit of God will abide in the homes of His people continually.

(Bruce D. Porter, *Ensign*, May 2001, 81.)

2 Ne. 15	**THE VINE AND THE VINEYARD**
	(Isa. 5; refer in *Latter-day Commentary on the Book of Mormon,* Bassett, to Jacob 5)

The fifth chapter of Isaiah speaks of Jehovah and the vines of his vineyard. The common grape, or biblical vine, *Vitis vinifera,* has a long history of cultivation in Israel. It is the first cultivated plant to be identified by name in the Bible (see Gen. 9:20) and continues to be an important crop in modern Israel. It was an important source of food and beverage in the ancient Near East. In ancient Israel the September grape harvest was a time of feasting, joy, and song.

In the Holy Land, the grapevine can be an exceptionally robust plant, capable of developing trunks up to one and one-half feet in diameter. They typically produce clusters of grapes weighing from ten to twelve pounds, although some approach thirty pounds in weight. To reach this fruit-producing potential, however, the vine requires a tremendous amount of care and attention. If left untended, it seldom survives. These characteristics made the vine an ideal metaphor for Israel.

(Terry Ball, *Thy People Shall Be My People and Thy God My God: The 22ⁿᵈ Annual Sidney B. Sperry Symposium* [Salt Lake City: Deseret Book Co., 1994], 18.)

In Isaiah's parable of the Vineyard, and in Christ's Parable of the Wicked Husbandman, taken together, we get an accurate picture of an Oriental vineyard. . . . (Isa. 5:1–2). . . . (Matt. 21:33). These two accounts list eight interesting facts that are true of many vineyards in Bible lands. They are often located on a hillside, they usually have a hedge or fence around them, the soil is cultivated by hoeing or spading, large stones are gathered out of the ground, choice vines are planted, a watch-tower is built, a winepress is constructed, and sometimes vineyards are rented. These points suggest the main features that need to be noticed in a study of the Oriental vineyard. . . .

Although vineyards are to be found in various locations in Palestine, it has been customary during past years for the hillsides to be utilized for the purpose, or the ground at the foot of a hill that slopes gently. Grapevines like a sandy or loose soil. They need plenty of sunshine and air by day, and dew by night, and their roots will penetrate deep crevices of rock to get nourishment. It was "in a very fruitful hill" that Isaiah's vineyard grew (Isa. 5:1). . . .

The favorite places for vineyards in Bible lands are Southern Palestine, especially in the vicinity of Hebron where there are many hillsides; and in Syria and the foothills of the Lebanon Mountains in the north. . . . The ground for hillside vineyards is not usually ploughed on account of its rocky character. Rather is the more arduous method of hoeing or spading by hand used. Isaiah pictures the process of cultivation of the soil in the word, ". . . [digged]".

(Fred H. Wight, *Manners and Customs of Bible Lands* [Chicago: Moody Press, 1953], 187–88, 190.)

2 Ne. 15:1–7   SONG OF THE VINEYARD
(Isa. 5:1–7; Jacob 5; Jer. 2:21; 12:10; Ps. 80:8; Matt. 20:1–16; 21:28–34; Mark 12:1–11; Luke 20:9–18; 13:6–9; John 15:1–8; Rom. 11:17–24)

The Israelites had a yearly festival, at the end of their year, called the feast of ingathering (Ex. 23:16; 34:22), because on that occasion the people were required to give thanks especially for the harvest of fields and vineyards. It has been suggested that this song, or poem, was composed and recited on such an occasion. It contains a parable in which Israel is represented as a vineyard (as in Isa. 3:14), and the consequences of the neglect of unfaithful keepers (Matt. 21:33–41).

(George Reynolds and Janne M. Sjodahl, *Commentary on the Book of Mormon*, ed. Philip C. Reynolds, 7 vols. [Salt Lake City: Deseret Book Co., 1955–1961], 1:333.)

This metaphor of the Lord's vineyard commences as a song, possibly like those sung by the men of Judah during the grape harvest. The husbandman of the vineyard is referred to as the "wellbeloved," who is identified as Jehovah, while the vineyard itself is clearly the house of Israel.

From the very beginning, it is evident that the "wellbeloved" invested all the care requisite for an abundant harvest from this vineyard. He planted it in an ideal location, on a *keren ben-shemen* (Heb., which is translated as "a very fruitful hill" in the KJV). Literally, *keren* means "a horn" and probably refers to a hornlike mountain peak or hillside. By planting the vineyard on such a *keren,* the wise husbandman would ensure that his vineyard would not be shadowed from essential sunlight. The phrase *ben-shemen* means, literally, "a child of fatness" and might refer to a location with exceptionally fertile soil. The husbandman prepared the soil by digging about it carefully and removing the stones. He then planted the vineyard, not with ordinary vines, or *gephen*, but rather with *soreq*, which is thought to be a variety of grapevine that produces one of the choicest of bluish-red grapes. To protect the vineyard, he built a watchtower and apparently placed a hedge or wall around it. Both the tower and the protective walls would probably be constructed from the stones gathered out of the fields. In anticipation of an abundant harvest, he even hewed out a winepress in the vineyard.

Surely the wellbeloved could have done nothing more to guarantee production from his vineyard. How bitter must his disappointment have been when, rather than bringing forth sweet juicy grapes—a faithful covenant people—the well-tended vineyard brought forth "wild grapes," or *beushim*, literally meaning "stinking, worthless things."

In frustration the husbandman determined to lay waste the vineyard but not by personally destroying the vines. Rather, he decided to cease taking care of the vineyard and withdraw his protection from it. Accordingly, he stopped pruning and cultivating the vineyard and commanded the clouds to rain no longer upon it. He also removed the protective wall from around it, thus allowing the vines to be trampled and ravaged. Eventually the vines were displaced from their choice location by noxious vegetation, including briars and thorns (see Isa. 7:23). Thus, the metaphor gives a powerful warning to Israel. If they do not respond to the nurturing direction and loving kindness of Jehovah, he will abandon them and allow another people to possess their choice land.

(Terry Ball, *Thy People Shall Be My People and Thy God My God:
The 22nd Annual Sidney B. Sperry Symposium* [Salt Lake City: Deseret Book Co., 1994], 19–20.)

These verses are part of the Song of the Vineyard. The song is about a caring master who shows great concern and love for his vineyard. The master is the Lord and the vineyard is the house of Israel, the Lord's covenant people. Grapes become plump, juicy, and sweet when the master of the vineyard has planted them in a fertile hill, removed stones and weeds, and prepared for the harvest. Members of the house of Israel, too, can flourish with the master's care.

Those who do not respond to care, however, become like wild or rotten grapes, which symbolize corrupt or evil people (Hosea 9:10). They will not partake of the atonement and abide in Christ. They will be trodden down by the Lord in great fury at his second coming, staining his robe red (D&C 133:50–51).

Those who follow Christ will bring forth good fruit (John 15). God made Israel the "choicest vine" so that it would be fruitful and become a righteous people among the nations. He built a tower in the vineyard so that watchmen, including the prophets, could watch for impending danger and then warn the children of Israel (Ezek. 3:17; 33:1–7; D&C 101:43–62). He also made a winepress in anticipation of a great harvest."

(Donald W. Parry, *Visualizing Isaiah*
[Provo, Utah: The Foundation for Ancient Research and Mormon Studies, 2001], 8.)

The parable of the vineyard has been given or told and enacted three times in history: once by Isaiah prior to the destruction of Jerusalem in 587 B.C. (Isa. 5:1–7), once by the Savior prior to the second destruction of Jerusalem in A.D. 70 (Matt. 21:33–46), and again by revelation through the prophet Joseph Smith in 1833 after the failure to establish a New Jerusalem in Missouri (D&C 101:43–62). All three parables use the same theme and speak of the same characters. Variations within the parables are appropriate to the time within which each was given. As an example, the first two talk about a "tower" (The Temple) which had been constructed by command of the Lord. The third parable speaks of a tower which the Lord commanded to be built but which the people never completed.

The Book of Mormon parable of the Olive tree in the fifth chapter of Jacob is similar in appearance and style but different in meaning. The story in Jacob is a historical parable of the scattering and the gathering of Israel.

(Loren D. Martin, *Isaiah: An Ensign to the Nations* [Salt Lake City: Valiant Publications, 1982], 117.)

2 Ne. 15:2   WINE-PRESS, WILD GRAPES
(Isa. 5:2)

He obviously anticipates a plentiful harvest because he also "hews" a winepress or vat in the middle of the vineyard. Such a wine vat consists of two basins or pits carved out of the rocks. The upper pit, where the grapes are trodden out, is shallow and large enough to accommodate the workers. A trench carries the pressed-out juices to a lower, deeper pit, where the wine accumulates until it is stored in clay jars or skin bags. The construction of this type of press is usually undertaken by wealthy landowners or by those who press grapes for many farmers. Thus, the fact that the master of this vineyard builds a vat in the middle of his own field indicates that he expects his harvest alone to justify its construction. To his disappointment, however, his vines yield only wild, sour grapes.

(Victor L. Ludlow, *Isaiah: Prophet, Seer, and Poet* [Salt Lake City: Deseret Book Co., 1982], 114.)

He likens the Lord to a "wellbeloved" husbandman who plants a vineyard in an exceptionally choice location and does everything requisite for producing a wonderful harvest of grapes. . . . He built a tower in the vineyard to protect it, and in anticipation of the abundant harvest, he hewed out a winepress within the vineyard itself. Imagine the husbandman's disappointment when, in spite of all his efforts, the vineyard refused to produce good grapes. Rather it brought forth "wild grapes," or in the Hebrew, *be'ushim*, literally meaning stinking, worthless things. When the house of Israel should have thrived in righteousness, it floundered in sin. Such failure to thrive was destroying the covenant people.

(Terry B. Ball, *Voices of Old Testament Prophets*:
The 26th Annual Sidney B. Sperry Symposium [Salt Lake City: Deseret Book Co., 1997], 51–52.)

2 Ne. 15:5   TAKE AWAY THE HEDGE . . . BREAK DOWN THE WALL
(Isa. 5:5)

His process of abandoning the vineyard exemplifies the judgments of God, who usually does not destroy or severely punish a wicked person; God simply leaves him alone to face the challenges of life and buffetings of Satan without the protection of the Spirit.

(Victor L. Ludlow, *Isaiah: Prophet, Seer, and Poet* [Salt Lake City: Deseret Book Co., 1982], 114.)

2 Ne. 15:6   BRIERS
(Isa. 5:6; refer in this text to 2 Ne. 20:17–19)

Briers surely would evoke negative memories for persons living close to the land. Everybody hates briers; they are an infuriating ground cover that trips, scratches and generally makes walking through them miserable. Briers don't just cause pain—they make you suffer. The scratches can make one's bare legs and ankles feel like they are on fire. In fact, briers and suffering are practically inseparable in the Bible. . . .

Briers are used metaphorically to depict the devastating result of God's judgment—turning pleasant and productive land into wasteland (cf. Isa. 5:6; 7:25; 32:13; Heb. 6:8). . . .

Being extremely hardy, briers are especially hard on the weak things. Small, delicate plants are no match for the voracious appetite of the brier. Jesus had this in mind when he told the parable of the sower (cf. Matt. 13:7; Mark 4:7; Luke 8:7). Finally, there is that ironic picture of the crown of thorns fashioned for Jesus as a way to mock him. The shameful tearing of his flesh is the outward display of inner suffering. Whether physical or metaphorical, briers and misery go hand in hand.

(*Dictionary of Biblical Imagery*, ed. Leland Ryken, James C. Wilhoit, and
Tremper Longman III, [Downers Grove, Illinois: InterVarsity Press, 1998], 123.)

2 Ne. 15:8–25   THE SIX WOES UPON THE WICKED
(Isa. 5:8–25)

What is that special form of sin which Isaiah sees? It is human selfishness—the unbrotherhood of man to man. . . . The cry which rises into his ears is the cry of stricken humanity—the cry of the poor and needy, the cry of the sad and weary. . . . He hears God calling him to lash the sins of the nation; but to him all the sins of the nation are forms of a single sin—*selfishness*. Does he deplore idolatry; it is because the idols of man are images of man's own glory. Does he repudiate extravagance in dress, and luxury in living; it is because this outlay of wealth might have been for the sake of the destitute. . . . To him the evil is not without but within, and can only be cured from within—by cultivating the barren spots in the life of the community. The burden of Isaiah is the burden of human compassion. It is the desire to right the wrongs which man has done to his brother. . . .

The preparation *he* proposed for meeting God was not [just] the attendance at the temple, not [just] the observance of the Sabbath, . . . but the sympathy of the heart with the wants and woes of man. . . . It seemed to him that before a man could begin to think of others, he must cease to think of himself—must become self-unconscious.

(George Matheson, *The Old Testament and the Fine Arts*,
comp. Cynthia Pearl Maus [New York: Harper & Row, 1954], 561–62.)

2 Ne. 15:8   WO UNTO THEM WHO JOIN HOUSE TO HOUSE
(Isa. 5:8; 3 Ne. 24:5; Gal. 6:17; D&C 19:26; Micah 2:1–2)

This woe is pronounced on the wealthy landowners who covet and buy up property, thus depriving the poor of their heritage. (See Micah 2:1–2.) The law of ancient Israel prescribed that land could not "be sold for ever" (Lev. 25:23; see also 1 Kgs. 21). It was to remain within families as a heritage for posterity. When economical circumstances necessitated the sale of land, it was to be returned to the original owners in the year of jubilee, which occurred every fifty years. (LDS Bible Dictionary, "Jubilee, Year of," 718).

(Hoyt W. Brewster, Jr., *Isaiah Plain and Simple* [Salt Lake City: Deseret Book Co., 1995], 46.)

Property acquired for selfish purposes is not a blessing. Greed is never satisfied. Ownership of property is not condemned. The only question is, how did the owner get it, and to what use does he put it?

(George Reynolds and Janne M. Sjodahl, *Commentary on the Book of Mormon*,
ed. Philip C. Reynolds, 7 vols. [Salt Lake City: Deseret Book Co., 1955–1961], 1:334.)

What are the things of this world? What are houses and lands . . . generally, to us? What are they to any Saints of God compared with eternal life? . . . There have been too much selfishness and division and every man for himself amongst us, and the devil for us all.

(Wilford Woodruff, *Discourses of Wilford Woodruff*, ed. G. Homer Durham [Salt Lake City: Bookcraft, 1946], 126.)

We are gathering to this beautiful land, to build up "Zion." . . . But since I have been here I perceive the spirit of selfishness. Covetousness exists in the hearts of the Saints. . . . Here are those who begin to spread out buying up all the land they are able to do, to the exclusion of the poorer ones who are not so much blessed with this worlds goods, thinking to lay foundations for themselves only, looking to their own individual families, and those who are to follow them.

(Brigham Young, as quoted in Hugh Nibley, *Brother Brigham Challenges the Saints*, ed. Don E. Norton and Shirley S. Ricks [Salt Lake City: Deseret Book Co., 1994], 47.)

The surplus property of this community, as poor as we are, has done more real mischief than everything else besides. . . . A man has no right with property, . . . [when the property doesn't] do good to himself and his fellow-man. . . . If the people of this community feel as though they wanted the whole world to themselves . . . and would hoard up their property, and place it in a situation where it would not benefit either themselves or the community, they are just as guilty as the man who steals my property.

(Brigham Young, *Journal of Discourses* 1:252, 255.)

Even when right is plainly on his side the poor man doesn't stand a chance, for "the churl . . . deviseth wicked devices to destroy the poor with lying words, even when the needy speaketh right," (32:7). "For the vile person will practice hypocrisy and utter error to make empty the soul of the hungry and he will cause the drink of the thirsty to fail." Real estate is a special province for such people and the ancient record is full of the slick and tricky deals by which they acquired their great estates. . . . "Wo unto them that join house to house, that lay field to field, till no place is left, till they be alone in the midst of the earth," and own it all themselves.

(Hugh W. Nibley, "Great Are the Words of Isaiah," *Sidney B. Sperry Symposium* [Provo, Utah: Religious Instruction, BYU, January 28, 1978], 202.)

This judgment falls upon wealthy landowners who buy up all the property they can until their lands border one another. This results in a monopoly of property that should be divided among others, especially the poor. This practice violates the spirit of the Law of the Jubilee, the property law of ancient Israel, which states that "the land shall not be sold forever." (Lev. 25:23.) Instead, land was to remain within families and clans as a perpetual inheritance. (See 1 Kgs. 21, in which Neboth refuses to sell his ancestral lands to King Ahab.) The hoarding of land described in verse 8 was in violation of this law, for when all property was purchased by a few wealthy individuals, there was no place for the original families to dwell. Having no homeland, they were forced to move to the cities or live on the property of the owner as indentured servants or slaves. Although drought, sickness, or economic setbacks might require a farmer to sell his land or indenture himself and family to cover losses, the Year of Jubilee every fifty years was instituted to correct the perpetual loss of land and the slavery of people by guaranteeing the periodic return of land to the original owners. Obviously, this law was severely abused by the landowners of Isaiah's time.

(Victor L. Ludlow, *Isaiah: Prophet, Seer, and Poet* [Salt Lake City: Deseret Book Co., 1982], 117.)

Wo is addressed to those who seek after, collect, acquire, or amass wealth; expanding their own personal power at the expense or neglect of all else. This is not a simple condemnation against the acquisition of wealth. It is a warning against the desire for the acquisition of wealth to an extreme degree, motivated by devotion or religious zeal. It is a warning against worshiping the god of this world, materialism.

The mania for acquisition is never quieted or satisfied by the gain. It is an unquenchable thirst or indulgence, and like an uncontrolled passion, indulgence is never sufficiency. The aspiration to acquire power, dominance, or conquest leaves the aspirant surrounded by his gods, earthy materialism, clamoring for constant attention. There is no place to be left alone in quiet solitude of soul.

(Loren D. Martin, *Isaiah: An Ensign to the Nations* [Salt Lake City: Valiant Publications, 1982], 124.)

2 Ne. 15:10   10 ACRES, 1 BATH, A HOMER, AN EPHAH
(Isa. 5:10)

In verse ten the seriousness of the desolation in the fields is demonstrated by the terms used. Ordinarily, a farmer would hope to get a thirty-, sixty-, or even a hundred-fold increase from the seed he planted. But instead he would only get one tenth back, because one homer of seed (equal to ten ephahs) would yield only one ephah of harvest. This is unique type of "reverse tithing."

(Victor L. Ludlow, *Unlocking the Old Testament* [Salt Lake City: Deseret Book Co., 1981], 149.)

The lands of the wealthy will become extremely unproductive. *Ten acres* represents the amount of land that ten yoke of oxen can plow in a day, or the equivalent of five acres of land by our modern measurement. From this acreage, the yield will be only one bath (four to eight gallons of wine). One homer of seed (about six bushels) will yield only an ephah of produce (four to six gallons of dry measure).

(Hoyt W. Brewster, Jr., *Isaiah Plain and Simple* [Salt Lake City: Deseret Book Co., 1995], 47.)

The land would become unproductive, so that five acres of a vineyard would produce only one bath (eight gallons) of wine, and a homer (six bushels) of seed, would yield only an ephah (four gallons) of grain. Isaiah's prognosis in these passages accurately describes the pitiful circumstances the remnant of Israel faced after the Babylonian and Assyrian deportations.

(Terry B. Ball, *Voices of Old Testament Prophets*:
The 26th Annual Sidney B. Sperry Symposium [Salt Lake City: Deseret Book Co., 1997], 54.)

The KJV . . . states ten acres, but the Hebrew reads ten yoke or the amount ten yoke of oxen could plow in a day, which is equivalent to about five acres.

(Terry B. Ball, *Voices of Old Testament Prophets*:
The 26th Annual Sidney B. Sperry Symposium [Salt Lake City: Deseret Book Co., 1997], 59.)

2 Ne. 15:11–12, 22   DRUNKENNESS
(Isa. 5:11–13, 22)

This passage indicates revelry and unholy merrymaking among those who spend time in immoral entertainment. It warns all against making strong drink their passion. A passage from the Book of Mormon presents a prophecy that corresponds in some ways to this verse of Isaiah: "There shall be many which shall say: Eat, drink, and be merry, for tomorrow we die; and it shall be well with us" (2 Nephi 28:7). But these are "false and vain and foolish doctrines" (Isa. 5:9). . . . The King James Version of the Bible uses the word "tabret," which is usually translated "tambourine" in modern English Bibles.

Instruments were used in worship. They were also played at banquets and feasts where merry-makers partook of wine and strong drink and participated in revelries. Apparently, harlots played their harps as they wandered around the city attempting to attract attention (Isa. 23:16).

(Donald W. Parry, *Visualizing Isaiah*
[Provo, Utah: The Foundation for Ancient Research and Mormon Studies, 2001], 46–47.)

The liquor fight is an eternal battle and moves from scene to scene and sin to sin.

There are numerous people who profit financially—some politicians, manufacturers, wholesalers, deliverers, dispensers, and the underworld. Added to that army are the rationalizers who demand their liquor, regardless of harm to others. Do they pray over their work?

The liquor traffic is sacrilege, for it seeks profit from the damnation of human souls." (Harry Emerson Fosdick.)

Arguments are specious, but to the gullible, unsuspecting, righteous, busy people, they are made to seem plausible. The tax argument, the employment one, the school lunch program, the freedom to do as one pleases—all are like sie ves with many holes. There is just enough truth in them to deceive. Satan deals in half truths.

(Spencer W. Kimball, *The Teachings of Spencer W. Kimball*, ed. Edward L. Kimball,
[Salt Lake City: Bookcraft, 1982], 206–207.)

2 Ne. 15:13   NO KNOWLEDGE . . . FAMISHED . . . DRIED UP
(Isa. 5:13; 2 Ne. 32:7; John 4:10)

Satan gains power over people because they lack gospel knowledge . . . (2 Ne. 32:7). Without the gospel individuals are deprived of the "bread of life" and the "living water" (John 6:48, 4:10). Thus, they are spiritually "famished" and "dried up with thirst." . . . Today individuals in the Church deceive others by their smooth words and scholarly language. . . . Some are led into inactivity and even apostasy because they do not search and understand the scriptures as they are illuminated by the light of the Spirit.

(Clyde J. Williams, *Doctrines of the Book of Mormon*,
ed. Bruce A. Van Orden and Brent L. Top [Salt Lake City: Deseret Book Co., 1992], 245–46.)

A person who has "no knowledge" is one who lacks intelligence or revelation. This is consistent with the statement that their honorable men are famished and their multitude dried up with thirst. . . . Without the constant rain from the heavens there is famine and thirst.

(Loren D. Martin, *Isaiah: An Ensign to the Nations* [Salt Lake City: Valiant Publications, 1982], 127.)

2 Ne. 15:14   HELL HATH ENLARGED HERSELF
(Isa. 5:14; D&C 122:7)

The term *hell* (Hebrew *sheol*) in this verse refers to the world of spirits. Hell opens her mouth wide enough to receive all who are pompous and wicked, as well as their pomp and glory; both the wicked *and* their evil traits will be cast down to hell. This "opened mouth" image that is connected to hell continues the symbolism of feasting ("strong drink," "wine," "feasts") and famine ("famished," "dried up with thirst"). The wicked open their mouths as they eat, drink, and are merry, while at the same time hell opens *her* mouth to swallow *them*. In the end, hell's mouth, not the mouths of the wicked, will be filled.

(Donald W. Parry, Jay A. Parry, and Tina M. Peterson,
Understanding Isaiah [Salt lake City: Deseret Book Co., 1998], 57.)

"My people are destroyed for lack of knowledge," said the prophet Hosea (see Hosea 4:6). Let us not let it happen to us. First, let us do our homework, because action without the proper education can lead to fanaticism. But after we have done our homework, let us take action, because education without action can only lead to frustration and failure.

(Ezra Taft Benson, *The Teachings of Ezra Taft Benson* [Salt Lake City: Bookcraft, 1988], 301.)

2 Ne. 15:14–15,21   PRIDE
(Isa. 5:14–15, 21; refer in *Latter-day Commentary on the Book of Mormon,* Bassett, to 2 Ne. 12:7–8; Jacob 2:13–17; 2 Ne. 9:28–30; 3 Ne. 6:10–16)

If the President of the Church or either of his counselors or of the apostles or any other man feels in his heart that God cannot do without him, and that he is especially important in order to carry on the work of the Lord, he stands upon slippery ground. I heard Joseph Smith say that Oliver Cowdery, who was the second apostle in this Church, said to him, "If I leave this Church it will fall."

Said Joseph, "Oliver, you try it." Oliver tried it. He fell; but the kingdom of God did not. I have been acquainted with other apostles in my day and time who felt that the Lord could not do without them; but the Lord got along with his work without them. I say to all men—Jew and Gentile, great and small, rich and poor—that the Lord Almighty has power within himself, and is not dependent upon any man to carry on his work; but when he does call men to do his work they have to trust in him.

(Wilford Woodruff, *The Discourses of Wilford Woodruff,*
ed. G. Homer Durham, [Salt Lake City: Bookcraft, 1946], 123–24.)

How can man believe and know that he can travel in man-made spaceships around the earth at thousands and thousands of miles an hour, communicate with man here upon the earth, and be directed in his course, with the knowledge that if he keeps in tune with home base he will be guided back to a safe landing; and that mere man can also construct implements such as the *Surveyor,* which he has sent to the moon, with which he has communicated in directing its activities, and from which he has received reports—and still say that it is impossible for God, the Creator of the world, to communicate with man, his own creation, who is traveling through space on a spaceship created by God and known as the earth, and that by keeping in touch with home base he can be assured of a safe return when he has completed his tour here upon the earth?

(N. Eldon Tanner, *Conference Report,* Oct. 1968, 49.)

2 Ne. 15:17   THE WASTE PLACES OF THE FAT ONES SHALL STRANGERS EAT
(Isa. 5:17)

Some commentaries suggest this verse should be placed next to verse 10. It is probably a reference to the desolate condition of the lands once inhabited by the wealthy. Rather than producing bountiful crops, their lands will provide forage for lambs and young goats or strangers. (The word "strangers" appears as "aliens" in early Hebrew texts while the Greek Septuagint uses "young goats.")

(Hoyt W. Brewster, Jr., *Isaiah Plain and Simple* [Salt Lake City: Deseret Book Co., 1995], 48.)

2 Ne. 15:18   **CART ROPE**
                     (Isa. 5:18)

Isaiah condemned those who think they can give up one sin and yet cling tenaciously to others. "Woe unto them that draw iniquity with cords of vanity, and sin as it were with a cart rope" (Isa. 5:18). Occasionally we cut the "cords of vanity" and let go of a favorite sin, but all too often we only periodically cast off from our cart a sin here and there rather than just letting go of the cart rope.

(Brent L. Top, *A Peculiar Treasure* [Salt Lake City: Bookcraft, 1997], 160.)

This verse creates an image of a beast of burden, such as a donkey or ox, pulling a cart of goods. The beast represents a wicked person and the cart represents sin. The wicked are burdened with sins, which they drag behind them, just as a beast of burden hauls its load from place to place.

The verse also suggests that vanity is the key component from which the cords are made. Many commit sins and then drag them after themselves because of vanity and pride. Sin is sometimes as difficult to break as a thick rope that is strong enough to pull a cart, but it is possible to break sin with the help of Christ. The Lord says, "Come unto me, all ye that labour and are heavy laden, and I will give you rest" (Matt. 11:28).

(Donald W. Parry, *Visualizing Isaiah*
[Provo, Utah: The Foundation for Ancient Research and Mormon Studies, 2001], 48.)

2 Ne. 15:20   **EVIL GOOD AND GOOD EVIL**
                     (Isa. 5:20; D&C 121:16–17; 2 Ne. 28:22; refer in *Latter-day
                     Commentary on the Book of Mormon*, Bassett, to Alma 30:12–28)

Satan uses his deceptive influence to change peoples' perception of evil. . . . The great switch in values has taken place in many areas, such as our music, movies, marriages, dress, and family size. Things that are wholesome, modest, or uplifting are often ridiculed or demeaned as worthless, outdated, or unrealistic. Things that bring fleeting, temporary pleasure are valued most in today's world. Concerning this moral inversion, Elder W. Grant Bangerter declared, "The voices and enticements of the world make good seem evil and evil, good. The false attractions to engage in immorality, to view that which is forbidden on your home video, to seek unbounded pleasure as if God did not exist, are, in reality, the yawning pit of hell, set there by the one who will try to bind you with his awful chains."

(Clyde J. Williams, *Doctrines of the Book of Mormon*,
ed. Bruce A. Van Orden and Brent L. Top [Salt Lake City: Deseret Book Co., 1992], 246–47.)

The fact that some governments and some churches and numerous corrupted individuals have tried to reduce such behavior from criminal offense to personal privilege does not change the nature nor the seriousness of the practice.

(Spencer W. Kimball, *Ensign*, Nov. 1980, 97.)

In the summertime one of our responsibilities was to haul hay from the fields into the barn for winter storage. . . . One day, in one of the loose bundles pitched onto the wagon was a rattlesnake! When I looked at it, I was concerned, excited, and afraid. The snake was laying in the nice, cool hay. The sun was glistening on its diamond back. After a few moments the snake stopped rattling, became still, and I became very curious. I started to get closer and leaned over for a better look, when suddenly I heard a call from my father: "David, my boy, you can't pet a rattlesnake!" . . .

I would like to talk to you about the dangers of petting poisonous snakes . . . today's popular entertainment often makes what is evil and wrong look enjoyable and right. Let us remember the Lord's counsel: "Woe unto them that call evil good, and good evil" (Isa. 5:20).

Pornography, though billed by Satan as entertainment, is a deeply poisonous, deceptive snake that lies coiled up in magazines, the Internet, and the television. Pornography destroys self-esteem and weakens self-discipline. It is far more deadly to the spirit than the rattlesnake my father warned me not to pet."

(David E. Sorensen, *Ensign,* May 2001, 41.)

Across the desk from me sat a handsome nineteen-year-old boy and a beautiful, shy, but charming eighteen-year-old girl. . . . They admitted they had broken the moral code and thus gone contrary to some standards, but they quoted magazines and papers and speakers approving premarital sex and emphasizing that sex was a fulfillment of human existence. . . .

Finally, the boy said, "Yes, we yielded to each other, but we do not think it was wrong because we *love* each other." I thought I had misunderstood him. Since the world began there have been countless immoralities, but to hear them justified by a Latter-day Saint youth shocked me. He repeated, "No, it is not wrong, because we *love* each other." . . .

The Savior said that if it were possible the very elect would be deceived by Lucifer. He uses his logic to confuse and his rationalizations to destroy. He will shade meanings, open doors an inch at a time, and lead from purest white through all the shades of gray to the darkest black.

This young couple looked up rather startled when I postulated firmly, "No, my beloved young people, you did not *love* each other. Rather, you *lusted* for each other." . . . As far back as Isaiah, deceivers and rationalizers were condemned: "Woe unto them that call evil good, and good evil; that put darkness for light, and light for darkness; that put bitter for sweet, and sweet for bitter!' (Isa. 5:20).

(Spencer W. Kimball, *The Teachings of Spencer W. Kimball,*
ed. Edward L. Kimball, [Salt Lake City: Bookcraft, 1982], 278–79.)

I speak of the importance of keeping covenants because they protect us in a world that is drifting from time-honored values that bring joy and happiness. In the future this loosening of moral fiber may even increase. The basic decency of society is decreasing. In the future our people, particularly our children and grandchildren, can expect to be bombarded more and more by the evils of Sodom and Gomorrah.

Too many families are being broken up. Good is called evil, and evil is called good. In our present "easiness of the way," have we forgotten the elements of sacrifice and consecration that our pioneer forebears demonstrated so well for us? . . .

Today the modern counterparts of Babylon, Sodom, and Gomorrah are alluringly and explicitly displayed on television, the Internet, in movies, books, magazines, and places of entertainment.

In the last general conference, President Gordon B. Hinckley warned us about moving too far toward the mainstream of society in some areas such as Sabbath day observance, family disintegration, and other matters. . . .

In our society many sacred values have been eroded in the name of freedom of expression. The vulgar and the obscene are protected in the name of freedom of speech. . . . Of course, as individuals and as a people we want to be liked and respected. But we cannot be in the mainstream of society if it means abandoning . . . righteous principles. . . .

All forms of evil are being masked. I speak of sexual immorality. I speak of wagering for money, which in many places is called gaming rather than gambling. This is typical of how many other evils are masked to make them more acceptable. . . .

The breakdown of parental authority erodes the most indispensable institution of society—the family. . . .

Many voices tell our children and grandchildren that evil is good and good is evil. . . . Daily scripture study, daily prayer, regular family home evening, obedience to priesthood authority in the home and in the Church constitute a great insurance policy against spiritual deterioration.

(James E. Faust, *Ensign*, May 1998, 21–22.)

I wonder if money earned upon the Sabbath, when it is unnecessary Sabbath earning, might . . . be unclean money. I realize that some people must work on the Sabbath; and when they do, if they are compelled, that is, of course, a different situation. But men and women who will deliberately use the Sabbath day to develop business propositions, to increase their holdings, to increase their income, I fear for them. I think the Lord was speaking to them when he said: "Woe unto them that call evil good." (Isa. 5:20.) Sometimes we salve our consciences by saying that the more we get the more we can give to the worthy causes, but that, of course, is a subterfuge. There are people who work on the Sabbath, not through compulsion but because the income is attractive. . . .

The Savior knew that the ox gets in the mire on the Sabbath, but he knew also that no ox deliberately goes into the mire every week. . . . Every time I see good folk who are willing to forego these profits, I rejoice and feel within my heart to bless them for their steadfastness, their courage, and their faith. . . . I know that men will never suffer, ultimately, for any seeming financial sacrifices that might be made.

(Spencer W. Kimball, *The Teachings of Spencer W. Kimball*, ed. Edward L. Kimball,
[Salt Lake City: Bookcraft, 1982], 227–29.)

Growing numbers of people now campaign to make spiritually dangerous life-styles legal and socially acceptable. Among them are abortion, the gay-lesbian movement, and drug addiction. . . .

Some challenge us to show where the scriptures specifically forbid abortion or a gay-lesbian or drug-centered life-style. "If they are so wrong," they ask, "why don't the scriptures tell us so in 'letter of the law' plainness?" These issues are not ignored in the revelations. (See Genesis 13:13 (footnote 13b); 18:20–22 (footnote 20b); 19:4–9 (footnote 5a); JST, Gen. 19:9–15; Lev. 18:22, 29; 20:13 (footnote 13a); Deut. 23:17 (footnote 17b); Rom. 1:24–27; 1 Cor. 6:9 (footnotes 9e, f); 1 Tim. 1:9–10 (footnote 10b, c).) The scriptures are generally positive rather than negative in their themes, and it is a mistake to assume that anything not specifically prohibited in the "*letter* of the law" is somehow approved of the Lord. . . .

Always when these destructive lifestyles are debated, *"individual right of choice"* is invoked as though it were the one sovereign virtue. That could be true only if there were but one of us. The rights of any individual bump up against the rights of another. And the simple truth is that we cannot be happy, nor saved, nor exalted, without one another.

The word *tolerance* is also invoked as though it overrules everything else. Tolerance may be a virtue, but it is not *the* commanding one. There is a difference between what one *is* and what one *does*. What one is may deserve unlimited tolerance; what one does, only a measured amount. A virtue when pressed to the extreme may turn into a vice. Unreasonable devotion to an ideal, without considering the practical application of it, ruins the ideal itself.

(Boyd K. Packer, *Ensign*, Nov. 1990, 84–85.)

Many modern professors of human behavior advocate as a cure to an afflicted conscience that we . . . change the standard to fit the circumstances so that there is no longer a conflict, thus easing the conscience. The followers of the divine Christ cannot subscribe to this evil and perverse philosophy with impunity. For the troubled conscience in conflict with right and wrong, the only permanent help is to change the behavior and follow a repentant path.

The prophet Isaiah taught, "Woe unto them that call evil good, and good evil; that put darkness for light, and light for darkness; that put bitter for sweet, and sweet for bitter!" (Isa. 5:20).

(James E. Faust, *Ensign*, Nov. 1986, 10.)

One of Satan's methods is to distract and entice us so that we will take our eyes off the danger. . . . He has succeeded to such an extent that many no longer recognize sin as sin. Movies, television, and magazines have glorified sin into what they think is an acceptable life-style: "[fornication], adultery, incest, . . . serial marriages, drug abuse, violence and double-dealing of every imaginable variety, [that is] often portrayed as [normal] behavior; where people who do good are not . . . rewarded and those who do evil are not punished" so stated a *Los Angeles Times* writer. . . .

Assuredly we live in a time spoken of by Isaiah when men "call evil good, and good evil" (Isa. 5:20).

(David B. Haight, *Ensign*, Nov. 1986, 37.)

Isaiah's description . . . of a people who call evil good and good evil is very descriptive of events in our days. The attitudes and tax laws against marriage and large families are based upon evil principles "considered to be good." . . . A news release in the BYU *Daily Universe* quoted a federal government representative calling the BYU dress standards "damaging and demeaning." Another sign of the times is the claim by some psychologists, and other misled individuals, that premarital sex relations are "good." Calling evil good and good evil is characteristic of an especially wicked world.

(L. La Mar Adams, *The Living Message of Isaiah* [Salt Lake City: Deseret Book Co., 1981], 66.)

Satan offers a strange mixture of just enough good to disguise the evil along his downward path to destruction. . . . He forges a Rembrandt-quality representation by calling evil good and good evil. He has confused many people, even nations and leaders, to the point of an immoral approach to moral issues. . . .

First, he says individual agency is justification for the destruction of a human life through abortion; second, same-gender intimate associations and even marriages are acceptable; and third, chastity and fidelity are old-fashioned and narrow-minded—to be sexually active with free expression is acceptable.

At this very moment, international heroes in sports, music, and movies not only live immoral lives but teach that immorality around the world through the powerful influence of the media. They are idolized and accepted by millions worldwide. The world in general seems to have lapsed into a coma of unrighteousness.

(Durrel A. Woolsey, *Ensign*, Nov. 1995, 84.)

2 Ne. 15:21	**WISE IN THEIR OWN EYES**
	(Isa. 5:21; Prov. 3:5–7; 2 Ne. 28:15; refer in *Latter-day*
	Commentary on the Book of Mormon, Bassett, to 2 Ne. 9:28–30)

Meekness requires genuine intellectual honesty, owning up to the learning experiences of the past and listening to the Holy Ghost as he preaches to us from the pulpit of memory.

As the Lord communicates with the meek and submissive, fewer decibels are required, and more nuances are received. . . . It is only the meek mind which can be so shown and so stretched—not those, as Isaiah wrote, who "are wise in their own eyes" (Isa. 5:21; see also 2 Ne. 9:29 and 15:21.)

God's counsel aligns us and conjoins us with the great realities of the universe; whereas sin empties, isolates, and separates us, confining us to the solitary cell of selfishness. Hence the lonely crowd in hell. . . .

Yielding one's heart to God signals the last stage in our spiritual development. Only then are we beginning to be fully useful to God! How can we sincerely pray to be an instrument in His hands if the instrument seeks to do the instructing?

(Neal A. Maxwell, *Ensign*, May 1985, 71.)

2 Ne. 15:23   JUSTIFY THE WICKED FOR REWARD
(Isa. 5:23)

This refers to those who take bribes. Because this statement immediately follows a woe pronounced against drunkenness, one wonders if Isaiah saw those well-known figures in sports, entertainment, or other positions of notoriety who accept payment for endorsing harmful products such as alcohol.

(Hoyt W. Brewster, Jr., *Isaiah Plain and Simple* [Salt Lake City: Deseret Book Co., 1995], 50.)

The false and misleading advertising of our day fits Isaiah's description. Famous athletes, movie stars, and other celebrities are paid large sums of money to endorse products which may well be harmful. Such advertising leads people away from righteousness.

(Monte S. Nyman, *Great Are the Words of Isaiah* [Salt Lake City: Bookcraft, 1980], 45.)

Naturally Isaiah takes us into the law courts: "Wo unto him that calleth evil good and good evil," that being the rhetorical art the art as Plato tells us "of making good seem bad and bad seem good by the use of words," which in the ancient world came to its own in the law courts. "Wo unto them that are wise in their own eyes and prudent in their own sight . . . which justify the wicked for a reward and take away the righteousness of the righteous from him." Which recalls how the Gadianton robbers when they finally got control of the government and the law courts, "when they did obtain the sole management of the government," at once 'turned their backs on the poor and needy. . .' (Hel. 6:39) filling the "judgment seats" with their own people (Hel. 7:4), "letting the guilty and the wicked go unpunished because of their money . . ." (7:5). "They justify the wicked for a reward," . . . serving their own interests by the laws and regulations which they make, "or turn aside the needy from judgment, and take away the right from the poor of my people, that widows may be their prey, and that they may rob the fatherless!" (10:1–2).

(Hugh W. Nibley, "Great Are the Words of Isaiah," *Sidney B. Sperry Symposium*
[Provo, Utah: Religious Instruction, BYU, January 28, 1978], 202.)

2 Ne. 15:24   STUBBLE AND CHAFF
(Isa. 5:24)

On blustery days after the harvest, the Israelite farmer took advantage of the wind to winnow his threshed grain. The threshed mixture of chaff, chopped stubble, and seed would be gathered upon a winnowing board or fork and tossed into the air. There the wind would catch the light chaff and stubble and blow it away while the heavy, clean kernels would fall back to the earth for the farmer to collect. Once the grains were removed, the remaining chaff and stubble would be dispersed by the wind or burned in a fire that was extremely hot, fast, and furious. Isaiah saw the fleeting chaff and stubble as a type of the temporality of the wicked. He warned that just as the "chaff of the mountains" is chased "before the wind" (Isa. 17:13) and as the "fire devoureth the stubble, and the flame consumeth the chaff" (Isa. 5:24), so shall Jehovah destroy the enemies of the covenant people and the apostates of Israel (see Isa. 29:5; 33:11; 40:24; 41:2, 15; 47:14).

(Terry Ball, *Thy People Shall Be My People and Thy God My God: The 22ⁿᵈ Annual Sidney B. Sperry Symposium* [Salt Lake City: Deseret Book Co., 1994], 25.)

Winnowing was accomplished by the use of either a broad shovel or of a wooden fork which had bent prongs. With this instrument, the mass of chaff, straw, and grain was thrown against the wind. Because there was generally a breeze blowing in the evening, this was the time when it was normally done. . . . (Ruth 3:2). . . .

(Jer. 15:7). When the grain and straw, not as yet separated, are thrown into the air, the wind causes the mass of material to fall as follows: Since the grain is the heaviest, it naturally falls beneath the fan. The straw is blown to the side into a heap, and the lighter chaff and the dust are carried beyond into a flattened windrow. . . . (Ps. 1:4). The chaff is burned as Scripture often indicates. "And the flame consumeth the chaff" (Isa. 5:24) . . . (Matt. 3:12; Luke 3:17).

(Fred H. Wight, *Manners and Customs of Bible Lands* [Chicago: Moody Press, 1953], 184–85.)

2 Ne. 15:25   THE HILLS DID TREMBLE
(Isa. 5:25; Moses 7:13)

Refers to an earthquake, as a result of which corpses littered the streets as refuse.

(George Reynolds and Janne M. Sjodahl, *Commentary on the Book of Mormon,* ed. Philip C. Reynolds, 7 vols. [Salt Lake City: Deseret Book Co., 1955–1961], 1:337.)

2 Ne. 15:26–30   AN ENSIGN TO THE NATIONS
(Isa. 5:26–30; D&C 115:5–6; 45:9; 2 Ne. 29:2; refer in this text to 2 Ne. 21:12)

In the last days the Lord "will lift up an ensign to the nations from far." Those who gather to this ensign will come quickly and with power. They will do so amidst contrasting conditions of light and darkness or good and evil.

A secondary interpretation of these verses focuses on the Assyrian invasion of Israel in 722–721 B.C. Commentators who subscribe to this belief identify the speed with which the Assyrian soldiers invaded the land and the quick destruction they brought about. Nevertheless, the major focus of these verses appears to align itself more closely with events of the last days.

(Hoyt W. Brewster, Jr., *Isaiah Plain and Simple* [Salt Lake City: Deseret Book Co., 1995], 51.)

Taken in historical context, these verses probably describe Assyrian soldiers in all their terrible power. They come with speed, need no rest, and do not even pause long enough to take off their shoes. Their weapons are ready, their roar is like that of the lion, and, when they lay hold of their prey, none can stop them. The destruction is so swift and complete that even in daylight, darkness (perhaps from the smoke of burning cities) and gloom (or defeat) hangs over the people. If these verses describe the Assyrian army and the fear and destruction it inflicted upon its enemies, this judgment was fulfilled upon Israel and Judah during Isaiah's day. In 722–721 B.C. Assyria conquered Israel, carrying the Ten Tribes into captivity, and in 701 B.C. she destroyed most of Judah and besieged Jerusalem. (See Isa. 36–37.)

In addition, the raised signal or ensign may represent the assemblage of a future spiritual force. . . . The ancient American prophet Nephi placed this chapter in a latter-day context when he quoted it in 2 Nephi 15. . . . We see that an ensign in the last days can refer to Zion, the gospel, missionary work, the gathering, and the Book of Mormon. . . . In short, the term *ensign* encompasses the Lord's whole work, and all aspects of his Church serve as his "standard" to the world.

(Victor L. Ludlow, *Isaiah: Prophet, Seer, and Poet* [Salt Lake City: Deseret Book Co., 1982], 122–123.)

Over 125 years ago, in the little town of Fayette, Seneca County, New York, the Lord set up an ensign to the nations. . . . *That ensign was the Church of Jesus Christ of Latter-day Saints*, which was established for the *last time*, never again to be destroyed or given to other people (Dan. 2:44). *It was the greatest event the world has seen since the day that the Redeemer was lifted upon the cross and worked out the infinite and eternal atonement.* It meant more to mankind than anything else that has occurred since that day.

No event should have been heralded among the people with greater effectiveness and received with greater evidence of joy and satisfaction. . . .

Following the raising of this *ensign*, the Lord sent forth his elders clothed with the priesthood and with power and authority, among the nations of the earth, bearing witness unto all peoples of the restoration of his Church.

(Joseph Fielding Smith, *Doctrines of Salvation: Sermons and Writings of Joseph Fielding Smith*, ed. Bruce R. McConkie, 3 vols. [Salt Lake City: Bookcraft, 1954–1956], 3:254–55.)

He warned the northern kingdom of Israel that they . . . could expect to be overrun by a terrifying army. He described the army's attack as one that would be so swift that none would escape and declared that it would leave darkness and sorrow in its wake (Isa. 5:26–30). This prophecy was fulfilled in 721 B.C. when the Assyrians conquered and deported many of the ten tribes of the kingdom of Israel. . . .

Isaiah 5:26–30 is a dualistic prophecy, meaning it applies to more than one time period and may have more than one interpretation. Latter-day Saints have traditionally placed the fulfillment of this prophecy in the last days and given it another interpretation. . . . Most commentators, however, see this as a prophecy that was fulfilled in Isaiah's day.

> (Terry B. Ball, *Voices of Old Testament Prophets*:
> *The 26th Annual Sidney B. Sperry Symposium* [Salt Lake City: Deseret Book Co., 1997], 53–54, 58.)

May I take you back 142 years when there was, of course, no tabernacle here, nor temple, nor Temple Square. On July 24, 1847, the pioneer company of our people came into this valley. An advance group had arrived a day or two earlier. Brigham Young arrived on Saturday. The next day, Sabbath services were held both in the morning and in the afternoon. . . . The season was late, and they were faced with a gargantuan and immediate task if they were to grow seed for the next season. But President Young pleaded with them not to violate the Sabbath then or in the future.

The next morning they divided into groups to explore their surroundings.

Brigham Young, Wilford Woodruff, and a handful of their associates hiked from their campground. . . . They climbed a dome-shaped peak, President Young having difficulty because of his recent illness.

When the Brethren stood on the summit, they looked over this valley to the south of them. It was largely barren, except for the willows and rushes that grew along the streams that carried water from the mountains to the lake. There was no building of any kind, but Brigham Young had said the previous Saturday, "This is the place."

The summit where they stood was named Ensign Peak out of reference to these great prophetic words of Isaiah: . . . (Isa. 5:26). . . . (Isa. 11:12).

There is some evidence to indicate that Wilford Woodruff took from his pocket a bandanna handkerchief and waved it as an ensign or a standard to the nations, that from this place should go the word of the Lord, and to this place should come the people of the earth.

I think they may also on that occasion have spoken of the building of the temple, which today stands a few feet east of here, in fulfillment of the words of Isaiah: . . . (Isa. 2:2–3).

How foolish, someone might have said, had he heard these men that July morning of 1847. . . . Here they were, almost a thousand miles from the nearest settlement to the east and almost eight hundred miles from the Pacific Coast. They were in an untried climate. The soil was different from that of the black loam of Illinois and Iowa, where they had most recently lived. They had never raised a crop here. They had never experienced a winter. They had not built a structure of any kind. These prophets, dressed in old, travel-worn clothes, standing in boots they had worn for more than a thousand miles from Nauvoo to this valley, spoke of a millennial vision. . . . They came down from the peak that day and went to work to bring reality to their dream.

> (Gordon B. Hinckley, *Ensign*, Nov. 1989, 51–52.)

2 Ne. 15:26–30   LATTER-DAY TRANSPORTATION
(Isa. 5:26–30)

In fixing the time of the great gathering, Isaiah seemed to indicate that it would take place in the day of the railroad train and the airplane (Isa. 5:26–29).

Since there were neither trains nor airplanes in that day, Isaiah could hardly have mentioned them by name. However, he seems to have described them in unmistakable words. How better could "their horses' hoofs be counted like flint, and "their wheels like a whirlwind" than in the modern train? How better could "their roaring . . . be like a lion" than in the roar of the airplane? Trains and airplanes do not stop for night. Therefore, was not Isaiah justified in saying: "none shall slumber nor sleep; neither shall the girdle of their loins be loosed, nor the latchet of their shoes be broken"? With this manner of transportation the Lord can really "hiss unto them from the end of the earth," that "they shall come with speed swiftly." Indicating that Isaiah must have foreseen the airplane, he stated: "Who are these that fly as a cloud, and as the doves to their windows? (Isa. 60:8).

(LeGrand Richards, *Israel! Do You Know?* [Salt Lake City: Deseret Book Co., 1973], 182.)

Isaiah saw many other things in connection with this gathering. He saw that the Lord would gather Israel quickly and with speed, that they would not even have time to loosen the shoe latchets of their shoes, or to slumber or sleep. (See Isa. 5:27.) Imagine a statement like that way back in the days of Isaiah, thousands of years ago, with their means of transportation at that time!

(LeGrand Richards, *Ensign*, Nov. 1975, 50.)

"Who are these that fly as a cloud, and as doves to their windows?" Sure enough we come with great speed. As Isaiah has said in the fifth chapter . . . they should come with speed swiftly; just as you emigrants do when you get on board of these railroads, when, instead of being ninety or a hundred days coming to this elevated region, as was the case for several years, you come in two or three days.

(Orson Pratt, *Journal of Discourses*, 16:84.)

They saw . . . our automobiles, our railroad trains; they saw, very probably, the communication that was taking place upon the face of the earth so wonderfully by wireless communication. . . . They saw, I believe, the airplanes flying in the midst of the heavens. . . . (Isa. 5:26–30; Nahum 2:2–5; Rev. 9:6–10.) . . .

The prophets saw the time in the latter days when an ensign should be lifted up that those gathering to Zion should come with speed swiftly; they should not be weary, neither should they be under the necessity of slumber, nor the loosing of their girdle or the shoes from off their feet. . . .

Not because we are any better or more worthy than the saints of former time, nor because we have greater intelligence, but because we are living in the dispensation of the fulness of times, when the Lord is gathering all things in one and preparing the earth for the great millennial reign. . . .

The Lord gave inspiration to Edison, to Franklin, to Morse, to Whitney and to all of the inventors and discoverers. . . . Without the help of the Lord they would have been just as helpless as the people were in other ages.

(Joseph Fielding Smith, *Doctrines of Salvation: Sermons and Writings of Joseph Fielding Smith,* ed. Bruce R. McConkie, 3 vols. [Salt Lake City: Bookcraft, 1954–1956], 1:146–47.)

I think that Isaiah was privileged to live almost more in our day than in the day he was actually here upon this earth. He was able to see so much of what the Lord would do in the latter days. . . . Isaiah saw the railroad train and the airplane and how the people would be gathered to Zion without even being able to loosen the latchets of their shoes.

A few years ago President McKay went to Scotland to help organize the first stake in his bonny Scotland. When he returned, he reported to us brethren of the Twelve, telling us that he left London at two o'clock in the afternoon, stopped for a short period in Chicago, and was here in Salt Lake City that night to sleep in his own bed. Then he compared this to the time his family crossed the ocean; they were 43 days on the water with a sailing vessel and then had to cross the plains the best they could.

Just think of the day in which we live.

(LeGrand Richards, *Conference Report,* Oct. 1966, 42–43.)

As promised in verses 26–30, the nation and people who are gathered to Zion will come so quickly that they will require neither rest nor a change of clothing. During Isaiah's day, any long journey required frequent rest stops and resulted in worn out clothing and sandals. . . .

Whereas verses 26–28 vividly describe nations (or missionaries) coming swiftly and powerfully from afar and verse 29 says that they will seize their prey (or converts) and take them safely away, verse 30 provides a perplexing conclusion to this section when interpreted in this way. It says that the nations will roar (or speak with authority) against their prey "in that day" (or in the last days), and as one looks upon the earth, there is "darkness and sorrow, and the light is darkened in the heavens thereof." . . . The "darkness and sorrow" might refer either to physical or spiritual conditions as destruction and apostasy rage upon the earth. The light "darkened in the heavens" seems to suggest the gospel or the Messiah himself coming forth out of obscure darkness. The verse describing the contrast between light and darkness follows the verse in which the ensign is raised by the Lord to the nations. Whereas one would expect that the ensign (v. 26), the manifestation of the Lord's army (v. 27–29), and other events of the Latter-day dispensation would bring forth glory and brightness over the whole earth, instead much evil and darkness will shroud the light of God's work in the last days (v. 30).

(Victor L. Ludlow, *Isaiah: Prophet, Seer, and Poet* [Salt Lake City: Deseret Book Co., 1982], 123–24.)

2 Ne. 15:26   HISS
(Isa. 5:26)

The Hebrew word from which hiss was translated means to quietly proclaim.

(Monte S. Nyman, *Isaiah: Prophecies of the Restoration* [Salt Lake City: Millennial Press, 1998], 28.)

Some commentators have supposed an allusion here, and in chapter 7, 18, to the custom of calling bees from their hives to the fields and back again by means of a hiss or whistle. Others, however, deny that any such custom existed, and claim that the allusion is to another custom prevalent in the East: that of calling the attention of any one in the street by a significant hiss. In the prophecy of Zechariah, the Lord says concerning the children of Ephraim, "I will hiss for them, and gather them" (Zech. 10:8). Here there is doubtless a reference to the same custom of calling attention by a hiss.

(James M. Freeman, *Manners and Customs of the Bible* [Plainfield, New Jersey: Logos International, 1972], 255.)

2 Ne. 15:28   HORSES' HOOFS SHALL BE COUNTED LIKE FLINT
(Isa. 5:28)

Hoofs of the Arab horses are never shod, this practice being made useless by the hot climate. In ancient days the same thing was true. In Scripture the quality of a horse was judged partially by the hardness of its hoofs. Isaiah said: Their horses' hoofs shall be counted like flint" (Isa. 5:28). Micah wrote: "I will make thy hoofs brass" (Micah 4:13).

(Fred H. Wight, *Manners and Customs of Bible Lands* [Chicago: Moody Press, 1953], 263–64.)

2 Ne. 15:29–30   THE PREY . . . CARRY AWAY SAFE
(Isa. 5:29–30)

While verses 26 through 28 seem to describe the messengers sent to the nations, verses 29 and 30 describe the "prey" leaving these lands. The prey are those of Israel, missionaries or members, who, because of the persecution and tribulation which come against them and the turmoil in the land, will be fleeing to Zion for safety. This seems to be describing the fulfilling of the times of the Gentiles, when the gentile nations will completely reject the gospel.

(Monte S. Nyman, *Great Are the Words of Isaiah* [Salt Lake City: Bookcraft, 1980], 46–47.)

2 Ne. 16   **ISAIAH'S CALL TO SERVE**
(Isa. 6; Rev. 4:2, 8; D&C 77:2–4)

Isaiah, writing in imagery difficult to the modern mind, describes his call to the prophetic office. Caught up in vision to the heavenly council, Isaiah is purged of his sins and granted his mission and commission as the Lord's anointed, with an accompanying admonition that a wayward people would be more than slow to hearken to his words. The chapter is consistent with what we know about prophetic calls generally, the pattern having been established with the Savior and others in the Grand Council of Heaven (Abr. 3:27; *Teachings,* 365).

(Joseph Fielding McConkie and Robert L. Millet,
Doctrinal Commentary on the Book of Mormon, 4 vols. [Salt Lake City: Bookcraft, 1987–1992], 1:279–80.)

Throughout King Uzziah's administration, Israel and Judah were wealthy and relatively powerful. Luxury had, however, brought about great social injustices—greed, envy, idleness, and drunkenness. The wealthy took advantage of the poor through heavy taxation. Rejection of the Lord and turning toward pagan gods became common. Religion became a matter of ritual and sacrificial offering. Immorality prevailed. Isaiah's call to the ministry came during the decline of Judah's and Israel's power, prosperity, and spirituality.

(Victor L. Ludlow, *Unlocking the Old Testament* [Salt Lake City: Deseret Book Co., 1981], 152.)

How can mortal prophets find language to unveil to the view of their fellow mortals the splendor and transcendent beauty of that eternal world of celestial might and glory? They speak of rainbows and jewels, of circling flames of fires, of burning coals of fire with lightning flashing forth therefrom; they tell of thunders and voices, of the sound of the rushing of many waters, and of majestic displays of might and beauty—all in an attempt to record in mortal words that which can be seen and known only by the power of the Spirit (Ezek. 1 and 10; Isa. 6). But the Lord be praised that they have made such attempts so that those who have not seen and heard may gain some meager knowledge of those things hidden behind the windows of heaven.

(Bruce R. McConkie, *Doctrinal New Testament Commentary,* 3 vols. [Salt Lake City: Bookcraft, 1973], 3:465–66.)

While Amos and Hosea were prophesying in the Northern Kingdom of Israel the messages entrusted to them by the Lord, a young man was growing up in Jerusalem in the Southern Kingdom. . . .

The Southern Kingdom of Judah was prosperous and outwardly happy during Isaiah's boyhood and youth in King Uzziah's long and successful reign. Uzziah encouraged agriculture and the raising of cattle and some men became rich and built up large estates. Commerce flourished and horses and chariots imported from Egypt were seen everywhere. King Uzziah had strengthened his kingdom's defenses and had won back one of Solomon's ports on the Red Sea. Crowds of worshipers thronged the Temple in Jerusalem and offered incense and sacrifices, confident that in so doing they found favor with the Lord. Judah was prosperous, powerful, and secure. . . .

Isaiah saw that the wealth of a few was obtained by the oppression of many. Great luxury and miserable poverty went hand in hand. Injustice and violence flourished. Religion had become a matter of observing the correct outward forms, instead of a thing of the understanding and the heart. All this Isaiah saw and he knew that Judah had become so self-complacent and satisfied with material things that she had all but forgotten her dependence upon the Lord her God.

One day during the year of King Uzziah's death while Isaiah was worshiping in the Temple in Jerusalem, he saw a vision which changed his whole life. In the sixth chapter of the Book of Isaiah he wrote of this great experience.

(Cynthia Pearl Maus, *The Old Testament and the Fine Arts* [New York: Harper & Row, 1954], 526–27.)

2 Ne. 16:1   **TRAIN**
                      (Isa. 6:1)

God's throne is exalted and his train, not to be taken as a literal extension of His robe, but rather as a symbol of his glory and majesty, fills His earthly palace.

(Paul Y. Hoskisson, *The Old Testament and the Latter-day Saints:*
Sperry Symposium 1986 [Randall Book Co., 1986], 196.)

2 Ne. 16:2   **SERAPHIM**
                      (Isa. 6:2)

The *seraphim*, in covering their faces and feet, symbolized reverence.

(Ellis T. Rasmussen, *A Latter-day Saint Commentary on the Old Testament*
[Salt Lake City: Deseret Book Co., 1993], 507.)

Hebrew dictionaries define a seraph in the Old Testament as a mythological being with six wings. The fact, however, that the word "seraphim" is not attested elsewhere in the Old Testament may suggest that Isaiah employed the word here in a unique meaning. As Isaiah and his schooled contemporaries knew, the meaning of the root from which this noun is formed denotes in its verbal aspect to burn or be fiery. Knowing this, Latter-day Saints should have no trouble recognizing that these wings represent celestial beings who attend God at his throne. (See the explanation of Revelation 4:6 in D&C 77:2.)

Based on the explanation in Doctrine and Covenants 77:4 of the three sets of wings of the beasts in Revelation 4:6, Latter-day Saints should recognize that the wings of the seraphim symbolize power. . . .

For instance, in Malachi 4:2 the Son of righteousness shall "arise with healing in his wings," i.e., the Son of righteousness will come with the power of healing.

(Paul Y. Hoskisson, *The Old Testament and the Latter-day Saints*:
Sperry Symposium 1986 [Randall Book Co., 1986], 196–97.)

2 Ne. 16:4   THE POSTS OF THE DOOR MOVED
(Isa. 6:4)

Large doors, such as the doors to a temple, did not have hinges as we know them; the leaves of the door were attached to a large post which itself pivoted in a socket (usually stone) top and bottom. Thus, if the post was to bear the weight of the large doors, often covered with metal, it had to be one of the more massive and solidly anchored wooden pieces in the structure. If this post moved at all, it could only be caused by a powerful force. In other words, the voice of the seraph, "the one who cried," was strong enough to cause the door post to move. The equivalent metaphorical statement in English would be that the roof was raised by the sound of his voice.

(Paul Y. Hoskisson, *The Old Testament and the Latter-day Saints*:
Sperry Symposium 1986 [Randall Book Co., 1986], 197.)

2 Ne. 16:5–7   COAL—LIPS
(Isa. 6:5–7)

A hot coal on the lips would literally be an unbearable ordeal. The footnote to verse 6 helps in understanding this symbolism by indicating that the coal is a symbol of cleansing. Matthew 3:11 relates the Holy Ghost to fire, and 2 Nephi 31:17 indicates that one may be cleansed by "fire, and by the Holy Ghost. The symbolism of a hot coal from the Lord's altar is indeed memorable and indicates not only the cleansing, or purity of Isaiah, but also that Isaiah (remember the coal was placed upon his lips) is now a "mouthpiece" for the Lord and may speak what the Lord himself would speak to the people. Whereas before, Isaiah was concerned that he dwelt among a people with unclean lips (see Isa. 6:5) and felt his inadequacy, now he has had a great spiritual experience and a calling which produced a change sufficient to create the confidence needed to answer the Lord's call (see v. 8), knowing that his lips would now echo the words of his Master.

(S. Brent Farley, *A Symposium on the Old Testament*
[Salt Lake City: The Church of Jesus Christ of Latter-day Saints, 1983], 63.)

To remove Isaiah's unworthiness, to make him fit to stand in the presence of the Lord, one of the seraphim touched his lips with a live coal from the altar. The realization of the significance of this symbolic act derives from an understanding of the altar and its use under the Law of Moses. The purpose of the sacrifices under the Law of Moses was to look forward through this similitude to the cleansing sacrifice of Jesus Christ and the atonement that would purge all sins from the lips of those who stand before God. The live coal from the sacrificial altar represents the element that makes the burnt offering possible, the element that cleanses our soul, fire. With this cleansing Isaiah is able to stand with confidence in the presence of the Lord.

(Paul Y. Hoskisson, *The Old Testament and the Latter-day Saints*:
Sperry Symposium 1986 [Randall Book Co., 1986], 198–99.)

What we say and how we act will create an atmosphere that is welcoming or hostile to the Holy Ghost. . . . The Lord . . . has asked us to so speak and so act that we edify or build one another. . . .(D&C 136:24). Nephi declared that the fruit of receiving the Holy Ghost and listening to the promptings of the Spirit is that we may "speak with the tongue of angels" (2 Ne. 32:2). Thus we create a spirit of reverence and of revelation.

I recently overheard a conversation among some of our young grandchildren. One of them apparently used the word *stupid*. Eight-year-old Nicholas, recently baptized, commented that perhaps one should not say that, as it was a "bad word." It was evident that there had been some good influence from Mom and Dad. . . .

Now some might think that these are small matters compared to the far more foul and demeaning expressions all around us. Yet, in small and in great ways, our words are creating an atmosphere in which we build or demolish. . . .

Over the years there has been an increase in sexual innuendos, raucous humor, violent expressions, and great noise in talk, in music, in gestures. Much of what is around us is crude and rude, with a corruption of moral behavior and sensitivity. Society has not been improved by our "light speeches" and our "light-mindedness." Instead, our expressions have polluted our communities and corrupted our souls.

President Spencer W. Kimball warned of vulgarity of speech and expression and particularly counseled against speaking of sex glibly, which he associated with immodesty. "Lewd talk and jokes," he said, "constitute another danger which lurks seeking as its prey any who will entertain it as the first step to dirtying the mind and thus the soul" (*The Miracle of Forgiveness,* [1969], 228). . . .

I've been struck by the fact that when Isaiah received his charge from the Lord, he bemoaned that he was 'a man of unclean lips' and dwelt 'in the midst of a people of unclean lips' (Isa. 6:5). This sin too had to be purged from Isaiah if he was to bear the word of the Lord. . . .

We need to eliminate from our conversations the immodest and the lewd, the violent and the threatening, the demeaning and the false.

(Robert S. Wood, *Ensign,* Nov. 1999, 83.)

2 Ne. 16:8   **HERE AM I**
                  (Isa. 6:8; 1 Sam. 3:4–8; Abr. 3:27; Gen. 22:1.)

"The door of history turns on small hinges," and so do people's lives.

Fathers, grandfathers, are we reading to our sons and grandsons the word of the Lord? Returned missionaries, do your messages and your lives inspire others to stand up and serve? Brethren, are we sufficiently in tune with the Spirit that when the Lord calls, we can hear, as did Samuel, and declare, "Here am I"? Do we have the fortitude and the faith, whatever our callings, to serve with unflinching courage and unshakable resolve? When we do, the Lord can work His mighty miracles through us.

(Thomas S. Monson, *Ensign,* Nov. 1992, 48.)

There is a great need for many more missionaries, including couples, as President Hinckley in his February 21, 1998, satellite broadcast said: 'With concerted effort, with recognition of the duty that falls upon each of us as members of the Church, and with sincere prayer to the Lord for help, we could double the number' of convert baptisms. . . .

There is not a work of greater importance or of greater joy and reward that we could do at this time. . . .

I believe our Heavenly Father and I trust Him, and when He reveals to us, speaking through our living prophet today, that we need to do more, and more of us need to become involved in the work of bringing souls unto Christ, then we need to step forward and say, "Here am I; send me" (Isa. 6:8).

(H. Bruce Stucki, *Ensign,* Nov. 1999, 44.)

2 Ne. 16:10   **HEART FAT, EARS HEAVY, SHUT EYES**
                  (Isa. 6:10)

The "making fat" of the hearts of the people seems to refer to Isaiah's being called to make the truth so plain that they would have to accept it or harden their hearts against it. . . .

The last half of Isaiah 6:10 may be misread that the Lord does not want the people to be converted and healed. The real meaning of the last part of the verse, as it is fully quoted in the New Testament [Acts 28:26–27; Matt. 13:14–15], is a declaration that the people did not *want* to understand, lest they should be converted so that the Lord could heal them.

(Monte S. Nyman, *Great Are the Words of Isaiah* [Salt Lake City: Bookcraft, 1980], 50–51.)

That did not mean, of course, that Isaiah was to make seeing people become blind. The blindness referred to in this book and by Jesus in his ministry refers to people who have eyes to see but who prefer to walk in darkness. When Isaiah provided revelation and light from God for that generation and they chose to walk in darkness, they, not God, inflicted blindness upon themselves (cf. John 9:40–41; see also Alma 29:4–5; D&C 93:31–32, 38–39; John 3:19–20). . . .

Isaiah . . . prepared a fallen people for the judgments at hand. According to the general sense of all scripture, a loving and merciful God encourages sinners to repent and return to him; he encourages rather than discourages repentance and conversion. Thus there must be something wrong with a translation or text that suggests that God wanted the Israelites to fail, so that they would not "see with their eyes, and hear with their ears, and understand with their heart, and convert, and be healed" by God (Isa. 6:10).

(Keith A Meservy, *Studies in Scripture, Vol. 4*, ed. Kent P. Jackson [Salt Lake City: Deseret Book Co., 1993], 87–88.)

In Hebrew literature the ear was the organ of understanding, the eye was the organ of perception, and the heart was the organ of thought. . . . Isaiah is told to tell the people that they have the physical capacity to understand and perceive God's message, but that they do not. If they have the ability to comprehend the message and they do not, it must mean that the people chose not to comprehend.

Isaiah is further told, according to the King James Version, to make the people's organs of thought dull, to cause their organs of understanding to be clumsy, and to close their organs of perception, so that the people would not use them and be cured by the divine message. . . .

How can a loving God commission His prophet to prevent the people from being cleansed from their uncleanness by causing their organs of comprehension to be ineffective? . . .

The best solution to this theological difficulty derives from a knowledge of the Hebrew grammatical forms used in this passage. The King James Version rests on the usual reading of the Hebrew *hiph'il* form of the three verbs involved. Normally the *hiph'il* conjugation has a causative meaning, and thus the translation "make the heart . . . fat." However, one of the modes of the *hiph'il* connotes a declarative, and would yield the translation "declare the heart of this people to be fat." Thus, the *New English Bible* for this passage reads, "This people's wits are dulled, their ears are deafened and their eyes blinded, so that they cannot see with their eyes nor listen with their ears nor understand with their wits, so that they may turn and be healed." This rendering would eliminate the theological difficulties imposed on the passage by reading a causative, because it would no longer be God through his prophet who makes the people incapable of realizing their moral turpitude. Isaiah becomes rather God's appointed accuser of the people.

(Paul Y. Hoskisson, *The Old Testament and the Latter-day Saints:*
Sperry Symposium 1986 [Randall Book Co., 1986], 199–200.)

2 Ne. 16:12–13 THEY SHALL RETURN . . . TEIL-TREE AND OAK
(Isa. 6:12–13)

Isaiah associated the oak and the terebinth not only with apostasy but also with restoration. Both kinds of trees are robust and cannot be destroyed merely by chopping them down, for the remaining stumps will regenerate the tree by sending forth new shoots. . . . (Isa. 6:12–13).

Accordingly, Isaiah taught that a part of Israel would return like the oak and terebinth, which, though they are eaten or consumed (*hayetah lebaer*) right to their substance or stumps (*matzebeth*), yet they possess a seed in them that can regenerate (see Isa. 6:13).

(Terry Ball, *Thy People Shall Be My People and Thy God My God:
The 22nd Annual Sidney B. Sperry Symposium* [Salt Lake City: Deseret Book Co., 1994], 29.)

This is clearly a prophecy that, although the cities of Judah will be destroyed and the inhabitants scattered, a remnant of that "holy seed" will return to inhabit the land. Further light is shed upon the phrase "shall be eaten" by a marginal reading in the KJV: "when it is returned, and hath been broused." This has reference to a purging of those who are to be scattered. Isaiah's analogy of a tree's being pruned by animals eating the leaves, and by the natural casting off of the dead leaves, indicates that the tenth to return will be of a new generation.

(Monte S. Nyman, *Great Are the Words of Isaiah* [Salt Lake City: Bookcraft, 1980], 52.)

The Lord declared to Isaiah that after he had given his message of accusation all the days of his life, and after the land had been devastated and Isaiah was dead, there would be a tenth of the people who would return to the land of Palestine.

This remnant is symbolized in the King James Version by dormant trees, signifying that this rest of the House of Israel will be spiritually fallow. The key to understanding that this verse also refers to Christ lies in the words "the holy seed." As Paul states in Galatians 3:16, the "seed" referred to in the Old Testament is Christ. And it is that "seed" that comprised the substance, that is the life of Israel, here symbolized by trees. In other words, the Messiah of Israel would be born of the spiritually dormant remnant of Israel living in the land of Palestine and he is the life substance of Israel.

(Paul Y. Hoskisson, *The Old Testament and the Latter-day Saints:
Sperry Symposium 1986* [Randall Book Co., 1986], 201–202.)

2 Ne. 17   **ISAIAH AND KING AHAZ**
                    (Isa. 7)

At this time, the southern kingdom of Judah was threatened by an alliance of the northern kingdom of Israel with Syria. The kings of these two countries wanted Ahaz to join them in an alliance against the Assyrians, but the king of Judah decided to cast his lot with the Assyrians.

In verse 3, the Lord sends Isaiah to counsel Ahaz against entering any alliances; instead, he is to depend on the protection of the God of Israel. Isaiah prophesies that the threat from the northern kingdom and from Syria will come to naught and that these two countries will be the ones that will be destroyed.

The Lord offers to give the disbelieving Ahaz a sign of the verity of His words, but the king refuses to ask for confirmation of the prophecy. The Lord gives the king a sign anyway: a sign involving the future birth of the Messiah through the house of David.

Because of rejecting divine counsel, Judah suffers consequences that could have been avoided. The people are oppressed, scattered, and taken into slavery. The once-fertile lands are left barren of crops and become useful only for wandering animals.

(Hoyt W. Brewster, Jr., *Isaiah Plain and Simple* [Salt Lake City: Deseret Book Co., 1995], 62.)

An Isaiah scholar explains that the prophecy in this section "was delivered on the occasion of Isaiah's first interview with King Ahaz, after the first alarm had reached Jerusalem that invasion was imminent. The king was apparently supervising the measures being taken to ensure a water-supply for the city in the event of a siege, when the prophet received the command to go with his son Shear-yashub."

Rezin king of Syria and Pekah king of Israel tried to persuade Ahaz king of Judah to ally with them against Assyria, their neighboring superpower. Meanwhile, Isaiah pleaded with Ahaz to trust the Lord for deliverance from the invading armies (7:1–10). Ahaz rejected Isaiah's spiritual counsel and won the support of Tiglathpileser III, king of Assyria, who in 732 B.C. invaded the Northern Kingdom of Israel and captured many cities (2 Kgs. 15:29; 16:7–9). Because Ahaz rejected Isaiah's (i.e., God's) plan, the armies of Rezin and Pekah invaded Judah, slew one hundred twenty thousand warriors, and carried away some two hundred thousand women and children. Judah was slaughtered, because, in part, of the great sins of her king and her people (2 Kgs. 16:5; 2 Chr. 28:5–8).

(Donald W. Parry, Jay A. Parry, and Tina M. Peterson,
Understanding Isaiah [Salt lake City: Deseret Book Co., 1998], 68–69.)

The Assyrians would eventually conquer Syria, Palestine, and even Egypt, but those conquests lay in the future as chapters 7 through 10 of Isaiah's record begin. At that point, Rezin, king of Syria, and Pekah, king of Israel (Ephraim), became allies and pressured Ahaz, king of Judah, to join their coalition (see Map 9, LDS Bible). When he refused, they agreed to conquer Judah and install someone named ben-Tabeal on Ahaz's throne (Isa. 7:1–6). In this threatening predicament, God tried to teach Ahaz that he should turn to Him for deliverance in times of need.

Not only did Ahaz refuse to believe in the Lord but he even sacrificed his children in his zeal to serve pagan gods. Moreover, he tried to eliminate any faith in Jehovah that remained in Judah by closing Solomon's temple and erecting altars throughout the country for his people to worship other gods (see 2 Chr. 28:2–4, 22–25).

With two enemies allied against him, Ahaz needed powers superior to his own. The Lord stood ready to help. . . . But apparently, if God granted Ahaz some kind of personal sign that he might request, Ahaz would be obliged to believe in Jehovah rather than in foreign gods. So Ahaz refused God's gracious offer.

(Keith A Meservy, *Studies in Scripture, Vol. 4,* ed. Kent P. Jackson, [Salt Lake City: Deseret Book Co., 1993], 95.)

In order to properly associate all the various names of places and persons, remember that the same country often carried different names. Just as the United States of America and its government might be identified in the press by a number of terms (the administration; the president; Washington, D.C.; the Capitol; Congress; America; etc.), the ancient powers also had a variety of names. The names of the three countries involved in this incident are:

Country:	Judah	Syria	Israel
Capital city	Jerusalem	Damascus	Samaria
Territory or tribe:	Judah	Aram	Ephraim
Leader:	Ahaz, of the House of David	Rezin	Pekah, son of Remaliah.

(Victor L. Ludlow, *Isaiah: Prophet, Seer, and Poet* [Salt Lake City: Deseret Book Co., 1982], 140.)

2 Ne. 17:3   SHEAR-JASHUB AND THE UPPER POOL
(Isa. 7:3)

The Lord's commandment for Isaiah to take his son Shearjashub with him to meet Ahaz is apparently purposeful. A marginal note in the KJV shows the meaning of his son's name to be "The remnant shall return." This meaning comes from the prophecy given by the Lord to Isaiah at the time of his call (6:13). The son's presence may have served either of two purposes. It may have been to remind Ahaz of the prophecy that Judah would not be utterly destroyed, or it may have been a reminder that the Lord had prophesied concerning Judah in order to prepare Ahaz for the prophecy which Isaiah was to deliver.

Their meeting at the "upper pool" may have not been coincidental either. Many biblical scholars have suggested that Ahaz was there inspecting the water supply and deciding how to protect it from the two invading forces. If this was the case, Ahaz's thinking on these matters would also prepare him to receive the prophecy Isaiah had been sent to deliver.

(Monte S. Nyman, *Great Are the Words of Isaiah* [Salt Lake City: Bookcraft, 1980], 54.)

The conduit or tunnel that carried water from the city's only water source, called Gihon Spring, still exists and is located just outside of what used to be the city wall. This made the city very vulnerable in time of siege. The king might have come to this upper pool of Gihon Spring to consider the means by which the city could be defended. But with his heart filled with apostasy and his mind muddled with anxiety over the imminent attack of a huge army from the north, Ahaz would certainly not be in a mood to feel sympathetic to what Isaiah was about to tell him.

(W. Cleon Skousen, *Isaiah Speaks to Modern Times* [Salt Lake City: Ensign Publishing Co., 1984], 201.)

2 Ne. 17:4   SMOKING FIREBRANDS
(Isa. 7:4)

The designation of the two kings as "the two tails of these smoking firebrands" also carries meaning. A firebrand was a torch. The description of these two kings as tails which are smoking indicates that their strength had been spent, as a torch smokes only when it is burned out.

(Monte S. Nyman, *Great Are the Words of Isaiah* [Salt Lake City: Bookcraft, 1980], 55.)

Isaiah was telling Ahaz to abandon his plans to arm the Jews and prepare a defense. Isaiah was also instructed to assure Ahaz that he had nothing to fear from these two kings from the north. The Lord compared their threat to the "tails of . . . smoking firebrands." A firebrand is a burning piece of wood, or a torch. When it has served its purpose and burned out, it becomes nothing but a "smoking firebrand" with little trails of smoke rising from its spent ashes. The Lord knew that both Ephraim (or the Ten Tribes under Ephraim) and Syria were soon to be conquered by the Assyrians, and that if Judah would simply "be quiet" and not provoke these northern enemies, their threatened attack on Judah would be aborted because they themselves would be under attack from Assyria."

(W. Cleon Skousen, *Isaiah Speaks to Modern Times*, [Salt Lake City: Ensign Publishing Co., 1984], 201.)

2 Ne. 17:6   SON OF TABEAL
(Isa. 7:6)

"The Lord even disclosed the plans of the enemy. He said they intended to "make a breach" in Judah's defenses and put a man of their own choosing on the throne. This would be a "son of Tabeal." Tabeal is described as "a man whose son went with the armies of Pekah, the king of Israel, and Rezin of Damascus, when they invaded Judah in the time of Ahaz" (Francis Nathan Peloubet, *Peloubet's Bible Dictionary* [Philadelphia: The John C. Winston company, 1925], p. 659.) The idea was to set up the son of Tabeal as a puppet king if Judah was conquered."

(W. Cleon Skousen, *Isaiah Speaks to Modern Times* [Salt Lake City: Ensign Publishing Co., 1984], 202.)

2 Ne. 17:8   SHALL EPHRAIM BE BROKEN
(Isa. 7:8)

What was happening in the political world of Isaiah's time? Assyria, the enemy of Israel, had embarked on a ruthless campaign to expand its borders. Isaiah's specific prophecy that in "threescore and five years" Ephraim, or the northern kingdom of Israel, would no longer be a kingdom or a nation was fulfilled. Ephraim fell in 721 B.C., midway through Isaiah's ministry.

King Sargon II of Assyria deported most of Ephraim's citizens, some of the ten tribes of Israel, to the north countries. The author of the book of Kings reports on the attack on Samaria, the capital of the northern kingdoms: "Then, the king of Assyria came up throughout all the land, and went up to Samaria, and besieged it three years. In the ninth year of Hoshea the king of Assyria took Samaria, and carried Israel away into Assyria" (2 Kgs. 17:5–6).

The deportation of ancient Israel occurred because of the people's great sins. "For so it was, that the children of Israel had sinned against the Lord their God . . . And walked in the statutes of the heathen. . . . And the children of Israel did secretly those things that were not right against the Lord their God" (vv. 7–10). Years later King Sennacherib campaigned against Judah, defeating many cities and villages, and again deporting many of its citizens.

(Donald W. Parry, *Visualizing Isaiah,*
[Provo, Utah: The Foundation for Ancient Research and Mormon Studies, 2001], 10.)

In this prophecy, Isaiah promises that the Syro-Israelite alliance will fail and that Israel will be scattered within sixty-five years. The fulfillment came about in successive stages. First, Tiglath-Pileser III (Pul) attacked Syria and Israel in 732 B.C. and took many Israelites captive to Assyria, especially those from the northern tribes. Secondly, in 730–727, Pul annexed the Transjordan area and deported large numbers of the Israelite tribes from that area to the far reaches of the Assyrian Empire. Third, in 726, Hoshea refused to pay Assyrian tribute, and Pul's successor, Shalmaneser, retaliated by attacking Israel and besieging Samaria, which fell in 722 B.C. Thus, within a dozen years of Isaiah's prophecy, the alliance had completely failed, and three major groups of Israelites had been deported. Finally, large groups of the Israelites fled from Assyria to the remote areas northward and became the lost Ten Tribes of Israel. Apparently, within about fifty years of their leaving Assyria, they were scattered so widely that many of them no longer existed as a cohesive group. Thereby Isaiah's prophecy to Ephraim was completely realized.

(Victor L. Ludlow, *Isaiah: Prophet, Seer, and Poet* [Salt Lake City: Deseret Book Co., 1982], 141–142.)

2 Ne. 17:10–12   ASK THEE A SIGN
(Isa. 7:10–12; D&C 63:10; refer in *Latter-day Commentary on the Book of Mormon,* Bassett, to Alma 30:43)

Ahaz's disbelief is indicated in Isaiah 7:9, and verse 11 is further evidence of his reluctance to follow the admonition of the Lord. The Lord challenges him to ask for a sign "either in the depth, or in the height above." The RSV renders this phrase "let it be deep as Sheol or high as heaven." In other words, let it be from the spirit world or from God in heaven. Ahaz gives an interesting rationalization for his refusal, quoting Deuteronomy 6:16 to justify his actions. The irony of quoting a scripture out of context in refusing to follow the prophet of the Lord further exemplifies his disbelief.

(Monte S. Nyman, *Great Are the Words of Isaiah* [Salt Lake City: Bookcraft, 1980], 56.)

2 Ne. 17:14–16   A VIRGIN SHALL CONCEIVE
(Isa. 7:14–16; refer in this text to 2 Ne. 18:18)

Isaiah and others often spoke in figures, using types and shadows to illustrate their points. Their messages were, in effect, hidden in parables (2 Ne. 25:1–8).

For instance, the virgin birth prophecy is dropped into the midst of a recitation of local historical occurrences so that to the spiritually untutored it could be interpreted as some ancient and unknown happening that had no relationship to the birth of the Lord Jehovah into mortality some 700 years later.

(Bruce R. McConkie, *Ensign,* Oct. 1973, 82–83.)

This sign was given to the Old Testament King Ahaz, encouraging him to take his strength from the Lord rather than military might of Damascus, Samaria, or other militant camps. Ahaz was slow to hear that counsel, but the Lord gave it anyway, declaring one of the signs to be a virgin's conception and birth of a son whose name would be called Immanuel.

There are plural or parallel elements to this prophecy, as with so much of Isaiah's writing. The most immediate meaning was probably focused on Isaiah's wife, a pure and good woman who brought forth a son about this time, the child becoming a type and shadow of the greater, later fulfillment of the prophecy that would be realized in the birth of Jesus Christ. The symbolism in the dual prophecy acquires additional importance when we realize that Isaiah's wife may have been of royal blood, and therefore her son would have been royalty of the line of David. Here again is a type, a prefiguration of the greater Immanuel, Jesus Christ, the ultimate son of David, the royal King who would be born of a literal virgin. Indeed, his title *Immanuel* would be carried forward to the latter days, being applied to the Savior in section 128, verse 22 of the Doctrine and Covenants.

(Jeffrey R. Holland, *Christ and the New Covenant* [Salt Lake City: Deseret Book Co., 1997], 79.)

Now if Immanuel of verse 14 is the Messiah, the Savior, what is his connection with the "child" of verses 15 and 16? Many Jewish commentators, not to mention some non-Jewish ones, think that the "virgin" or "young woman" of verse 14 may be a woman of the royal family, or any other young woman of Judah, and that her son, a boy whom she called Immanuel, does not refer to the Christ. Personally, I am inclined to accept Immanuel as a reference to the Savior, and especially in the light of [Isa. 8:8], where Judah is referred to as Immanuel's land. The allusion to Immanuel suggests that the land of Judah (about which Ahaz was concerned) had a great destiny to fulfill, and hence that it was not about to be destroyed by Syria and Ephraim. Verses 15 and 16 of [Isaiah 7] simply make our Lord's infancy a symbolical representation of the short-lived nature of the threat to Judah.

(Sidney B. Sperry, *Book of Mormon Compendium* [Salt Lake City: Bookcraft, 1968], 199.)

Isaiah, then, declared that the Lord would, nevertheless, give him a sign: Behold, a virgin—a young wife, possibly the wife of the Prophet—would become the mother of a son, whom she would call Emmanuel, meaning, "God is with us." Syria and the land of Ephraim. Both would be overrun by the Assyrians before the child would be old enough to discern between evil and good. This prophecy was literally fulfilled in the days of Ahaz, but it had another fulfillment in the person of our Lord. According to Matthew 1:20–24, Joseph, when thinking of leaving Mary secretly, without causing a public scandal, had a dream, in which an angel appeared to him and explained that he had no cause against Mary. The evangelist adds that, all this was done, that it might be fulfilled which was spoken of the Lord by the Prophet, saying: "Behold, a virgin shall be with child, and shall bring forth a son, and they shall call his name Emmanuel." A most notable instance of the double application of a prophetic utterance!

(George Reynolds and Janne M. Sjodahl, *Commentary on the Book of Mormon*,
ed. Philip C. Reynolds, 7 vols. [Salt Lake City: Deseret Book Co., 1955–1961], 1:342.)

Within the prophetic context, any act of divine deliverance foreshadows God's ultimate deliverance—salvation. Therefore, there should be no problem in seeing how God used the birth of a baby in Isaiah's time to foretell deliverance for that generation, while focusing attention on the birth of another baby, through whom all the world will be delivered (Isa. 9:6). And Isaiah himself was chosen by the Lord to be the father, just as the faithful witness recorded (Isa. 8:1–3, 18). How honored Isaiah must have felt when his own son was called to typify the birth of God's own Son. . . . Indeed, the Lord's message of deliverance is contained in their names: "Isaiah," Hebrew *yesa'yahu*, means "Jehovah saves." "Maher-shalal-hash-baz" (Isa. 8:1) represents an earthly deliverance that points to salvation, and "Shear-jashub" (Isa. 7:3) means "a remnant will return."

(Keith A Meservy, *Studies in Scripture, Vol. 4,* ed. Kent P. Jackson, [Salt Lake City: Deseret Book Co., 1993], 97.)

2 Ne. 17:15   BUTTER AND HONEY
(Isa. 7:15, 22)

Honey is frequently mixed with various forms of milk-preparations and used upon bread. . . . It is considered very palatable, especially by the children. The context shows that the reference in the text is made particularly to the days of childhood.

(James M. Freeman, *Manners and Customs of the Bible* [Plainfield, New Jersey: Logos International, 1972], 255.)

2 Ne. 17:17–25   RESULTS OF KING AHAZ REJECTING ISAIAH'S WORDS
(Isa. 7:17–25)

With King Ahaz having rejected the word of the Lord, the prophet now proceeds to pronounce the penalties that would befall the king and the people of Judah. Instead of becoming a partner with the Assyrians, Ahaz and his people would become their prey. They would experience a devastation such as they had not seen since the days the northern tribes broke away from the united kingdom of the twelve tribes. Flies and bees would infest the land, and thorns and briers would take over the once-productive land. The people would be taken into captivity, and those who remain would have to forage for food.

(Hoyt W. Brewster, Jr., *Isaiah Plain and Simple* [Salt Lake City: Deseret Book Co., 1995], 70.)

Ahaz's failure to believe in the Lord led to the devastation of his land by the Assyrians, the same source to which he, in his twisted wisdom, had looked for deliverance. In fact, Isaiah said that God sent the Assyrians against his people to humble them (Isa. 10:5–11). The account of this appears in Isaiah 36–37 and 2 Kings 18–19, in which the writer explains: the "king of Assyria came against all the defenced cities of Judah, and took them" (Isa. 36:1). Sennacherib, the Assyrian king, boasted in his own records about how he conquered forty-six fortified cities plus innumerable smaller cities in their environs and carried their inhabitants into captivity. The kingdom of Judah was devastated. Of its cities, only Jerusalem survived."

(Keith A Meservy, *Studies in Scripture, Vol. 4,* ed. Kent P. Jackson, [Salt Lake City: Deseret Book Co., 1993], 98.)

King Ahaz wants to ask the king of Assyria to come and help him. Isaiah prophesies that the Lord is going to bring the king of Assyria upon Ahaz and all of Judah. The king's coming against them would be the worst devastation they had experienced since the twelve tribes had divided into the two nations of Ephraim and Judah (approximately 975 B.C.). The prophecy states that the land which has been cultivated for agricultural purposes will be left uncultivated following the Assyrian conquest. The fly and the bee are usually interpreted to be the armies of Egypt and Assyria, which would come upon Judah as a swarm. However, the invasion by Egypt is historically questionable. The prophecy therefore seems to refer to literal swarms of flies and bees inhabiting the land. The fly was and still is notorious in Egypt, and the honeybee was apparently notorious is Assyria. When the land remains uncultivated, the Lord will bring the insects from these lands, where they will find a permanent home in the desolate valleys. The Lord's "shaving with a razor that is hired" symbolizes the comfort of having someone else perform a tedious or unpleasant task, such as shaving every morning, and the Lord's using the king of Assyria to do the unpleasant task of punishing the wickedness of Judah. This punishment will be very thorough, as the whole body (land of Judah) will be shaved. Following the devastating "shaving" of the agricultural land, it will be used to graze a few animals. The cow will produce milk, which will be used for making butter, and the honey gathered from the bees will supplement the diet. The main diet for the few nomadic people who remain upon the land will then be milk, or butter, and honey. Thus the land will become a land of milk and honey. The vineyards will be left unpruned or uncared for and will quickly turn into briers and thorns, and only the hunters shall go among them seeking wild animals for food. Small areas will be digged with the mattock (the hoe) for a few vegetables, but the formerly cultivated land will be primarily a grazing land for a few cattle. When Assyria came and conquered northern Israel, she also came upon the regions round about Jerusalem and thus fulfilled this prophecy.

(Monte S. Nyman, *Great Are the Words of Isaiah* [Salt Lake City: Bookcraft, 1980], 59–60.)

After Ahaz turned down Isaiah's advice, he went straight to the temple, stripped it of all its precious ornaments, and sent them to the king of Assyria as a bribe to induce him to immediately attack Syria and the northern Ten Tribes before they attacked Judah. In this verse [20] Isaiah is assuring Ahaz that although the Assyrians were like a "razor that is hired" (hired by Ahaz, in fact!), they would nevertheless turn around and shave Judah.

(W. Cleon Skousen, *Isaiah Speaks to Modern Times* [Salt Lake City: Ensign Publishing Co., 1984], 206.)

The seriousness of the devastation in the land is expressed in verses 22–25. People will be able to retain only a fraction of their original herds and flocks, . . . yet the population will be so decimated that the limited livestock will provide plentiful milk and curds to the survivors. . . . The abundance of honey in these devastating circumstances comes from the large land areas that are left uncultivated and quickly turn to wild flowers, weeds, and other blossom-producing plants. Thus, ironically, the few who remain in the land will enjoy milk and honey because of the relatively large numbers of food-producing animals. They will still have problems and dangers, however, since they must fight off the weeds, thorny bushes, and wild animals. All in all, Isaiah describes serious conditions that will beset the people.

(Victor L. Ludlow, *Isaiah: Prophet, Seer, and Poet* [Salt Lake City: Deseret Book Co., 1982], 146.)

2 Ne. 17:18   BEE
(Isa. 7:18)

The Lord will signal or prompt the Assyrian armies (here referred to as "bees") to come down on Judah. The *Lord shall whistle* to the bees is a symbol built on an actual ancient practice, for Cyrillus of Alexandria (ca. A.D. 400) wrote about beekeepers who whistled to bees to get them to return to their hives.

(Donald W. Parry, Jay A. Parry, and Tina M. Peterson,
Understanding Isaiah [Salt Lake City: Deseret Book Co., 1998], 78.)

The fly and the bee often symbolize fighting soldiers (Deut. 1:44; Ps. 118:12). These symbols are well chosen because "the flooding of the Nile brought . . . swarms of flies," and "the hill districts of Assyria were well known for their bees" (J. Alec Motyer, *The Prophecy of Isaiah: An Introduction and Commentary*, 89).

(Donald W. Parry, *Visualizing Isaiah*
[Provo, Utah: The Foundation for Ancient Research and Mormon Studies, 2001], 26.)

2 Ne. 17:20   RAZOR
(Isa. 7:20)

Isaiah records that the Lord would use a razor to shave the head, beard, and hair of the feet of members of the house of Israel. The razor represents the Assyrian king and his armies who customarily forced war prisoners to become slaves, and then humiliated and dishonored them by shaving them from head to toe.

(Donald W. Parry, *Visualizing Isaiah*
[Provo, Utah: The Foundation for Ancient Research and Mormon Studies, 2001], 27.)

The humiliation and slavery that will befall the people is represented in verse 20 by the razor cutting off their hair. The Assyrians cut off all the hair from their captives for three reasons: humiliation, sanitation (especially while traveling under crude conditions to Assyria), and separation (if any slaves escaped while being moved from their homeland, they could not blend in with other peoples since their baldness would give them away; thus they usually were quickly recaptured, punished, and returned to their captors).

(Victor L. Ludlow, *Isaiah: Prophet, Seer, and Poet* [Salt Lake City: Deseret Book Co., 1982], 145.)

The full, rounded beard was a sign of manhood and a source of pride to Hebrew men. It was considered an ornament, and much care was given to its maintenance. In fact, the wealthy and important made a ceremony of caring for their beards. Custom did not allow the beard to be shaved, only trimmed (Lev. 19:27; 21:5), except in special circumstances. . . .

An attack on the beard is an attack on the person. Because the beard was a symbol of manhood, it was a great insult to degrade someone's beard. Thus David's men suffer grave humiliation when they return from a diplomatic mission with half of each man's beard shaven by the Ammonites. In fact, they did not return to Jerusalem until their beards had grown back (2 Sam 10:4–5). Similarly, Isaiah warns Israel that they will suffer a figurative emasculation at the hand of the king of Assyria (Isa. 7:20).

(*Dictionary of Biblical Imagery,* ed. Leland Ryken, James C. Wilhoit, and
Tremper Longman III, [Downers Grove, Illinois: InterVarsity Press, 1998], 80–81.)

2 Ne. 17:24–25   BRIERS AND THORNS
(Isa. 7:24–25; refer in this text to 2 Ne. 15:6)

This whole territory would be used by hunters, who would come among the briars and bushes with bows and arrows to seek game.

The luxurious, terraced hills, which were so carefully cultivated and weeded to keep out thorns and briars, would no longer be used for the vine or the tree. These hills would all be occupied by oxen, sheep, and goats.

(W. Cleon Skousen, *Isaiah Speaks to Modern Times* [Salt Lake City: Ensign Publishing Co., 1984], 207.)

2 Ne. 18   GOD IS A ROCK OF OFFENSE FOR HIS PEOPLE
(Isa. 8)

We have seen, in Chapter 17, Isaiah's failure to influence King Ahaz of Judah. Now the prophet turns to the people, and in prophecies that parallel those in Chapter 17 he assures them that their present enemies, Israel and Syria, will fall before Assyria. But since they refuse to believe, like their king in this respect, he prophesies disaster, the coming of Assyrian forces to overrun their land like a flood. Despite Assyria's success in overrunning Judah, Isaiah makes clear that God will not permit the entire destruction of His people. On the contrary, the peoples (the reference is to Assyria) will be overthrown and a remnant of Israel will survive, "for God is with us," a play on the name Immanuel. The Lord's plan, not Assyria's will prevail.

(Sidney B. Sperry, *Book of Mormon Compendium* [Salt Lake City: Bookcraft, 1968], 201–03.)

2 Ne. 18:1–4   SYMBOLIC NAMES
(Isa. 8:1–4; refer in this text to 2 Ne. 18:18)

Isaiah was the father of two sons, Maher-shalal-hash-baz (see 2 Ne. 18:3) and Shear-jashub (see 2 Ne. 17:3). Both names are symbolic of the Lord's intentions for the northern kingdom of Israel. Maher-shalal-hash-baz is a Hebrew term meaning "to speed to the spoil, he hasteneth the prey" (Isa. 8:1*d*; see also 2 Ne. 18:1*b*). This name describes the events spoken of in 2 Nephi 18:4. The ten tribes were overrun and despoiled by the Assyrians when Samaria, the capital of the northern kingdom, was besieged. Shear-jashub is a Hebrew term meaning "the remnant shall return" (Isa. 7:3*a*). This is a reference to the day when Israel will be gathered from her scattered condition. Thus Isaiah could report: "Behold, I and the children whom the Lord hath given me are for signs and for wonders in Israel from the Lord of Hosts" (2 Ne. 18:18).

(*Book of Mormon Student Manual, Religion 121 and 122*
[Salt Lake City: The Church of Jesus Christ of Latter-day Saints, 1989], 33.)

The message Isaiah carried to the people was "Maher-Shalal-Hash-Baz" or, "quick to the plunder, swift to the spoil." (See Isa. 8, footnote 1d.) This message was written on a large tablet or parchment to warn the people that an Assyrian attack was imminent. The message was also embodied in Isaiah's son, who received the message as his given name. The nearness of fulfillment was also to be seen in the son because before he could "call out" or speak to his parents, the invasion would come upon Damascus and Samaria, and their wealth would go to Assyria. . . .

Isaiah had the warning witnessed by leaders of Jerusalem, and thus after his wife conceived and they named their son, the people waited for him to learn to speak. It appears that before he did, the attack came, and the Judeans received a confirmation of Isaiah's peophetic powers.

With a witness of Isaiah's prophecy about the Assyrian attack upon the northern countries, the people of Jerusalem could study his prophecy given about them and know that it was also to be fulfilled.

(Victor L. Ludlow, *Isaiah: Prophet, Seer, and Poet* [Salt Lake City: Deseret Book Co., 1982], 147.)

2 Ne. 18:3   PROPHETESS
(Isa. 8:3; Ex. 15:20; Judges 4:4–5; Luke 2:36–38)

The Isaiah that has floated before our eyes has been commonly a stately form treading the upper circles, walking amid courts and breathing the air of kings. The dignity of his rhythm has seemed incompatible with a modest sphere; the strength of his denunciations has appeared to imply the voice of one who moved upon the mountains. But look beneath the surface and you will change your view. There will stand before you a new Isaiah, a humble-minded Isaiah, an Isaiah whose heart is in the valley. His very house was in the valley—in the lower part of Jerusalem. Men called the spot "the Valley of Vision"—perhaps by way of a sneer. . . . Down in his Valley of Vision Isaiah lived, far from the madding crowd—divorced from public sympathy, almost in social ostracism. But not divorced from family life. No—there the brightness comes in. Isaiah had the joy of wedded happiness. He had a wife whose mind was in tune with his own. She was familiarly called "the prophetess"—a great compliment to her, and a great testimony to her unity with her husband. And there were two sons born to them . . . sons whose names he had fondly recorded.

(George Matheson, *The Old Testament and the Fine Arts,*
comp. Cynthia Pearl Maus [New York: Harper & Row, 1954], 562.)

2 Ne. 18:5–8   WATERS OF SHILOAH . . . WATERS OF THE RIVER
(Isa. 8:5–8; Gen. 49:10).

Isaiah describes and then contrasts two forms of waters—the soft, rolling waters of Shiloah, located near the temple mount of Jerusalem, and the waters of the Euphrates, a great river that often floods out of control. The waters of Shiloah are controlled and inviting, whereas the Euphrates is dangerous and destructive. The waters of Shiloah bring life to those who drink them; the Euphrates brings death to those who are swept up in its flood. Isaiah's images of the two waters are symbolic: the former represents Jesus, the King of Heaven, who is likened to the waters of life; the latter is the king of Assyria, who leads his great, destructive armies and "cover the earth [like a flood . . . and] destroy the inhabitants thereof" (Jer. 46:8). Inasmuch as the inhabitants of Judah had rejected Jesus, or the waters of Shiloah, the Lord set upon them the king of Assyria, or the strong and mighty waters of the river that would overflow their banks and cover the entire land with its destruction.

(Donald W. Parry, Jay A. Parry, and Tina M. Peterson,
Understanding Isaiah [Salt Lake City: Deseret Book Co., 1998], 83.)

The gentle waters of Shiloah (v. 6) were the major water source for ancient Jerusalem. Located at the Gihon spring in the Kidron Valley east of the fortified city, they ebb and flow continually throughout the year. . . . During Isaiah's life, the waters were brought into a fortified area of the city when King Hezekiah, the son of Ahaz, built a tunnel through Mount Ophel, which still carries from eight to forty inches of running water. . . . This cool, flowing spring supplied more than enough water for the city of Jerusalem.

The "waters of Shiloah" also represent the continuous tender care that the Lord provided for his people as he sought to lead them with gentle promptings of the Spirit. The Judean leaders rejected the Lord's advice offered through Isaiah, who foretold how the raging floodwaters of the Euphrates River would replace the waters of Shiloah. Instead of gentle water around their knees, the raging torrent of the Assyrian army would gather around their necks (v. 8).

(Victor L. Ludlow, *Isaiah: Prophet, Seer, and Poet*
[Salt Lake City: Deseret Book Co., 1982], 147–48.)

President Wilford Woodruff, the apostle who became the fourth President of the Church I represent, said this to the Jews in the year 1879:

> "And this is the will of your great Elohim, O house of Judah, and whenever you shall be called upon to perform this work, the God of Israel will help you. You have a great future and destiny before you. . . . The God of your father's house has kept you distinct as a nation for eighteen hundred years, under all the oppression of the whole Gentile world. You may not wait until you believe on Jesus of Nazareth, but when you meet with *Shiloh* your king, you will know him. . . . It is true that after you return and gather your nation home, and rebuild your City and Temple, that the Gentiles may gather together their armies to go against you to battle . . .; but when this affliction comes, the living God, that led Moses through the wilderness, will deliver you, and *your Shiloh will come* and stand in your midst and will fight your battles; and you will know him, and the afflictions of the Jews will be at an end, while the destruction of the Gentiles will be so great that it will take the whole house of Israel who are gathered about Jerusalem, seven months to bury the dead of their enemies.". . .

The Book of Mormon, which was also written to the Jew, testifies *who* the Shiloh is, "for there is save one Messiah spoken of by the prophets" (2 Ne. 25:18).

(Ezra Taft Benson, *Ensign*, Dec. 1976, 71.)

2 Ne. 18:9   YE SHALL BE BROKEN IN PIECES
(Isa. 8:9)

The repetition of phrases at the end of verse 9 accentuates the message and provides a form of the comparative. The comparative degree in Hebrew was formed by simply repeating a word or phrase. To repeat the item three or more times made it superlative. Whereas in English one would say "good," "better," and "best" to indicate comparative degrees, in Hebrew one could say "good,"

"good, good," and "good, good, good." Thus, in the verse above, Isaiah is warning the nations that if they prepare for battle, they will be devastated.

(Victor L. Ludlow, *Isaiah: Prophet, Seer, and Poet* [Salt Lake City: Deseret Book Co., 1982], 148.)

2 Ne. 18:14–15   STONE OF STUMBLING
(Isa. 8:14)

Because the Lord would save Judah, the prophet advised against a confederacy with other nations for security; the king and people should make the Lord their "sanctuary." Isaiah knew, however, that the Lord as Savior in those times, as also later during the Lord's life on earth, would be "a stone of stumbling," upon whom many unbelievers would "stumble, and fall, and be broken, and be snared, and be taken" (Isa. 8:14–15).

Neither the king nor the people would accept the testimony given to the Lord's disciples, nor would they understand the "signs" and wonders provided through Isaiah.

(Ellis T. Rasmussen, *A Latter-day Saint Commentary on the Old Testament*
[Salt Lake City: Deseret Book Co., 1993], 510.)

The phrase "both the houses of Israel" refers to the northern kindgom of Israel and the southern kingdom of Judah. During times of apostasy, citizens of these kingdoms viewed Jesus Christ as a stumbling stone, or someone who got in their way during their journey through mortality.

(Donald W. Parry, *Visualizing Isaiah*,
[Provo, Utah, The Foundation for Ancient Research and Mormon Studies, 2001], 77.)

Both Peter and Paul quoted verse 14 to the Jews as evidence of their stumbling over Christ (see 1 Pet. 2:8; Rom. 9:33; 1 Cor. 1:23). Jacob, the Book of Mormon prophet, also foretold that the Jews would stumble over Christ (see Jacob 4:15).

(Monte S. Nyman, *Great Are the Words of Isaiah* [Salt Lake City: Bookcraft, 1980], 65.)

2 Ne. 18:16   BIND UP THE TESTIMONY
(Isa. 8:16; D&C 88:84; 109:46; 133:71–72)

The threatened disaster predicted by Isaiah (the invasion of Syria and Israel) having taken place, and other prophecies having been partly fulfilled, the prophet finds himself vindicated by events.

The meaning of these events, like a document legally drawn up and signed, is to be bound and signed in the hearts of his disciples.

(Sidney B. Sperry, *Book of Mormon Compendium* [Salt Lake City: Bookcraft, 1968], 204.)

One commentary indicates that the binding and sealing of the law is a symbolic process whereby one actually ties up a parchment roll, whereon the teachings of the prophets are recorded, as a witness against those to whom the message was delivered.

(J. R. Dummelow, as quoted in Hoyt W. Brewster, Jr., *Isaiah Plain and Simple*
[Salt Lake City: Deseret Book Co., 1995], 81.)

Prophets both ancient and modern are given power to bind and seal something on earth and have it sealed in heaven (see Matt. 16:19; 18:18; D&C 1:8; 68:12). The wording of verse 16 is reversed in D&C 88:84, wherein the Lord sent his disciples among the Gentiles, and in the Appendix to the Doctrine and Covenants, referring to those who refused to believe in the Lord's servants (see D&C 133:71–72). The wording therein is to bind up the law and seal up the testimony instead of binding the testimony and sealing up the law. However, the meaning is the same in either case. While the sealing may be a sealing unto heaven or a sealing against heaven, as shown in the various references cited, Isaiah's charge was to seal up the disciples to heaven.

(Monte S. Nyman, *Great Are the Words of Isaiah* [Salt Lake City: Bookcraft, 1980], 65.)

2 Ne. 18:17   [PATIENCE] . . . WAIT UPON THE LORD
(Isa. 8:17; Eccl. 3:1–7; D&C 64:31–32; 88:68.)

Attentive doctors, nurses, therapists, a loving spouse, parents, children, and friends comfort us when we are ill and speed our recovery process. There are times when, no matter how independent we may be, we must entrust others with our care. We must surrender ourselves to them. Our caregivers are those who assist in the healing process.

The Lord is the ultimate caregiver. We must surrender ourselves to the Lord. In doing so, we give up whatever is causing our pain and turn everything over to Him. . . .

As we put our faith and trust in the Lord, we must battle our pain day by day and sometimes hour by hour, even moment by moment; but in the end, we understand that marvelous counsel given to the Prophet Joseph Smith as he struggled with his pain of feeling forgotten and isolated in Liberty Jail:

"My son, peace be unto thy soul; thine adversity and thine afflictions shall be but a small moment;
"And then, if thou endure it well, God shall exalt thee on high; thou shalt triumph over all thy foes"
(D&C 121:7–8). . . .

When pain, tests, and trials come in life, draw near to the Savior. "Wait upon the Lord, . . . look for him" (Isa. 8:17; 2 Ne. 18:17). "They that wait upon the Lord shall renew their strength; they shall mount up with wings as eagles; they shall run, and not be weary; and they shall walk, and not faint" (Isa. 40:31). Healing comes in the Lord's time and the Lord's way; be patient.

Our Savior waits for us to come to Him through our scripture study, pondering, and prayer to our Heavenly Father. . . . As we are strengthened and healed, we can then lift and strengthen others with our faith.

(Robert D. Hales, *Ensign,* Oct. 1998, 18–19.)

Being human, we would expel from our lives physical pain and mental anguish and assure ourselves of continual ease and comfort, but if we were to close the doors upon sorrow and distress, we might be excluding our greatest friends and benefactors. Suffering can make saints of people as they learn patience, long-suffering, and self-mastery. The sufferings of our Savior were part of his education.

(Spencer W. Kimball, *Faith Precedes the Miracle* [Salt Lake City: Deseret Book Co., 1973], 98.)

No pang that is suffered by man or woman upon the earth will be without its compensating effect . . . if it be met with patience.

(James E. Talmage, as quoted in Spencer W. Kimball, *Faith Precedes the Miracle* [Salt Lake City: Deseret Book Co., 1972], 98.)

No pain that we suffer, no trial that we experience is wasted. It ministers to our education, to the development of such qualities as patience, faith, fortitude and humility. All that we suffer and all that we endure, especially when we endure it patiently, builds up our characters, purifies our hearts, expands our souls, and makes us more tender and charitable, more worthy to be called the children of God . . . and it is through sorrow and suffering, toil and tribulation, that we gain the education that we come here to acquire and which will make us more like our Father and Mother in heaven.

(Orson F. Whitney as quoted in Spencer W. Kimball, *Faith Precedes the Miracle* [Salt Lake City: Deseret Book Co., 1973], 98.)

To appreciate this story, you have to realize that it occurred when he was nearly eighty and had bone cancer. He had bone cancer so badly in his hips that he could hardly move. The pain was great. . . .

He had the responsibility for the welfare farm. An assignment was given to weed a field of onions, so Dad assigned himself to go work on the farm. . . . I have met several people who were with him that day. I talked to one of them on the phone, and he said that he was weeding in the row next to Dad. . . . He said that the pain was so great that Dad was pulling himself along on his stomach with his elbows. He couldn't kneel. The pain was too great for him to kneel. Everyone who has talked to me about that day has remarked how Dad smiled and laughed and talked happily with them as they worked in that field of onions. . . .

After all the work was finished and the onions were all weeded, someone said to him, "Henry, good heavens! You didn't pull those weeds, did you? Those weeds were sprayed two days ago, and they were going to die anyway."

Dad just roared. He thought that was the funniest thing. He thought it was a great joke on himself. He had worked through the day in the wrong weeds. They had been sprayed and would have died anyway.

When Dad told me this story, I knew how tough it was. So I asked him, "Dad, how could you make a joke out of that? How could you take it so pleasantly?" He said something to me that I will never forget, and I hope you won't. He said, "Hal, I wasn't there for the weeds."

Now, you'll be in an onion patch much of your life. So will I. It will be hard to see the powers of heaven magnifying us or our efforts. It may even be hard to see our work being of any value at all. And sometimes our work won't go well.

But you didn't come for the weeds. You came for the Savior. . . . I promise you that if you will be patient and diligent, you will have the blessing of knowing that you are doing what the Lord would have you do. And you will remember that while you're in that onion patch, you are not there for the weeds. (That will be important sometimes when the weeds don't come out easily.) You will feel the approval of God.

"But they that wait upon the Lord shall renew their strength; they shall mount up with wings as eagles; they shall run, and not be weary; and they shall walk, and not faint" (Isa. 40:31).

Dad never got better. He just got worse. So you might say, "Well, he waited upon the Lord, but he couldn't run and he couldn't walk." But that was true only in this life. There will be a day for you and me when, whatever difficulties and limitations we have here, we will have that promise fulfilled for us. We will be lifted up as on eagles wings if we have waited upon the Lord. . . .

One night when I was not with him and the pain seemed more than he could bear, he somehow got out of bed and on his knees beside it—I know not how. He pled with God to know why he was suffering so. And the next morning he said, with quiet firmness, "I know why now. God needs brave sons."

(Henry B. Eyring, *To Draw Closer To God* [Salt Lake City: Deseret Book Co., 1997], 101–103, 116.)

Since the Lord wants a people "tried in all things" (D&C 136:31), how specifically will we be tried? He tells us, I will try the faith and the patience of my people (see Mosiah 23:21). Since faith in the timing of the Lord may be tried, let us learn to say not only, "Thy will be done," but patiently also, "Thy timing be done." . . .

In the agonizing atoning process, Jesus let His will be "swallowed up in the will of the Father" (Mosiah 15:7). As sovereigns, choosing to yield to the Highest Sovereign is our highest act of choice. It is the only surrender which is also a victory! . . .

So, brothers and sister, given what Jesus *died for,* are we willing to *live with* the challenges allotted to us? (See Alma 29:4, 6). Trembling is sometimes both permissible and understandable. . . .

We are to . . . finish the work we personally have been given to do; to be able to partake of a bitter cup without becoming bitter . . . to let our wills increasingly be swallowed up in the will of the Father; to acknowledge . . . that, indeed, "All these things shall give thee experience, and shall be for thy good" (D&C 122:7).

(Neal A. Maxwell, *Ensign,* May 2001, 59–61.)

In all the important decisions in our lives, what is most important is to *do the right thing.* Second, and only slightly behind the first, is to *do the right thing at the right time.* People who do the right thing at the wrong time can be frustrated and ineffective. They can even be confused about whether they made the right choice when what was wrong was not their choice but their timing. . . .

Indeed, we cannot have true faith in the Lord without also having complete trust in the Lord's will and in the Lord's timing. . . . In our service in the Lord's church we should remember that *when* is just as important as *who, what, where,* and *how.* . . .

People who do not accept continuing revelation sometimes get into trouble by doing things too soon or too late or too long. The practice of polygamy is an example. . . .

This principle [of timing] applies to revelation . . . and to all of the most important events in our lives: birth, marriage, death, and even our moves from place to place. . . .

Faith in the Lord Jesus Christ prepares us for whatever life brings. . . .

If we have faith in God and if we are committed to the fundamentals of keeping His commandments and putting Him first in our lives, we do not need to plan every single event—even every important event—and we should not feel rejected or depressed if some things—even some very important things—do not happen at the time we had planned or hoped or prayed. . . .

Plan, of course, but fix your planning on personal commitments that will carry you through no matter what happens. Anchor your life to eternal principles, and act upon those principles whatever the circumstances and whatever the actions of others. Then you can await the Lord's timing and be sure of the outcome in eternity.

(Dallin H. Oaks, *Brigham Young University 2001–2002 Speeches*
[Provo, Utah: Brigham Young University Publications & Graphics, 2002], 188–92.)

Patience is another form of self-control. It is the ability to postpone gratification and to bridle one's passions. In his relationships with loved ones, a patient man does not engage in impetuous behavior that he will later regret. Patience is composure under stress. A patient man is understanding of others' faults.

A patient man also waits on the Lord. We sometimes read or hear of people who seek a blessing from the Lord, then grow impatient when it does not come swiftly. Part of the divine nature is to trust in the Lord enough to "be still and know that [he is] God" (D&C 101:16).

A priesthood holder who is patient will be tolerant of the mistakes and failings of his loved ones. Because he loves them, he will not find fault nor criticize nor blame.

(Ezra Taft Benson, *Ensign,* Nov. 1986, 47.)

2 Ne. 18:18   I AND THE CHIDREN
(Isa. 8:18; refer in this text to 2 Ne. 18:1–4)

The Prophet reminds the people of the fact that both he and his children were signs and wonders given them by the Lord as testimonies of his predictions. The names of two of his sons are recorded: Shear-jashub (Isa. 7:3) and Maher-shalal-hash-baz (Isa. 8:3). Whether Immanuel, mentioned in Isaiah 7:14 and 8:8, was the second son of Isaiah is a debated question. . . . It seems to me that the context of Isaiah 7:14 compels us to regard the virgin, the "alma" of that text as a young woman living at the time of King Ahaz and the prophet; for, how could her motherhood otherwise have been a sign to the skeptic king, for whom it was intended? . . . We notice that Isaiah, before the birth of Maher-shalal-hash-baz, undoubtedly following divine instructions, summoned two competent witnesses to accompany him to the mother of the expected child, to ascertain to their own satisfaction and to disarm public criticism, that she, the "prophetess," was the legal wife of the Prophet. And, is it not probable that she was given that title, because she was the mother of the prophetic child Immanuel,—the type of the Messiah?

(George Reynolds and Janne M. Sjodahl, *Commentary on the Book of Mormon,* 7 vols.,
ed. Philip C. Reynolds [Salt Lake City: Deseret Book Co., 1955–1961], 1:346.)

2 Ne. 18:19   PEEP—FAMILIAR SPIRITS
(Isa. 8:19; Ex. 22:18; Deut. 18:10–12; D&C 46:7–9)

There can be no good or wholesome purpose accomplished in this kind of entertainment [ouija boards], therefore it should not be indulged in by members of the Church. . . . When a person is baptized and receives the laying on of hands for the gift of the Holy Ghost, he is promised that he will receive the necessary guidance for his spiritual and temporal good, provided he is true to his covenants. . . .

There is no need for any member seeking inspiration or knowledge through any unsavory or evil source which is coming from Satan or one of his emissaries. Those who have the light of the Spirit, or Holy Ghost, will avoid any contacts from any evil source. No doubt it is true that the use of these instruments is in the spirit of fun and for amusement. Let it be remembered that the Spirit of the Lord does not and will not dwell in unclean or disobedient tabernacles. . . .

The disobedient and wayward become the prey of deception; and as darkness enters their souls, the true light is driven out. . . . To seek for information through ouija boards or any way contrary to the instruction the Lord has given is a sin. . . .

All through the Bible, the New Testament as well as the Old, the Lord and his prophets have expressed their displeasure when the people turned from the Lord to "familiar spirits."

(Joseph Fielding Smith, *Answers to Gospel Questions,* 5 vols.,
[Salt Lake City: Deseret Book Co., 1957–1966], 4:30–33.)

2 Ne. 18:19–22   SEEK UNTO THEIR GOD
(Isa. 8:19–22)

The main point of this passage is that turning to any sort of spiritualism, such as turning to the dead on behalf of the living, is forbidden. People of faith should turn "to the law and to the testimony," which are the scriptures. If other sources do not agree, "it is because there is no light in them."

They of Israel who had ceased to seek the true God were about to pass into the bondage their king had led them to. Trouble, darkness, and the dimness of anguish lay ahead.

(Ellis T. Rasmussen, *A Latter-day Saint Commentary on the Old Testament*
[Salt Lake City: Deseret Book Co., 1993], 510.)

2 Ne. 18:20   THE LAW
(Isa. 8:20; refer in *Latter-day Commentary on the Book of Mormon,* Bassett, to 3 Ne. 15:5–6, 10)

2 Ne. 18:20   NO LIGHT IN THEM
(Isa. 8:20; 2 Ne. 12:5)

There are two great scriptural tests which show whether men have the light and are walking therein, one pertaining to beliefs, the other to conduct. Isaiah challenged false teachers with this test: "To the law and to the testimony: if they speak not according to this word, it is because there is no light in them" (Isa. 8:20). And John, speaking particularly to members of the Church, those upon whom "the true light now shineth," said: "He that saith he is in the light, and hateth his brother, is in darkness even until now. He that loveth his brother abideth in the light, and there is none occasion of stumbling in him. But he that hateth his brother is in darkness, and walketh in darkness, and knoweth not whither he goeth, because that darkness hath blinded his eyes" (1 Jn. 2:8–11).

(Bruce R. McConkie, *Mormon Doctrine,* 2d ed. [Salt Lake City: Bookcraft, 1966], 445–46.)

May I suggest three short tests to avoid being deceived. . . .

1. What do the standard works have to say about it? "To the law and to the testimony: if they speak not according to this word, it is because there is no light in them," said Isaiah (Isa. 8:20).

This is one of the great truths of Isaiah so important that it was included in the Book of Mormon scriptures. . . .

2. The second guide is: what do the latter-day Presidents of the Church have to say on the subject—particularly the living President? . . .

3. The third and final test is the Holy Ghost—the test of the Spirit. By that Spirit we ". . . may know the truth of all things" (Moro. 10:5).

(Ezra Taft Benson, *Conference Report*, Oct. 1963, 16–17.)

To those in quest of spiritual light—this word of counsel: Seek it only in God's appointed way. Follow the advice of the Apostle James and the example of Joseph the Prophet. (James 1:5; *Hist. Ch.* vol.1, 4, 5.) Never go upon the Devil's ground. Keep away from all deceptive influence. One may believe in hypnotism, without being a hypnotist, without surrendering one's will to the will of the person exercising that power—a very dangerous power when wielded by an unprincipled possessor. In like manner, one may believe spiritualism real, without becoming a spiritualist, without attending "seances," without consulting "mediums," without putting trust in planchettes, ouija boards, automatic pencils, false impersonations, etc., or in any way encouraging the advances of designing spirits, who thus gain an ascendancy over their victims, leading them into mazes of delusion, and often into depths of despair. Go not after them; and if they come to you, put them to the test "Try the spirits" (1 Jn. 4:1). If they speak not according to revealed truth,—if they conform not to divine standards, "it is because there is no light in them" (Isa. 8:20).

(Orson F. Whitney, *Saturday Night Thoughts* [Salt Lake City: The Deseret News, 1921], 312.)

2 Ne. 19   MESSIANIC PROPHECIES
(Isa. 9)

Chapters 9 and 10 of Isaiah are a natural continuation of chapters 7 and 8; the historical context still centers upon the Assyrian crisis of 734–701 B.C., although the situation worsens after Ahaz ignores Isaiah's counsel. In chapters 7 and 8, Isaiah told Ahaz that an Assyrian alliance would bring problems. Now, in chapters 9 and 10, with the alliance an accomplished fact, Isaiah prophesies more specifically about the Assyrian punishments coming upon Israel and Judah. He warns the ten tribes in the north of their impending captivity and foretells a later Assyrian attack upon the southern tribes.

The messianic prophecies of chapters 7 and 8 are also developed further in chapters 9 and 10. The Immanuel prophecy is amplified in chapter 9 as Isaiah promises a "new light" and a new leader for Israel. This promised child could be the young King Hezekiah, who would help deliver Judah from the Assyrians, but if Hezekiah is the object of Isaiah's prophecy, he is only a foreshadowing of Jesus Christ, the greater light and deliverer of all nations.

(Victor L. Ludlow, *Isaiah: Prophet, Seer, and Poet* [Salt Lake City: Deseret Book Co., 1982], 151.)

2 Ne. 19:1   GALILEE OF THE NATIONS
(Isa. 9:1)

The northern part of Palestine, allotted to Zebulon and Naphtali and bordering on Phoenicia and Syria, was known as the "Galilee of the Nations," or, Gentiles, because of its mixed population. The manners and customs of the people, and even the dialect spoken became affected by foreign settlers.

(George Reynolds and Janne M. Sjodahl, *Commentary on the Book of Mormon*, |ed. Philip C. Reynolds, 7 vols. [Salt Lake City: Deseret Book Co., 1955–1961], 1:348.)

When the land of Canaan was divided among the twelve tribes of Israel, the tribes of Zebulun and Naphtali lay to the west of the Sea of Galilee and formed the northern border of Israel next to the gentile nations of the Galilee. . . . The land of Naphtali and Zebulun was the first area captured by the Assyrians in the time of Isaiah (see 2 Kgs. 15:29). The phrase "afterwards did more grievously afflict by the way of the Red Sea beyond Jordan in Galilee of the nations" . . . probably has reference to a later captivity by Assyria. . . . The blessing which was to have come to this area, but which had been lost by Israel's wickedness and subsequent subjection by Assyria, would come through the "light" of Christ as he ministered unto Judah in Galilee, as noted in Matthew.

(Monte S. Nyman, *Great Are the Words of Isaiah* [Salt Lake City: Bookcraft, 1980], 67.)

2 Ne. 19:2   THE LIGHT SHINED
(Isa. 9:2; D&C 138:18)

The land of the shadow of death is a land peopled by those who do not know Jesus Christ, the "great light," and his gospel. These people walk in darkness. Jesus was the great light that shone upon the inhabitants of Galilee during his mortal mission. Matthew 4:13–16 contains the fulfillment of this prophecy found in Isaiah 9:1–2. As those who follow Christ walk through mortality in the latter days, they will receive great hope, comfort, and joy when they accept Jesus as the "great light."

(Donald W. Parry, *Visualizing Isaiah*
[Provo, Utah: The Foundation for Ancient Research and Mormon Studies, 2001], 78.)

2 Ne. 19:3   JOY OF THE HARVEST
(Isa. 9:3)

In the Orient, the harvest time is always a time of great festivity. To the Jews of Bible days, it was also a time of great joy. . . . The law provided two feasts that were harvest festivals (Exod.

23:16). The first of these was called at one time The Feast of the Harvest, and later named The Feast of Pentecost. This feast was celebrated after the grain harvest. . . . The second of these feasts was sometimes called The Feast of Ingathering, being held after all the grain, fruit, wine, and oil had been gathered in. . . . It was also called the Feast of Tabernacles (Lev. 23:39–43), because they dwelt in booths to remind them of the wilderness days of the past.

(Fred H. Wight, *Manners and Customs of Bible Lands* [Chicago: Moody Press, 1953], 136–37.)

The entire process of harvesting caused much joy among the people, as it ensured them food for the coming year. . . . The Lord's victory over Israel's enemies and his coming will bring Israel a joy similar to that experienced by a farmer at an abundant harvest.

(Donald W. Parry, *Visualizing Isaiah*
[Provo, Utah: The Foundation for Ancient Research and Mormon Studies, 2001], 78–79.)

In the King James Version this verse states that the people would NOT increase their joy, but the Book of Mormon gives the correct rendition. In fact, the King James translators inserted a marginal note indicating there was some question about the word "not." The Revised Standard Version leaves out the "not" just as the Book of Mormon did nearly a century earlier. The word "not" obviously contradicts the next two phrases, which say that the joy of the people will be so exuberant that it will be similar to the happiness which always accompanies the gathering in of the harvest, or the happiness of those occasions when the booty is about to be distributed after a long, hard-fought campaign for victory.

(W. Cleon Skousen, *Isaiah Speaks to Modern Times* [Salt Lake City: Ensign Publishing Co., 1984], 222.)

2 Ne. 19:3–7   A CHILD IS BORN
(Isa. 9:3–7)

If Isaiah is prophesying about Hezekiah [the king of Judah who helped deliver Israel from the Assyrians], then verse 3 describes the Israelites' joy at their deliverance; verse 4 portrays how the Assyrians were defeated in spite of their greater numbers, just as the many Midianites were by Gideon and his 300 men (Judg. 7); verse 5 describes the Assyrian casualties; and verses 6 and 7 tell us about Hezekiah's titles and righteous, peaceful rule as king.

If the verses describe a righteous people fighting against wickedness, then verse 3 describes their joy at success, verses 4 and 5 portray the defeat of the enemy, and verses 6 and 7 describe a new age of millennial peace that may be assisted or ushered in by a messianic figure.

Finally, the identification of the ruler in verses 3–7 with Jesus Christ has a number of possibilities, as verse 3 talks about his many followers who rejoice at the spiritual blessings he has provided; verse 4 describes how he was able to overcome the temptations of Satan, break the yoke of sin, and maintain power over the legions of Satan's devils; verse 5 symbolizes his atonement and the cleansing powers of baptism and the Holy Ghost; verse 6 presents some of his titles and roles; and verse 7 describes his eternal position as the Lord and King of this earth.

(Victor L. Ludlow, *Isaiah: Prophet, Seer, and Poet* [Salt Lake City: Deseret Book Co., 1982], 154.)

2 Ne. 19:4   YOKE, STAFF, ROD
(Isa. 9:4; 1 Ne. 3:27–29)

In biblical times, the staff and rod were used by taskmasters on slaves. A yoke was a wooden frame designed to harness together beasts of burden. These three items—the yoke, staff, and rod—signify oppression, or the burdens placed on Israel by its neighbors (Isa. 10:5, 24–27).

In particular, the language of this verse recalls the manner in which Egypt oppressed the Israelites before Moses led them out of captivity. (For example, see "yoke" in Leviticus 26:13; "burden" in Exodus 1:11; 2:11; 5:4–5; 6:6–7; and "taskmasters" in Exodus 3:7; 5:6, 10–14). Just as Moses delivered ancient Israel from the Egyptian yoke of physical bondage, Jesus Christ delivers his followers from the yoke of spiritual bondage.

(Donald W. Parry, *Visualizing Isaiah*
[Provo, Utah: The Foundation for Ancient Research and Mormon Studies, 2001], 79.)

Is it any wonder that Laman and Lemuel worked off their pent-up frustration by beating their younger brother with a stick when they were once hiding in a cave? Every free man in the East carries a stick, the immemorial badge of independence and of authority; and every man asserts his authority over his inferiors by his stick, which "shows that the holder is a man of position, superior to the workman or day-labourers. The government officials, superior officers, tax-gatherers, and schoolmasters use this short rod to threaten —or if necessary to beat—their inferiors, whoever they may be." The usage is very ancient. "A blow for a slave," is the ancient maxim in Ahikar, and the proper designation of an underling is *'abd-ad-'asa*, "stick-servant." This is exactly the sense in which Laman and Lemuel intended their little lesson to Nephi, for when the angel turned the tables he said to them, "Why do ye smite your younger brother with a rod? Know ye not that the Lord hath chosen *him* to be a ruler over *you?*" (1 Ne. 3:29).

(Hugh Nibley, *Lehi in the Desert/ The World of the Jaredites/ There were Jaredites*,
ed. John W. Welch [Salt Lake City: Deseret Book Co., 1988], 69–70.)

2 Ne. 19:6–7   THE GOVERNMENT SHALL BE UPON HIS SHOULDER
(Isa. 9:6–7; Luke 2:10–11)

We know that the government was not placed on Christ's shoulders during his first coming, but it will be when he comes the second time to fulfill his complete messianic role. When he came as a baby, it was important for his believers to know what his overall role would be. As Gabriel told Mary, 'the Lord God shall give unto him the throne of his father David: and . . . of his kingdom there shall be no end' (Luke 1:32–33; reiterated by Zacharias in Luke 1:69–74. Inspired people have always kept Christ's overall ministry in mind to comprehend the full nature of his earthly mission (see Luke 1:33, 68–71).

(Keith A Meservy, *Studies in Scripture, Vol. 4,* ed. Kent P. Jackson [Salt Lake City: Deseret Book Co., 1993], 99.)

One of the beautiful reminders in this magnificent passage . . . is the gentle declaration that through all of his power and majesty, Christ is still "the Son"—the Son as taught by Abinadi and other Book of Mormon prophets. . . . We are reminded here that he is, gloriously, the Son of God, a child of heaven.

The fact that the government would eventually be upon his shoulders affirms what all the world will one day acknowledge–that he is Lord of lords and King of kings and will one day rule over the earth and his Church in person. . . . All can take comfort from the fact that because the government–and the burdens thereof–will be upon his shoulders, they will be lifted in great measure from our own. This is yet another reference in Isaiah to the Atonement, the bearing away of our sins (or at very least in this reference, our temporal burdens) on the shoulders of Christ.

As "Wonderful Counselor," he will be our mediator, our intercessor, defending our cause in the courts of heaven. . . .

Of course, as noted by Isaiah, Christ is not only a mediator but also a judge. . . . It is as if the judge in that great courtroom in heaven, unwilling to ask anyone but himself to bear the burdens of the guilty people standing in the dock, takes off his judicial robes and comes down to earth to bear their stripes personally. Christ as merciful judge is as beautiful and wonderful a concept as that of Christ as counselor, mediator, and advocate.

"Mighty God" conveys something of the power of God, his strength, omnipotence, and unconquerable influence . . .

"Everlasting Father" underscores the fundamental doctrine that Christ is a Father—Creator of worlds without number, the Father of restored physical life through the Resurrection, the Father of eternal life for his spiritually begotten sons and daughters, and the One acting for the Father (Elohim) through divine investiture of authority. . .

Lastly, with the phrase "Prince of Peace," we rejoice that when the King shall come, there will be no more war in the human heart or among the nations of the world."

(Jeffrey R. Holland, *Christ and the New Covenant* [Salt Lake City: Deseret Book Co., 1997], 80–81.)

Some scholars believe that the leader promised by Isaiah in chapter 9 was Hezekiah. Hezekiah was indeed a righteous king, for he both helped bring Judah to a higher spiritual plane and brought a partial peace to the land. Hezekiah listened to the counsel of Isaiah and tried to follow it. He seems particularly righteous when contrasted with his father, Ahaz, and his son Mannaseh. Still, Isaiah was merely using Hezekiah as a type, a figure of the future Messiah. . . . When the Israelites heard of Isaiah's prophecy, they knew it applied to Hezekiah and that they would enjoy a period of peace, but some of them also knew that its full realization would come only in the birth and life of the Messiah, the perfect king.

(Victor L. Ludlow, *Isaiah: Prophet, Seer, and Poet* [Salt Lake City: Deseret Book Co., 1982], 155.)

2 Ne. 19:6   **THE EVERLASTING FATHER**
                        (Isa. 9:6; refer in *Latter-day Commentary on the Book of Mormon*, Bassett, to 1 Ne. 19:10)

2 Ne. 19:8–20:4 JUDGEMENT AGAINST ISRAEL
            (Isa. 9:8–10:4)

Isaiah 9:8–10:4 is divided into four subsections. The first subsection deals with pride (9:8–12), and the fourth refers to social injustice (10:1–4). The four subsections are part of a single prophecy but are divided structurally with an identical poetic refrain at the end of each section: "For all this his anger is not turned away, but his hand is stretched out still" (9:12, 17, 21; 10:4; see also 5:25).

This prophecy has a dual fulfillment: first, when the ancient kingdom of Israel was destroyed, and second, when the world will be destroyed at the time of the second coming of Christ.

(Donald W. Parry, Jay A. Parry, and Tina M. Peterson,
Understanding Isaiah [Salt Lake City: Deseret Book Co., 1998], 97.)

Isaiah now turns his attention to the rebellious northern kingdom of Israel, whose ruling tribe is represented by Ephraim and whose capital is Samaria. The historical setting is the same as in verses 1–7: the northern tribes have already been placed under direct Assyrian control, and many leading citizens have been taken captive to Assyria. The campaign of Tiglath-Pileser III in 732 B.C. brought about the deportation of the major portions of the northernmost Israelite tribes, Zebulun and Naphtali. Still, the invasion and deportation did not bring the stubborn Israelites to the realization that the prophecies uttered against them would all surely come to pass unless they repented. They had had a taste of the Lord's judgment, but learned nothing from it, since Isaiah still levels four major accusations against them: pride [19:8–12], evil leaders [19:13–17], selfishness [19:18–21], and injustice [20:1–4].

(Victor L. Ludlow, *Isaiah: Prophet, Seer, and Poet* [Salt Lake City: Deseret Book Co., 1982], 156.)

2 Ne. 19:9–10   BRICKS - HEWN STONES-SYCAMORES - CEDARS
(Isa. 9:9–10)

In Isaiah's time, bricks were made of mud or clay mixed with sand, straw, or other material, and then baked in a kiln or dried by the sun. Bricks were inferior to hewn stone because bricks were more breakable. Additionally, hewn stone was more expensive to prepare. . . . The sycamore is a fruit-bearing tree valued for its figs and lumber. The Egyptians used its wood to make coffins, but apparently sycamore wood was not as precious as that of a cedar (Isa. 9:10). The sycamore grows to a height of forty feet. Its branches spread widely from a short trunk.

(Donald W. Parry, *Visualizing Isaiah*
[Provo, Utah: The Foundation for Ancient Research and Mormon Studies, 2001], 11.)

The doors as well as windows were ordinarily built of sycamore wood. It was only for ornamental purposes of the wealthy that cedar wood was used.

(Fred H. Wight, *Manners and Customs of Bible Lands* [Chicago: Moody Press, 1953], 25.)

2 Ne. 19:11   ADVERSARIES OF REZIN
(Isa. 9:11)

Perhaps we should read [as do some Hebrew manuscripts] 'the princes of Rezin' [the king of Syria]; the meaning would then be that the Syrian allies of Israel [Isaiah 7:1–2] will turn against it.

(J. R. Dummelow, *The One Volume Bible Commentary* [New York: Macmillan, 1936], 421–22.)

2 Ne. 19:12, 17, 21; 20:4   HIS HAND IS STRETCHED OUT STILL
2 Ne. 19:8 through 20:4 comprises a prophetic poem. (2 Ne. 7:2; 15:25; 24:26–27; 28:32; Jacob 6:4–5; Alma 19:36; Mosiah 14:1; 16:12; 29:20; 3 Ne. 9:13–14; D&C 35:8; Ezek. 6:14; 14:9; 2 Ne. 1:4)

Before we leave this prophetic poem (19:8–20:4) it should be pointed out that the last clause of the four refrains (19:12, 17, 21; 20:4), "but his hand is stretched out still," is usually interpreted to mean that God's wrath against his people is unappeasable, that Isaiah has no word of hope for his people, still unrepentant. Some commentators express the meaning of the clause in this manner: "But his hand is stretched out still to strike." I may be wrong, but I feel that Isaiah was by no means completely a prophet of doom, that he still held out to his people a note of encouragement intended to bring about their repentance (cf. Isa. 1:16–20). Let me express it this way: "But his hand is stretched out still if only you but change your ways."

(Sidney B. Sperry, *Book of Mormon Compendium* [Salt Lake City: Bookcraft, 1968], 213.)

His grasp is galactic.

(Neal A. Maxwell, *Ensign*, May 1976, 26.)

Our merciful and long-suffering Lord is ever ready to help. His "arm is lengthened out all the day long" (2 Ne. 28:32), and even if His arm goes ungrasped, it was unarguably there! In the same redemptive reaching out, our desiring to improve our human relationships usually requires some long-suffering. Sometimes reaching out is like trying to pat a porcupine. Even so, the accumulated quill marks are evidence that our hands of fellowship have been stretched out, too!

(Neal A. Maxwell, *Ensign,* Nov. 1996, 22.)

Isaiah frequently used an interesting phrase when discussing Judah's sins and God's continued acts of judgment against her: "For all this his anger is not turned away, but his hand is stretched out still" (Isa. 5:25; 9:12, 17, 21; 10:4). Despite repeated punishments, Isaiah's people refused to repent. This reminds us of the words of Amos, Isaiah's contemporary, when he repeated after a whole series of devastating experiences, "Yet have ye not returned unto me" (Amos 4:6, 8, 11). These phrases imply that God uses judgments as chastening tools to accomplish his divine purpose. As Mormon wrote, "And thus we see that except the Lord doth chasten his people with many afflictions, yea, except he doth visit them with death and with terror, and with famine and with all manner of pestilence, they will not remember him" (Hel. 12:3).

(Keith A Meservy, *Studies in Scripture, Vol. 4*, ed. Kent P. Jackson [Salt Lake City: Deseret Book Co., 1993], 99.)

2 Ne. 19:13–17   THE HEAD AND THE TAIL
(Isa. 9:13–17)

The second evil to bring the destructive judgments of God upon Israel is her wicked leaders, both the political and the religious leaders. The "head" (government) and the "tail" (false prophets) are identified in verse 15. The phrase "and honourable" is not given in the Book of Mormon as characteristic of the head. Under the government of Israel, the Lord's prophet was to instruct the king or the government leaders (for example, Isaiah taught Ahaz, as Nathan had taught David), but Israel's future prophets will cause her to err. The entire people will be hypocrites. The Book of

Mormon phrase "of them" in verse 17, identifying the young men and the fatherless and widows specifically as hypocrites, points out the justice of God in not showing mercy to them.

(Monte S. Nyman, *Great Are the Words of Isaiah* [Salt Lake City: Bookcraft, 1980], 69.)

2 Ne. 19:18–21   NO MAN SHALL SPARE HIS BROTHER
(Jer. 19:9; Moro. 9:10; refer in Latter-day Commentary
on the Book of Mormon, Bassett, to Moro. 9:20)

The third evil to visit Israel is the wickedness which is likened to a forest fire. The fire of wickedness will sweep on, using the people for fuel. All will be consumed in wickedness. This wickedness is so severe that brothers will "consume" brothers, members of their own families, and even themselves—and will still not be satisfied.

(Monte S. Nyman, *Great Are the Words of Isaiah* [Salt Lake City: Bookcraft, 1980], 69.)

2 Ne. 20   CHIASMUS
(refer in Latter-day Commentary on
the Book of Mormon, Bassett, to Alma 36)

If chiasmus can be convincingly identified in the Book of Mormon, it will testify of the book's ancient origin. No one in America, let alone in western New York, fully understood chiasmus in 1830. Joseph Smith had been dead ten full years before John Forbes's book was published in Scotland. Even many prominent Bible scholars today know little about chiastic forms beyond the name and a few passages where they might be found. The possibility of Joseph Smith's noticing the form accidentally is also remote, since most biblical passages containing inverted word orders have been rearranged into natural word orders in the King James translation. Even had he known of the form, he would still have had the overwhelming task of writing original, artistic chiastic sentences. . . . If the Book of Mormon is found to contain true chiastic forms in an ancient style, then is not the book's own repeated claim to be the product of an ancient culture veritably substantiated?

(John W. Welch, *Book of Mormon Authorship*, ed. Noel B. Reynolds
[Provo: Religious Studies Center, Brigham Young University, 1982], 41–42.)

A. The wicked will bow down (vs. 1–4)
B. Assyria raised by the Lord (5)
C. The Assyrian king speaks against Jerusalem (6–11)
D. The Lord will punish proud Assyria (12–14)
E. An ax is used as a tool (15)

F. The Lord is a burning fire in the land (16–17)

G. Out of all the [multitudes]—only a remnant remains (18–19)

H. A remnant of Israel shall return to the Lord (20–21)

G. Out of the "sands of the sea"—only a remnant returns (22)

F. A divine consumption is in the land (23)

E. A rod is used as an instrument (24–26)

D. Assyria's yoke will be lifted (27)

C. Assyrian army approaches Jerusalem (28–32)

B. Assyria humbled by the Lord (33)

A. The haughty will be cut down (34)

(Victor L. Ludlow, *Isaiah: Prophet, Seer, and Poet* [Salt Lake City: Deseret Book Co., 1982], 161.)

2 Ne. 20   **ASSYRIA AND THE LAST DAYS**
(Isa. 10)

The first portion of this chapter prophesies of the coming destruction of Assyria, and the last part compares this destruction to what will happen to the wicked in the last days.

(Daniel H. Ludlow, *A Companion to Your Study of the Old Testament* [Salt Lake City: Deseret Book Co., 1981], 289.)

Judah was the hypocritical nation referred to in Isaiah 10:6. It would be brought down, for "the eyes of the lofty shall be humbled" (Isa. 5:15). In Isaiah 10, we see how God's divine purpose was accomplished, even though the principal agent by which it was done was evil. God used the Assyrians to bring about his judgments on Judah. The Assyrians intended to conquer and plunder (Isa. 10:7–11, 13–14), but God intended to humble his hypocritical, proud, and rebellious people (Isa. 10:5–6). They both intended to devastate Judah, though their reasons differed. Still, God empowered the Assyrians to do it (cf. Deut. 28:47–52).

Ahaz's successor was the faithful king Hezekiah, who vainly tried to turn his people back to God after his father had led them astray (see Isa. 36–37; 2 Kgs. 18–19). The Assyrian king Sennacherib rightly claimed that God had called him to attack Judah (Isa. 36:10). Thus, he "came up against all the defenced [fortified] cities of Judah, and took them" (Isa. 36:1). . . . Sennacherib glorified himself by crediting his mighty armies and superior leaders for his victory over Judah; he boasted, "By the strength of my hand I have done it, and by my wisdom; for I am prudent" (Isa. 10:13).

The Lord had foretold what would happen if the Assyrians took the honor to themselves: "When the Lord hath performed his whole work upon mount Zion and on Jerusalem, I will punish the fruit of the stout heart of the king of Assyria, and the glory of his high looks" (Isa. 10:12). . . . The Lord humbled Sennacherib by devastating his army and preserving Jerusalem intact, in answer to the faith of Hezekiah and his people (Isa. 37:33–37).

In chapter 10 (vv. 20–27), Isaiah again referred to the day when a remnant would escape and return, a theme reflected in the name of his son Shear-jashub (Isa. 7:3; 10:21–22).

(Keith A Meservy, *Studies in Scripture, Vol. 4,* ed. Kent P. Jackson,
[Salt Lake City: Deseret Book Co., 1993], 99–100.)

The "floods" [Isa. 28:2; 8:6–7] mentioned by Isaiah surely did come, engulfing the Kingdom of Israel and nearly swamping the Kingdom of Judah, as God's judgment began to play out on a nation that had largely abandoned Yahweh. . . .

The reason why God commissioned Assyria as the "rod of My anger" [2 Ne. 20:5] . . . [was because] Rehoboam had installed idolatrous calf worship as the official religion of the state, and all of the kings subscribed to it. Worse, the Ahab dynasty instituted Baal worship as the state religion. . . . The Kingdom of Judah also had its share of idolatry, and Baal worship made its inroads there too, especially in the days of Queen Athaliah, daughter of Ahab and Jezebel, and wife of King Jehoram. She spread the infection into the southern kingdom!

No doubt many Bible students think that Assyrian deportation of Hebrews from Palestine was much like Nazi deportations of Jews and political prisoners during World War II, where the goal was to inflict suffering and to exterminate. But that is not how the Assyrians treated their prisoners of war. In the first place, the Assyrians maintained no death camps or concentration camps. In the second place, the Assyrians wanted the labor of captive peoples; they did not seek to destroy them. They settled some deportees in cities to carry out building projects or provide skilled craftsmen. Others they sent to rural areas to maintain or expand the region of cultivation. Yet others peopled regions depopulated by punitive action after a rebellion (e.g., 2 Kgs. 17:24). . . .

The Assyrians took care that their deportees arrived in good condition. They fed them adequately on the way, provided footwear to protect their feet on the march, and made carts or donkeys available for the transport of women and children. Moreover, they did not break up families, but commonly deported families and whole communities as a group. . . .

The Assyrian army laid siege to Jerusalem during the reign of Hezekiah. Sennacherib, the Assyrian king, taunted the defenders of Jerusalem, threatening to deport them. But he also promised them that he would settle them in a new land similar to their own. And he could do that, for Assyria had a lot of similarities to Palestine. Moreover, Assyrians found it advantageous to settle deported peoples in lands similar to the ones they came from, since then they could immediately adapt to the agricultural possibilities of their new homes and quickly achieve maximum production.

Though Assyria was originally quite small, it was expansionistic. . . . In 732 B.C. Assyrians defeated Syria and deported the population of its capital, Damascus (2 Kgs. 16:9). In the same year Assyria annexed the northern part of Israel. About the same time she engaged in a running struggle with Babylon and established her mastery there with the destruction of Babylon in 689. Then she turned her attention to Egypt and subsequently to Elam (Persia) and for some decades controlled both kingdoms. So at Assyria's height as a nation during the seventh century, its control stretched from Iran or Persia on the east to Egypt on the west. . . .

Some ancient historians suggest that the Assyrians may not have been more cruel than other Near Eastern peoples; they just kept better records of their actions. . . . Life was cheap in the ancient

Near East, as it seems to be in the modern Near East, with the terrorist acts. . . . A Western or Christian mentality of the sanctity of life should not be imposed on the ancient Near East. . . . They were not unduly severe with defeated peoples who were for the first time coming under Assyrian control. They vented their full fury against the rebellious, however, with punishments so severe that they would not dare to rebel again. . . . Those who dared to rebel might have their hands chopped off or be skinned alive and have their skins publicly displayed on a pole.

The Assyrians often used their actions as propaganda or psychological warfare. If they could sufficiently impress their enemies with the terror of their might, possibly they would not have to fight. The opponents would just wilt before their awesome terror. That was, of course, the approach of Sennacherib's men before the walls of Jerusalem in Hezekiah's day (see 2 Kgs. 18 and Isa. 36). . . .

When Sennacherib's men stood before the walls of Jerusalem, they promised the people a new life in a pleasant land (2 Kgs. 18:32). In captivity they would not be thrown in jail or killed but would contribute to the Assyrian economy and to Assyrian power.

> (Howard F. Vos, *Nelson's New Illustrated Bible Manners and Customs*
> [Nashville: Thomas Nelson Publishers, 1999], 251–252; 260–61.)

The scattering occurred in three primary phases: (1) the Assyrian captivity of the northern kingdom of ten of the tribes of Israel (c. 722 B.C.); (2) the Babylonian captivity of the kingdom of Judah (c. 587 B.C.); and (3) the destruction of the Judean state and second temple by Rome (A.D. 66–70). While other cases of scattering occurred, these phases accomplished the Lord's purposes of punishing his covenant people by scattering them; but he mercifully made preparation for gathering their descendants in the latter years when they "come to the knowledge of their Redeemer" (2 Ne. 6:8–14).

> (Douglas A. Stewart, *Encyclopedia of Mormonism*,
> edited by Daniel H. Ludlow, 4 vols. [New York: Macmillan Publishing Co., 1992], 2:708.)

The Lord said that Israel's wickedness would cause him to send Assyria, "the rod of [his] anger" (2 Ne. 20:5), against his people "to take the spoil, and to take the prey, and to tread them down like the mire of the streets" (v.6). This prophecy was literally fulfilled when Assyria captured the northern kingdom of Israel and took the people captive to Assyria. This prophecy further revealed that when Assyria became lifted up in pride the Lord would "punish the fruit of the stout heart of the king of Assyria, and the glory of his high looks" (v. 12). The Lord made it clear that even though Assyria accomplished his purposes against Israel, they had no reason to be proud. As the ax cannot boast of itself against the one who uses it, so the Assyrians could not think of themselves as being higher than the Lord (see v. 15). Assyria was but an instrument in the hand of the Lord in fulfilling his purposes.

> (*Book of Mormon Student Manual, Religion 121 and 122*
> [Salt Lake City: The Church of Jesus Christ of Latter-day Saints, 1989], 33.)

For a time the confederated tribes were a united monarchy under Saul, David, and Solomon, but ultimately they divided into two major kingdoms. The kingdom to the north—which comprised 10 ? tribes, including the descendants of Joseph—retained the designation *Israel*. The kingdom to the south—made up primarily of the tribe of Judah—adopted the name of *Judah*. (See 1 Kgs. 11:31–32; 12:19–24.)

(Ezra Taft Benson, *Ensign*, Dec. 1976, 69.)

2 Ne. 20:2 **NEEDY, POOR, WIDOWS**
(Isa. 10:2; Acts 6:1–3; Tim. 5:3, 8; D&C 83:2–6;
136:8; James 1:27; D&C 104:15–18.)

The term *widows* is used 34 times in the scriptures. In 23 of these passages, the term refers to widows and the fatherless. I believe the Lord has a tender feeling toward widows and the fatherless, or orphans. He knows that they may have to rely more completely on Him than on others. Their prayers will be more personal and lasting, service to fellowmen more genuine, and faith greater. . . .

To you wonderful sisters who find yourselves as widows, please know that God loves you. You are the choice among the choice. . . . Dear sisters, your very lives, as an example of righteous living, continue to inspire younger family members to do better. You continue as teachers.

At some period in God's timetable, you will join your eternal companion and serve together, forever, in the great work in the spirit world.

For you young widows with ever-increasing family responsibilities, know that God is aware of your needs and that He will provide. Continue to exercise faith and good works. Faithful family and Church members will assist. Be willing to receive assistance from others as necessary. Your children will know that you provide them with a double measure of love. It is my testimony that our Heavenly Father will abundantly compensate your family with eternal blessings because of the goodness of your hearts.

To the family and friends of widows, God knows of your service and He may judge your works by how well you assist the widow. President James E. Faust once shared with the General Authorities a wonderful story about how neighbors and friends in a small farming community in central Utah treated the widows. They each had so many hours or minutes to take water turns to irrigate their home gardens. They agreed that they could each take a little less water so that the widows of the neighborhood could have more water for their gardens.

I recently observed five elderly widows drive together to a Church meeting in a modest car. They entered the meeting together and sat down beside each other. They seemed to draw strength and protection from one another. I felt the goodness of their noble lives as I watched their tender association with one another in the twilight of their lives.

Brothers and sisters, the Lord loves widows. I know that the leaders of the Church are concerned about the welfare of the widows. We members should care for and assist the widows within our family, home, ward, and neighborhood. I urge you young people—members of the Primary, youth, and young adults–to take the opportunity to assist and draw strength from the widows in your community.

(Elder Earl C. Tingey, *Ensign*, May 2000, 76–78.)

We hear reports from time to time of older men and women who, in the sunset of their lives, are neglected by their families and their neighbors. Those who are both poor and old often suffer doubly. . . . Please don't assume that such individuals will always make their needs known. Often those who need help most are the last to make it known.

The ones about whom I am particularly speaking are those who will suffer in silence because they are proud or because they do not know what to do. Surely sensitive home teachers, visiting teachers, quorum leaders, and bishops can be more effective in both ascertaining and responding to the needs of these individuals.

(Spencer W. Kimball, *The Teachings of Spencer W. Kimball*, ed. Edward L. Kimball [Salt Lake City: Bookcraft, 1982], 367–68.)

To be justified before God we must love one another . . . we must visit the fatherless and the widow in their affiction, . . . for such virtues flow from the great fountain of pure religion. . . . We can love our neighbor as ourselves, and be faithful in tribulation, knowing that the reward of such is greater in the kingdom of heaven. What a consolation! What a joy! Let me live the life of the righteous, and let my reward be like this!

(Joseph Smith, *History of the Church of Jesus Christ*, 2:229.)

Blessed of the Lord is Brother Whitney, even the Bishop of the Church of Latter-day Saints, . . . the time cometh that . . . he shall deal with a liberal hand to the poor and the needy, the sick and afflicted, the widow and the fatherless. And marvelously and miraculously shall the Lord his God provide for him, even that he shall be blessed with a fullness of the good things of this earth. . . . And it shall come to pass, that according to the measure that he meteth out with a liberal hand to the poor, so shall it be measured to him again by the hand of his God, even an hundred fold. Angels shall guard his house, and shall guard the lives of his posterity. . . . As a lion goeth forth among the lesser beasts, so shall the going forth of him be whom the Lord hath anointed to exalt the poor.

(Joseph Smith, *History of the Church of Jesus Christ*, 2:289.)

The rich cannot be saved without charity, giving to feed the poor.

(Joseph Smith, *History of the Church of Jesus Christ*, 4:608.)

The man who is hungry and destitute has as good a right to my food as any other person, and I should feel as happy in associating with him, if he had a good heart, as with those who have an abundance, or with the princes of the earth. They all are esteemed by me, not according to the wealth and position they hold, but according to the character they have. . . .

It is a disgrace to every man and woman that has sense enough to live, not to take care of their own relatives, their own poor.

(*Discourses of Brigham Young*, comp. John A. Widtsoe [Salt Lake City: Deseret Book Co., 1954], 317–18.)

When we begin to think of those whom we would help as being useful for something instead of being objects of pity, we will then begin to plan ways by which the . . . thriftiness of widowhood and the youthful vigor of the able-bodied might be utilized toward the solving of their own problems and for the blessing of the lives of those less fortunate than they. . . .

The Prophet Joseph Smith declared: "It has always been a cardinal teaching with the Latter-day Saints that a religion that has not the power to save people temporally and make them prosperous and happy here cannot be depended upon to save them spiritually and exalt them in the life to come." . . .

Said Brigham Young: "It is never any benefit to give out and out to man or woman, money, food, clothing or anything else, if they are able-bodied, and can work to earn what they need, when there is anything on earth for them to do. . . . To pursue a contrary course would ruin any community in the world and make them idlers. People trained in this way have no interest in working. . . . Teach this girl to do housework and that woman to sew and do other kinds of work . . . for the bone and sinew of men and women are the capital of the world" (Brigham Young, *J. D.,* 11:297).

(Harold B. Lee, *Decisions for Successful Living* [Salt Lake City: Deseret Book Co., 1973], 203–204.)

We urge you, particularly priesthood brethren and Relief Society sisters, to be sensitive to the needs of the poor, the sick, and the needy. We have a Christian responsibility to see that the widows and fatherless are assisted. "Pure religion and undefiled before God and the Father is this, to visit the fatherless and widows in their affliction, and to keep himself unspotted from the world" (James 1:27).

(Ezra Taft Benson, *The Teachings of Ezra Taft Benson* [Salt Lake City: Bookcraft, 1988], 449.)

2 Ne. 20:3   **WHAT WILL YE DO . . . ?**
                   (Isa. 10:3)

But the Lord wants Isaiah to ask these wicked judges and bureaucrats a question. What are they going to do in the coming crisis when destruction descends on them by an enemy who has come from afar? What good will their ill-gotten wealth be to them in that threatening situation? To whom will they flee for help? And since there is going to be a universal destruction of the wicked, to whom will they leave the glory of their inheritance?

(W. Cleon Skousen, *Isaiah Speaks to Modern Times* [Salt Lake City: Ensign Publishing Co., 1984], 231.)

2 Ne. 20:7   **HE MEANETH NOT SO**

(Isa. 10:7)

Of course, the Lord knew that Sennacherib had no intention of accomplishing GOD'S purposes. The intent of his heart would be to destroy, desolate, and cut off many nations which would lie in his path. He would do it for what he thought were his own purposes.

(W. Cleon Skousen, *Isaiah Speaks to Modern Times* [Salt Lake City: Ensign Publishing Co., 1984], 232.)

2 Ne. 20:8   **PRINCES ALTOGETHER KINGS**

(Isa. 10:8)

Assyria now boasts that even the commanders in its army are vassal kings. . . . Not only that, but he boasts of the ease with which he has gathered the wealth of the peoples and has claimed the whole earth as his dominion. In their fear none of the inhabitants gave any resistance, not even a "chirp."

(Sidney B. Sperry, *Book of Mormon Compendium* [Salt Lake City: Bookcraft, 1968], 214–15.)

2 Ne. 20:9–11   **CALNO AS CARCHEMISH, ETC.**

(Isa. 10:9–11)

In his pride, the Assyrian looks over his conquests. Carchemish (Fort of Chemosh) was the chief city of the Hittites from 1100 to 850 B.C. It was there that Pharaoh Necho was defeated in 605 B.C., five years before Lehi left Jerusalem. See Jer. 46:2; 2 Chron. 25:20).

The Assyrian king is represented as saying, Since I have made myself the master of kingdoms, the images of which were more powerful than those of Jerusalem and Samaria, why should I not gain possession of Jerusalem and her idols?

(George Reynolds and Janne M. Sjodahl, *Commentary on the Book of Mormon*, 7 vols., ed. Philip C. Reynolds [Salt Lake City: Deseret book Co., 1955–1961], 1:353.)

Sargon records how he conquered and destroyed these cities:

> The king's throne would be set up before the gates of the city and the prisoners would be paraded before him, led by the monarch of the captured town, who would undergo the most agonizing torture, such as having his eyes put out or confinement in a cage, until the king of Assyria set a term to his long-drawn agony. Sargon had the defeated king of Damascus burned alive before his eyes. The wives and daughters of the captured king were destined for the Assyrian harems and those who were not of noble blood were condemned to slavery. Meanwhile the soldiery had been massacring the population,

and brought the heads of their victims in into the king's presence, where they were counted up by the scribes. Not all the male prisoners were put to death, for the boys and craftsmen were led into captivity, where they would be assigned to the hardest tasks on the royal building projects, where the swamps which cover so much of Mesopotamia must have caused an enormously high rate of mortality. The remainder of the population were uprooted and sent to the other end of the empire. (Quoted in A. Heschel, *The Prophets* [New York: Jewish Publ. Soc. of America, 1962], 163.)

The arrogant boasting of Assyria would eventually bring God's wrath upon her, but only after she had completed her task against Jerusalem.

(Victor L. Ludlow, *Isaiah: Prophet, Seer, and Poet* [Salt Lake City: Deseret Book Co., 1982], 162–63.)

2 Ne. 20:12   I WILL PUNISH THE STOUT HEART
(Isa. 10:12; 2 Kgs. 19:32–37)

The Assyrians will attack Mount Zion, the hill upon which Solomon built his temple. (1 Kings 8:1). (This attack occurred in 701 B.C., under the Assyrian king Sennacherib). Yet the Lord will punish the king of Assyria for his "stout heart" and "high looks" (arrogance, pride, and boasting). This prophecy was fulfilled when a desolating sickness was sent into the Assyrian camps, causing many deaths, and the king was later slain by his own sons. (2 Kings 19:32–37; Isaiah 37:33–38.)

(Hoyt W. Brewster, Jr., *Isaiah Plain and Simple* [Salt Lake City: Deseret Book Co., 1995], 100.)

He describes Assyria as coming from the North; oppressive and ruthless; a law unto itself; militaristic and bent on world domination; imposing its yoke of servitude on other nations; encroaching on the world by degrees, swallowing up territories; and setting all the surrounding peoples in fear of it. When the world is ripe in iniquity, Assyria suddenly bursts forth like a flood. With its alliance of nations, it sweeps over the entire earth, conquering, destroying by fire and by the sword, leaving havoc and disaster in its wake—capturing the whole world. Only Zion/Jerusalem, a safe place for the Lord's righteous, does Assyria not conquer. Assyria invades even Egypt, the other great superpower; Assyria penetrates Egypt and ravages her land.

After a few years of war and oppression, Assyria lays siege to Zion/Jerusalem, where a remnant of Israel takes refuge. Then occurs Assyria's demise. Because of his covenant with Israel, and because the righteous of his people remain faithful through much trial and tribulation, the Lord utterly destroys the Assyrian army. The 185,000 men who perished overnight in the days of King Hezekiah . . . serve as the historical type of a latter-day Armageddon. . . . The first [kind of divine protection], based on the Sinai covenant, requires that all the Lord's army consist of righteous men. Joshua's army, at the conquest of Canaan, forms its historical type. The second kind of divine protection rests on the Davidic covenant. . . . This requires the exemplary righteousness of the Davidic king.

He merits the Lord's protection by proxy on behalf of those loyal to the king. King Hezekiah and the people who fled to Jerusalem from the Assyrians serve as its historical type.

(Avraham Gileadi, *The Book of Isaiah: A New Translation with Interpretive Keys from the Book of Mormon* [Salt Lake City: Deseret Book Co., 1988], 72–73.)

2 Ne. 20:14   **NEST—EGGS—PEEP**
                       (Isa. 10:14)

Israel is compared to a bird's nest, eggs, wings, and call. (See 3 Ne. 10:4–6; D&C 10:65; 29:1–2 for other examples of bird symbolism.) The eggs in the nest represent Israel's riches, which Assyria has raided. Israel's inability to move its wings or to make a peep signifies that it, like a little chick, is helpless before Assyria's ravening armies.

(Donald W. Parry, *Visualizing Isaiah*
[Provo, Utah: The Foundation for Ancient Research and Mormon Studies, 2001], 33.)

2 Ne. 20:15   **THE AXE BOAST ITSELF**
                       (Isa. 10:15; refer in *Latter-day Commentary on
                       the Book of Mormon,* Bassett, to Alma 39:2 & Morm. 3:9)

Not long after I was ordained a deacon, my bishop, Leon Walker, asked me into his office to give me an assignment. He handed me a bright key, the key to the chapel, and charged me with responsibility to help look after the building. I considered myself one of the most fortunate boys in the world to have an assignment from my priesthood president. I thought this would not be a difficult task. My home was just a one-minute bicycle ride away from the building. But I soon learned what I suppose all bishops know, and that is, everybody in the ward seems to have a key to the building. As soon as I had the building locked up of an evening, someone came along behind me and opened a door. As soon as I had opened a Primary classroom, some diligent soul was there behind me to lock it up again. I could hardly stay on top of that job.

But I began to learn then, as I have come to understand since, that any call, any service in our Lord's cause sanctifies us. Whether it is performed in the glare of the public eye or in a quiet corner known only to God is of no consequence. What matters is that we do serve, for by serving we keep our covenants with deity. . . .

I acknowledge that anything I may achieve will be by virtue of the power and the grace and the gift of God. I am not, in Isaiah's words, the axe that shall "boast itself against him that heweth therewith"; I am not the saw that shall "magnify itself against him that shaketh it" (Isaiah 10:15). With Nephi, "I know in whom I have trusted" (See 2 Ne. 4:19.)

(D. Todd Christofferson, *Ensign,* May 1993, 83.)

2 Ne. 20:17–19   TREES, BRIARS, AND THORNS
(Isa. 10:17–19; refer in this text to 2 Ne. 15:6)

Trees in general were highly valued by the inhabitants of the ancient Near East as sources of food, fuel, and building material. . . . The loftiness of trees, along with the great value men placed upon them, made trees an ideal metaphor for arrogance and materialism.

In the same fashion, characteristics of the lowly briars and thorns render them an appropriate metaphor for pride and worldliness. . . . All thistles . . . are invasive, noxious, and unruly, doing harm to any that would touch them–traits commonly found in the proud and worldly as well.

Isaiah coupled the lowly briars and thorns with the lofty trees of the forest to illustrate and foretell the fate of the ungrateful, rebellious, and worldly, be they rich or poor, great or small. For example, in speaking of the destruction of the boastful Assyrians, Isaiah prophesied that the flame of the Holy One would devour Assyria's thorns and briars "in one day" and also "consume the glory of his [Assyria's] forest," so that the remaining trees would be so few even a child could count them (see Isa. 10:17–19).

(Terry Ball, *Thy People Shall Be My People and Thy God My God:
The 22ⁿᵈ Annual Sidney B. Sperry Symposium* [Salt Lake City: Deseret Book Co., 1994], 23.)

The "forest" (people) of Assyria shall be destroyed so completely that a child will be able to count those ('trees') who remain. The Babylonians and Persians later fulfilled this prophesy, destroying completely the Assyrians as a nation and people.

(Hoyt W. Brewster, Jr., *Isaiah Plain and Simple* [Salt Lake City: Deseret Book Co., 1995], 102.)

2 Ne. 20:22–23   CONSUMPTION DECREED
(Isa. 10:22–23)

The Saints have not too much time to save and redeem their dead, and gather together their living relatives, that they may be saved also, before the earth will be smitten, and the consumption decreed falls upon the world.

(Joseph Smith, *Teachings of the Prophet Joseph Smith,*
comp. Jospeh Fielding Smith [Salt Lake City: Deseret Book Co., 1976], 330.)

2 Ne. 20:22   SAND OF THE SEA
(Isa. 10:22)

The Old Testament formula for an apostate people's return to God is found in 2 Chronicles 30:6–9. These verses speak of Israel's return to the promised land, to God through repentance, and to true temple worship. The expression "as the sands of the sea" recalls the Abrahamic covenant that speaks of Abraham's posterity becoming as numerous as the sands of the sea (Gen. 22:17; Abr. 3:14). Although the number of children of Israel will be exceedingly high, only a remnant will return. . . . The great stretch of sandy seashore next to the Mediterranean Sea together with the immense deserts of sand throughout the Near East have made sand the subject of many similes in the scriptures.

(Donald W. Parry, *Visualizing Isaiah*
[Provo, Utah: The Foundation for Ancient Research and Mormon Studies, 2001], 101.)

Isaiah declared that the people of Israel will have become so numerous that Jacob's descendants will be as the countless sands of the sea. He also hints that out of these many millions of heirs to the latter-day kingdom, only a "remnant" will elect to return. After that, God's great "consumption" or cleansing will take place so that the earth can overflow with righteousness.

(W. Cleon Skousen, *Isaiah Speaks to Modern Times* [Salt Lake City: Ensign Publishing Co., 1984], 236.)

2 Ne. 20:24–25   ZION
(Isa. 10:24–25; refer in this text to 2 Ne. 12:3 and 2 Ne. 14:5–6)

These verses are a plea to the people who will dwell in Zion in the future. The Zion spoken of by the Old Testament prophets was identified by the Prophet Joseph Smith as the whole of North and South America. . . . The "Assyrians" in verse 24 would thus symbolize the Gentiles who were inhabiting that land and were ruling over the blood of Israel scattered among them or living under their rule. The plea is for the Israelites to rely upon the Lord. While they may have trials and tribulations, these will be short-lived and the promised blessings of Israel will be restored.

(Monte S. Nyman, *Great Are the Words of Isaiah* [Salt Lake City: Bookcraft, 1980], 70.)

The whole of America is Zion itself from north to south, and is described by the Prophets, who declare that it is the Zion where the mountain of the Lord should be, and that it should be in the center of the land.

(Joseph Smith, *Teachings of the Prophet Joseph Smith*,
comp. Jospeh Fielding Smith [Salt Lake City: Deseret Book Co., 1976], 362.)

2 Ne. 20:26   SLAUGHTER OF MIDIAN
(Isa. 10:26; 9:4)

The Midianites sprang from Midian, a son of Abraham by Keturah, whom he married after the death of Sarah. But Abraham did not permit Midian's sons to inherit with Isaac. Instead he gave them gifts and sent them away "to the country of the east" (Gen. 2:6), which probably included the desert fringes of Moab, Edom, and parts of the Sinai Peninsula.

Midianites next appear as tribes who bought Joseph and sold him into slavery in Egypt (Gen. 37:25–36). Later as Moses fled from Egypt, he went to the land of Midian, where he married Zipporah, daughter of Jethro, a Midianite priest (Ex. 2:15–22; 3:1). Relations with the Midianites were therefore friendly, and Jethro helped Moses with certain organizational tasks (Ex. 18).

Midianites soon became enemies of Israel, however. Feeling threatened when Israel attempted to penetrate the Transjordan region at the end of the wilderness wanderings, they and the Moabites hired Baalam to curse Israel (Num. 22:4–7). When the curse did not succeed, the Midianites involved their women in an attempt to lead Israel into apostasy and initially succeeded. The judgment fell on the Midianites, associated Moabites, and defecting Israelites (Num. 25). Midianites were singled out for destruction (Num. 25:16–18). And Israel enjoyed a great victory over them (Num. 31).

Thereafter the Midianites remained adversaries of Israel, and during the period of the judges periodically harassed some of the Israelite tribes. During the days of Gideon they raided the stockpiles of new grain during harvest time, but Gideon dealt them an overwhelming defeat (Judges 7–8). Scripture later cited this defeat as an example of God's deliverance of His people from oppression (Ps. 83:9, 11; Isa. 9:4; 10:26).

(Howard F. Vos, *Nelson's New Illustrated Bible Manners and Custom,*
[Nashville: Thomas Nelson Publishers, 1999], 130.)

2 Ne. 20:28–34   ASSYRIAN MARCH TOWARD JERUSALEM
(Isa. 10:28–34)

Having given a message of hope and comfort to Israel's "remnant," he now gives us a prophetic but graphic description of the Assyrian invasion through towns or near towns on the northern approaches to Jerusalem. We do not know the exact location of all the towns mentioned, but suffice it to say that most of them were in the vicinity of Jerusalem. Aiath (Josh. 7:2) is supposed to have been about nine miles to the north and east of Jerusalem and about two miles northwest of Michmash, which in turn was a little over seven miles from the capital city of Judah. Migron was probably situated between Ai and Mishmash, but has not been identified. Ramath was located just a short distance north of Jerusalem, and Anathoth, the birthplace of Jeremiah, is about three miles northeast of the capital. Nob (city of priests; 1 Sam. 22:19) was obviously near Jerusalem (v. 32), near enough that an enemy leader could be seen waving his hand or shaking his fist at her. Many scholars think that it may have been situated on Mt. Scopus, a hill to the north of Jerusalem.

Isaiah describes the rapid advance of the enemy and pictures the fear and panic that grip the inhabitants of the towns and villages that lie in the immediate path of the Assyrians. In verse 32 we have the climax—at Jerusalem. . . .

Isaiah knows that the power of Israel's enemies is but temporary; he doubtless keeps constantly in mind the eventual redemption of a remnant of Israel free from enemy oppression. And so he ends this particular prophecy with a prediction of the sudden destruction of Assyria by the Lord. He uses the metaphor of a forest being cut down by the forester's cutting instrument. The Lord is the divine forester who cuts down and humbles the pride of the forest (Assyria). The boughs of the trees may represent the young men who are slain in battle. The tall trees of the forest would then represent the haughty ruling classes, and the thickets the common people (cf. 19:18; 12:12, 13). The Lord does his work with terrifying power. Some authorities think that these verses (33, 34) refer to the destruction of Judah, but the general context of the chapter convinces many others besides myself that the destruction of Assyria is the theme.

(Sidney B. Sperry, *Book of Mormon Compendium* [Salt Lake City: Bookcraft, 1968], 219–221.)

2 Ne. 20:30   CAUSE IT TO BE HEARD
(Isa. 10:30)

Scriptures recorded in all dispensations teach that we show our *love* of God as we *hearken* to His commandments and *obey* them. These actions are closely connected. In fact, the Hebrew language of the Old Testament in most instances uses the same term for both *hearkening* (to the Lord) and *obedience* (to His word). . . .

That term was . . . (shâma), which means "to hear intelligently. The term was used hundreds of times in the Hebrew Old Testament, as Israel was counseled to *hearken* to the word of the Lord and *obey* it.

Different terms were used in some instances in the Hebrew text whenever reference was made to hearing or responding *without* implied obedience. Examples:

"They have ears, but they *hear* not" (Ps. 135:17; see also 140:6; italics added) . . . (azan) to give ear—to listen. . . .

"Lift up thy voice, O daughter . . . cause it to be *heard*" (Isa. 10:30; italics added; see also Ps. 10:17). (qashav) to give heed.

(Russell M. Nelson, *Ensign*, May 1991, 24–25.)

2 Ne. 20:33–34   HIGH ONES HEWN DOWN
(Isa. 10:33–34)

Fulfillment of this prophecy can be seen in the subsequent conquest of Assyria by the Babylonians and the Medes, after which the proud Assyrians ceased to be a people.

(Terry Ball, *Thy People Shall Be My People and Thy God My God: The 22nd Annual Sidney B. Sperry Symposium* [Salt Lake City: Deseret Book Co., 1994], 23.)

2 Ne. 21   **ISAIAH VIEWS LATTER DAYS & MILLENNIAL CONDITIONS**
(Isa. 11; D&C 87:6; 63:51; 101:30–31; Isa. 51:6;
refer in this text to 2 Ne. 12:4, 11)

In addition to the Old Testament and Book of Mormon accounts, portions of these writings are found in the New Testament (Rev. 2:16; 5:5; 19:15; and Rom. 15:12) and the D&C (19:15; 113:1–6; and 133:26–29); and in Joseph Smith's history as found in the Pearl of Great Price, he tells us that the entire chapter of Isaiah 11 was quoted to him by the Angel Moroni (JS–H 1:40). Additionally, on several occasions the Prophet provided commentary on verses in this chapter. (See *TPJS*, 14–15, 71, 93, 316.)

(Hoyt W. Brewster, Jr., *Isaiah Plain and Simple* [Salt Lake City: Deseret Book Co., 1995], 107.)

Isaiah testified that "then the eyes of the blind shall be opened, and the ears of the deaf shall be unstopped. Then shall the lame man leap as an hart, and the tongue of the dumb sing" (Isa. 35:5–6). Great blessings will come to those who have been prisoners in their own bodies, which blessings will prepare the way for freedom to act upon their righteous desires. Along with blindness and deafness, all other physical hindrances will be removed.

(Craig J. Ostler, *Voices of Old Testament Prophets*:
The 26th Annual Sidney B. Sperry Symposium [Salt Lake City: Deseret Book Co., 1997], 76–77.)

The Millennium consists in this—every heart in the Church and Kingdom of God being united in one; the Kingdom increasing to the overcoming of everything opposed to the economy of heaven, and Satan being bound, and having a seal set upon him. All things else will be as they are now, we shall eat, drink, and wear clothing.

(Brigham Young, *Journal of Discourses*, 1:203.)

The Lord has said through his servants that during the millennium those who have passed beyond and have attained the resurrection will reveal in person to those who are still in mortality all the information which is required to complete the work of these who have passed from this life. Then the dead will have the privilege of making known the things they desire and are entitled to receive. In this way no soul will be neglected and the work of the Lord will be perfected.

(Joseph Fielding Smith, *Doctrines of Salvation: Sermons and Writings of Joseph Fielding Smith*,
ed. Bruce R. McConkie, 3 vols. [Salt Lake City: Bookcraft, 1954–1956], 3:65.)

[As to children born during the Millennium,] Elder Bruce R. McConkie wrote that as the Millennium proceeds, "Earth's main inhabitants . . . will be those who continue to come here from celestial realms to gain their bodies and to prepare themselves for immortal glory" (*Millennial Messiah*, 640). These are they who will be born during the Millennium, raised in millennial conditions, and "grow up without sin unto salvation" (D&C 45:58). These children "shall die an hundred years old" (Isa. 65:20), at which time they "shall be changed in the twinkling of an eye, and shall be caught up" (D&C 101:31) to dwell with other resurrected beings awaiting the end of the Millennium and the change of the earth to a celestial globe.

(Craig J. Ostler, *Voices of Old Testament Prophets*:
The 26th Annual Sidney B. Sperry Symposium [Salt Lake City: Deseret Book Co., 1997], 70–71.)

2 Ne. 21:1, 10   STEM, ROD, & ROOT
(Isa. 11:1, 10; D&C 113:1–6; JS–H 1:40;
Book of Mormon Compendium, Sperry, 223, 226–227)

Isaiah testifies of Christ as both the "stem of Jesse" (mortal Messiah) and the righteous judge (millennial Messiah). He further testifies of a rod and root of Jesse (Joseph Smith), "a servant in the hands of Christ, who is partly a descendant of Jesse as well as of Ephraim, or of the house of Joseph, on whom there is laid much power," a man "unto whom rightly belongs the priesthood, and the keys of the kingdom, for an ensign, and for the gathering of [the Lord's] people in the last days" (D&C 113:1–2, 4–6; cf. JS–H 1:40).

(Joseph Fielding McConkie and Robert L. Millet,
Doctrinal Commentary on the Book of Mormon, 4 vols. [Salt Lake City: Bookcraft, 1987–1992], 1:281.)

As to the identity of the Stem of Jesse, the revealed word says: "Verily thus saith the Lord: It is Christ" (D&C 133:1–2). . . . The King who shall reign personally upon the earth during the Millennium shall be the Branch who grew out of the house of David. He shall execute judgment and justice in all the earth because he is the Lord Jehovah, even him whom we call Christ.

Through Zechariah the Lord spoke similarly: "Thus saith the Lord of hosts: . . . I will bring forth my servant the BRANCH . . . I will remove the iniquity of the land in one day [meaning that the wicked shall be destroyed and the millennial era of peace and righteousness commence]. In that day, saith the Lord of hosts, shall ye call every man his neighbour under the vine and under the fig tree" (Zech. 3:7–10). Of that glorious millennial day the Lord says also: "Behold the man whose name is The BRANCH; and he shall grow up out of his place, and he shall build the temple of the Lord: Even he shall build the temple of the Lord; and he shall bear the glory, and shall sit and rule upon his throne" (Zech. 6:12–13).

That the Branch of David is Christ is perfectly clear. We shall now see that he is also called David, that he is a new David, an Eternal David, who shall reign forever on the throne of his ancient ancestor. . . .

David's temporal throne fell long centuries before our Lord was born, and that portion of Israel which had not been scattered to the ends of the earth was in bondage to the iron yoke of Rome. But the promises remain. The eternal throne shall be restored in due course with a new David sitting thereon, and he shall reign forever and ever. . . .

How glorious shall be the coming day when the second David, who is Christ, reigns on the throne of the first David; when all men shall dwell safely; when the earth shall be dotted with temples; and when the gospel covenant shall have full force and validity in all the earth!

(Bruce R. McConkie, *The Promised Messiah* [Salt Lake City: Deseret Book Co., 1978], 192–95.)

"*Root of Jesse.*" The Doctrine and Covenants identifies this individual as "a descendant of Jesse, as well as of Joseph, unto whom rightly belongs the priesthood, and the keys of the kingdom, for an ensign, and for the gathering of my people in the last days" (D&C 113:5–6). The apostle Paul mistakenly identified the "root" as Christ (Rom. 15:12). Dr. Sidney B. Sperry explained the reason for this mistake:

"Examination of Romans 15:12 demonstrates that Paul was closely following the Septuagint LXX, Greek translation) text of Isaiah 11:10 rather than the Hebrew. As a matter of fact, the LXX version is only a paraphrase of the original Hebrew. We notice that the Greek version of Isaiah 11:1 translates the Hebrew text, 'stem of Jesse,' as the 'root of Jesse' and uses the same phrase in Isaiah 11:10. Of interest is the fact that the Greek word *riza* (root) is used in both verses to translate different Hebrew words. Paul would be quick to discern that the 'root of Jesse' of the LXX text of Isaiah 11:1–5 was the Christ. And when he observed that the phrase 'root of Jesse' was used again in verse 10, he would naturally assume that it, too, had reference to the Christ. Hence the reason for his quotation in Romans 15:12."

Who, then, is the "root of Jesse"? It appears that the Prophet Joseph Smith is both the "rod" and the "root" that will come from Jesse . . .

However, Victor Ludlow suggested that "Joseph Smith might not be the only 'root of Jesse' in these last days. Many presidents of the Church have been related to him by blood, and all have held the priesthood and the keys of the kingdom that he held . . . The 'root of Jesse' could also be that particular prophet who will hold the keys when Christ returns to preside personally over his kingdom. The term could even represent the office of the president of the Church. In any case, the 'root of Jesse' designates a great leader in the Church of Jesus Christ in this dispensation."

(Hoyt W. Brewster, Jr., *Isaiah Plain and Simple* [Salt Lake City: Deseret Book Co., 1995], 112–13.)

The discussion of the tree, its rod, stem, branch, and roots in Isaiah 11:1 is a continuation of the prophecy regarding the cutting down of the forest from the previous chapter. The Lord will "lop the bough," hew down the "high ones," and "cut down the thickets of the forest" (Isa. 10:33–34). The Lord, or forester, will trim the boughs and cut down the trees to clean out the forest and prepare the way for the stem of Jesse to flourish. This trimming and cutting symbolizes the Lord's severing the power and glory of unrighteous leaders and their nations.

The stem of Jesse is Christ. The Doctrine and Covenants is explicit: "Who is the Stem of Jesse spoken of in the 1st, 2d, 3d, 4th, and 5th verses of the 11th chapter of Isaiah? Verily thus saith the Lord: It is Christ" (D&C 113:1–2). The Davidic royal family, then, is compared to the stump or "stem" of an olive tree. Just as an olive tree is able to send forth a shoot or "rod," so would the family of David send forth a leader who would have wisdom, understanding, counsel, might, and knowledge (Isa. 11:2). That leader is Jesus Christ.

(Donald W. Parry, *Visualizing Isaiah*
[Provo, Utah: The Foundation for Ancient Research and Mormon Studies, 2001], 80.)

2 Ne. 21:1–5   MILLENNIAL CHRIST
(Isa. 11:1–5)

It is clear from the Book of Mormon and the Doctrine and Covenants that the principal character in this passage is Jesus Christ. Joseph Smith, recalling the visit of the angel Moroni on the night of September 21, 1823, wrote that Moroni "quoted the eleventh chapter of Isaiah, saying that it was about to be fulfilled."

The imagery of the tree in this passage is a natural continuation of the figure used in relationship to Christ and the children of Israel throughout the scriptures. . . . Heaven's Forester carefully trims his trees (consider Zenos' allegory quoted by Jacob) and in this manner cleans out the evil of his forest. With God's cleansing of Israel—cutting down boughs here, leveling thickets there, especially the lofty and arrogant ones—all that remains of the people of covenant at this reading is a stump. This prepares the way for flourishing new shoots to come out of the heritage of Jesse. . . .

There is warning for all in the language here that speaks of God smiting the earth with the rod of his mouth and the very breath of his lips slaying the wicked. . . . In those last days Christ's judgment will be the truth he speaks and an acknowledgment of that truth from all who hear him.

In that millennial moment the Messiah will usher in the peace for which all the righteous have wished, worked, and waited."

(Jeffrey R. Holland, *Christ and the New Covenant* [Salt Lake City: Deseret Book Co., 1997], 86–87.)

2 Ne. 21:4; 2 Ne. 30:9   SMITE THE EARTH WITH THE ROD OF HIS MOUTH
(Isa. 11:4; 16:5; D&C 29:11–12; 43:29; 38:21–22)

When that time shall come, the "earth shall be full of the knowledge of the Lord, as the waters cover the sea." Wickedness shall be destroyed, for with righteousness shall Jehovah "judge the poor, and reprove with equity for the meek of the earth: and he shall smite the earth with the rod of his mouth, and with the breath of his lips shall he slay the wicked."

In that day there shall be *no "divided Christianity." All who will not repent and receive the gospel shall soon be removed, and they who shall remain shall learn to worship the true and living God in spirit and in truth. The Church of Jesus Christ shall have sway over all the earth, for Christ shall be the King and Deliverer.* Peace shall prevail both among men and among beasts. Satan shall be bound and his dominion, which he has held by usurpation and fraud since the beginning of the earth's temporal existence, shall come to an end. The rightful King shall reign and his saints shall possess the kingdom according to the vision of Daniel (Isa. 65:17–25; D&C 101:23–31; Dan. 7:14, 22, 27).

Jerusalem shall become a righteous city when Israel is gathered and redeemed. Zion also shall be cleansed of all iniquity, and in that day, when Christ shall rule, the word of the Lord to Isaiah shall be fulfilled, "for out of Zion shall go forth the law, and the word of the Lord from Jerusalem" (Isa. 2:3).

(Joseph Fielding Smith, Doctrines of Salvation: Sermons and Writings of Joseph Fielding Smith,
ed. Bruce R. McConkie, 3 vols. [Salt Lake City: Bookcraft, 1954–1956], 1:168–69.)

For the righteous and the meek, the judgment shall be a blessing. The coming of Jesus Christ as Judge will improve the justice system of nations and peoples. The courts will not be influenced by the wickedness of corrupt laws and judges that are now part of the fallen earth. As the Prophet Joseph Smith explained, "The world has had a fair trial for six thousand years; the Lord will try the seventh thousand Himself; 'He whose right it is, will possess the kingdom, . . . Satan will be bound, and the works of darkness destroyed; . . . and he that fears the Lord will alone be exalted in that day.'" (Smith, *History of the Church*, 5:64–65; see also Isa. 28:17.) The hopes and dreams of good people through the ages will be realized as righteousness becomes the standard of judgment and equity is bestowed upon all of the inhabitants of the earth. . . .

Isaiah wrote that those who have not known the Lord's name will also be spared at the beginning of the Millennium (see Isa. 66:19). Those who have not known the name of Jesus Christ, or the non-Christian peoples, are referred to as heathen nations. Concerning those who have not known his name, God revealed further clarification to the Prophet Joseph Smith saying that "the heathen nations [shall] be redeemed, and they that knew no law shall have part in the first resurrection; and it shall be tolerable for them" (D&C 45:54). It should be remembered that those who lived in wickedness in mortality or "the spirits of men who are to be judged, and are found under condemnation . . . live not again until the thousand years are ended" (D&C 88:100–101). But many among the heathen nations will be able to abide a terrestrial law and enjoy the blessings of the Millennium. They are good, honorable people who have been "blinded by the craftiness of men" (D&C 76:75). Further, they will receive a testimony of Jesus in the millennial day or will have received this testimony as spirits prior to coming forth in the resurrection from the dead (D&C 76:72–74).

(Craig J. Ostler, Voices of Old Testament Prophets:
The 26th Annual Sidney B. Sperry Symposium [Salt Lake City: Deseret Book Co., 1997], 65–66, 68–69, 83.)

During all these years men dwelling in mortality will have the privilege of associating with those who have received their resurrection. Our Lord and Savior will be a familiar figure among the righteous saints. Instruction will be given by resurrected prophets. How could wickedness remain under such conditions? Those who have passed through the resurrection will not, however, dwell with those in mortality. They will not stay in earthly, or human homes nor sleep in the beds of mortals. Such a thing would be inconsistent. Joseph Smith has said:

> Christ and the resurrected Saints will reign over the earth during the thousand years. They will not probably dwell on the earth, but will visit it when they please, or when it is necessary to govern it. There will be wicked men on the earth during the thousand years. The heathen nations who will not come up to worship will be visited with the judgments of God, and must eventually be destroyed from the earth. . . .

The question naturally will arise, if the wicked are to be destroyed when Christ comes, then how can there be wicked men on the earth during the Millennium, as stated by Joseph Smith and Isaiah? It is quite evident that the "wickedness" during that time will be among those who are heathen, or have not come into the Church, and their wickedness consists of failure to receive the Gospel of Jesus Christ . . . (D&C 84:50–53).

Men will be free from the temptations of Satan; peace will be in the hearts of all men, and it is decreed that in time all will receive the truth, for the Gospel is to cover the earth as the waters do the sea.

(Joseph Fielding Smith, *The Way to Perfection* [Salt Lake City: Deseret Book Co., 1968], 312–14.)

2 Ne. 21:5   RIGHTEOUSNESS . . . THE GIRDLE OF HIS LOINS
(Isa. 21:5)

If the tunic was ungirded it would interfere with a person's ability to walk freely, and so a girdle was always worn when leaving home for any kind of a journey (See 2 Kgs. 4:29; Acts 12:8). There were and are today two kinds of girdles. One, a common variety, is of leather, usually six inches broad and furnished with clasps. This was the kind of girdle worn by Elijah (2 Kgs. 1:8), and by John the Baptist (Matt. 3:4). The other, a more valuable variety, is of linen (See Jer. 13:1), or sometimes of silk or embroidered material. It is generally a handbreadth wide. The girdle served as a pouch in which to keep money (2 Sam. 18:11) and other things that might be needed (Mark 6:8). The girdle was used to fasten a man's sword to his body (1 Sam. 25:13). . . .

The Scriptures often make symbolic use of the girdle. When Jesus said to His disciples: "Let your loins be girded about" (Luke 12:35), it was as if He had said: "Be as men who have a long race to run; gather up the folds of your flowing robes, and fasten them with your girdle; that nothing may keep you back or impede your steps." In Bible language, "to be girded" means: "to be ready for action" (cf. Ps. 18:39) . . . Paul calls truth to be the Christian's girdle in his warfare with Satan (Eph. 6:14).

(Fred H. Wight, *Manners and Customs of Bible Lands* [Chicago: Moody Press, 1953], 93–94.)

2 Ne. 21:6   **A LITTLE CHILD SHALL LEAD THEM**
(Isa. 21:6; Ps. 8:2; Matt. 21:16; Alma 32:23; refer in *Latter-day Commentary on the Book of Mormon,* Bassett, to 3 Ne. 17:11–24)

Inspired children often show the way through the wilderness. . . . Children often have the "thoughts and [the] intents of [their] hearts" focused on the Master. Though not full of years, such children are full of faith! . . .

It has been a privilege to seal several adopted children to Nan and Dan Barker, now of Arizona. Some time ago Nate, then just over three, said: "Mommy, there is another little girl who is supposed to come to our family. She has dark hair and dark eyes and lives a long way from here."

The wise mother asked, "How do you know this?"

"Jesus told me, upstairs."

> The mother noted, "We don't have an upstairs," but quickly sensed the significance of what had been communicated. After much travail and many prayers, the Barker family were in a sealing room in the Salt Lake Temple in the fall of 1995—where a little girl with dark hair and dark eyes, from Kazakhstan, was sealed to them for time and eternity. Inspired children still tell parents "great and marvelous things" (3 Ne. 26:14).

Benjamin Ballam is the special, spina bifida child of Michael and Laurie Ballam. He has been such a blessing to them and many others. Also spiritually precocious, Benjamin is a constant source of love and reassurance. Having had 17 surgeries, resilient Benjamin knows all about hospitals and doctors. Once, when an overwhelmed attendant became vocally upset—not at Benjamin, but over stressful circumstances—little three-year-old Benjamin exemplified the words of another Benjamin about our need to be childlike and "full of love" (Mosiah 3:19). Little Benjamin reached out, tenderly patted the irritated attendant, and said, "I love you anyway." . . . No wonder . . . in certain moments we feel children are our spiritual superiors. . . .

Elder Craig Zwick and I shared a precious moment in Fortaleza, Brazil, where we were privileged to bless a special seven-year-old boy who was dying of leukemia. His names—Jared Ammon—tell you much about his parents and family. . . . Jared Ammon's faithful 14-year-old sister held him in her arms. His stomach was so severely swollen. When the stake president lifted the oxygen mask to ask if he would like a blessing, Jared said, "Yes, please." It was a privilege to bless him and to call him to serve beyond the veil. Tears flowed, for the Spirit was strong. The oxygen mask was then lifted again, and Jared Ammon was asked if there was anything else we could do for him. Jared meekly requested that we sing for him "I Am a Child of God" (*Hymns,* no. 301). Weepingly, we responded to a submissive Jared Ammon's last request, and two hours later he was released from this life.

Before emplaning the next day, we went to the viewing at the chapel. His wonderful parents were full of faith, composed, and reverently "willing to submit" (Mosiah 3:19). The sister who held Jared plans to serve a mission later on this side of the veil while Jared serves on the other.

Brothers and sisters, no wonder the divine direction is for each of us to "becometh as a child" (Mosiah 3:19) . . . Only "after the trial of [our] faith" does the full witness come; meanwhile, often "a little child shall lead [us]" (Ether 12:6; Isa. 11:6).

(Neal A. Maxwell, *Ensign,* May 1996, 69–70.)

We ourselves can learn from our children and grandchildren. . . . Our grandson, six-year-old Jeffrey Monson Dibb, . . . along with his girlfriend, went for a walk one day. They marched up the front steps of a home, not knowing who lived there or what affiliation they might have with the Church. They knocked on the front door, and a woman answered. Without the slightest hesitation, Jeff Dibb said to her, "We are the visiting home teachers. May we come in?" They were ushered into the living room and were asked to be seated. With total faith the children addressed the woman, "Do you have a treat for us?" What could she do? She produced a treat, and they had a nice conversation. The impromptu teachers departed uttering a sincere "Thank you."

"Come back again," they heard the woman say, with a smile on her face.

"We will," came the reply.

The parents of the two youngsters heard of the incident. I am certain they were restrained in counseling the little ones. Perhaps they remembered the words from the scriptures: "And a little child shall lead them."

(Thomas S. Monson, *Ensign*, Nov. 1997, 19.)

You, my sisters, set the example through your lives and through your teachings that influence children to set proper examples for others. "A little child shall lead them" (Isaiah 11:6). No one is too young to exert influence. We begin to lead others, appreciably, as soon as we have character of our own. There is a certain innocence of heart, purity of soul, and refinement of feeling peculiar to children, to youth, which affects other people, ofttimes more vitally and potently than we are accustomed to think. These are mature spirits in infant bodies, in child bodies—precious, eternal souls. Let us ever consider them as such. So, as you teach these children, remember this is our first obligation, to implant in their hearts a testimony of the divinity of this great work.

(Ezra Taft Benson, *The Teachings of Ezra Taft Benson* [Salt Lake City: Bookcraft, 1988], 551.)

Last summer I received a letter from a woman who has emerged from a long period of Church inactivity. She is ever so anxious for her husband, who as yet is not a member of the Church, to share the joy she now feels.

She wrote of a trip which she, her husband, and their three sons made from the family home to Grandmother's home in Idaho. While driving through Salt Lake City, they were attracted by the message which appeared on a billboard. The message invited them to visit Temple Square. Bob, the nonmember husband, made the suggestion that a visit would be pleasant. The family entered the visitors' center, and Father took two sons up a ramp that one called "the ramp to heaven." Mother and three-year-old Tyler were a bit behind the others, they having paused to appreciate the beautiful paintings which adorned the walls. As they walked toward the magnificent sculpture of Thorvaldsen's *Christus*, tiny Tyler bolted from his mother and ran to the base of the *Christus*, while exclaiming, "It's Jesus! It's Jesus!" As Mother attempted to restrain her son, Tyler looked back toward her and his father and said, "Don't worry. He likes children."

After departing the center and again making their way along the freeway toward Grandmother's, Tyler moved to the front seat next to his father. Dad asked him what he liked best about their adventure on Temple Square. Tyler smiled up at him and said, "Jesus."

"How do you know that Jesus likes you, Tyler?"

Tyler, with a most serious expression on his face, looked up at his father's eyes and answered, "Dad, didn't you see his face?" Nothing else needed to be said.

As I read this account, I thought of the statement from the book of Isaiah: "And a little child shall lead them" (Isa. 11:6).

(Thomas S. Monson, *Ensign*, May 1990, 53.)

One who fulfilled in his life this admonition of the Savior was a missionary, Thomas Michael Wilson. . . . When he was but a teenager, and he and his family were not yet members of the Church, he was stricken with cancer, followed by painful radiation therapy, and then blessed remission. . . . The family began to look to religion to help them through this time of tribulation. Subsequently they were introduced to the Church and baptized. After accepting the gospel, young Brother Wilson yearned for the opportunity of being a missionary. A mission call came for him to serve in the Utah Salt Lake City Mission. . . .

Elder Wilson's missionary companions described his faith as like that of a child. . . . After eleven months, illness returned. Bone cancer now required the amputation of his arm and shoulder. Yet he persisted in his missionary labors. . . .

I learned that an investigator whom Elder Wilson had taught was baptized at the baptistry on Temple Square but then wanted to be confirmed by Elder Wilson, whom she respected so much. She, with a few others, journeyed to Elder Wilson's bedside in the hospital. There, with his remaining hand resting upon her head, Elder Wilson confirmed her a member of The Church of Jesus Christ of Latter-day Saints.

Elder Wilson continued month after month his precious but painful service as a missionary. . . .

Elder Wilson's physical condition deteriorated. The end drew near. He was to return home. He asked to serve but one additional month. . . . Like a child trusting implicitly its parents, Elder Wilson put his trust in God. . . . His parents, Willie and Julia Wilson, and his brother Tony came to Salt Lake City to help their son and brother home to Alabama. However, there was yet a prayed-for, a yearned-for, blessing to be bestowed. The family invited me to come with them to the Jordan River Temple, where those sacred ordinances which bind families for eternity, as well as for time, were performed.

I said good-bye to the Wilson family. I can see Elder Wilson yet as he thanked me for being with him and his loved ones. He said, "It doesn't matter what happens to us in this life as long as we have the gospel of Jesus Christ and live it." What courage. What confidence. What love. The Wilson family made the long trek home to Lafayette, where Elder Thomas Michael Wilson slipped from here to eternity. . . .

Elder Thomas Michael Wilson was buried with his missionary name tag in place.

When Elder Wilson's mother and his father visit that rural cemetery and place flowers of remembrance on the grave of their son, I feel certain they will remember the day he was born, the pride they felt, and the genuine joy that was theirs. This tiny child they will remember became the mighty man who later brought to them the opportunity to achieve celestial glory. Perhaps on these pilgrimages, when emotions are close to the surface and tears cannot be restrained, they will again thank God for their missionary son, who never lost the faith of a child, and then ponder deep within their hearts the Master's words, "And a little child shall lead them" (Isa. 11:6).

(Thomas S. Monson, *Ensign*, May 1990, 53.)

2 Ne. 21:6–9   A NEW EDEN
(Isa. 11:6–9; 65:25; Abr. 4:29–30; D&C 101:26, 29)

Wolf/leopard/lion/lamb/kid/calf. Six animals are listed (not counting the fatling, see below); three are wild carnivores (*wolf, leopard, lion*) that feed on the three tame animals (*lamb, kid, calf*). The wild animals, which are ferocious, aggressive, and vicious, are a threat to mankind; the tame animals are docile, submissive, and useful to man. This passage may be taken literally; or the wolf, leopard, and lion may represent those who foment war and murder; the lamb, kid, and calf may symbolize meek and peaceful people.

Fatling. The King James Version translation of *fatling* is probably incorrect. The Jerusalem Bible suggests "calf and lion cub feed together," replacing *fatling* with the verb *feed*.

Little child shall lead them. Small children will not only feel safe among the ferocious beasts but will have control over them and lead them.

Cow/bear/lion/ox. Isaiah continues to compare wild, carnivorous animals (*bear* and *lion*) with tame animals (*cow* and *ox*). His prophecy that the lion will pasture like the ox suggests that there will be no shedding of blood during the Millennium by man or beast. During the Millennium, "the enmity of man, and the enmity of beasts, yea, the enmity of all flesh, shall cease from before my face" (D&C 101:26).

Their young ones. This refers to the offspring of the cow and the bear and indicates that the subsequent generations of beasts will have no hostilities toward one another. This peaceful state of affairs, wherein no blood is shed, will endure. . . .

Both the nursing infant and the weaned toddler are completely helpless in the face of danger, but during the Millennium, both will be able to play at the asp (possibly the cobra) and the cockatrice's (possibly the viper's) dens, for poisonous snakes that once harmed and destroyed will be harmless. The curse between the seed of the woman (the child) and the serpent (Gen. 3:15) will be gone. The serpents here call to mind "that old serpent, called the Devil, and Satan" (Rev. 12:9), whose intent it is to harm and destroy the souls of mankind. Satan, however, will be bound during the Millennium, with all of his angels, so that peaceful conditions can hold sway.

They shall not hurt nor destroy in all my holy mountain. Enmity will be removed from the earth, and peace, love, and kindness will be the rule. *Holy mountain* may refer to the entire earth in its temple-like condition.

(Donald W. Parry, Jay A. Parry, and Tina M. Peterson,
Understanding Isaiah [Salt Lake City: Deseret Book Co., 1998], 119–20.)

"Isaiah often equates the growing wickedness of the world with the brutal and wasteful exploitation of nature, which has reached an alltime climax in the present generation. We all know his most poetic lines: "The leopard shall lie down with the kid, the calf and the young lion, the fatling together, and a little child shall lead them. The cow and the bear shall feed, their young ones lie down together. The lion shall eat straw like the ox." In my school days this was the prize illustration of the unrealistic Isaiah, zoological nonsense. It was not the "nature red in tooth and claw" of our own neo-Darwinian world. Since then a lot has been learned about the true nature of certain savage beasts.

(Hugh W. Nibley, "Great Are the Words of Isaiah," *Sidney B. Sperry Symposium*
[Provo, Utah: Religious Instruction, BYU, January 28, 1978], 206.)

The peace that will exist among all creatures on the earth is exciting. Flesh-eating and plant-eating animals will be at peace with each other, because all living creatures in that day will be herbivorous, as they were in the Garden of Eden.

(Keith A Meservy, *Studies in Scripture, Vol. 4,* ed. Kent P. Jackson [Salt Lake City: Deseret Book Co., 1993], 101.)

[The following occurred while Zion's Camp was on the march from Kirtland to Missouri.] In pitching my tent we found three massasaugas or prairie rattlesnakes, which the brethren were about to kill, but I said, "Let them alone—don't hurt them! How will the serpent ever lose its venom, while the servants of God possess the same disposition, and continue to make war upon it? Men must become harmless before the brute creation, and when men lose their viscious dispositions and cease to destroy the animal race, the lion and the lamb can dwell together, and the sucking child can play with the serpent in safety." The brethren took the serpents carefully on sticks and carried them across the creek. I exhorted the brethren not to kill a serpent, bird, or an animal of any kind during our journey unless it became necessary in order to preserve ourselves from hunger.

(Joseph Smith, *Teachings of the Prophet Joseph Smith*,
comp. Joseph Fielding Smith [Salt Lake City: Deseret Book Co., 1976], 71.)

One of the instructions given by the Prophet during this journey was that his brethren should not kill an animal of any kind, unless it became absolutely necessary to save themselves from starvation. On one occasion . . . the men saw three rattlesnakes and were about to kill them, but Joseph forbade the act. He asked the elders how would the serpent ever lose its venom while the servants of God made war upon it with desire to kill. He said: "Men themselves must first become harmless before they can expect the brute creation to be so. When man shall lose his own vicious disposition and cease to destroy the inferior animals, the lion and lamb may dwell together and the suckling child play with the serpent in safety." It was a deep philosophy and contrary to the preconceived notions and early lessons of his brethren; but they obeyed. And soon they experienced the truth of his words. One of the members of the camp by the name of Solomon Humphrey lay down on the prairie one day to rest. He fell asleep with his hat in hand. While he slumbered a large rattlesnake crawled up and coiled between him and his hat, and when Elder Humphrey awoke he found the serpent's head not a foot from his own. He did not harm it, and when some of his brethren would have killed it, he stayed their hands, saying: "No, I will protect him, for he and I have had a good nap together." Although the rattlesnake was roused it made no effort to strike.

(George Q. Cannon, *Life of Joseph Smith the Prophet,* [Salt Lake City: Deseret Book Co., 1972], 174–75.)

During the general conference when we were sustained, President Gordon B. Hinckley described some of the terrible atrocities that have been inflicted on children throughout the world. We read in news-papers and periodicals of the evil influences that are invading our homes.

As a new and very concerned Primary presidency, we prayed and searched the scriptures and were led to a verse in Isaiah that describes conditions during the Millennium: "They shall not hurt nor destroy in all my holy mountain: for the earth shall be full of the knowledge of the Lord" (Isa. 11:9). That was exactly what we wanted to have happen. We didn't want any child to be hurt or destroyed, but we didn't want to wait for the Millennium. We wanted that to happen right now. If our Primaries were full of the knowledge of the Lord, if our homes were full of the knowledge of the Lord, there would be peace and righteousness and the children would not be hurt in any way. . . .

The world is not a safe place. It is not a place where children will feel peace, hope, and direction unless they are taught to love and follow the Savior. Please help them know that these great blessings can be theirs, and show them what they need to do to receive these blessings."

(Patricia P. Pinegar, *Ensign*, Nov. 1999, 67.)

I opened the Old Testament randomly and . . . came upon a prophecy of Zechariah regarding the city of Jerusalem in the millennial day: "And the streets of the city shall be full of boys and girls playing in the streets thereof" (Zech. 8:5). That verse for me has ever since personified the joy and peace of the earth's Sabbath Day—a time to come in which children will grow up free from fear, from neglect and abuse, from darkness and ignorance; a time in which the little ones of the world will live under the seal of a higher law and a loving Lord. I yearn for the day when in every village and city of the world, boys and girls will play in innocence, and every child know the peace of a happy home. For me, that is the Millennium.

(Bruce D. Porter, *The King of Kings* [Salt Lake City: Deseret Book Co., 2000], 181.)

2 Ne. 21:9   **THE EARTH FULL OF KNOWLEDGE**
                        (Isa. 11:9; 54:13)

Advances in communication and travel during this last century have hastened the pace at which the word of the Lord goes out from Zion. (See Micah 4:2.) I feel much like Isaiah, who spoke of our time, when "the earth shall be full of the knowledge of the Lord, as the waters cover the sea" (Isa. 11:9). I believe that this marvelous outpouring of knowledge has heightened our ability to take the Lord's saving message to the world, "that repentance and remission of sins should be preached in his name among all nations." (Luke 24:47.)

(James E. Faust, *Ensign*, May 1999, 19.)

[2 Ne. 30:8.] Has he fulfilled that promise? If there be anybody in this house past seventy-five years of age who will take the time to think of what has occurred since the Book of Mormon was first published, he will discover that almost every implement, almost every convenience now enjoyed by mankind, has come since the Book of Mormon issued from the press in the year 1830. We are witnesses this day that in a hundred years this world has made progress along most lines greater than in all the previous centuries since the earth was created and our first parents came upon it. The Lord said he would commence his work among the nations. Man had had his trial; men for thousands of years had worked at it. But when the Lord set his hand and when he began to quicken the minds of men by the inspiration of his holy power men began to work out wonderful inventions that have changed the entire condition of this world. I say to you that after a hundred years we are living in a new world. But the work of the Lord has only just begun.

(George Albert Smith, *Conference Report*, Apr. 1930, 67–68.)

In our day we are experiencing an explosion of knowledge about the world and its people. But the people of the world are not experiencing a comparable expansion of knowledge about God and his plan for his children. On that subject, what the world needs is not more scholarship and technology but more righteousness and revelation.

I long for the day prophesied by Isaiah when "the earth shall be full of the knowledge of the Lord" (Isa. 11:9; 2 Ne. 21:9). In an inspired utterance, the Prophet Joseph Smith described the Lord's "pouring down knowledge from heaven upon the heads of the Latter-day Saints" (D&C 121:33). This will not happen for those whose "hearts are set so much upon the things of this world, and aspire to the honors of men." (v. 35) . . . The Lord makes this great promise to the faithful:

> "The doctrine of the priesthood shall distil upon thy soul as the dews from heaven.

> "The Holy Ghost shall be thy constant companion, and thy scepter an unchanging scepter of righteousness and truth; and thy dominion shall be an everlasting dominion, and without compulsory means it shall flow into thee forever and ever" (D&C 121:45–46).

(Dallin H. Oaks, *Ensign*, May 1989, 30.)

The gospel will be taught far more intensely and with greater power during the millennium, *until all the inhabitants of the earth shall embrace it.* Satan shall be bound so that he cannot tempt any man. Should any man refuse to repent and accept the gospel under those conditions then he would be *accursed.* Through the revelations given to the prophets, we learn that during the reign of Jesus Christ for a thousand years *eventually all people will embrace the truth. . . .*

If the knowledge of the Lord covers the earth as the waters do the sea, then it must be universally received. Moreover, the promise of the Lord through Jeremiah is that it will no longer be necessary for anyone to teach his neighbor, "saying, Know the Lord: for they shall all know me, from the least of them unto the greatest of them, saith the Lord." (*Era,* vol. 58, 142, 176; Jer. 31:34.)

(Joseph Fielding Smith, *Doctrines of Salvation: Sermons and Writings of Joseph Fielding Smith,*
ed. Bruce R. McConkie, 3 vols. [Salt Lake City: Bookcraft, 1954–1956], 3:64–65.)

It will be thus when Jesus descends in the clouds of glory . . . You are made new creatures. So the earth will be made new, and great knowledge will be imparted to the inhabitants thereof . . . The knowledge of God will then cover the earth as the waters cover the mighty deep. There will be no place of ignorance, no place of darkness, no place for those that will not serve God. Why? Because Jesus, the Great Creator, and also the Great Redeemer, will be himself on the earth, and his holy angels will be on the earth, and all the resurrected Saints that have died in former dispensations will all come forth, and they will be on the earth. What a happy earth this creation will be, when this purifying process shall come, and the earth be filled with the knowledge of God as the waters cover the great deep! What a change! Travel, then, from one end of the earth to another, you can find no wicked man, no drunken man, no man to blaspheme the name of the Great Creator, no one to lay hold on his neighbor's goods, and steal them, no one to commit whoredoms. . . . But, inquires one, can they sin? Yes; their agency will still be left . . .

Children will grow up without sin unto salvation, as a general thing, . . . mortality still continues, that people are subject to plagues, subject to pain, and subject to be afflicted . . . When Jesus has been here in person a thousand years, and all the ancient Saints that have been resurrected, and the modern Saints also, after they have lived upon the earth for the space of a thousand years, it seems that Satan is to be loosed out of his prison, and permitted to go forth and tempt. Whom shall he tempt? Those whom Jesus has brought from heaven? No, they are beyond temptation. Whom will he tempt? Those that are yet mortal—the innumerable inhabitants of the earth . . . He will go out into the four quarters of the earth, and gather together all that he can overcome . . .

Satan will gather up his hosts, that have apostatized from the truth . . . and fire will descend from God out of heaven, and devour that portion of the army of Satan that is still mortal. . . . They will be consumed, the same as the wicked will have been consumed over a thousand years before that.

(Orson Pratt, *Journal of Discourses,* 21: 324–26.)

Some members of the Church have an erroneous idea that when the millennium comes all of the people are going to be swept off the earth except righteous members of the Church. That is not so. There will be millions of people, Catholics, Protestants, agnostics, Mohammedans, people of all classes, and of all beliefs, still permitted to remain upon the face of the earth, but they will be those who have lived clean lives, those who have been free from wickedness and corruption. All who belong, by virtue of their good lives, to the terrestrial order, as well as those who have kept the celestial law, will remain upon the face of the earth during the millennium.

Eventually, however, the knowledge of the Lord will cover the earth as the waters do the sea. But there will be need for the preaching of the gospel, after the millennium is brought in, until all men are either converted or pass away. In the course of the thousand years all men will either come into the Church, or kingdom of God, or they will die and pass away. In that day there will be no death until men are old. Children will not die but will live to the age of a tree. Isaiah says this is 100 years. When the time comes for men to die, they will be changed in the twinkling of an eye, and there will be no graves.

(Joseph Fielding Smith, *Doctrines of Salvation: Sermons and Writings of Joseph Fielding Smith*, ed. Bruce R. McConkie, 3 vols. [Salt Lake City: Bookcraft, 1954–1956], 1:86–87.)

2 Ne. 21:10–12   TWO GATHERINGS
(Isa. 21:10–12; A of F 10)

From this scripture we learn that the events described were to be in the future: "The Lord shall set his hand again the second time to recover the remnant of his people." There could not be a "second time" unless there had been a first. The first time as when the Lord led Israel out of Egyptian bondage and captivity.

(LeGrand Richards, *A Marvelous Work and a Wonder*, rev. ed. [Salt Lake City: Deseret Book Co., 1979], 202.)

The time has at last arrived when the God of Abraham, of Isaac, and of Jacob, has set His hand again the second time to recover the remnants of his people, which have been left from Assyria, and from Egypt, and from Pathros, and from Cush, and from Elam, and from Shinar, and from Hamath, and from the islands of the sea, and with them to bring in the fulness of the Gentiles, and establish that covenant with them, which was promised when their sins should be taken away. . . . This covenant has never been established with the house of Israel, nor with the house of Judah. . . . Christ, in the days of His flesh, proposed to make a covenant with them, but they rejected Him and His proposals, and in consequence thereof, they were broken off, and no covenant was made with them at that time. . . . Thus after this chosen family had rejected Christ and His proposals, the heralds of salvation said to them, "Lo, we turn unto the Gentiles;" and the Gentiles received the covenant, and were grafted in from whence the chosen family were broken off.

(Joseph Smith, *History of the Church*, Vol. 1, [Salt Lake City: Deseret Book Co., 1976], 313.)

The latter-day gathering is the second gathering . . . whereas the first was the gathering of Israel out of Egypt, making Moses the official holder of the gathering keys (see D&C 110:11). Not only will Israel be gathered, but many among the Gentile nations will also join the gathered remnant to learn of God (see Isa. 11:10, 12; 14:1; Jer. 16:14–16). The Church and the restored gospel will be the rallying standard, or "ensign," to which Israel and these others will come (cf. 2 Ne. 6:14; 25:17; 29:1).

(Keith A Meservy, *Studies in Scripture, Vol. 4,* ed. Kent P. Jackson [Salt Lake City: Deseret Book Co., 1993], 103.)

The second gathering will see remnants return from all directions (as symbolized by different countries: Assyria = Modern Iraq; Egypt, Pathros = Egypt; Cush = Ethiopia; Elam = Iran; Shinar = Iraq; Hamath = Syria) and from various continents (islands of the sea). The Lord will also set up a church (or ensign) for the nations and the scattered outcasts of Israel.

(Victor L. Ludlow, *Unlocking the Old Testament* [Salt Lake City: Deseret Book Co., 1981], 158–59.)

Isaiah prophesied "that the Lord shall set his hand again . . . to recover the remnant of his people" (Isa. 11:11). Jeremiah declared that "remnants" would come from "the land of the north" (Jer. 3:18; 16:14–15; cf. 23:7–8; 31:8) and that the Lord would "make a new covenant" with them (Jer. 31:31).

Book of Mormon prophets affirmed that the Lord had not forgotten the ten tribes, and that they are keeping records that will yet be revealed (2 Ne. 29:12–14). When the resurrected Jesus Christ appeared in the Americas, he spoke of being commanded of the Father to minister unto the lost tribes, "for they are not lost unto the Father" (3 Ne. 17:4). Jesus also promised that the Lord's redemptive work in the last days would include "the tribes which have been lost" (3 Ne. 21:26). . . .

On April 3, 1836, Moses appeared to the Prophet Joseph Smith and Oliver Cowdery in the Kirtland Temple and committed to them the "keys of the gathering of Israel . . . and the leading of the ten tribes from the land of the north" (D&C 110:11). These keys still rest with the President of the Church. In time, the ten tribes are to be "crowned with glory . . . by the hands of the servants of the Lord, even the children of Ephraim" (D&C 133:26–34) . . . Plainly, according to scripture and teachings of LDS leaders, descendants of the lost tribes—wherever they may be—have continued to receive divine attention and will receive future blessings.

(David L. Bolliger, *Encyclopedia of Mormonism,* ed. Daniel H. Ludlow, 4 vols.
[New York: Macmillan Publishing Company, 1992], 2:709.)

In the LDS perspective, gathering Israel in the latter days consists of the following: (1) the spiritual gathering, which includes coming to know that Jesus is the Christ and joining The Church of Jesus Christ of Latter-day Saints; (2) the assembling of Church members to organized Stakes; and (3) the gathering of the descendants of Jacob's twelve sons—including the lost ten tribes (D&C 110:11)—to the lands of their inheritance. These gatherings are necessary because of ancient apostasies that resulted in the dispersion of Israel into all nations (Deut. 4:27; 28:64; Jer. 16:13; Hosea 9:17). . . .

Anciently, the Lord brought Israel out of Egypt, and Isaiah prophesied a future recovery of Israel from many lands (Isa. 11:11–13; cf. 2 Ne. 6:14).

(Terry L. Niederhauser, *Encyclopedia of Mormonism*, ed. Daniel H. Ludlow, 4 vols. [New York: Macmillan Publishing Company, 1992], 710.)

2 Ne. 21:12   AN ENSIGN
(D&C 45:9; refer in this text to 2 Ne. 15:26–30)

What that Statue of Liberty has symbolized to the oppressed and downtrodden of Europe, the gospel of Jesus Christ is to the world.

The restored gospel, the Church, has reared an ensign to the nations . . . and invites the world to peace, to rest, to contentment.

(David O. McKay, *Conference Report*, Apr. 1963, 97.)

This Church is the standard which Isaiah said the Lord would set up for the people in the latter days. . . . This Church is the ensign on the mountain spoken of by the Old Testament prophets.

(Marion G. Romney, *Conference Report*, Apr. 1961, 119.)

"Rising above the Salt Lake Valley is a dome-shaped peak. Brigham Young saw it in a vision before the Saints left Nauvoo. He saw an ensign descend upon the hill and heard the voice of Joseph Smith say, "Build under [that] point . . . and you will prosper and have peace" (quoted by George A. Smith, in *Deseret News* [semiweekly], 29 June 1869, 3).

When Brigham Young first arrived in the valley, he immediately recognized the peak. On the morning of July 26, 1847, the men who would eventually comprise the new First Presidency, along with several members of the Twelve, climbed its slopes.

This small group of priesthood leaders gazed out upon the valley below. "This is whereon we will plant the soles of our feet," President Young said, "and where the Lord will place his name among his people" (quoted by Erastus Snow, in *Deseret News*, 22 Oct. 1873, 5).

As I now stand at Ensign Peak and see the valley below, I marvel at the foresight of that little group. These prophets, dressed in old, travel-worn clothes, standing in boots they had worn for more than a thousand miles, spoke of a millennial vision. It was both bold and audacious. It was almost unbelievable.

Here they were, almost a thousand miles from the nearest settlement to the east and almost eight hundred miles from the Pacific coast. They were in an untried climate. They had never raised a crop here. They had not built a structure of any kind.

They were exiles, driven from their fair city on the Mississippi into this desert region of the West. But they were possessed of a vision drawn from the scriptures and words of revelation: "And he shall set up an ensign for the nations, and shall assemble the outcasts of Israel, and gather together the dispersed of Judah from the four corners of the earth" (Isa. 11:12).

(Gordon B. Hinckley, Ensign, May 1997, 63.)

2 Ne. 21:12   GATHER ISRAEL & JUDAH
              (Isa. 11:12; refer in *Latter-day Commentary on the Book of Mormon,*
              Bassett to, 2 Ne. 6:10–11 & 2 Ne. 30:7 & 3 Ne. 20:13, 29–33)

Here is a declaration that the two great kingdoms of Israel—its "out-casts," the ten tribes, scattered seven hundred and twenty years before Christ, and the "dispersed of Judah," dispersed among all nations, shall be gathered. But before he gathers them he will set up an ensign—an ensign is to be raised in the latter-days especially for the gathering of Israel. . . . The Lord has never said that he will lift it up before the time comes to gather Israel. . . . He must begin it among the Gentiles, . . . as Isaiah tells us in the 49th chapter— a standard or ensign, to which the people will gather, will be reared among the Gentiles. Recollect this is something to be commenced among the Gentiles, not among the Jewish nation, not away yonder in Palestine or Jerusalem.

(Orson Pratt, Journal of Discourses, 14:66–67.)

The Jews have got to gather to their own land in unbelief. They will go and rebuild Jerusalem and their temple. . . . When they have done this and rebuilt their city, the Gentiles, in fulfillment of the words of Ezekiel, Jeremiah, and other prophets, will go up against Jerusalem to battle and to take a spoil and a prey; and then, when they have taken one-half of Jerusalem captive and distressed the Jews for the last time on the earth, their Great Deliverer, Shiloh, will come. They do not believe in Jesus of Nazareth now, nor ever will, until he comes and sets his foot on Mount Olivet and it cleaves in twain, one part going towards the east, and the other towards the west. Then, when they behold the wounds in his hands and in his feet, they will say, "Where did you get them?" And he will reply, "I am Jesus of Nazareth, King of the Jews, your Shiloh, Him whom you crucified." Then, for the first time will the eyes of Judah be opened. They will remain in unbelief until that day.

(Wilford Woodruff, The Discourses of Wilford Woodruff,
ed. G. Homer Durham, [Salt Lake City: Bookcraft, 1946], 118–119.)

We are all Gentiles by nationality, we are of the Gentile nations who hold the sway of the earth. Not only will the Jews have blessings again, but these poor despised Indians will enjoy the light and glory of the gospel of Christ; their fathers proclaimed blessings upon them, by the spirit of prophecy and revelation . . . A remnant of them will embrace the gospel, and their eyes will be opened and they will understand that they are of Israel. Our missionaries have labored among them, and what effect has it had? But little . . .

We cannot do a great deal for that people, only pray for them, and treat them kindly, until the power of God begins to rest upon them, and they are waked up by the visions of heaven, and the angels begin to converse with them. They will be inspired by the spirit of the power of God, like other branches of Israel, and the day will come when the . . . tribes in these mountains will again feel they possess souls among men as their fathers did before them. The ten tribes will also come in remembrance before the Lord, and they will again return with outstretched arms to their lands, and be led by leaders inspired by the Spirit and power of God, and they will come with visions, revelations, and prophets, and they will be baptized and ordained under the hands of the children of Ephraim, who bear the Holy Priesthood.

(Wilford Woodruff, *The Discourses of Wilford Woodruff,*
ed. G. Homer Durham, [Salt Lake City: Bookcraft, 1946], 119–20.)

2 Ne. 21:12–13   JUDAH AND EPHRAIM
(Isa. 11:12–13)

It is important to know biblical history in order to understand how significant it is that Judah and Ephraim will be at peace in that day (Isa. 11:12–13). In biblical times, Ephraim, the Northern Kingdom (also called Israel), and Judah, the Southern Kingdom, often fought each other (Isa. 11:13), as we have seen (Isa. 7–8). Things will be otherwise in the Millennium, when they will come together amicably. As the scattered bones of a body will be reunited into one body, so scattered Israelites will become one nation under one king (see Ezek. 37:1–14).

(Keith A Meservy, *Studies in Scripture, Vol. 4*, ed. Kent P. Jackson [Salt Lake City: Deseret Book Co., 1993], 103.)

The entire verse recalls the tensions and hostilities that existed between Ephraim (the Northern Kingdom) and Judah (the Southern Kingdom), beginning with Jeroboam's break with Rehoboam (1 Kgs. 11–12). God's latter-day gathering will result in the uniting of the kingdoms of Judah and Israel, made possible because the gospel teaches peace and love and because the Messiah, who is the true king of Israel and Judah, rules with justice and righteousness (11:1–5). The Book of Mormon also plays a prominent role in reuniting Ephraim and Judah (Ezek. 37:15–28).

(Donald W. Parry, Jay A. Parry, and Tina M. Peterson,
Understanding Isaiah [Salt Lake City: Deseret Book Co., 1998], 124.)

[Isaiah 11:13–14.] These verses describe a return to a united kingdom of Israel as it was before the division following the reign of Solomon. Ephraim was the name by which the northern 10? tribes were called, and Judah consisted of the southern 1? tribes. Ephraim will at the time of this reuniting occupy the promised land of Joseph, the Americas (see 3 Nephi 15:12–13). This prophecy speaks of more than a geographical uniting; it is a spiritual and political reuniting. Abraham was promised the land "from the river of Egypt unto the great river, the river Euphrates" (Genesis 15:18), which has never as yet been completely occupied by Abraham's children under one head. In Isaiah's time the Philistines occupied the area of the present-day Gaza Strip on the Mediterranean coast, which falls within the geography of Abraham's promised land; and Edom, the descendants of Esau, occupied the area of Mt. Seir to the south and the east. Moab, the descendants of Lot and his eldest daughter, occupied the territory directly north of Edom on the east side of the Jordan. Together, the Edomites and the Moabites represented the expansion of the land of Abraham on the east. The children of Ammon, the descendants of Lot and his younger daughter, occupied the land directly north of Moab on the east side of the Jordan. Today these all constitute the modern nation of Jordan. That this prophecy is yet to be fulfilled is shown by the declaration that the children of Ammon will obey the house of Israel. None of this land east of the Jordan is under the rule of the house of Israel, nor has the envy yet departed from between Ephraim and Judah to bring about a united rule.

(Monte S. Nyman, *Great Are the Words of Isaiah* [Salt Lake City: Bookcraft, 1980], 75–76.)

Who is Judah? The Jews. Who is Ephraim? Those of the birthright, the leaders of the kingdom, the Church. This harmony between Judah and Ephraim is something never before experienced, due to the early envy and jealousy inherited from Judah himself toward the chosen son of Joseph. News releases of the day confirm and fulfill this latter-day prophecy. Judah has given Ephraim a position on its famous Mount Olivet for a historical monument of peace, the Orson Hyde Memorial. The *Jerusalem Post* referred to President Spencer W. Kimball as a "prophet in the line of Abraham and Moses." (*Church News*, Dec. 29, 1979, 5.)

(L. La Mar Adams, *The Living Message of Isaiah* [Salt Lake City: Deseret Book Co., 1981], 73–74.)

2 Ne. 21:14   THE SHOULDERS OF PHILISTINES
(Isa. 11:14)

"They shall fly upon the shoulders of the Philistines toward the West." We recognize the fulfillment of that prophecy in the founding of this Church by Joseph Smith, a lineal descendant of Abraham, Isaac and Jacob, who thus lifted the Ensign for the gathering of their descendants from their long dispersion among the nations. But a part of the fulfillment rests with the Gentiles. Their steamships, their railroads, their means of rapid transit and communication—these are "the shoulders of the Philistines," upon which the children of Ephraim have been and are being brought to the West, to the land of Zion, where the New Jerusalem is to rise, where the pure in heart will assemble, and the necessary preparation be made for the coming of the Lord in his glory. God works outside as well as inside his Church, and uses big things and little things for the accomplishment of his purposes.

(Orson F. Whitney, *Conference Report*, Oct. 1919, 69.)

Compare the translation in the New International Version: "They will swoop down on the slopes of Philistia." As Israel gathers to God's signal (ensign) and possesses righteousness, the priesthood, and the power received in the temple, then Israel's former enemies, the Philistines, Edomites, Moabites, and Ammonites—symbols for the nations of our day—will be subject to them.

(Donald W. Parry, Jay A. Parry, and Tina M. Peterson,
Understanding Isaiah [Salt Lake City: Deseret Book Co., 1998], 124.)

2 Ne. 21:15–16   THE TONGUE OF THE EGYPTIAN SEA - HIGHWAY
(Isa. 11:15–16; 35:8–10; Jer. 23:7–8; D&C 133:26–32;
Isaiah Speaks to Modern Times, Skousen, 114–119.)

The word *tongue* should be translated "gulf." This phrase recalls the occasion when Moses and the Israelites crossed the Red Sea on dry ground (Ex. 14:21–22), an event that anticipates the gathering in the last days, when no powerful nation, mortal tyrant, or army will stop the promised events of the gathering of the saints around God's standard.

With his mighty wind shall he shake his hand over the river . . . and make men go over dryshod. Three elements in this passage, *mighty wind, hand,* and *go over dryshod*, recall the Israelites' crossing of the Red Sea. "Moses stretched out his *hand* over the sea; and the Lord caused the sea to go back by a *strong east wind* all that night, and made the sea dry land . . . And the children of Israel went into the midst of the sea upon the *dry ground*" (Ex. 14:21–22; emphasis added). The same powers that guided the ancient Israelites out of Egypt will guide modern Israel out of symbolic Egypt (the world) to their gathering places.

(Donald W. Parry, Jay A. Parry, and Tina M. Peterson,
Understanding Isaiah [Salt Lake City: Deseret Book Co., 1998], 124.)

Various interpretations have been rendered for the term "tongue of the Egyptian sea" in verse fifteen. It might be the western arm of the Red Sea (or Gulf of Suez) near the Suez Canal. Another possibility is the delta (or tongue) of the Nile that protrudes into the Mediterranean Sea along Egypt's north coast. The most likely explanation would be the large inland sea created late each spring as the Nile overflows its banks and floods a large part of the valley, like a tongue sticking far inland. Isaiah 19:5–10 describes this event in greater detail. This prophecy has been fulfilled since the building of the Aswan Dam and the destruction of the traditional way of life along the Nile.

The Lord will also divert "the river" (usually understood to be the Euphrates River) into seven streams so travelers can walk across without getting their feet wet. Verse sixteen says that a highway will be prepared for the remnant of Israel coming from Assyria (the land on the other side of the Euphrates). Isaiah 19:23–25 prophesies of a highway all the way from Assyria (through Israel) to Egypt. Other prophecies also describe a great highway for the righteous in the last days (Isa. 35:8–10; 51:9–11; D&C 133:27).

Although this highway could be a literal, physical road, it may represent any means of transportation, such as an airway or railroad. The Lord did not create a literal road for ancient Israel, but he did prepare the way for them so they would reach their destination. He will do the same for Israel in the last days, and they will recognize his hand in their return (Jer. 16:14–15; 30; 31).

(Victor L. Ludlow, *Unlocking The Old Testament* [Salt Lake City: Deseret Book Co., 1981], 159–60.)

I often think when I see gentlemen and ladies sitting in our tabernacles, who have come over this great highway that has been cast up, whether they realize that they are fulfilling the prophecies of Isaiah. . . . I am satisfied that they do not realize it, but they are fulfilling the revelations of God. The Gentiles are coming to the light of Zion. . . . When we have got our eyes opened, and our hearts set upon building up the kingdom of God, then will we return and rebuild the waste places of Zion.

(Wilford Woodruff, *The Discourses of Wilford Woodruff*, ed. G. Homer Durham, [Salt Lake City: Bookcraft, 1946], 226–27.)

It appears that a way will be provided to assemble the outcasts of Israel again in their promised land. The safe and secure physical arrangements, whatever they may be, will, in fact, be but symbolical of the way of holiness whereon only the righteous can find footing. The way of holiness cannot be other than the strait and narrow path. The wayward tribes, having forsaken the ancient holy way, having been scattered for their wickedness, shall now be gathered because they forsake the world and seek again that whereon the footprints of their fathers are found . . .

Once forsaken, left alone, now they shall be enfolded in the arms of his love. And oh, what blessings await them!

(Bruce R. McConkie, *The Millennial Messiah* [Salt Lake City: Deseret Book Co., 1982], 327.)

In the last two verses (15, 16) of this prophecy, Isaiah desires to let us know that when the remnant of Israel returns, it shall be aided by God's power, even as he showed forth his power at the exodus from Egypt under Moses. Notice that Isaiah singles out Egypt and Assyria, two countries that held Israelites in bondage, in connection with his symbolic description of God's power that shall provide a highway or means for the return of His people in the latter days. He symbolizes the use of the power of the

Almighty by telling us that He will cut off or separate the tongue of the Egyptian sea, shake his hand over the Euphrates, smite it into many streams and cause men to go over it dryshod. Perhaps "Egyptian sea" and "River" (vs. 15) are metonyms for places of exile and bondage. Such shall be overthrown when the time of redemption comes. In connection with this verse, see D&C 133:26–34.

(Sidney B. Sperry, *Book of Mormon Compendium* [Salt Lake City: Bookcraft, 1968], 229.)

As the Lord smote the tongue of the Egyptian sea in ancient days, and caused his people to go through on a highway in the midst of those mighty waters which stood like walls on each side of the assembly of Israel. So in the latter days he will not only cut off the tongue of the Egyptian sea, but the river in its seven streams will also be divided and men will go through dryshod. This is the testimony of the prophets concerning the events that are to take place when the times of the Gentiles are fulfilled.

(Orson Pratt, *Journal of Discourses*, 14:66.)

All that God has said with regard to the ten tribes of Israel, strange as it may appear, will come to pass. They will, as has been said concerning them, smite the rock, and the mountains of ice will flow before them, and a great highway will be cast up, and their enemies will become a prey to them; and their records, and their choice treasures they will bring with them to Zion. These things are as true as God lives.

(Wilford Woodruff, *Journal of Discourses*, 21:301.)

The Jews will be moved upon by and by, and they will return to the land of their fathers, and they will rebuild Jerusalem. These Lamanites here will receive the Gospel of Christ in fulfillment of the revelations of God. The Prophets which have been shut up in the north country with the nine and a half tribes led away by Shalmanezer, King of Assyria, thousands of years ago, will come in remembrance before God; they will smite the rocks and mountains of ice will flow down before them, and those long lost tribes will come forth . . . and they will be crowned under the hands of the children of Ephraim—the Elders of Israel who dwell in the land of Zion.

(Wilford Woodruff, *Journal of Discourses*, 18:38.)

Here are the ten tribes of Israel, we know nothing about them only what the Lord has said by His Prophets. There are Prophets among them, and by and by they will come along, and they will smite the rocks, and the mountains of ice will flow down at their presence, and a highway will be cast up before them, and they will come to Zion, receive their endowments, and be crowned under the hands of the children of Ephraim . . . They will receive their blessings and endowments, from under the children Ephraim.

(Wilford Woodruff, *Journal of Discourses*, 4:231–32.)

Isaiah . . . in an apparent reference to the joining of the continents, and using that prophetic imagery for which he has such great renown, says: "Thy land shall be married" (Isa. 62:4). Also in a setting relative to the Millennium and the gathering of Israel, Isaiah says, "There shall be an highway for the remnant of his people, which shall be left." That is, those who are left because they have abided the day of our Lord's coming shall find a highway to lead them to their appointed gathering places. It shall then be, Isaiah says, "like as it was to Israel in the day that he came up out of the land of Egypt" (Isa. 11:16). As the Lord provided a highway through the Red Sea for his people anciently, as they traveled to their promised land, so will he provide a way for them to travel in the latter days. Our latter-day revelation, after stating that the great deep shall be driven back into the north countries and that the continents shall become one land, states that "they who are in the north countries," meaning the Ten Tribes, shall return. "And an highway shall be cast up in the midst of the great deep" for them (D&C 133:23–27). Would we go too far astray if we were to suggest that the highway is created by the joined landmasses, and that as ancient Israel found a dry path through the Red Sea, so latter-day Israel will find a dry path where the Atlantic Ocean once was?

(Bruce R. McConkie, *The Millennial Messiah* [Salt Lake City: Deseret Book Co., 1982], 624–25.)

2 Ne. 22

(Isa. 12) *This chapter is a hymn consisting of two short psalms. It is uncertain whether verse 3 belongs at the end of the first psalm (a thanks psalm) or the beginning of the second psalm (a praise hymn).*

Two brief psalms comprise the whole of chapter 12, and they provide a suitable conclusion to the messianic images of chapter 11. This short chapter is also a positive, inspirational capstone for the first dozen chapters of Isaiah's writings. . . . In the two psalms of chapter 12, Isaiah speaks for all Israel as he gives thanks and praise to the Lord for providing salvation and millennial blessings.

(Victor L. Ludlow, *Isaiah: Prophet, Seer, and Poet* [Salt Lake City: Deseret Book Co., 1982], 177–78.)

This song of praise unto Jehovah will be sung in the day of Israel's great restoration. Paul, in writing to the Hebrews, may have been quoting a part of verse 2 to show a brotherhood between Christ and his people (see Heb. 2:13). The water which is drawn "out of the wells of salvation" is similarly promised by John the Revelator (see Rev. 21:6); the "water" which is promised and given through Christ is identified by John as the Holy Ghost (see John 7:38–39).

(Monte S. Nyman, *Great Are the Words of Isaiah* [Salt Lake City: Bookcraft, 1980], 77.)

2 Ne. 22:1   **I WILL PRAISE THEE—THOU WAST ANGRY**
                 (Isa. 12:1)

The Targum says, "I sing because although when I had sinned You were angry with me, yet, when I returned to Your law, You showed me mercy." Rashi: "I sing because my exile was an atonement for my sins." The thought expressed by Rashi is analogous to that in Psalm 119:71: "It is good for me that I have been afflicted for thus have I learned Thy precepts." Kimchi says, "The reason for my singing is that You did not let me remain in the exile, as I had deserved."

(Solomon B. Freehof, *Book of Isaiah* [New York: Union of American Hebrew Congregation, 1972], 81.)

2 Ne. 22:2   **JEHOVAH**
                 (Isa. 12:2; 26:4; Exodus 6:3; Ps. 83:18; Moro. 10:34;
                 D&C 109:34, 42, 56, 68; 110:3; 128:9; Abr. 1:16)

The covenant or proper name of the God of the Old Testament was so highly reverenced that it was rarely spoken. In fact, the original pronunciation of the name may be unknown to mortal man. When reading orally, the Israelites substituted the name *Adonai,* meaning literally, *my Lord.* Elder James E. Talmage tells us that "*Jehovah* is the Anglicized rendering of the Hebrew, *Yahveh* or *Jahveh,* signifying the *Self-existent One,* or *The Eternal.* This name is generally rendered in our English version of the Old Testament as LORD, printed in [small] capitals." . . . Of the four times the sacred name appears unchanged in the Old Testament, Isaiah uses it twice. Latter-day Saints affirm that this holy name is the premortal name of Jesus Christ and has been used in behalf of the Savior in sacred places during His postmortal ministry.

(Hoyt W. Brewster, Jr., *Isaiah Plain and Simple* [Salt Lake City: Deseret Book Co., 1995], 121.)

2 Ne. 22:3   **DRAW WATER OUT OF THE WELLS OF SALVATION**
                 (Isa. 12:3)

The "water out of the wells of salvation" is a symbol also used in Jeremiah 2:13 and John 4:7–14. It is life-giving "water" of new birth unto salvation and atonement.

(Ellis T. Rasmussen, *A Latter-day Saint Commentary on the Old Testament*
[Salt Lake City: Deseret Book Co., 1993], 512–513.)

By comparing the punctuation, especially the quotation marks, with the King James Version, a major problem with this short psalm becomes apparent. Although the beginning of the psalm is clearly defined in verse 1, the conclusion of the psalm remains indefinite. Scholars agree that verse 3 is the most important verse in this set, but they disagree as to whether or not it should be included within the psalm. Unfortunately, the original Hebrew provides no help with this problem because it contains no punctuation at all. Indeed, most early Hebrew writings had no punctuation, since such symbols were not developed or even encouraged because space on writing materials (scrolls of parchment, clay tablets, metal plates, etc.) was at a premium, and most readers of the materials were familiar enough with it that they could supply the necessary breaks, pauses, and inflections. Therefore, context becomes the best clue for interpretation.

(Victor L. Ludlow, *Isaiah: Prophet, Seer, and Poet* [Salt Lake City: Deseret Book Co., 1982], 178.)

Wells of Salvation. Has reference to the feast of tabernacles, or tents, celebrated by the Jews at the close of the year in grateful remembrance of the goodness of God to their fathers in the wilderness, and to themselves, as evidenced by abundant harvests and other blessings in the land of Rest (Lev. 23:34). The observance lasted for seven days. A libation was an important part of the services every day. It was at the close of such a festival that our Lord stood on the temple ground and invited the people to come unto him. It was the last day. The water was perhaps flowing gently in the trench. But the crowd was about to disperse. Each one had to go to his own home and leave the life-giving stream for, perhaps, less pleasant water containers. Then Jesus cried with a loud voice: "If any man thirst, let him come unto me, and drink. He that believeth on me, as the scripture hath said, out of his innermost parts shall flow rivers of living water." You need not thirst, because you cannot always stay by this stream (John 7:37, 38; cf. John 4:14) Jesus spoke of the spirit which they that believe on him should receive (John 7:39).

(George Reynolds and Janne M. Sjodahl, *Commentary on the Book of Mormon,*
ed. Philip C. Reynolds, 7 vols. [Salt Lake City: Deseret Book Co., 1955–1961], 1:360.)

As one who, by special assignment, has been given authority in the house of Israel today, I ask the God of Abraham, Isaac, and Jacob to bless my brethren of Judah and have mercy on them; that the land to which Judah has returned after a long night of dispersion shall be fruitful, prosperous, and become the envy to her neighbors; that the nation Israel shall be delivered from all her oppressors and enemies; that Judah will "draw water out of the wells of salvation" (Isa. 12:3), and fulfill all those prophecies that God declared through his prophets Isaiah, Ezekiel, and Jeremiah, even that prophecy through Zechariah that "the Lord shall inherit Judah his portion in the holy land, and shall choose Jerusalem again" (Zech, 2:12).

(Ezra Taft Benson, *Ensign*, Dec. 1976, 72.)

Brothers and sisters, let us be anxiously engaged in good causes. Let us love God the Father and His Son, Jesus Christ. Let us sustain and live by the revelations of the restored gospel. Let us love our fellow beings and fill our hearts and souls with the light of the gospel of Jesus Christ. Then we will sing with Isaiah:

> "Behold, God is my salvation; I will trust, and not be afraid; . . .
> "Therefore with joy shall [I] draw water out of the wells of salvation" (Isaiah 12:2–3). . . .

Each of us needs to model what it truly means to be a believing and behaving Latter-day Saint. . . . Let us . . . radiate to others the joy, confidence, love, and warmth of being part of the true Church of Christ.

Our discipleship is not something to be endured with long face and heavy heart. Nor is it something to be jealously clutched to our bosoms and not shared with others . . .

Remember, too often our behavior is a bigger deterrent to others than is our doctrine.

(M. Russell Ballard, *Ensign*, Oct. 1999, 62.)

2 Ne. 22:4   HIS NAME IS EXALTED
(Isa. 12:4)

It will be in the latter days that the gathered hosts of Israel will praise the Lord and call upon his name. They will have learned that the beginning of repentance and the turning away from stubborn apostasy starts with humble prayers, and calling upon God to forgive and guide his wayward children. No longer will they be atheistic or agnostic, or seek to hold God in derision. No longer will they be humanistic or "man centered" in seeking happiness and the true meaning of life. Finally, they will acknowledge the Lord as the Supreme and Exalted One.

(W. Cleon Skousen, *Isaiah Speaks to Modern Times* [Salt Lake City: Ensign Publishing Co., 1984], 256.)

2 Ne. 22:5   SING UNTO THE LORD
(Isa. 12:5)

The admonition to "sing unto the Lord" is not one that is reserved for the redeemed remnant of the future. Sacred music invites the Spirit of the Lord into our midst and is a wonderful way in which to worship Deity. Modern revelation reminds us that the Lord's "soul delighteth in the song of the heart; yea, the song of the righteous is a prayer unto [Him]" (D&C 25:12).

(Hoyt W. Brewster, Jr., *Isaiah Plain and Simple* [Salt Lake City: Deseret Book Co., 1995], 122.)

2 Ne. 23–24   **DESTRUCTION OF BABYLON–DESTRUCTION AT SECOND COMING**
(Isa. 13–14; *Commentary on the Book of Mormon*,
Reynolds and Sjodahl, 1:364)

As the Medes conquered the Babylonians in 538 B.C., so shall the conquest of the wicked by the destroying angels be accomplished at the coming of the great and dreadful day of the Lord. As ancient Israel was left to marvel at the once mighty but now deposed and displaced king of Babylon, so latter-day Israel will marvel at the dethronement of Lucifer, the despot of darkness and king of evil. . . . Thus the past becomes the key that unlocks the future. As history has its cycles, so prophecies have multiple ful-fillments and repeated applications. Isaiah's prophecies of events now past foretell events yet future. The past is the stage upon which the future is portrayed.

(Joseph Fielding McConkie and Robert L. Millet,
Doctrinal Commentary on the Book of Mormon, 4 vols. [Salt Lake City: Bookcraft, 1987–1992], 1:282.)

I. The fall of Babylon (13:1–22, 14:1–23)
    A. Introduction (13:1)
    B. The Lord gathers his forces (13:2–5)
    C. The Lord brings his power against (spiritual) Babylon (13:6–13)
    D. The Lord brings the Medes against (physical) Babylon (13:14–22)
    B'. The Lord will be merciful to Israel (14:1–3)
    C'. A taunt song against the king of (spiritual) Babylon (14:4–21)
    D'. The destruction of (physical) Babylon (14:22–23)

II. The fall of Assyria (14:24–27)

III. The fall of Philistia (14:28–32)

(Victor L. Ludlow, *Isaiah: Prophet, Seer, and Poet* [Salt Lake City: Deseret Book Co., 1982], 182.)

[Isaiah] Chapters 13 and 14 both concern Babylon and are by far the longest of the series. They are also the only two chapters of this series which are quoted in the Book of Mormon. There is undoubtedly a dual message within them. The basic message is against the old Babylon, which existed before Isaiah's time and became a world power under King Nebuchadnezzar after Assyria's downfall and after the ministry of Isaiah. Babylon became the epitome of wickedness in the ancient world, and was used in both the New Testament and the Doctrine and Covenants as the symbol of the wicked world (see Rev. 14:8; D&C 133:14). Thus a greater message is to modern-day Babylon, the wickedness of our world. It is often difficult to know which Babylon the text is referring to, and it may be that sometimes it refers to both at the same time. Because Nephi included these two chapters in the Book of Mormon record, it would appear that the majority of the text refers to the latter days.

Chapter 14 is an interesting proverb against the king of Babylon. Babylon represents the wicked world, and the king of that wickedness is none other than Satan himself. The graphic description in this chapter of Satan's *fall* is most interesting.

(Monte S. Nyman, *Great Are the Words of Isaiah* [Salt Lake City: Bookcraft, 1980], 78.)

2 Ne. 23   **BABYLON**
                  (Isa. 13)

In [Isaiah] chapter 13, Isaiah first addresses Babylon, the ancient country that had ruled over the Middle East until displaced by the Assyrians. . . . Although Babylon was subject to Assyrian rule during Isaiah's lifetime, she gradually regained power and independence until the New Babylonian Empire replaced Assyria as the major power in the Fertile Crescent at the end of the seventh century B.C. . . . But even during the so-called Assyrian period, Babylon still represented the best of culture, learning, literature, and religion (in the same way that Greek culture was sustained and imitated during the Roman period). Therefore, Isaiah often uses Babylon and her king as symbols of the world and its wickedness.

(Victor L. Ludlow, *Isaiah: Prophet, Seer, and Poet* [Salt Lake City: Deseret Book Co., 1982], 180.)

The authorship of this chapter is disputed by some of the uninspired worldly scholars, who rely on their academic learning but do not recognize the role of the Spirit in understanding scripture and prophetic utterances. Because Isaiah focuses on the destruction of Babylon, an event that occurred long after his time, and because these so-called scholars do not believe in prophecy, they assume that this chapter was written by someone after the event had come to pass.

(Hoyt W. Brewster, Jr., *Isaiah Plain and Simple* [Salt Lake City: Deseret Book Co., 1995], 123.)

2 Ne. 23:1   **BURDEN**
                  (Isa. 13:1)

A *burden* is a prophecy of doom or judgment against a people. The Hebrew root (*masa'*) literally means "lifting" or "a lifting up," perhaps indicating that the prophecy or judgment is lifted up by the voice of the prophet against the people. Isaiah's prophetic calling included uttering a prophecy of doom against many peoples or nations, including Moab (15:1), Damascus (17:1), Egypt (19:1), the desert of the sea (21:1), Dumah (21:11), Arabia (21:13), the valley of vision (22:1), Tyre (23:1), and the beasts of the south (30:6). Similarly, the *burden* of the word of the Lord also came to Nahum (1:1), Habakkuk (1:1), Zechariah (12:1), and Malachi (1:1).

The same Hebrew root is also used in connection with the lifting of the ensign (5:26; 11:12; 13:2) upon a high mountain. Hence, the Lord will "lift up" judgment against the wicked and will "lift up" an ensign to the righteous.

(Donald W. Parry, Jay A. Parry, and Tina M. Peterson,
Understanding Isaiah [Salt Lake City: Deseret Book Co., 1998], 130.)

Burden is used several times in Isaiah's prophetic addresses to several of Israel's neighboring nations and to Jerusalem itself . . . It is used to translate the Hebrew *massa*, meaning "something lifted up" against the wicked, with a call for their repentance. While addressed to nations known in history, the messages have symbolic meanings also for peoples having like faults in later times.

This burden is addressed to Babylon, an ancient nation thriving first in patriarchal times but arising again after Isaiah's time.

(Ellis T. Rasmussen, *A Latter-day Saint Commentary on the Old Testament*
[Salt Lake City: Deseret Book Co., 1993], 513.)

2 Ne. 23:1   BABYLON
(Isa. 13:1; refer in this text to 2 Ne. 23:14–22.)

Babylon was the ancient capital city of Babylonia, a society noted for its wickedness and cruelty. In our day it is a representation of the wickedness of the world. In fact, the Lord Himself equated the "midst of wickedness" with "spiritual Babylon." (D&C 133:14.) The ancient city appeared to be impregnable to attack, with walls said to be 56 miles in circumference, 335 feet high, and 85 feet wide. Yet, as foreseen by Isaiah, this fortress of ancient Babylonia fell. The plea to come forth out of today's Babylon (D&C 133:5, 7, 14) is the clarion call to modern Israel to escape from the Babylonian bondage of wickedness to the freedom and light of the gospel of Jesus Christ (D&C 45:9; 50:24; 88:86.)

(Hoyt W. Brewster, Jr., *Isaiah Plain and Simple* [Salt Lake City: Deseret Book Co., 1995], 124.)

That the Babylon spoken of in this verse includes more than ancient Babylon is obvious from the rest of the chapter, which clearly speaks of the time of the second coming of Christ. Another Babylon is identified in the Doctrine and Covenants as "spiritual Babylon" and is defined as wickedness (see D&C 133:14). Various other sections in the Doctrine and Covenants use Babylon in this context (see D&C 1:16; 35:11; 64:24; 86:3). The Book of Revelation also speaks repeatedly of the fall of Babylon in the last days, which has reference to the fall of the kingdom of the devil (see Rev. 14:8; 16:19; 17:5;

18:2–4, 10, 21). Jeremiah chapters 50 and 51 contain the words of the Lord against Babylon by Jeremiah the prophet; these sayings are more detailed than Isaiah's and seem directed toward ancient Babylon.

(Monte S. Nyman, *Great Are the Words of Isaiah* [Salt Lake City: Bookcraft, 1980], 80.)

Babylon became the dominant political and military power in the world when she completely destroyed the Assyrians in 605 B.C. Most of the building of the Babylonian empire occurred under King Nebuchadnezzar. Incidental to his conquests along the Mediterranean, he conquered the Jews. He tried to be kind to them, but the Jewish kings continually rebelled, so Nebuchadnezzar came in 587 B.C. and completely demolished Jerusalem. He destroyed the beautiful temple of Solomon and carried off to Babylon those Jews who were not slain or scattered during the siege. Babylon would have probably kept the Jews in captivity forever, but she became so wicked that her power over the surrounding nations lasted only until 539 B.C. That was the year the Medes and Persians came sweeping down from the mountains and high plateaus to the east and conquered Babylon in a single night. They were led by Cyrus, whom Isaiah identified by name around 175 years before Cyrus was born (see Isa. 44:28; 45:1). After Babylon was overthrown, Cyrus allowed the Jews to return to Jerusalem in 538 B.C.

(W. Cleon Skousen, *Isaiah Speaks To Modern Times* [Salt Lake City: Ensign Publishing Co., 1984], 260.)

2 Ne. 23:2   BANNER—GATES OF THE NOBLES
(Isa. 13:2; refer in this text to 2 Ne. 15:26–30 & 2 Ne. 21:12)

The word "banner" is translated from the same Hebrew word as is translated "ensign." In Isaiah 5:26 . . . The banner is therefore the Book of Mormon. The high mountain upon which the book is to be lifted is the Americas. . . .
Those who lifted up the banner were to exalt the voice and wave the hand or give a signal to go into the gates of the nobles (see footnote in the Book of Mormon under 2 Nephi 23:2). The nobles at the time of the coming forth of the Book of Mormon were the Gentiles, the ones who were living in the Americas upon the land promised to Joseph (Morm. 5:19–20).

(Monte S. Nyman, *Isaiah: Prophecies of the Restoration* [Salt Lake City: Millennial Press, Inc., 1998], 32–33.)

The gates of Eastern cities were an important part of ancient city life. They were not only places of entrance and exit, but also served as places of private and public business transactions. The gates were often taken as representing the city itself. . . . In the Isaiah context, the meaning is probably an invitation for those who are fleeing Babylon to enter the holy cities of Jerusalem and Zion (the new Jerusalem). (See D&C 133:12–14.)

(Hoyt W. Brewster, Jr., *Isaiah Plain and Simple* [Salt Lake City: Deseret Book Co., 1995], 125–26.)

The "battle flag" could be used to rally the forces of the world against Jerusalem (see Isa. 10), or it might serve as an "ensign" . . . around which the Lord's servants and saints gather against the evil forces of the world. (See Isa. 11:10; 62:10, where the same word is used.) In either case, it will assemble a mighty force that will fulfill some of the Lord's judgments against the wicked.

(Victor L. Ludlow, *Isaiah:Prophet, Seer, and Poet* [Salt Lake City: Deseret Book Co., 1982], 183.)

This verse is addressed to Cyrus and the hosts of Medes and Persians whom Cyrus would assemble in the highlands east of the Tigris River. They were to raise up the banner and descend on the nobles of Babylon. It is interesting that in the Joseph Smith Translation it says "MY banner," suggesting that Cyrus is representing the rod of God's wrath as he goes forth to conquer Babylon. . . .

In the latter days the Lord's banner is raised up, but for a different purpose. It is to lead God's people out of Babylon or the wickedness of the world.

(W. Cleon Skousen, *Isaiah Speaks to Modern Times* [Salt Lake City: Ensign Publishing Co., 1984], 260–61.)

Because city gates were public passageways, they took on the nature of a "public square" where legal and civil events occurred. . . . Immediately inside many city gates was an area where officials met and deliberated. To "sit in the gate" (or its variant "sit in the seat") implied one's prominence in the community. . . . Even kings sometimes positioned themselves "in the gate" (2 Sam. 18:24; 19:8). . . .

The pattern was established even before the Israelites settled in cities, with Moses judging the people "in the gate of the camp" during their wilderness wanderings (Ex. 32:26). . . .

Because so much commercial and civil business was transacted at the city gate, it became a prime image for prophetic denunciations of a corrupt society. . . . While the majority of biblical references are to literal gates, they also assume figurative qualities. Sometimes they are a synecdoche for an entire city: "Her gates shall lament and mourn; ravaged, she shall sit upon the ground" (Isa. 3:26 NRSV); \"Wail, O gate; cry, O city" (Isa. 14:31 NRSV).

(*Dictionary of Biblical Imagery*, ed. Leland Ryken, James C. Wilhoit, and Tremper Longman III [Downers Grove, Illinois: InterVarsity Press, 1998], 321–22.)

2 Ne. 23:3   MY SANCTIFIED ONES
(Isa. 13:3)

Jehovah's *sanctified ones* (Josh. 3:5) are those who are temple worthy, who actually attend the temple, and who are made holy by Christ's power. In ancient Israel the soldiers prepared for the holy war by participating in holy rituals connected with the temple (Deut. 23:10–15). In this dispensation, Jesus

Christ's soldiers (members of the Church) prepare for the battle against Babylon by participating in temple rituals.

(Donald W. Parry, Jay A. Parry, and Tina M. Peterson
Understanding Isaiah, [Salt Lake City: Deseret Book Co., 1998], 131.)

The "sanctified ones" are those whom God will bless. In ancient times these were Cyrus and his Medes and Persians, who were blessed in putting down the wickedness of Babylon. In the latter days it will be the leaders of the gathering hosts of Israel.

"For mine anger IS NOT UPON them that rejoice in my highness" (2 Ne. 23:3; emphasis added). This is a great compliment to Cyrus because he was reared among pagans and never did hear the full message of the Gospel. Nevertheless, the Lord assures him that he will be blessed because he, in his limited way, honored God.

(W. Cleon Skousen, Isaiah Speaks to Modern Times [Salt Lake City: Ensign Publishing Co., 1984], 261.)

2 Ne. 23:4   NOISE
(Isa. 13:4)

The word *noise* in this verse may also be translated "voice," such as in "the voice of many people in the mountains." Elsewhere Isaiah likens the noise of a great multitude of people to the "noise of the seas" (17:12) and "the rushing of mighty waters" (17:12). The saints, or *multitude*, will gather together from the world's nations and kingdoms with the intent of building Zion (Matt. 24:30–31; D&C 29:7–11; 45:66–71; 103:22–25).

(Donald W. Parry, Jay A. Parry, and Tina M. Peterson,
Understanding Isaiah [Salt Lake City: Deseret Book Co., 1998], 131.)

2 Ne. 23:4   IN THE MOUNTAINS LIKE AS OF A GREAT PEOPLE
(Isa. 13:4)

This has reference to gathering of the Saints in the Rocky Mountains. On 6 August 1842, Joseph Smith prophesied that some of the Saints would "live to go and assist in making settlements and build cities and see the saints become a *mighty people in the midst of the Rocky Mountains.*" (*Teachings of the Prophet Joseph Smith*, 255; emphasis added.)

(Donald W. Parry, Jay A. Parry, and Tina M. Peterson,
Understanding Isaiah [Salt Lake City: Deseret Book Co., 1998], 131–132.)

2 Ne. 23:5   **THE END OF HEAVEN**
(Isa. 13:5)

The end of heaven may simply suggest the farthest reaches of the earth.

(Donald W. Parry, Jay A. Parry, and Tina M. Peterson,
Understanding Isaiah [Salt Lake City: Deseret Book Co., 1998], 132.)

2 Ne. 23:5   **TO DESTROY THE WHOLE LAND**
(Isa. 13:5)

Isaiah seems to be saying here that the Lord's valiant servants will successfully battle evil during this time period. A modern revelation adds light to this phrase of Isaiah: "Wherefore, I [the Lord] call upon the weak things of the world, those who are unlearned and despised, to thrash the nations by the power of my Spirit; And their arm shall be my arm, and I will be their shield and their buckler; and I will gird up their loins, and they shall fight manfully for me; and their enemies shall be under their feet; and I will let fall the sword in their behalf, and by the fire of mine indignation will I preserve them" (D&C 35:13–14; 133:58–59).

(Donald W. Parry, Jay A. Parry, and Tina M. Peterson,
Understanding Isaiah [Salt Lake City: Deseret Book Co., 1998], 132.)

2 Ne. 23:6–9   **DAY OF THE LORD**
(Isa. 13:6–9; 1 Ne. 11:35–36; Isa. 2:12; Amos 5:18; 3 Ne. 25:5–6)

The phrase "day of the Lord" first appears in the writings of the eighth-century prophets Amos and Isaiah (Amos 5:18–20; Isa. 2:6–22) to refer to a day of judgment that is so extremely severe that the people will howl with fear. Isaiah compares the trembling fear and shaking terror of the men to the anguish of a woman in labor. . . .

Verse 9 explains that the purpose of the day of the Lord is to purge the earth of all sinners. (See D&C 133:50–51; Joel 2:1–2; Mal. 4:1; 2 Thes. 1:7–9.) In his later writings, Isaiah elaborates upon the intensity and completeness with which the Lord will cleanse the earth (Isa. 24:1–6; 34:2–8; 63:4; 64:1–2; 66:15–16).

(Victor L. Ludlow, *Isaiah: Prophet, Seer, and Poet* [Salt Lake City: Deseret Book Co., 1982], 184.)

In general, this is that period of time just preceding the return of the resurrected Lord to this earth, as well as the time of His actual coming. . . .

Although the righteous will ultimately be saved in the kingdom of God, it should be pointed out that even some of them will fall prey to the war and pestilence that will precede the Second Coming.

"It is a false idea," said the Prophet Joseph Smith, "that the Saints will escape all the judgments, whilst the wicked suffer; for all flesh is subject to suffer, and 'the righteous shall hardly escape;' still many of the Saints will escape, for the just shall live by faith; yet many of the righteous shall fall a prey to disease, to pestilence, etc., by reason of the weakness of the flesh and yet be saved in the Kingdom of God." *(HC* 4:11.)

(Hoyt W. Brewster Jr., *Isaiah Plain and Simple* [Salt Lake City: Deseret Book Co., 1995], 127–28.)

2 Ne. 23:9   FACES SHALL BE AN FLAMES
(Isa. 13:9)

Rashi says that means their faces (i.e., of the Babylonians) will be yellow with fear. Kimshi says, red with shame. And Ibn Ezra, stressing the root of the word which means "fire" or "flame," says that it means the face burned with intense pain.

(Solomon B. Freehof, *Book of Isaiah* [New York: Union of American Hebrew Congregation, 1972), 84.)

2 Ne. 23:11   THE WORLD
(Isa. 13:11)

The encroachment of the world into our lives is threatening! How hard it seems for many of us to live *in* the world and yet not *of* the world.
Through Isaiah the word of the Lord comes:

> "And I will punish the world for their evil, and the wicked for their iniquity; and I will cause the arrogancy of the proud to cease, and will lay low the haughtiness of the terrible." (Isa. 13:11.) . . .

Every man should love his wife and cherish and protect her all the days of their lives and she should love, honor, and appreciate her husband. . . .
Analyze the divorces of which you know, and you will find so often selfishness is in them. . . . Certainly, selfishness is near its greatest peak when innocent children must suffer for the sins of their parents. . . .
It was found in . . . [a] survey that about 90 percent gave as the reason for the breakup immorality on the part of one or both of the participants.
Immorality is totally selfish. Can you think of a single unselfish element in that sin? Accordingly, if two good people will discard selfishness, generally they can be compatible. . . .
"Sex can be a wonderful servant but a terrible master: that it can be a creative force more powerful than any other in the fostering of a love, companionship, happiness or can be the most destructive of all of life's forces." (Billy Graham, "What the Bible Says About Sex," *Reader's Digest*, May 1970, 118.) . . .
This, then, is our program: to reaffirm and boldly carry forward the work of God in cleanliness.

(Spencer W. Kimball, *Ensign*, May 1974, 5–8.)

2 Ne. 23:12　　**MORE PRECIOUS THAN GOLD**
　　　　　　　　(Isa. 13:12)

To survive in a day of such universal destruction will indeed make the life of any person who survives more precious than fine gold. The gold of Ophir was so fine that Solomon had his merchant ships import it to Israel. Ophir is believed to have been in southern Arabia, but some scholars think it might have been in India or Africa.

(W. Cleon Skousen, *Isaiah Speaks to Modern Times* [Salt Lake City: Ensign Publishing Co., 1984], 265.)

2 Ne. 23:13–14　**I WILL SHAKE THE HEAVENS**
　　　　　　　　　(Isa. 13:13–14)

This verse, which notes cosmological changes that will affect the earth at the time of Christ's second coming, is partially quoted or paraphrased in Doctrine and Covenants 21:6 and 35:24. It was also quoted by Oliver Cowdery. (See Messenger and Advocate, Apr. 1835, 111–12.) . . . Beginning with verse 14, Isaiah seems to describe the literal conquest of Babylon by the Medes, although this also appears to be a dual prophecy including spiritual Babylon."

(Monte S. Nyman, *Great Are the Words of Isaiah*, [Salt Lake City: Bookcraft, 1980], 82–83.)

"The earth will be removed out of its orbit in the present solar system and given a new location. It shall "remove" out of its "place." . . . But at the time of Christ's coming it will apparently be the intention of the Lord to return the earth to its original environment. To do this quickly would require that the earth be returned to Kolob faster than the speed of light. Such a phenomenon would seem to fit the words of the Lord in this verse. He said he would shake the heavens, and the earth would remove out of her place. Of course the earth's present place is about 30,000 light years out from the center of our galaxy. To pull the earth back toward Kolob in a very short time would give the appearance of all the stars falling from heaven as earth went rushing by. . . .

The earth will be as a chased roe (which is famous for its fleetness and tremendous speed). This implies that the planet will not only be moved out of its place, but it will flee back toward Kolob at a fantastic speed. The Lord says the earth will be like an abandoned sheep which no man takes up or claims. For the earth to seem to be running loose through the night sky will be a terrifying experience for those who are then living upon this planet. Many will perish. The hearts of many will fail them because of their terror.

Here is the way the Lord describes these coming events in a modern scripture: "For not many days hence and the earth shall tremble AND REEL TO AND FRO AS A DRUNKEN MAN; and the sun shall hide his face, and shall refuse to give light; and the moon shall be bathed in blood; and the stars shall become exceedingly angry, and shall cast themselves down as a fig that falleth from off a fig-tree" (D&C 88:87; emphasis added). No doubt this is exactly what it will seem like for all those living on the earth. The planet will be moving too fast for the light of the sun to reach it; in fact, the prophetic writings suggest it will have departed out of our present solar system altogether. The light of the stars will go rushing past, giving the impression that they are falling.

As we have quoted earlier, the Lord goes on to say, "And all things shall be in commotion; and surely, men's hearts shall fail them; for fear shall come upon all people" (D&C 88:91). The Lord says that as this period of commotion commences, every man will hasten to get home to his own people and flee into his own land."

(W. Cleon Skousen, *Isaiah Speaks to Modern Times* [Salt Lake City: Ensign Publishing Co., 1984], 266–68.)

When the earth was framed and brought into existence and man was placed upon it, it was near the throne of our Father in heaven . . . When man fell, the earth fell into space, and took up its abode in this planetary system . . . This is the glory the earth came from, and when it is glorified it will return again unto the presence of the Father.

(Brigham Young, *Journal of Discourses*, 17:143.)

It may be that the changes on the earth, of which Isaiah spoke, will cause the heavens to appear to move above the inhabitants of the earth as if the stars in the heavens are actually falling. Elder Bruce R. McConkie wrote that "it shall appear to man on earth as though the stars in the sidereal heavens are falling. And in addition, as here recorded, some heavenly meteors or other objects, appearing as stars, will fall 'unto the earth.' Indeed, the events of that day shall be so unprecedented and so beyond human experience, that the prophets are and have been at an almost total loss for words to describe those realities pressed in upon them by the spirit of revelation (*Doctrinal New Testament Commentary*, 3:486.)

(Craig J. Ostler, *Voices of Old Testament Prophets*:
The 26th Annual Sidney B. Sperry Symposium [Salt Lake City: Deseret Book Co., 1997], 71.)

2 Ne. 23:14   ROE
(Isa. 13:14, footnote 14a)

This word is used in nearly a dozen verses. . . . In most instances, the word [means] "gazelle."

(*The New Compact Bible Dictionary*, ed. T. Alton Bryant
[Grand Rapids, Michigan: Zondervan Publishing House, 1967], 44.)

2 Ne. 23:14–22   DESTRUCTION OF BABYLON
(Isa. 13:14–22; refer in this text to 2 Ne. 23:1 & 2 Ne. 24:22–23.)

[Babylon] was the greatest city in all the world. . . . Yet Isaiah announced that that city would be destroyed; he said that it would never be rebuilt, that it would never be inhabited from generation to generation, that it would become the abode of reptiles and wild animals and that the Arabs would no more pitch their tents there. That was a declaration that the greatest city in the world would not only be destroyed, but it would also never be rebuilt.

(LeGrand Richards, *Conference Report*, Apr. 1954, 54.)

You remember the prophecy of Isaiah, when he declared the destruction of Babylon, which was at that time the greatest city in all the world. . . . Isaiah said that it would never be rebuilt, that it should become the abode of wild animals and reptiles, that the Arab would no more pitch his tent there. (See Isa. 13:19–22.)

When Brother [Howard W.] Hunter and Brother [Spencer W.] Kimball came back from the Holy Land after Christmas 1961, I asked Brother Hunter if he saw Babylon. He said he saw what there was left of it. Just think of anyone but a prophet of God being able to say that one of the great cities of the world today would be destroyed and never be rebuilt.

(LeGrand Richards, *Conference Report*, Oct. 1966, 42.)

Isaiah prophesied a literal new exodus for some of the Lord's people in the last days that resembles the ancient exodus out of Egypt. He predicted that the Lord's people will exit "Babylon" on the eve of a cataclysmic destruction, a destruction like that which struck Sodom and Gomorrah. To Isaiah, however, "Babylon" in the latter days consists of a world ripening in iniquity and the wicked who make up its citizenry. Both the exodus out of Egypt, therefore, and also the name Babylon serve as types. First, the Lord will miraculously intervene to save his people from bondage and destruction as he did in Egypt. Second, the ancient Babylonian world, which was known for its idolatry and oppression, here becomes a symbol of latter-day wickedness. Third, there will occur a Sodom-and-Gomorrah type of destruction (by fire rained down from the sky) in the last days.

(Avraham Gileadi, *Rediscovering The Book of Mormon*,
ed. John L. Sorenson and Melvin J. Thorne [Salt Lake City: Deseret Book Co. 1991], 198–99.)

Babylon was one of the great cities of the ancient world, perhaps the greatest. Its walls were, for height and width, one of the wonders of the world. The temple of Bel, the terraced ("hanging") gardens, the immense copper gates, and the artificial lake were, up to that time, the greatest achievements of human skill and ingenuity. The fields and farms and flocks yielded almost incredible returns, and the wealth, luxury and power of the ruling classes were correspondingly great. If any city, or country, could be regarded as invincible, Babylonia and Babylon might be so considered. But centuries before their fall Isaiah predicted, with supernatural knowledge of the details, the destruction of the city and the overthrow of the government.

It was done by means of strategy. After a long siege, apparently without effect, Cyrus, who led the besieging Medes and Persians, decided to turn the Euphrates out of its course and enter on the dry river bed. That was a gigantic undertaking. The river was 1500 feet wide and 12 feet deep. However, the undertaking was successful. The invaders entered from two sides, the former inflow and outflow of the river, and so quietly did they take possession that most of the people did not know what was happening till it was too late to make resistance. Aristotle had been informed that some of the inhabitants did not know until three days afterwards that the city had fallen. When the king of Babylon learned that Cyrus was at the gate of the palace, he commanded that he be admitted. He was. The king and all the revelers surrounding him perished. Many Babylonian princes, at that time, ended their useless earthly lives, in a drunken debauch. The kingdom was divided and given to the Medes and the Persians. Comp. Dan. 5.

(George Reynolds and Janne M. Sjodahl, *Commentary on the Book of Mormon*, ed. Philip C. Reynolds, 7 vols. [Salt Lake City: Deseret Book Co., 1955–1961], 1:364.)

2 Ne. 23:17   THE MEDES
(Isa. 13:17)

The Medes . . . came from Persia and easily conquered Babylon in 538 B.C. The walls were destroyed twenty years later, after which the city never again became the capital of an independent, strong Mesopotamian power. Two centuries later, after the Greeks, under Alexander the Great, conquered the Persians, Babylon rapidly declined in commercial and cultural importance as Seleucia became the major city in the area. By the time of Christ, only a few astronomers and mathematicians continued to live in the ancient, sparsely populated city. After they left, Babylon became a deserted *tell* (mound), which sand and brush gradually covered until it became a hill used only by wild animals and as grazing land for nomadic flocks

(Victor L. Ludlow, *Isaiah: Prophet, Seer, and Poet* [Salt Lake City: Deseret Book Co., 1982], 185.)

God used Assyria as a rod to destroy many ancient Near East peoples; now he uses the wickedness of the Medes to kill each other (the Medes were located in the mountainous region north and east of Babylon) . . .

Historically, the Medes, having formed an alliance with the Persians under Cyrus the Great's leadership, conquered the great Babylonian empire by damming the Euphrates River, marching through its riverbed, going under the city walls, and subsequently capturing Babylon. This event took place more than one hundred sixty years after Isaiah's prophecy. The phrase *shall not regard silver and gold* indicates that the Medes did not go into battle to obtain plunder (silver and gold); instead, their motivation was to kill, and gain power and control. Perhaps ancient Media points forward to all nations of the last days who have the same wicked designs.

(Donald W. Parry, Jay A. Parry, and Tina M. Peterson,
Understanding Isaiah [Salt Lake City: Deseret Book Co., 1998], 137–38.)

The man who led the Medes and the confederation of nearby nations against Babylon turned out to be Cyrus. His mother was the daughter of the king of the Medes, and according to tradition the old king was so cruel to his people that Cyrus rose up and overthrew him. Cyrus was supported by the Persians. He combined the two peoples. He also conquered all of the tributaries of the old Assyrian empire and formed many of them into a confederation before attacking Babylon in 539 B.C. Cyrus was not a cruel or brutal king, but generous with his subjects and wise in his administration of their affairs. The Lord therefore blessed him with success in putting down the wickedness of Babylon. It was not Cyrus, but subsequent Persian kings, who fulfilled Isaiah's prophecies concerning the total devastation of Babylon.

(W. Cleon Skousen, *Isaiah Speaks to Modern Times* [Salt Lake City: Ensign Publishing Co., 1984], 269.)

2 Ne. 23:19   CHALDEES

Chaldean is often "used as a synonym for Babylonian" (New Bible Dictionary, 203) (Isa. 13:19; 47:1, 5; 48:14, 20). "The *Chaldeans* were a group of tribes in the lower delta of the twin rivers below the most southerly Babylonian cities" who "had gained a leading position within Babylonia by the time of Isaiah; Merodachbaladan and Nebuchadrezzar were both Chaldeans. It was under Nebuchadrezzar (605–562 B.C.) that Babylonia reached its zenith of power, pomp and splendour, but his empire fell only a generation after his death.

(Donald W. Parry, Jay A. Parry, and Tina M. Peterson,
Understanding Isaiah [Salt Lake City: Deseret Book Co., 1998], 138.)

2 Ne. 24:1–3   THE STRANGERS SHALL BE JOINED
(Isa. 14:1–3; 2 Ne. 6:6–7; 10:8–9)

The Lord's mercy will be shown by his gathering his people back to their own land. The strangers who will be joined with them are most probably the Gentiles who will have accepted the gospel while the house of Israel is being gathered. The second verse in the Book of Mormon contains an eighteen-word retention which emphasizes the extent of the gathering of Israel—from "the ends of the earth"—and establishes that there will be more than one land for the gathering . . .

Verse 2 also shows a reversal of the ruling class: whereas Israel had been captive and in bondage to the Gentiles, the Israelites will now rule (in righteousness) over their former oppressors. Verse 3 retains the wording "*that* day" instead of KJV "the day," clearly designating the time when Israel will be gathered and freed from bondage.

(Monte S. Nyman, *Great Are the Words of Isaiah* [Salt Lake City: Bookcraft, 1980], 83–84.)

These verses were fulfilled when Cyrus the Great of Persia issued an order allowing all captive people in Babylon to return to their place of origin. The first group of Jews returned in 538 B.C. and started to rebuild Jerusalem and Judea. Another great exodus of Jews began in 520 B.C., and the group eventually was able to rebuild the walls of Jerusalem, the city itself, and the temple. Later, under the Maccabees (167–70 B.C.), the Jews enjoyed autonomy and prosperity, being so successful that they began to proselyte other people in the area and to grow in numbers. Indeed, the body of Jews grew into the millions by the time of Christ; while Babylon became desolate, Judea flourished. . . .

These verses can also find two fulfillments in the latter days. First, they may refer to The Church of Jesus Christ of Latter-day Saints, whose missionary work spreads to all nations and prepares for the peaceful conditions under which the Savior will establish his kingdom at the time of his second coming. Second, these verses may refer to the modern-day return of the Jews to the Holy Land and their building of the modern state of Israel. However, the full blessings of these verses will not be realized until the second coming of Christ, when the Jews will accept him as their Savior.

(Victor L. Ludlow, *Isaiah: Prophet, Seer, and Poet* [Salt Lake City: Deseret Book Co., 1982], 186.)

2 Ne. 24:2   LANDS OF PROMISE
(Isa. 14:2)

In the original text of this verse there were 18 words which have been left out of the King James Version. The brass plates contained these words and clarified three others: "And the people shall take them and bring them to their place; YEA, FROM FAR UNTO THE ENDS OF THE EARTH; AND THEY SHALL RETURN TO THEIR LANDS [note the plural] OF PROMISE. And the house of Israel shall possess them, and the land of the Lord SHALL BE for servants and handmaids; and they shall take them captives UNTO WHOM they were captives; and they shall rule over their oppressors" (2 Ne. 24:2; emphasis added).

Note how extensive the gathering will be. Also note that the two lands of promise (Palestine and America) will be exclusively for the servants and handmaids of the Lord. Those who formerly persecuted the people of Israel will now find themselves depending on the children of Israel for the administration of the government in righteousness.

(W. Cleon Skousen, *Isaiah Speaks to Modern Times* [Salt Lake City: Ensign Publishing Co., 1984], 275–76.)

2 Ne. 24:4–8   BABYLON—HOW HATH THE OPPRESSOR CEASED
(Isa. 14:4–8)

"The traits and the behavior which Isaiah denounces as the worst of vices are without exception those of successful people . . . The very wickedest people in the Book of Mormon are the Zoramites. A very proud, independent, courageous, industrious, enterprising, patriotic, prosperous, people who attended strictly to their weekly religious duties with the proper observance of dress standards. Thanking God for all he had given them and bearing testimony to his goodness. They were sustained in all their doings by a perfectly beautiful self-image. Well, what is wrong with any of that? There is just one thing that spoils it all and that is the very thing that puts Israel in bad with the Lord. . . . and yet . . . By far the commonest charge Isaiah brings against the wicked is "oppression" *'ashaq*. The word means to choke, to grab by the neck and squeeze, grasp, or press, to take the fullest advantage of someone in your power, in short, to maximize profits. It is all centralized in "Babylon . . . the golden city, the oppressor," (14:4). Which gives us instant insight into the social and economic structure of Isaiah's world. It is a competitive and predatory society, "Yea, they are greedy dogs which can never have enough. And (leaders) they are shepherds that cannot understand (they do not know what is going on): because everyone is looking out for himself —'they all look to their own way, every one for his gain, from his quarter'" (56:11).

The charge applies to our own day when ". . . every man walketh in his own way, and after the image of his own God, whose image is in the likeness of the world, and whose substance is that of an idol, which waxeth old and shall perish in Babylon, even Babylon the great which shall fall." (D&C 1:16). Babylon had flourished long before Isaiah's day and it was to flourish long after. . . . Its philosophy is no where better expressed than in the words of Korihor: " . . . every man fared in this life according to the management of the creature; therefore every man prospered according to his genius, and that every man conquered according to his strength . . . and whatsoever a man did was no crime" (Alma 30:17).

(Hugh W. Nibley, "Great Are the Words of Isaiah," *Sidney B. Sperry Symposium*
[Provo, Utah: Religious Instruction, BYU, January 28, 1978], 198–99.)

This section of the poem describes the beginning of the Millennium, when Satan will be bound and the earth will rest. The reference is to rulers who have come under the influence of Satan and not solely to Nebuchadnezzar or one of his successors. The binding of Satan at the beginning of the thousand years is also prophesied in the New Testament (see Rev. 20:1–3), the Book of Mormon (see 1 Ne. 22:26), and the Doctrine and Covenants (see 43:31; 88:110; 101:28). First Nephi 22:15 suggests that the prophecy of the binding of Satan used by Nephi may have been taken from Isaiah.

(Monte S. Nyman, *Great Are the Words of Isaiah* [Salt Lake City: Bookcraft, 1980], 85.)

There were three notable occasions when this verse was literally fulfilled for the Jews. The first was when they were liberated along with the rest of Israel from captivity and hard bondage under the Egyptians. The second was when they were liberated from the Babylonians by Cyrus and the Persians. The third has been in modern times when powerful dictators such as Adolf Hitler and Benito Mussolini established a policy of slave labor camps for Jews, and said they would eventually exterminate all Jews coming within their power. In each of these instances the terrible desolation hanging over the people was suddenly lifted. It was virtually unbelievable at first. And so it will yet be when the Jews face their Armageddon. After much tribulation, it will suddenly end. As with the fall of ancient Babylon in a single night, so shall it be in the latter days. Their oppressors will dissolve into nothing just as the golden city of the Babylonians ceased to be a threat once the Persians had taken over.

(W. Cleon Skousen, *Isaiah Speaks to Modern Times* [Salt Lake City: Ensign Publishing Co., 1984], 276–277.)

2 Ne. 24:4–21   TAUNT–SONG
(Isa. 14:4–8; D&C 88:110)

These verses begin the *taunt-song* aimed at the once-powerful king of Babylon. Even the trees rejoice in the demise of this once-powerful king. Although the historical context of these verses is couched in ancient Babylon, the application extends to the latter days as well. It could apply to the ultimate removal of any wicked leader, particularly Satan. He will be bound at the commencement of the Millennium, reducing him to the role of a powerless prisoner for one thousand years (see D&C 88:110).

(Hoyt W. Brewster, Jr., *Isaiah Plain and Simple* [Salt Lake City: Deseret Book Co., 1995], 136–137.)

2 Ne. 24:8   CEDARS OF LEBANON
(Isa. 24:8; refer in this text to 2 Ne. 12:13)

It is a well-known fact that the trees of Lebanon were cut down by the kings of Assyria (cf. Habakkuk 2:17), and inscriptions found in the district of Lebanon seem to confirm the Babylonian guilt in this respect.

(Sidney B. Sperry, *Book of Mormon Compendium* [Salt Lake City: Bookcraft, 1968], 175.)

The various destructions described by Isaiah always involve destruction of the forests. Therefore, now that he described the land at peace, he pictured the forests themselves as feeling secure.

(Solomon B. Freehof, *Book of Isaiah* [New York: Union of American Hebrew Congregation, 1972], 88.)

2 Ne. 24:9–11   ART THOU ALSO BECOME WEAK AS WE
(Isa. 14:9–11)

This section of the poem predicts Satan's being restricted to the spirit world of hell during the millennial years of peace on earth, and describes the reaction of hell's inhabitants when it is announced that he is assigned there. That he will have influence there is shown by the Prophet Joseph Smith's statement that "when we have power to put all enemies under our feet in this world, and a knowledge to *triumph over all evil spirits in the world to come*, then we are saved" (*TPJS*, 297). Alma 34:34–35 also shows that the spirit of the devil will have power to possess the unrepentant in the spirit world. When he is bound in the spirit world, "the chief ones of the earth"—those leaders who were influential in the devil's kingdom while they lived upon the earth—will assemble to greet him. When they see him, they will be amazed at his having lost his power.

(Monte S. Nyman, *Great Are the Words of Isaiah* [Salt Lake City: Bookcraft, 1980], 85.)

2 Ne. 24:12–17   LUCIFER - SHALT BE BROUGHT DOWN
(Isa. 14:12–17; D&C 76:25–26; 29:36; Moses 4:3–4;
1 Ne. 22:26; 2 Ne. 2:17–18)

The only places in the Bible and the Book of Mormon where the title *Lucifer* is used are Isaiah 14:12 and 2 Nephi 24:12. In Doctrine and Covenants 76:25–28 we learn that Lucifer (which means "light bearer") was the premortal name of Satan. Because of his rebellion against God he fell from his position of "authority in the presence of God" (v. 25) and "was called Perdition" (v. 26), which means "destruction."

(*Book of Mormon Student Manual, Religion 121 and 122*
[Salt Lake City: The Church of Jesus Christ of Latter-day Saints, 1989], 34.)

The name Lucifer (Hebrew *helel*) means "shining one." If the name is given different vowels (*helal*), it signifies the crescent of the moon, having possible meaning that Lucifer had less light (symbolically) than the full moon, or Lucifer's light waned as does the light of the moon during its cycle. Further, Lucifer's light was far less than the light of Jesus Christ, whose light is the sun (Ps. 84:11; D&C 88:7–9). Isaiah may also be using a play on words, for Lucifer's name (*helel*) sounds like a word Isaiah uses in 13:6 where he commands those of Babylon to "Howl!" (Hebrew *helili*).

(Donald W. Parry, Jay A. Parry, and Tina M. Peterson,
Understanding Isaiah [Salt Lake City: Deseret Book Co., 1998], 148.)

Perhaps there are principles here that few men have thought of. No person can have this salvation except through a tabernacle.

Now, in this world, mankind are naturally selfish, ambitious and striving to excel one above another; yet some are willing to build up others as well as themselves. So in the other world there are a variety of spirits. Some seek to excel. And this was the case with Lucifer when he fell. He sought for things which were unlawful. Hence he was sent down, and it is said he drew many away with him; and the greatness of his punishment is that he shall not have a tabernacle. This is his punishment. So the devil, thinking to thwart the decree of God, by going up and down in the earth, seeking whom he may destroy—any person that he can find that will yield to him, he will bind him, and take possession of the body and reign there, glorying in it mightily, not caring that he had got merely a stolen body; and by and by some one having authority will come along and cast him out and restore the tabernacle to its rightful owner. The devil steals a tabernacle because he has not one of his own: but if he steals one, he is always liable to be turned out of doors.

(Joseph Smith, *Teachings of the Prophet Joseph Smith*,
comp. Joseph Fielding Smith [Salt Lake City: Deseret Book Co., 1976], 297–98.)

Most scholars identify the "morning star" or Lucifer as a mythical figure or as a figurative representation of a Babylonian king. Latter-day Saints are fortunate to have modern scripture that explains who Lucifer is. Additional modern scripture explains his actions and attitude in greater detail. (Compare Isa. 14:12–14 with D&C 76:25–27; 29:36–37; Moses 4:1–4.)

(Victor L. Ludlow, *Isaiah: Prophet, Seer, and Poet* [Salt Lake City: Deseret Book Co., 1982], 188.)

As people fill their hearts with the Spirit of God, there will be no room in their hearts for Satan's influence. Isaiah delighted in the future binding of Satan for one thousand years and the eventual banishment of Satan to outer darkness following the Millennium.

In teaching this concept Isaiah employed a satirical song. He portrayed the ancient king of Babylon as a type for Lucifer. Similar to the king of Babylon, Lucifer has ruled over an empire built upon tyranny and oppression . . . (Isa. 14:13–14). Isaiah prophesied that the day will come when Lucifer will "be brought down to hell, to the sides of the pit" (Isa. 14:15). John the Revelator was shown an angel who had the key of a bottomless pit. "He laid hold on . . . that old serpent, which is the Devil, and Satan, and bound him a thousand years, and cast him into the bottomless pit, and shut him up, and set a seal upon him, that he should deceive the nations no more, till the thousand years should be fulfilled" (Rev. 20:2–3). Satan will be held in such low regard that people will mock him, saying, "Is this the man that made the earth to tremble, that did shake kingdoms; . . . that opened not the house of his prisoners?" (Isa. 14:16–17). Truly, during the Millennium Lucifer will be bound and will "not have power to tempt any man" (D&C 101:28). Therefore, he will "have no place in the hearts of the children of men" (D&C 45:55).

(Craig J. Ostler, *Voices of Old Testament Prophets*:
The 26th Annual Sidney B. Sperry Symposium [Salt Lake City: Deseret Book Co., 1997], 75–76.)

2 Ne. 24:19   THRUST THROUGH WITH A SWORD
(Isa. 24:19)

This became literally true. Nabonadius, the last king of Babylonia, fled to Borsippa, after having been defeated in battle by Cyrus, and left his son, Belshazzar, in Babylon to look after the affairs of state. The young prince was surprised by the invaders, in the midst of revelry, and slain in the confusion, at the gate of his magnificent palace, "thrust through with a sword"; whereupon Nabonadius, his father, crushed in body and spirit by his losses, surrendered to the conqueror.

(George Reynolds and Janne M. Sjodahl, *Commentary on the Book of Mormon*,
ed. Philip C. Reynolds, 7 vols. [Salt Lake City: Deseret Book Co., 1955–1961], 1:367.)

2 Ne. 24:22–23   DESTRUCTION OF BABYLON
(Isa. 14:22–23)

Isaiah prophesies that God would put an end to Babylon, the great city of ancient Babylonia known for its huge walls, celebrated gardens and parks, and beautiful temples. Babylon's destruction would be so great that both "son" and "nephew"—those who would produce additional generations to inhabit Babylon—would be destroyed.

Isaiah's words were fulfilled in 539 B.C. when Cyrus, king of Persia, defeated Babylon together with its evil rulers and residents. How complete was Babylon's destruction? The Lord said, "I will sweep it with the broom of destruction." Just as one sweeps a house to eliminate dust and dirt, so God swept Babylon of its foulness so that nothing, not even dust, remained. Its temples and gardens are gone, and Babylon now stands in ruins, a testimony that Isaiah's words were fulfilled.

Babylon is a perfect example of an evil place that was destroyed by the power of God. As such, Babylon is a type and a shadow of the wicked world that will be destroyed by God's power in the last days (D&C 1:16).

(Donald W. Parry, *Visualizing Isaiah*
[Provo, Utah: The Foundation for Ancient Research and Mormon Studies, 2001], 35.)

2 Ne. 24:23   POOLS OF WATER
(Isa. 14:23)

At the beginning of our era, Babylon was still partly inhabited and the surrounding country was cultivated. In the second century, the walls were still standing. During the fourth century they served as an enclosure for wild animals, and Persian monarchs went there to amuse themselves hunting. By and by the location was lost sight of and forgotten. More modern writers—Dr. Alexander Keith, among others—note the utter desolation of the once famous city. From the place where once the temple of Bel and the royal palaces rose in majestic heights, to the streets, everything has been reduced to gravel hills. Some are large; others are smaller. One who sees the innumerable parallel hills and the depressions between them does not know whether they are remnants of streets or canals. Babylon is fallen. Its foundations could not have been brought lower. Its "pomp has been brought down to the grave." It has literally become "pools of water." For laborers have made innumerable excavations to get gravel, or clay, for industrial purposes, and when the Euphrates overflows its banks, its water fills these hollows forming pools, or swamps. Such was the glory of Babylon less than a century ago (cf. Jer. 51:42).

(George Reynolds and Janne M. Sjodahl, *Commentary on the Book of Mormon,*
ed. Philip C. Reynolds, 7 vols. [Salt Lake City: Deseret Book Co., 1955–1961], 1:367.)

When Cyrus conquered Babylon, he destroyed her irrigation works, turning the once lush and fruitful land into fetid pools of water (swamps or bogs).

(Hoyt W. Brewster, Jr., *Isaiah Plain and Simple* [Salt Lake City: Deseret Book Co., 1995], 144.)

2 Ne. 24:24   AS I HAVE PURPOSED, SO SHALL IT STAND
(Isa. 14:24.)

This must be the foundation of our instruction: love of God and love for and service to others. . . . That which we teach must be constantly gauged against these two standards established by the Lord. If we shall do so, this work will continue to roll forward. . . .

You and I may fail as individuals and miss the blessing. But his work cannot fail. There will always be those he will raise up to accomplish it. He has declared: "Surely as I have thought, so shall it come to pass; and as I have purposed, so shall it stand" (Isa. 14:24).

I bear witness to you . . . that he, watching over Israel, slumbers not nor sleeps. God help us to be faithful to the great trust he has placed in us.

(Gordon B. Hinckley, *Ensign*, May 1983, 8.)

2 Ne. 24:25   BRING THE ASSYRIANS IN MY LAND
(Isa. 14:25; 36)

It is difficult to determine whether Isaiah is prophesying about the destruction of Sennacherib's Assyrian army in 701 B.C. or the defeat of the army of the nations led by King Gog in the last days. (Compare Isa. 36–37 with Ezek. 38–39.) In both cases, the Lord's punishment is felt by the wicked nations of the earth.

(Victor L. Ludlow, *Isaiah: Prophet, Seer, and Poet* [Salt Lake City: Deseret Book Co., 1982], 189.)

The Lord has not only determined to destroy Babylon in due time, but he has already programmed the means by which a more immediate threat to Israel will be eliminated. This was the Assyrian Empire, which preceded Babylon and was the terror of the world in Isaiah's day. In this verse the King James Version says the Lord will "break" the Assyrians, but in the brass plates it says the Lord will "BRING" the Assyrians into the promised land (2 Ne. 24:25). This makes the rest of the verse more sensible. For it says these Assyrians will pour into the mountains of Israel and tread them under foot (conquer them). It turned out that the Assyrians did not storm the mountains of Judah but only the mountains of Ephraim, where the Ten Tribes were located. These were trodden under foot from around 735 to 721 B.C., when the surviving remnants were carried off to Assyria. There they remained as virtual captives or hostages until Babylon came along in 605 B.C. and virtually annihilated the Assyrian people as a nation. This allowed the Ten Tribes to escape from their Assyrian captors and flee northward over the Caucasus Mountains, where they disappeared and became known as the lost tribes.

(W. Cleon Skousen, *Isaiah Speaks to Modern Times* [Salt Lake City: Ensign Publishing Co., 1984], 284.)

2 Ne. 24:26–27   HAND STRETCHED OUT UPON ALL NATIONS
(Isa. 14:26–27; refer in this text to 2 Ne. 19:12, 17)

What we mortals encounter as the unforeseen, God has already seen, such as how the oil deposits of this earth would shape the latter-day conflicts among nations. God's "is the hand that is stretched out upon all the nations" (Isa. 14:26). He likewise foresaw all the awful famines, some resulting from the unwise, unnecessary erosions of precious topsoil. He surely foresaw the terrible persecutions of the Jews. Having created the earth, He had anticipated the impact of continental drifts on the frequency and intensity of latter-day earthquakes. He who analogized that "the wicked are like the troubled sea, when it cannot rest" (Isa. 57:20) also knows where and when, in latter days, the seas' tidal waves will heave themselves savagely "beyond their bounds" (D&C 88:90).

Without the revelations, however, the answers as to the why of our existence and the why of human suffering would elude even the best intellectual excursions.

(Neal A. Maxwell, *Ensign*, Nov. 1987, 37.)

2 Ne. 24:28–31   PALESTINA
(Isa. 14:28–31)

The country of Philistia consisted essentially of five city-states, each governed by its own lord. The nation was home of the Philistines, detested enemies of Judah and the Israelites. This country was at the height of its power at the time of King Saul's death, but declined during the reign of King David. The Philistines were conquered by the Assyrians in 734 B.C., later they became part of the Persian Empire, and finally the land was annexed to Syria by the Romans.

(Hoyt W. Brewster, Jr., *Isaiah Plain and Simple* [Salt Lake City: Deseret Book Co., 1995], 148.)

A number of thorny, unresolved historical problems prevent the giving of a reasonably exact interpretation of some parts of the prophecy. But Isaiah seems to be telling Philistia not to rejoice over his predictions of the ruin and downfall of Judah, her traditional enemy. For whereas the kingdom of Judah will fall, there will come a glorious day when the people of Israel will rise above their troubles. . . . On the other hand, Philistia is to be ruined and to fall without having any prospects of recovery.

(Sidney B. Sperry, *Book of Mormon Compendium* [Salt Lake City: Bookcraft, 1968], 244–45.)

"Philistia, the country of the Philistines (Heb. Peleshet), the southern part of the coast plain of Canaan. This country was once one of the most flourishing, and, consequently, one of the most important and wealthy in Syria. Its cities, particularly Gaza, Askelon and Ashdod, were famous in the Old World, when the prophets predicted their destruction. Even long after their doom was proclaimed, they continued to prosper. Alexander the Great, the conqueror of the Persian army, was halted outside Gaza and delayed for two months. Askelon was famous for its flourishing vineyards, which made it an important commercial center. Ashdod was a strongly fortified city, strong enough to hold the Egyptian conquerors at bay for twenty years. It was demolished by the Turks in 1270 A.D., and Ibrahim Pasha carried away a considerable part of the ruins, to use for building material elsewhere. The surrounding country was fertile enough for many years. Wheat, peas, beans, fig trees, almonds and pomegranates were produced in abundance, but gradually the curse seemed to settle upon the soil. It became barren, and the few inhabitants who survived eked out a precarious existence by taking care of a few sheep and goats. Gaza was destroyed by Alexander the Great, 333 B.C. Strabo, at the beginning of our era, refers to it as a "desert." That is the very expression the angel of the Lord used when he sent Philip to go and meet the Ethiopian. He said "rise and go . . . unto the way that goeth down from Jerusalem unto Gaza, which is desert." (Acts 8:26) True, Constantine rebuilt Gaza, and established an ecclesiastic see there, but not on the old site but some distance from it. It was the new Gaza, known as "Ghuzze," which figured in the world war and fell into the hands of General Sir Henry Allenby, Nov. 6, 1917.

(George Reynolds and Janne M. Sjodahl, *Commentary on the Book of Mormon*,
ed. Philip C. Reynolds, 7 vols. [Salt Lake City: Deseret Book Co., 1955–1961], 1:369.)

2 Ne. 24:29   SERPENT'S ROOT–COCKATRICE–FIERY SERPENT
(Isa. 14:29)

Sidney Sperry points out the *serpent's root, cockatrice* (venomous viper), and *fiery flying serpent* are "all symbolic of evil to come upon her [Philistia]." (*BMC*, 245). Each of these represents a more deadly threat than the previous one mentioned. J. R. Dummelow identified Sargon (Assyrian king from 722 to 705 B.C.) and Sennacherib (Assyrian king from 705 to 681 B.C.) as the cockatrice and fiery serpent, "each one proving more terrible and formidable to the nations of Western Asia than his predecessor."

(Hoyt W. Brewster, Jr., *Isaiah Plain and Simple* [Salt Lake City: Deseret Book Co., 1995], 149.)

2 Ne. 24:32   **THE LORD HATH FOUNDED ZION**
                    (Isa. 14:32)

Isaiah also knew that ultimately the whole Philistine coast would be occupied by a righteous people who would say: "The Lord hath founded Zion, and the poor of his people shall trust in it." The word "Zion" refers to a place and a condition. Modern prophets have been told that the place called Zion is North and South America, to which Isaiah referred frequently in his writings (Smith, *Teachings*, 362). However, "Zion" as a condition can be anywhere. As the Lord has declared, "This is Zion—the pure in heart" (D&C 97:21). Isaiah knew that ultimately Palestine would belong to the pure in heart.

(W. Cleon Skousen, *Isaiah Speaks to Modern Times* [Salt Lake City: Ensign Publishing Co., 1984], 286.)

Why is Isaiah hard to understand? (Nephi gives us the answer in 2 Ne. 25:1–5.)

2 Ne. 25:17   **RESTORE HIS PEOPLE–MARVELOUS WORK**
                    (Isa. 11:11; 29:14; refer in this text to 2 Ne. 21:10–12 & 2 Ne. 27:26)

2 Ne. 26:15–16 **LOW OUT OF THE DUST**
                    (Isa. 29:3–4)

These verses could refer to the nations of Judah and Israel being brought low, or destroyed. The ancient covenant people would then speak "low out of the dust" in the sense that they would speak out of the depths of their humbled condition.

A more probable interpretation of these verses would be their application to the destruction of the ancient Nephite civilization. This is obviously the interpretation Nephi had in mind. This people, because of iniquity and unbelief, were to be "brought down low in the dust, even that they are not." Yet, even though destroyed as a people without posterity, their words "shall speak . . . out of the ground, and their speech shall be low out of the dust." . . .

The last survivor of that ancient Nephite society was a prophet, scribe, and warrior named Moroni. He was charged with safeguarding those sacred writings. He discharged that duty by concluding the record and safely burying it in a protected place to which he was undoubtedly led. Over fourteen hundred years later, then a resurrected being, he was divinely directed to deliver the plates "out of the ground" to the young Prophet Joseph Smith. Joseph, in turn, was called to translate the sacred record into what is now known to millions throughout the earth as the Book of Mormon: Another Testament of Jesus Christ. (See JS–H 1:27–54, 59–60.)

Because Nephi is expounding on Isaiah, rather than simply quoting, his words cast a great deal of light on this passage.

(Hoyt W. Brewster, Jr., *Isaiah Plain and Simple* [Salt Lake City: Deseret Book Co., 1995], 152–53.)

Never was a prophecy more truly fulfilled than this, in the coming forth of the Book of Mormon. Joseph Smith took that sacred history "out of the ground." It is the voice of the ancient prophets of America speaking "out of the ground"; their speech is "low out of the dust"; it speaks in a most familiar manner of the doings of bygone ages; it is the voice of those who slumber in the dust. It is the voice of prophets speaking from the dead, crying repentance in the ears of the living. In what manner could a nation, after they were brought down and destroyed, "speak out of the ground?" Could their dead bodies or their dust, or their ashes speak? Verily, no: they can only speak by their writings or their books that they wrote while living. Their voice, speech or words, can only "speak out of the ground," or "whisper out of the dust" by their books or writings being discovered.

(Orson Pratt, *Orson Pratt's Works: The Light of Understanding* [Salt Lake City, Deseret News Press, 1945], 271.)

The Lord designed from the beginning to bring the Book of Mormon forth from the ground as a voice from the dust, as truth springing out of the earth. The symbolism and imagery in this are beautiful. As revelation pours down from above to water the earth, so the gospel plant grows out of the earth to bear witness that the heavenly rains contain the life-giving power. Heaven and earth join hands in testifying of the truths of salvation. Their combined voices are the voice of restoration, the voice of glory and honor and eternal life, the voice from heaven, and the voice out of the earth.

(Bruce R. McConkie, *The Millennial Messiah* [Salt Lake City: Deseret Book Co., 1982], 150.)

[Enoch] was told that following a period of great apostasy, "righteousness [would come] down out of heaven; and truth [would come] forth out of the earth, to bear testimony of [the] Only Begotten." And then the Lord said to Enoch that, in the day of refreshing, "righteousness and truth will I cause to sweep the earth as with a flood, to gather out mine elect from the four quarters of the earth" (Moses 7:62).

Righteousness and truth descended from the heavens when the Father and the Son appeared to Joseph Smith, when Moroni brought the plates, and when other prophets and apostles returned to the earth. Truth came forth out of the earth with the publication of the Book of Mormon.

(Merrill J. Bateman, "Truth and Righteousness Will Sweep the Earth,"
BYU Women's Conference address, 27 Apr. 2000, 2.)

2 Ne. 26:16   FAMILIAR SPIRIT
(Isa. 29:4; refer in this text to 2 Ne. 18:19.)

Elder LeGrand Richards called our attention to a minister of another religion who said that the Book of Mormon read with the same sweet feeling as the New Testament (see *CR*, Apr. 1976, 124). In other words, the message of the Book of Mormon sounds familiar to those who have received the message of the Bible, the gospel, or the Spirit of God. On the other hand, "familiar spirits" in Old Testament times referred to a form of spiritualism wherein spirits from the dead were called back out of the ground through witchcraft or enchantment (see 1 Sam. 28; Isa. 8:19–20). Some have used this meaning to disclaim the Book of Mormon. However, a careful reading of Isaiah shows that the words of the record would be "as" a familiar spirit. Just as the spirits came "out of the ground," so would the record of a people who had been destroyed. Nephi in 2 Nephi 26:16 shows that the power of God would be given to these people to "whisper . . . even as it were out of the ground."

(Monte S. Nyman, *Great Are the Words of Isaiah* [Salt Lake City: Bookcraft, 1980], 107–108.)

Some biblical scholars have maintained that witchcraft is being referred to in that portion of Isaiah 29:4 which says that the voice shall be "as one that hath a familiar spirit." These scholars evidently arrived at this interpretation because of similar wording in other parts of the Bible. For example, in Leviticus we read: "Regard not them that have familiar spirits, neither seek after wizards, to be defiled by them" (Leviticus 19:31), and "A man also or woman that hath a familiar spirit, or that is a wizard, shall surely be put to death" (Leviticus 20:27). (For further biblical references indicating that the term "familiar spirits" might sometimes refer to witches, see 1 Sam. 28:7; 2 Kgs. 21:6; 1 Chron. 10:13; Isa. 8:19 and 19:3.)

However, a careful reading of this scripture, particularly when read together with Nephi's explanation, would indicate that the term it "hath a familiar spirit" means that this record (the Book of Mormon) would speak with a "familiar voice" to those who already have the Bible. In other words, Nephi is evidently saying here that the doctrinal teachings of the Book of Mormon would seem familiar to people who had already read and accepted the Bible."

(Daniel H. Ludlow, *A Companion To Your Study of The Book of Mormon*
[Salt Lake City: Deseret Book Co., 1976], 138–139.)

2 Ne. 26:18; 27:2 AN INSTANT SUDDENLY
(Isa. 29:5)

An ancient nation which lived in America actually was destroyed suddenly, just as Isaiah foretold. Its population numbered in the millions. These people once had been righteous and had prophets among them who kept a sacred history engraved on metal plates. Before their final destruction, one of their prophets buried that record in the ground in a stone container for safe-keeping. Hence, when this book was found, translated, and published in modern times, that early nation literally spoke out of the ground just as Isaiah said it would.

(Mark E. Petersen, *Ensign*, Nov. 1977, 12.)

These predictions of Isaiah could not refer to Ariel, or Jerusalem, because their speech has not been "out of the ground," or "low out of the dust," but it refers to the remnant of Joseph who were destroyed in America. . . . The Book of Mormon describes their downfall, and truly it was great and terrible. At the crucifixion of Christ, "the multitude of their terrible ones," as Isaiah predicted "became as chaff that passeth away," and it took place, as he further predicts, "at an instant suddenly." Many of their great and magnificent cities were destroyed by fire, others by earthquakes, others by being sunk and buried in the depths of the earth. This sudden destruction came upon them because they had stoned and killed the prophets sent among them. Between three and four hundred years after Christ, they again fell into great wickedness, and the principal nation fell in battle. Forts were raised in all parts of the land, the remains of which may be seen at the present day. Millions of people perished in battle and they suffered just as the Lord foretold by Isaiah.

(Orson Pratt, *Orson Pratt's Works: The Light of Understanding*
[Salt Lake City: The Deseret News Press, 1945], 270–71.)

In what form or shape or by what method did Moroni restore the everlasting gospel? . . . God could do only one thing, and that was to raise up a new prophet for this particular purpose, and this He did in the person of the Prophet Joseph Smith, Jr.

In what way did the angel deliver the gospel to Joseph Smith? . . . The prophet Isaiah explains. In the twenty-ninth chapter of his book, he tells of an ancient record that would come out of the ground in the latter days, in a time preceding the restoration of Palestine as a fruitful field. (See verse 17.) This record would be in the form of a book, he said, having to do with a people who had been destroyed suddenly. (See Isa. 29:5.)

(Mark E. Petersen, *Ensign*, Nov. 1983, 31.)

2 Ne. 26:25   BUY . . . WITHOUT MONEY AND WITHOUT PRICE
(Isa. 55:1; refer in this text to 2 Ne. 9:50–51.)

A beautiful illustration of the customary mode of addressing purchasers in the East is given by Miss Rogers, who thus describes her walk through one of the streets of Jerusalem: "The shopkeepers were crying to the passers-by, 'Ho, every one that hath money, let him come and buy! Ho, such a one, come and buy!' But some of them seemed to be more disinterested, and one of the fruiterers, offering me preserves and fruit, said; 'O lady, take of our fruit without money and without price; it is yours, take all that you will,' and he would gladly have laden our *kawas* with the good things of his store and then have claimed double their value."—*Domestic Life in Palestine*, 49. There is more sincerity in the Gospel invitations than in those of the traders.

(James M. Freeman, *Manners and Customs of the Bible* [Plainfield, New Jersey: Logos International, 1972], 275.)

2 Ne. 27
Even though each verse of 2 Nephi 27 does not parallel Isaiah 29, the entire chapter will be included because each verse of 2 Nephi 27 gives effective commentary for Isaiah 29.

2 Ne. 27:1–2 THE LAST DAYS–THE DAYS OF THE GENTILES
(Isa. 29:6; Eth. 2:11; 3 Ne. 30:1–2; D&C 18:6; 29:9; 45:28–33; 61:31; Luke 21:24; JS–H 1:41; refer in *Latter-day Commentary on the Book of Mormon,* Bassett, to 3 Ne. 16:10–16 & 3 Ne. 20:15–20, 22)

We are living in the days of the Gentiles when this prediction was to be fulfilled. . . . If we are living the religion which the Lord has revealed and which we have received, we do not belong to the world. We should have no part in all its foolishness. . . . If I sometimes, and once in a while I do, go to a football game or a baseball game or some other place of amusement, invariably I will be surrounded by men and women who are puffing on cigarettes or cigars or dirty pipes. It gets very annoying, and I get a little disturbed. I will turn to Sister Smith, and I will say something to her, and she will say, "Well, now, you know what you have taught me. You are in their world. This is their world." And that sort of brings me back to my senses. Yes, we are in their world, but we do not have to be of it. So, as this is their world we are living in, they prosper, but, my good brethren and sisters, their world is coming to its end.

(Joseph Fielding Smith, *Conference Report,* Apr. 1952, 27–28.)

Speaking of the overthrow of the Jews and the destruction of Jerusalem, the Lord said to his disciples: "And they shall fall by the edge of the sword, and shall be led away captive into all nations: and *Jerusalem shall be trodden down of the Gentiles, until the times of the Gentiles be fulfilled. . . .*"

This scripture was also referred to by Moroni when he visited Joseph Smith in September, 1823, which scripture he said was soon to be fulfilled. He said that the fulness of the Gentiles was soon to come in. . . .

We all know that from the time of the destruction of Jerusalem in the year 70 A.D. until near the close of World War I, Jerusalem was trodden down of the Gentiles, and during all of that time the Jews were scattered and almost without privileges in the Holy Land. The Lord said they should remain scattered among the nations *until* the times of the Gentiles were fulfilled. Moroni said the times of the Gentiles were about to be fulfilled. Today we are living in the *transition* period; *the day of the Gentiles has come in, and the day of Judah and the remnant of downtrodden Israel is now at hand.*

(Joseph Fielding Smith, *Doctrines of Salvation: Sermons and Writings of Joseph Fielding Smith,* ed. Bruce R. McConkie, 3 vols. [Salt Lake City: Bookcraft, 1954–1956], 3:258–59.)

Now is the great day of the Gentiles, and it has been for centuries since the Savior's first coming when Israel was rejected by him. From that time forward world history has been centered in the Gentile nations, largely in the Christian Gentile nations. Certainly all modern history has been centered in the Christian Gentile nations, which are the ones the Book of Mormon speaks of. The whole colonization of the world, all of the major wars, have concerned the Gentile nations. The Germans, the British and their allies, fought World War I. All of them were Christian nations. Who fought the second World War? Essentially the same division. What nations are now fighting the war that is going on in the world continually? Russia which was a Christian nation although her government has now rejected Christianity, and the United States and their allies. This is the time of the Gentiles. The Gentiles still speak of their various spheres of influence, but the number of uncommitted nations of the world is growing. The time of the Gentiles obviously is coming to an end. No longer does what the European nations say go without question from the Orientals, the Africans. Can you imagine the Egyptians taking over the Suez Canal fifty years ago or even Africans rising up in revolt against their masters? They have done it. Or the people of Indonesia, formerly the Dutch East Indies, rising up against the Dutch and throwing them off? Again they have done it. This is the time of the end of the Gentiles domination of the world. Historians recognize this.

(F. Kent Nielsen, *Book of Mormon Teachings*, [Provo, Utah: Extension Publications, Adult Education and Extension Services, 1960], 27. As found in *The Fulfillment of Book of Mormon Prophecies*, Warner, Hawkes Pub., 1975, 108.)

What do you mean by their times being fulfilled, and the fullness of the Gentiles coming in? . . . This Gospel, which God sends by the ministration of "another angel" from heaven, must be preached to all nations, kindreds, tongues and people, to the Gentiles first; and when they get through with them, it will go to Israel, for the times of the Gentiles will then be fulfilled; in other words, when God shall speak to his servants,—and say unto them—"It is enough, you have been faithful in your ministry, you have warned the nations, kindreds and tongues of the Gentiles sufficiently, now I call you to a still greater work, and will give you a new mission, not to go and preach to the Gentiles, but go to the remnants of the House of Israel wherever they can be found, and let your testimony be to them. Hunt them up from the four quarters of the earth, gather them out with a mighty hand and with an outstretched arm, and bring them back to their own land." When that time shall come Israel will be gathered and not till then.

(Orson Pratt, *Journal of Discourses*, 16:352.)

The Gentiles have not continued in the goodness of God, but have departed from the faith that was once delivered to the Saints, and have broken the covenant in which their fathers were established (see Isa. 24:5); and have become high-minded, and have not feared; therefore, but few of them will be gathered with the chosen family. Have not the pride, high-mindedness, and unbelief of the Gentiles, provoked the Holy One of Israel to withdraw His Holy Spirit from them, and send forth His judgments to scourge them for their wickedness? This is certainly the case.

(Joseph Smith, *History of the Church*, 1:313–14.)

How does our nation stand?

Are not many of us materialistic? Do we not find it well-nigh impossible to raise our sights above the dollar sign? . . .

Are not many of us status-seekers—measuring the worth of a man by the size of his bank account, his house, his automobile?

Are we not . . . willing to co-exist with evil . . . so long as it does not touch us personally?

If the answer to these questions is, "yes" . . . then surely these are among the many reasons why this is truly an era of peril. . . .

Many of us imagine in the foolishness of pride, that our manifold blessings are due not to God's goodness, but to our own wisdom and virtue. Too many of us have been so drunk with self-sufficiency as no longer to feel the need of prayer. . . .

This is a sad commentary on a civilization which has given to mankind the greatest achievements and progress ever known. But it is an even sadder commentary on those of us who call ourselves Christians, who thus betray the ideals given to us by the Son of God himself.

(Ezra Taft Benson, *Conference Report*, Oct. 1960, 103, 105.)

Taking the meridian of time as a starting point, the gospel was preached first to the Jews and thereafter to the Gentiles. In our dispensation, the dispensation of the fulness of times, the gospel was, according to prophecy, brought forth by Gentiles who in turn will take it to all the nations of the earth. After the Gentiles have had ample opportunity to receive it and then turn on it in wickedness, it will be taken from them and given back to its original stewards. Thus, the first shall be last and the last first (see 1 Ne. 13:42).

When we speak of the day of the Gentiles being fulfilled, we are speaking of that time when "the consumption decreed" will make "a full end of all nations" (D&C 87:6), and a messianic kingdom established in their stead. Thus, the day of the Gentile will end—its power, authority, and influence will be no more.

(Joseph Fielding McConkie, *Third Nephi 9–30, This Is My Gospel*, ed. Monte S. Nyman and Charles D. Tate, Jr. [Provo: Religious Studies Center, BYU, 1993], 174–75.)

2 Ne. 27:3–5   DREAM OF A NIGHT VISION
(Isa. 29:7–10)

With all my heart I implore those who are walking on the fringes of our faith to seek the safety of the center. This can be done best by counseling with your leaders and remaining within the fellowshipping circle of the Saints, and receiving nourishment from the good word of God. Do not permit faithless people to turn you out of the right way. . . .

And I pray for those who deal in the highest form of larceny—that of stripping people of their precious testimonies. Such action, if continued, will lead only to the futility and emptiness of the dream of a night vision. (See 2 Ne. 27:3; Acts 5:33–39.)

(Carlos E. Asay, *Ensign,* Nov. 1981, 69.)

Many who are without the fulness of the gospel but who reject that fulness when it is available wander in a stupor of sin (see D&C 84:51); they are frequently among those who have imbibed the liquors of a licentious world and are intoxicated with immorality and idolatry and inebriated with apathy. Their vision is dim and their judgment faulty. They are without the living God in the world, having chosen to live after the manner of that world. . . .

Those who choose to reject the prophets and thereby spurn living oracles sleep on, long after the glorious dawn of heaven-sent revelation has brought an end to the night of apostate darkness and the vapor of ignorance and sin. In their pitiable plight they have become comatose as to the things of righteousness.

(Joseph Fielding McConkie and Robert L. Millet,
Doctrinal Commentary on the Book of Mormon, 4 vols. [Salt Lake City: Bookcraft, 1992], 314.)

2 Ne. 27:6–11   SEALED PORTION OF THE PLATES
(Isa. 29:4, 11; Eth. 4:4–6; 3 Ne. 26:9–10; *Millennial Messiah,*
McConkie, 114; *History of the Church,* 4:537)

What is in the sealed portion of the Gold Plates? _____ *v.7; Eth. 1:3; 3:25, 27*

How will it be made available to us? _____
v.11

When will we receive it? _____ *Eth. 4:6–7; 2 Ne. 30:17; 3 Ne. 26:8–10*

The people of Limhi brought to Mosiah a record, "engraven on plates of ore" (Mosiah 21:27), which record Mosiah translated, by the aid of "two stones which were fastened into the two rims of a bow," and which gave an account of the Jaredites, (Mosiah 28:11–19.) In translating this record Mosiah kept from going forth to the people that particular part forbidden by the Lord to be revealed until after he was lifted up upon the cross (Ether 4:1). These sacred revelations given to the Brother of Jared were kept from the Nephite people, as well as many other things, until after the resurrection of Christ (Alma 63:12). After the appearing of the Savior to the Nephites, the vision of the Brother of Jared was revealed to the Nephites. When Moroni made his abridgment of the record of Ether, he copied on his record the vision of the Brother of Jared (Ether 4:2–7).

At the command of the Lord, however, Moroni also sealed up the greater things in this vision and also the *interpreters—which were the same "two stones" had by the Brother of Jared*—so that this vision should not be made known even in our day among the Gentiles, in the day of their wickedness (2 Ne. 27:8); it could not be revealed "until the day that they shall repent of their iniquity, and become clean before the Lord." (Ether 4:6.) So we today do not have the fulness of the account written and sealed up by the Brother of Jared and again sealed by Moroni. This part of the record the Prophet Joseph Smith was forbidden to translate. We have, then, received but the "lesser part" (3 Ne. 26:8–11).

(Joseph Fielding Smith, *Doctrines of Salvation: Sermons and Writings of Joseph Fielding Smith,*
ed. Bruce R. McConkie, 3 vols. [Salt Lake City: Bookcraft, 1954–1956], 3:224–25.)

Now the Lord has placed us on probation as members of the Church. He has given us the Book of Mormon, which is the lesser part, to build up our faith through our obedience to the counsels which it contains, and when we ourselves, members of the Church, are willing to keep the commandments as they have been given to us and show our faith as the Nephites did for a short period of time, then the Lord is ready to bring forth the other record and give it to us, but we are not ready to receive it. Why? Because we have not lived up to the requirements in this probationary state in the reading of the record which had been given to us and in following its counsels.

(Joseph Fielding Smith, *Conference Report*, Oct. 1961, 19–20.)

I have had many people ask me through the years, "When do you think we will get the balance of the Book of Mormon records?" And I have said, "How many in the congregation would like to read the sealed portion of the plates?" And almost always there is a 100-percent response. And then I ask the same congregation, "How many of you have read the part that has been opened to us?" And there are many who have not read the Book of Mormon, the unsealed portion. We are quite often looking for the spectacular, the unobtainable. I have found many people who want to live the higher laws when they do not live the lower laws.

(Spencer W. Kimball, *The Teachings of Spencer W. Kimball,*
ed. Edward L. Kimball [Salt Lake City: Bookcraft, 1982], 531–32.)

When, during the Millennium, the sealed portion of the Book of Mormon is translated, it will give an account of life in the premortal existence; of the creation of all things; of the fall and the Atonement and the Second Coming; of temple ordinances, in their fulness; of the ministry and mission of translated beings; of life in the spirit world, in both paradise and hell; of the kingdoms of glory to be inhabited by resurrected beings; and many such like things.

(Bruce R. McConkie, CES Symposium, Aug. 1984, 1.)

Note that there are two parts of the book which were to be brought forth: the words of those that have slumbered and a revelation of God from the beginning of the world to the ending thereof. The King James Version "vision of all" (Isa. 29:11) had reference to the second part, the revelation of the world from the beginning to the end. This revelation was given to the brother of Jared. As the Nephite prophet Moroni abridged the Jaredite records, he stated that the Lord "showed unto the brother of Jared all the inhabitants of the earth which had been, and also all that would be" and that the Lord commanded the brother of Jared to "write these things and seal them up; and I will show them in mine own due time unto the children of men" (Ether 3:25, 27). Thus, the King James Version "version of all" could also be referring to this account of all the inhabitants of the earth.

(Monte S. Nyman, *Symposium on the Old Testament*
[Salt Lake City: The Church of Jesus Christ of Latter-day Saints, 1983], 126.)

2 Ne. 27:9   **SLUMBERED IN THE DUST**
                   (Isa. 29:11; refer in this text to 2 Ne. 26:15–16)

Now, obviously, the only way a dead people could speak "out of the ground" or "out of the dust" would be by the written word which was accomplished through the "Stick of Joseph." Truly it has a familiar spirit, for it contains the words of the Nephite and Lamanite prophets of God.

(LeGrand Richards, *Israel! Do You Know?* [Salt Lake City: Deseret Book Co., 1973], 38.)

The image of a voice from the dead is first found in Genesis 4:10, where Abel's spilled blood cries from the ground to the Lord for vengeance. In Mosaic ritual, the blood of sacrifices was poured on the ground and covered with dust (see Lev. 17:10–14; Deut. 15:23; compare Ezek. 24:7). When death was unwarranted, as in the case of Abel, the blood of the victim continued to speak for him, as if he were still alive.

(Robert A. Cloward, *Isaiah in the Book of Mormon*, ed. Donald W. Parry and John W. Welch,
[Provo, Utah: Foundation for Ancient Research and Mormon Studies, 1998], 193–94.)

2 Ne. 27:12–14   **THE THREE WITNESSES**
                   (2 Ne. 11:3; 2 Cor. 13:1; Deut. 19:15; Eth. 5:2–3; D&C 17:1–3;
                   History of the Church, 1:52–57

A murder trial was in progress in the town where Mr. Barrington then lived, and walking along the main street one day Mr. B. noticed a great many people walking up to the county courthouse, and not knowing what was going on there, he says, 'I became inquisitive, and made up my mind to go there also, and on entering the courtroom I found that the same was crowded to overflowing, but being young and strong I soon made my way up to the railing in front of the bench and jury box, and then I learned from a friend that it was murder trial on before the court, and that the young attorney who was then addressing or making his opening argument to the jury was the county attorney, Oliver Cowdery; as soon as Mr. Cowdery closed his opening argument the attorney fro the prisoner arose, and, in a sneering way, said: "May it please the Court, and gentlemen of the jury, I challenge Mr. Cowdery, since he seems to know so much about this poor defendant, to tell us something about his connection with Joe Smith, and the digging out of the hill of the Mormon Bible, and how Mr. Cowdery helped Joe Smith to defraud the American people out of a whole lot of money by selling the Mormon Bible, and telling them that an angel appeared to them from heaven, dressed in white clothes." After having kept on for a while in this way, abusing Mr. Cowdery, he (attorney for the defendant) began to argue the case to the jury; but all interest was shifted from the prisoner and his case and directed towards Oliver Cowdery; everybody was wondering in what manner he would reply to the accusation just made. The people did not believe, or know before this, that they had elected a county prosecutor who had been an associate of the 'Mormon Prophet,' Joseph Smith. Finally, when the defendant's attorney had completed his argument, Oliver Cowdery's turn came to reply, and everybody in the courtroom strained their necks to catch a glimpse of Mr. Cowdery.

"He arose as calm as a summer morning, and in a low but clear voice which gradually rose in pitch and volume as he proceeded, said: 'If your honor please, and gentlemen of the jury, the attorney of the opposite side has challenged me to state my connection with Joseph Smith and the Book of Mormon; as I cannot now avoid the responsibility, I must admit to you that I am the very Oliver Cowdery whose name is attached to the testimony, with others, as to the appearance of the angel Moroni; and let me tell you that it is not because of my good deeds that I am here, away from the body of the Mormon church, but because I have broken the covenants I once made, and I was cut off from the church; but, gentlemen of the jury, I have never denied my testimony, which is attached to the front page of the Book of Mormon, and I declare to you here that these eyes saw an angel, and these ears of mine heard the voice of an angel, and he told us his name was Moroni; that the book was true, and contained the fulness of the gospel, and we were also told that if we ever denied what we had heard and seen that there would be no forgiveness for us, neither in this world nor in the world to come.'" (Affidavit-files, Church Historian's Office as quoted in Berrett and Burton, *Readings in LDS Church History*, vol. 1, pp. 59–61.)

(Alma P. Burton and Clea M. Burton, *Stories From Mormon History*
[Salt Lake City: Deseret Book Co., 1972], 49–50.)

I do not believe that in any court of justice in the world if a man were being tried for murder and twelve reputable citizens testified of their knowledge of the circumstances leading to the murder, and there were no one who could testify against what they said, there would be failure to convict the man. We have the testimony of Joseph Smith and the testimony of three witnesses to the effect that God gave them a knowledge regarding the Book of Mormon, that an angel of God declared from heaven that the book had been translated by the gift and power of God. These men were Oliver Cowdery, David Whitmer, and Martin Harris. They left the Church, but to the day of their death they maintained their testimony regarding the declaration of the angel, and that they were commanded to bear witness of the divinity of this book, and they did so. Eight men, some of whom were excommunicated from the Church, maintained their testimony that they had seen and handled the plates from which the Book of Mormon was translated, and they remained true to that testimony to the day of their death. The disbelief of all the world does not prove that those men did not tell the truth.

(Heber J. Grant, *Gospel Standards* [Salt Lake City: Improvement Era Publication, 1942], 27.)

Upon hearing the story of golden plates delivered by an angel, some people today ask: "Where are the plates now?" They seem to think if they could see the plates, it would make the testimony of the witnesses more credible. But this is not the way the Lord works. He operates through a law called the law of witnesses. This law provides that in the mouth of two or three witnesses shall the truth of His word be established in all ages (see D&C 6:28; 2 Ne. 27:12–14).

(Ezra Taft Benson, *The Teachings of Ezra Taft Benson* [Salt Lake City: Bookcraft, 1988], 50.)

David Whitmer published a declaration in 1887 which contains the following:
It is recorded in the American Encyclopaedia and the Encyclopaedia Brittanica, that I, David Whitmer, have denied my testimony as one of the three witnesses to the divinity of the *Book of Mormon*, and that the other two witnesses, Oliver Cowdery and Martin Harris, denied their testimony of that book. I will say once more to all mankind, that I have never at any time denied that testimony or any part thereof. I also testify to the world, that neither Oliver Cowdery nor Martin Harris ever at any time denied their testimony. They both died reaffirming the truth of the divine authenticity of the *Book of Mormon*.

(William E. Berrett and Alma P. Burton, *Readings in L.D.S. Church History*, 3 vols.
[Salt Lake City: Deseret Book Co., 1953–1958], 1:62.)

It was in Clarkston, Utah, July, 1875.
Early in the morning a thought came to my mind, that I would go and see brother Harris. It was only three blocks from my home. I heard that he was not feeling well, and people came from other towns to see him, and hear his testimony on the Book of Mormon. But when I arrived, there were two men present. Brother Harris lay on his bed leaning on his elbow. I said, "How are you brother Harris?" He answered slowly, "Pretty well."
"We came to hear your testimony on the Book of Mormon." "Yes," he said in a loud voice, as he sat up in bed, "I wish that I could speak loud enough that the whole world could hear my testimony. Brother, I believe there is an angel here to hear what I shall tell you, and you shall never forget what I shall say. The Prophet and Oliver Cowdery, David Whitmer and myself went into a little grove to pray; to obtain a promise that we should behold it with our own eyes. That we could testify of it to the world. We prayed two or three times, and at length the angel stood before Oliver and David, and

showed them the plates. But, behold I had gone to myself to pray and in my desperation I asked the Prophet to kneel down with me, and pray for me, that I might also see the plates. And we did so, and immediately the angel stood before me and said, "Look." And when I glanced at him I fell; but I stood on my feet and saw the angel turn the golden leaves over, and I said, "It is enough, my Lord, my God!" Then I heard the voice of God say, "The book is true, and translated correctly." . . . "As sure as you are standing here and see me, just so sure did I see the angel with the golden plates in his hand; and he showed them to me." . . . His lips trembled and tears came into his eyes. . . . I refreshed myself and shook hands with him and thanked him and left.

When I think of the day I stood before Martin Harris, and saw him stretch forth his hand and raise his voice and bear his testimony, the feeling that thrilled my whole being I can never forget, nor can I express the joy that filled my soul. This is true testament.

        (Signed)   Ole A. Jensen
                          John Godfrey
                          James Keep

(William E. Berrett and Alma P. Burton, *Readings in L.D.S. Church History: from Original Manuscripts*, 3 vols. [Salt Lake City: Deseret Book Co., 1953], 1:62–63.)

David Whitmer, in 1881, as reported in the Richmond *Conservator*, of March 25, that year, made this statement:

> Those who know me best know well that I have always adhered to that testimony. And that no man may be misled or doubt my present views in regard to the same, I do again affirm the truth of all my statements as then made and published. . . .
>
> In the spirit of Christ, who hath said, "Follow thou me, for I am the Life, the Light, and the Way," I submit this statement to the world; God in whom I trust being my judge as to the sincerity of my motives and the faith and hope that is in me of eternal life.

On Sept. 7, 1878, David Whitmer, in the presence of Elder Joseph F. Smith, Elder Orson Pratt, and a number of other persons, including his eldest son, a grandson, and a son, Jacob Whitmer, bore this testimony:

> He (the angel) stood before us. Our testimony, as recorded in the Book of Mormon, is strictly and absolutely true.

In 1886, David Whitmer said to Elder Edward Stevenson:

> As sure as the sun shines and I live, just so sure did the angel appear unto me and Joseph Smith and I heard his voice and did see the angel standing before us.

(Francis W. Kirkham, *A New Witness for Christ in America*, 2 vols., rev. ed. [Salt Lake City: Utah Printing Co., 1942–1959], 248–49.)

The testimony of the Three Witnesses to the Book of Mormon stands forth in great strength. Each of the three had ample reason and opportunity to renounce his testimony if it had been false, or to equivocate on details if any had been inaccurate. As is well known, because of disagreements or jealousies involving other leaders of the Church, each one of these three witnesses was excommunicated from The Church of Jesus Christ of Latter-day Saints by about eight years after the publication of their testimony. All three went their separate ways, with no common interest to support a collusive effort. Yet to the end of their lives—periods ranging from 12 to 50 years after their excommunications—not one of these witnesses deviated from his published testimony or said anything that cast any shadow on its truthfulness.

(Dallin H. Oaks, *Ensign*, May 1999, 36.)

2 Ne. 27:14   HIM THAT REJECTETH THE WORD

Such rejection occurs not only when the book is spurned by unbelievers but also when Latter-day Saints—those who have accepted the book as the word of God–fail to take it seriously. Regarding such neglect, consider the warnings of two latter-day prophets.

President Joseph Fielding Smith, tenth prophet of the Lord in these latter days, stated: No member of [The Church of Jesus Christ of Latter-day Saints] can stand approved in the presence of God who has not seriously and carefully read the Book of Mormon (*CR*, October 1961, 18).

President Ezra Taft Benson, the thirteenth man to wear the prophet's mantle in this dispensation, declared: "Every Latter-day Saint should make the study of this book a lifetime pursuit. Otherwise he is placing his soul in jeopardy and neglecting that which could give spiritual and intellectual unity to his whole life" (*CR*, April 1975, 97).

(Hoyt W. Brewster, Jr., *Isaiah Plain and Simple* [Salt Lake City: Deseret Book Co., 1995], 160.)

2 Ne. 27:15–19   CHARLES ANTHON
(Isa. 29:11–12; JS–H 1:61–65)

This is the brilliant and scholarly gentleman who turned out to be the "one that is learned," spoken of in Isaiah 29:11 and in 2 Nephi 27:15–18.

It was to this learned professor of Columbia that Martin Harris took the characters which had been copied from the plates of the Book of Mormon.

Charles Anthon was professor of classical studies at Columbia College (later Columbia University) for forty-seven years—1820–1867. In earlier years he attended Columbia as a student and is described as probably the most brilliant scholar ever to attend Columbia College.

The Dictionary of American Biography describes Professor Anthon as a prolific writer. During a period of thirty years he produced at least one volume annually. "Each of his text books passed through several editions, and for thirty years his influence upon the study of the classics in the United States was probably greater than that of any other man." (vol. 1, 314)

Edgar Allen Poe wrote of Anthon: "If not absolutely the best, he is at least generally considered the best classicist in America . . . " (The Literati, New York, 1859, 45–47).

Harper's Weekly, August 17, 1867, said Professor Anthon was "more widely known in Europe than any other American commentator on classical authors."

Charles Anthon was a bachelor and lived in a wing of Columbia College. It is believed that it was there, in his study, that Martin Harris interviewed him.

(The above information was abstracted from "The Anthon Transcript," by Professor Stanley B. Kimball of Southern Illinois University, BYU Studies, Spring, 1970, 331.)

(W. Cleon Skousen, Hidden Treasures from the Book of Mormon, 1:1367.)

I went to the city of New York, and presented the characters which had been translated, with the translation thereof, to Professor Charles Anthon, a gentleman celebrated for his literary attainments. Professor Anthon stated that the translation was correct, more so than any he had before seen translated from the Egyptian. I then showed him those which were not yet translated, and he said that they were Egyptian, Chaldaic, Assyric, and Arabic; and he said they were true characters. He gave me a certificate, certifying to the people of Palmyra that they were true characters, and that the translation of such of them as had been translated was also correct. I took the certificate and put it into my pocket, and was just leaving the house, when Mr. Anthon called me back, and asked me how the young man found out that there were gold plates in the place where he found them. I answered that an angel of God had revealed it unto him.

He then said to me, "Let me see that certificate." I accordingly took it out of my pocket and gave it to him, when he took it and tore it to pieces, saying, that there was no such thing now as ministering of angels, and that if I would bring the plates to him, he would translate them. I informed him that part of the plates were sealed, and that I was forbidden to bring them. He replied, "I cannot read a sealed book." I left him and went to Dr. Mitchell, who sanctioned what Professor Anthon had said respecting both the characters and the translation."

(Martin Harris, History of the Church, 1:20.)

Dr. Anthon's unfortunate role in these important events was a source of great embarrassment to him in later years. This would tend to verify the statement of Nephi that his motives were not entirely sincere [v. 16]. For example, he wrote a letter to E. D. Howe on February 17, 1834, verifying the visit of Martin Harris but ridiculing the claim that he had given Mr. Harris a certificate vouching for the accuracy of the translation or the authenticity of the writings. Said Professor Anthon, "He [Martin Harris] requested an opinion from me in writing, which, of course, I declined to give, and he then took his leave, taking his paper with him." Seven years later, on April 3, 1841, Professor Anthon wrote a letter to the Rev. Dr. T. W. Coit in which he said, "He requested me to give him my opinion in writing about the paper which he had shown me. **I did so without hesitation**, partly for the man's sake, and partly to let the individual 'behind the curtain' see that the trick was discovered.

The import of what I wrote was, as far as I can now recollect, simply this, that the marks in the paper appeared to be merely an imitation of various alphabetical characters, and had, in my opinion, no meaning at all connected with them." At that point the duplicity of Dr. Anthon becomes fully evident as he verifies the very thing which he had formerly denied, all of which lends great credence to the simple and direct statement of Martin Harris as to what really happened.

At the time of the above visit, neither Martin Harris nor Joseph Smith was aware that the Book of Mormon contained a commentary on chapter 29 of Isaiah, or that it impugned the motives of Dr. Anthon. In later years, when Professor Anthon was told that he had been identified as the "learned" scholar in Isaiah 19:11, he was intellectually horrified. Martin Harris became aware of this when he made a special trip to New York a second time to personally present a copy of the newly published Book of Mormon to him. Professor Anthon would not even allow Martin Harris to leave a copy in the house!

(W. Cleon Skousen, *Isaiah Speaks to Modern Time*, [Salt Lake City: Ensign Publishing Co., 1984], 100–101.)

2 Ne. 27:19   UNLEARNED
(Isa. 29:12; JS–H 1:63–65; 2 Ne. 3:7–9, 11, 13–15, 17–19)

Let us stop and reflect how Joseph Smith the man "unlearned" according to the Lord's prediction, has confounded the wise and the learned, the professors of science and of religion, and how their theories and doctrines have crumbled before the truth. False teachings have been exposed. The humble have had the Gospel taught to them, while the wise in their own conceit have stood astounded but unrepentant before the onslaughts of this youth against the citadel of their superstitions and false philosophy. We should humbly thank our Father in Heaven for the fulfillment of Isaiah's prophecy.

(Joseph Fielding Smith, *Church History and Modern Revelation,* 4 vols.
[Salt Lake City: The Deseret News Press, 1946–1949], 1:21–22.)

Joseph Smith (as a young man) . . . could neither write nor dictate a coherent and well-worded letter, let alone dictate a book like the Book of Mormon, and though I was an active participant in the scenes that transpired, was present during the translation of the plates, and had cognizance of things as they transpired, it is marvelous to me—a marvel and a wonder—as much as to anyone else. . . . My belief is that the Book of Mormon is of divine authenticity—I have not the slightest doubt of it . . . when acting as his scribe, your father (she was being interrogated by her son) would dictate to me hour after hour; and when returning after meals, or interruptions, he would at once begin where he had left off, without either seeing the manuscript or having any portion of it read to him. This was an unusual thing for him to do. It would have been improbable that a learned man could do this and for one so ignorant and unlearned as he was, it was simply impossible.

(Emma Smith, *The Witnesses of the Book of Mormon,* comp. Preston Nibley
[Salt Lake City: Deseret Book Co., 1968], 28–29.)

Joseph was, by the standards of the world, "not learned." Isaiah foresaw it. . . . Joseph did not have the skilled, formal tutoring young Saul had at the feet of Gamaliel. (See Acts 22:3.)

Emma Smith reportedly said that Joseph, at the time of the translation of the Book of Mormon, could not compose a "well-worded letter, let alone dictating a book like the Book of Mormon . . . [which was] marvelous to me—a marvel and a wonder—as much as to anyone else" (Preston Nibley, *The Witnesses of the Book of Mormon,* Salt Lake City: Deseret Book Co., 1968, 28.)

This obscure young man apparently paused while translating the dicating to Emma—probably from the fourth chapter of 1 Nephi—concerning the "wall of Jerusalem"—and said, in effect, "Emma, I didn't know there was a wall around Jerusalem."

(Neal A. Maxwell, *Ensign*, Nov. 1983, 54.)

A man asked me awhile ago—"Why did the Lord choose Joseph Smith to build up his kingdom? Why did he not choose Dr. Porter, Henry Ward Beecher, or some such men?" Said I—"Such men would sell the kingdom of God and everything in it for money and popularity, and as the Lord lives he never could rule and handle them, none of them would work with him, they are too much like the Pharisees, Sadducees, High Priests and Rabbis of Judea and Jerusalem." Did the Lord ever choose such men to perform his work? Go through the whole history of the world, and you will find that whenever God wanted a servant, an Apostle or a Prophet, he chose the very humblest man that could be found. When a king was wanted for Israel, he could not find one out of all the tall sons of Jesse; and when the Prophet asked if Jesse had not another son, he was told no, only the boy that looked after the sheep. Nobody thought anything about him, he was of no consequence. "Let me see him," said the man of God; and when he was brought, the Prophet poured oil on his head and anointed him King of Israel. So it has been all the way through. Take Moses, the leader of Israel. . . . When the Lord called Moses to deliver Israel from Egypt, said he—"How can I do this? I am a man of a hard language and slow of speech. . . .

So all the way through the Lord has chosen the weak things of the world to confound the wise, and the things that are nought, to bring to nought the things that are. Jesus Christ himself was born in a stable and cradled in a manger; and who were his Apostles? Illiterate fishermen, men of the lowest calling almost in Judea. . . .

The Lord called Joseph Smith because he was foreordained before the world was to build up this Church and Kingdom. . . . He was an illiterate youth, but the Lord used him, and he lived to fulfill the measure of his appointment.

(Wilford Woodruff, *Journal of Discourses*, 18:118.)

In 1856, Emma recalled that Joseph dictated the translation to her word for word, spelled out the proper names, and would correct her scribal errors even though he could not see what she had written. At one point while translating, Joseph was surprised to learn that Jerusalem had walls around it (E. C. Briggs, "Interview with David Whitmer," *Saints' Herald* 31 [June 21, 1884]: 396–97). Emma was once asked in a later interview if Joseph had read from any books or notes while dictating. She answered, "He had neither," and when pressed, added: "If he had anything of the kind he could not have concealed it from me" (*Saints' Herald* 26 [Oct. 1, 1879]: 290).

(John W. Welch and Tim Rathbone, *Encyclopedia of Mormonism,*
ed. Daniel H. Ludlow, 4 vols., [New York: Macmillan Publishing Co., 1992], 1:210.)

When the Lord commenced his work . . . he passed over the learned institutions of the day, and went into a field and laid his hand on the head of Joseph Smith, a ploughboy,—upon one who cultivated the earth, and had scarcely education enough to read his Bible. . . .

When the early Elders of this Church began to preach the first principles of the Gospel, how oft have we heard the question asked—Why did not the Lord call upon some learned man—upon the presidents of theological seminaries, or upon some of our learned missionaries? Why, if this work be true, did he call upon a person so low—so uneducated—so foolish? This inquiry was made in every direction by hundreds and by thousands, and was laid down by them as a sufficient reason for rejecting the Book of Mormon and the testimony of the servants of God.

(George A. Smith, *Journal of Discourses*, 7:111.)

Why did God choose an unschooled rustic to be the tool in his hand to build up the last dispensation? Why did he not take of the wise men of the earth . . . ?

We will answer that question by another. Why did God choose the family of a humble Nazarene carpenter in which to rear his Son . . . ?

Why did not Jesus, beginning his work and choosing those who should follow him, seek out those of great learning, from among the scribes, the Pharisees, the Sadducees, the elders, why did he not choose them that were schooled in the law and in its refinements and perversions. . . . Why instead of that, did he go along the seashore among the humble fishermen . . . ?

Men would choose the wise and confound the weak, but God chooses the weak things of the earth to confound the mighty. Nor does he put new wine into old bottles. . . .

So the Son of God chose the fishermen on the seashore to march with him, and the Father and the Son chose the humble rustic to lead the way into a new and the last dispensation. They chose a virgin mind that, unpolluted by heresies and sensitive to the promptings of the Spirit, could be taught and led. . . .

So, as time went on, God revealed to the boy prophet the things he should know in order to restore and again build up the Church of Christ on earth.

(J. Reuben Clark, Jr., *On the Way to Immortality and Eternal Life* [Salt Lake City: Deseret Book Co., 1961], 120–22.)

2 Ne. 27:20–21   I AM ABLE TO DO MINE OWN WORK

Because the centerpiece of the Atonement is already in place, we know that everything else in God's plan will likewise finally succeed. God is surely able to do His own work! (See 2 Ne. 27:20–21.) In His plans for the human family, long ago God made ample provision for all mortal mistakes. His purposes will all triumph and without abrogating man's moral agency. Moreover, all His purposes will come to pass in their time (see D&C 64:32).

Take away an acknowledgment of divine design and then watch the selfish scurrying to redesign political and economic systems to make life pain-free and pleasure-filled. Misguided governments mean to live, even if they live beyond their means, thereby mortgaging future generations.

(Neal A. Maxwell, *Ensign*, Nov. 1990, 17.)

2 Ne. 27:20   THEY HAVE REJECTED THEM
(refer in *Latter-day Commentary on the Book of Mormon,* Bassett, to 2 Ne. 9:28–30)

This is not solely a reference to professor Anthon, since the plural pronoun *they* is used. The reference suggests a mind-set of most of the learned of the world, who, by and large, do not take the Book of Mormon seriously. Even when they read it, they do not *really* read it, except with a mind-set which excludes miracles, including the miracle of the book's coming forth by the "gift and power of God."

(Neal A. Maxwell, *First Nephi, The Doctrinal Foundation*, ed. Monte S. Nyman and Charles D. Tate, Jr. [Provo: BYU Religious Studies Center, 1988], 9.)

2 Ne. 27:21   TOUCH NOT THE THINGS WHICH ARE SEALED
(Eth. 1:4; 5:1; refer in *Latter-day Commentary on the Book of Mormon,* Bassett, to Eth. 5)

2 Ne. 27:23   THE SAME YESTERDAY, TODAY, AND FOREVER

What teaching can compare in priceless value and in far-reaching effect with that which deals with man as he was in the eternity of yesterday, as he is in the mortality of today, and as he will be in the for-ever of tomorrow. . . . You are to teach this Gospel using as your sources and authorities the Standard Works of the Church and the words of those whom God has called to lead His people in these last days. You are not, whether high or low, to intrude into your work your own peculiar philosophy, no matter what its source or how pleasing or rational it seems to you to be. . . .

You are not, whether high or low, to change the doctrines of the Church or to modify them, as they are declared by and in the Standard Works of the Church and by those whose authority it is to declare the mind and the will of the Lord to the Church. The Lord has declared that he is "the same yesterday, today, and forever." . . .

We are clear upon this point, namely, that we shall not feel justified in appropriating one further tithing dollar to the upkeep of our seminaries and institutes of religion unless they can be used to teach the gospel in the manner prescribed.

(J. Reuben Clark, Jr., as quoted in Boyd K. Packer, *Teach Ye Diligently*, rev. ed.
[Salt Lake City: deseret Book co., 1991], 374–76.)

2 Ne. 27:25   HAVE REMOVED THEIR HEARTS FAR FROM ME . . . FEAR TOWARD ME TAUGHT BY THE PRECEPTS OF MEN
(Isa. 29:13; JS–H 1:17–19; Matt. 7:21–23)

What was the condition of the religious world, which professed to believe in and practice the doctrines of the Redeemer, when the Father and the Son appeared to Joseph Smith and instructed him? . . . Some of the leading teachings and practices were as follows:

1. That God the Father, the Son, and the Holy Ghost are not three personages, but one ethereal, immaterial God, unknown and unknowable to man, who fills the immensity of space.
2. That the canon of scripture is full and complete, and since the passing of the apostles there was to be no more revelation, no opening of the heavens and communications by angels, but the people were left to rely on what was written in the *Bible* or taught by their priests.
3. That baptism is to cleanse us from "original sin," and that all little children had to be "regenerated" by baptism and if not baptized they will perish.
4. That baptism is an ordinance acceptable to the Lord by sprinkling or pouring water on the heads of unbaptized adults or infants.
5. That men may take upon themselves the authority to be ministers of the word of God, without a divine appointment by one duly authorized by Jesus Christ.
6. That the organization of the Church as established in the days of Jesus Christ and his apostles is no longer necessary; there were to be no more apostles, prophets, and gifts of the spirit.
7. That man was not created in the image of God in form, for God is not an anthropomorphic being.
8. Other doctrines, such as the necessity for keys for the restoration of Israel, the need of the coming of Elijah, as proclaimed in the scriptures, are not necessary.

(Joseph Fielding Smith, *Doctrines of Salvation: Sermons and Writings of Joseph Fielding Smith*,
ed. Bruce R. McConkie, 3 vols. [Salt Lake City: Bookcraft, 1954–1956], 3:284–85.)

As I finished my first mission over in Amsterdam, . . . I was invited into the home of one of the Saints to talk to her neighbor. When my companion and I arrived, the neighbor was there but she had her minister with her . . . and right there he challenged me to a debate in his church the next Saturday night.

When we arrived, the church was full. . . . The minister stood up and said, "Now, inasmuch as Mr. Richards is a guest in our church, we will accord him the privilege of opening this debate, and we will each talk for twenty minutes. Is that agreeable with you, Mr. Richards?" . . .

I hurried over faith and repentance—I thought they believed in them. I spoke on baptism by immersion for the remission of sin until everybody was giving me accord.

Then it came to the laying on of hands for the gift of the Holy Ghost. And they didn't believe that. I never found a church that did believe it outside of our Church—they think the Holy Ghost comes just like the breezes that blow over the head. I quoted them the passage saying that when the Apostles at Jerusalem heard that Samaria had accepted the word of God through the preaching of Philip, they sent Peter and John. And when they came, they prayed for them, they laid their hands upon them, and they received the Holy Ghost. . . .(Acts 8:19–20.)

And then I gave them a few more references on the laying on of hands for the gift of the Holy Ghost, and sat down.

The minister stood up and talked for twenty minutes, and he never once mentioned a word I had said. He started on the Mountain Meadows Massacre and the "Mormon Bible," and stated that Joseph Smith had admitted he had made many mistakes; and then in a most courteous manner, he said: "Now if Mr. Richards will enlighten us on these matters, I am sure this audience will be most appreciative."

I was on my feet just like that. . . . I said, "If I understand a debate, it is the presentation of argument and the answering of those presentations. Has this man answered any of my arguments?" Everybody said, "No."

I said, "All right, my friend, you may have your twenty minutes over again." He couldn't do it, and I knew he couldn't.

Finally his wife stood up in the audience, and she said, "What Mr. Richards is asking you is fair. You ought to answer him."

But he couldn't do it. . . . I met him on the street a number of times after that, but he would duck his head so he didn't need to speak to me!

Now that is what Isaiah meant when he said they would teach for doctrines the precepts of men.

(LeGrand Richards, *Ensign*, May 1982, 30–31.)

Some people are weak in their faith and testimonies but are not even aware of how precarious their situation is. Many of them likely would be offended at the suggestion. They raise their right hand to sustain Church leaders and then murmur and complain when a decision does not square with their way of thinking. They claim to be obedient to God's commandments but do not feel at all uncomfortable about purchasing food at the store on Sunday and then asking the Lord to bless it. Some say they would give their lives for the Lord, yet they refuse to serve in the nursery.

The Savior spoke very explicitly about people who "draw near me with their mouth, and with their lips do honour me, but have removed their heart far from me" (Isa. 29:13).

(Joseph B. Wirthlin, *Ensign*, Nov. 1992, 35.)

The Lord has stated that His Church will never again be taken from the earth because of apostasy (see D&C 138:44). But He has also stated that some members of His Church will fall away. There has been individual apostasy in the past; it is going on now, and there will be an ever-increasing amount in the future. While we cannot save all the flock from being deceived, we should, without compromising our doctrine, strive to save as many as we can. For, as President J. Reuben Clark, Jr., said, "We are in the midst of the greatest exhibition of propaganda that the world has ever seen." Do not believe all you hear.

(Ezra Taft Benson, *The Teachings of Ezra Taft Benson* [Salt Lake City: Bookcraft, 1988], 90.)

2 Ne. 27:26   A MARVELOUS WORK AND A WONDER
(Isa. 29:14; D&C 4:1; 6:1; 11:1; 12:1; 14:1; 18:44; 3 Ne. 21:9)

More than seven hundred years before the birth of Jesus Christ the Lord spoke through Isaiah of the coming forth of the Book of Mormon and the restoration of the Gospel. Isaiah, by prophecy, spoke of the restoration of the new and everlasting covenant, and the Lord performing a "marvelous work and a wonder," which should cause "the wisdom of their wise men" to perish, and "the understanding of their prudent men" to be hid. . . . This marvelous work is the restoration of the Church and the Gospel with all the power and authority, keys and blessings which pertain to this great work for the salvation of the children of men.

(Joseph Fielding Smith, as quote in Hoyt W. Brewster, Jr., *Isaiah Plain and Simple*
[Salt Lake City: Deseret Book Co., 1995], 168.)

April 6, 1830, in the state of New York, The Church of Jesus Christ of Latter-day Saints had its beginning in this dispensation, a beginning that went largely unnoticed by the world. A small number of the men and women, including the Prophet Joseph Smith, gathered in the home of Peter Whitmer, Sr., to witness and participate in the official organization of the Church. Today [1980] there are over 4 ? million members in eighty-one countries. We now look in retrospect of 150 years of the history of the Church and are led to exclaim with Isaiah, "Truly the work is marvelous and wonderful!"

That the Church of Jesus Christ would have an inconspicuous beginning and then enjoy phenomenal growth was likewise predicted. Jesus used the comparison of the small mustard seed to describe the early beginning of His church. But eventually, He declared, that insignificant seed would become a great tree and many would find refuge in its branches (see Matt. 13:31–32).

The prophet Daniel described the beginning and remarkable growth of the Church as a small stone which would become a great mountain and fill the entire earth! (see Dan. 2:34–35, 44).

As men have attempted to assess the Church at a given period of time, in many instances they have not been able to see its forward movement and potential. The growth of the Church, like the growth of grass or trees, has been almost imperceptible to the eye, but little by little, line by line, precept by precept, the Church has matured.

(Ezra Taft Benson, *Ensign*, May 1980, 32.)

There are no wise men in this world today nor prudent men who can understand all of the prophecies like we Latter-day Saints can because of the restoration of this gospel. . . . [Isaiah] said . . . that the wisdom of their wise men shall perish and the understanding of their prudent men shall be hid. There are so many things that have transpired in this day that the wise men of this world cannot understand.

(LeGrand Richards, *Ensign*, Nov. 1980, 65.)

In August of 1852 . . . a special conference was held in the old tabernacle on this square. President Heber C. Kimball opened by saying:

> "We have come together today . . . to hold a special conference to transact business, . . . inasmuch as there are elders to be selected to go to the missions of the earth.
>
> "The missions we will call for during this conference are, generally, not to be very long ones; probably from three to seven years will be as long as any man will be absent from his family."
>
> The clerk then read ninety-eight names of individuals who had been proposed for foreign missions. . . .

To me it is a thing of wonder that at a time when our people were struggling to gain a foothold in these mountains, they put the spread of the gospel ahead of comfort, security, the well-being of their families, and all other considerations. . . .

It has gone on ever since, and it goes on today at an accelerated pace. In a hundred nations missionaries of the Church are teaching the doctrines of salvation. . . . They are fulfilling the declarations of ancient prophets who spoke in the name of the Lord concerning the "marvellous work and a wonder" that should come to pass in the dispensation of the fulness of times (Isa. 29:14).

(Gordon B. Hinckley, *Ensign*, Nov. 1989, 53.)

Joseph was a seer. He had the gift to translate ancient records (see *History of the Church*, 1:238), and a "seer is greater than a prophet" (Mosiah 8:13–17).

The process of translation was truly "a marvellous work and a wonder," or, as rendered in Hebrew, "a miraculous miracle" (Isa. 29:14). Depending upon his sequence of translation, scholars estimate Joseph in 1829 was translating at a rapid daily equivalent of from eight to thirteen of today's printed pages. . . . An able, professional translator recently told me he considers one page a day productive.

(Neal A. Maxwell, *Ensign*, May 1992, 38.)

2 Ne. 27:27   **I KNOW ALL THEIR WORKS**
                         (Isa. 29:15; 2 Ne. 28:9; D&C 38:1–2; refer in *Latter-day*
                         Commentary on the Book of Mormon, Bassett, to 2 Ne. 9:20)

Not only does our Heavenly Father see all we do, but he sees us with such eyes of love that Enoch, who saw God's reaction to sin in the time of Noah in vision, asked of God in surprise, "How is it that thou canst weep, seeing thou are holy, and from all eternity to all eternity?" (Moses 7:29). Explaining that he saw the terrible, inescapable consequences of unrepented and unforgiven sins, God said to Enoch: "And the whole heavens shall weep over them, even all the workmanship of mine hands; wherefore should not the heavens weep, seeing these shall suffer?" (Moses 7:37).

God knows all we have done. And while he cannot look on sin with the least degree of allowance, he looks on us with compassion beyond our capacity to measure. When the scripture speaks of the whole heavens weeping, I think of another picture, given to us by the Prophet Joseph Smith. This is what he said: "The spirits of the just are . . . blessed in their departure to the world of spirits. Enveloped in flaming fire, they are not far from us, and know and understand our thoughts, feelings, and motions, and are often pained therewith." (*History of the Church of Jesus Christ of Latter-day Saints*, ed. B. H. Roberts, 2d ed. rev., 7 vols. [Salt Lake City: Deseret Book Co., 1974], 6:52.)

These words pain me when I think of those I have loved and who loved me who are surely now among the spirits of the just. The realization that they feel pain for us and that the God of Heaven weeps because of our unrepented sin is surely enough to soften our hearts and move us to action.

(Henry B. Eyring, *To Draw Closer to God* [Salt Lake City: Deseret book Co., 1997], 122–23.)

In the beginning, God, the father of our spirits, "formed man of the dust of the ground" (Gen. 2:7). Because the Hebrew verb *ysr* ("to form") is often used to describe pot-making, the original image intended may have been the Lord shaping man out of the clay. Those who seek to hide their counsels from their Creator rationalize, "Who seeth us? and who knoweth us?" (Isa. 29:15). The Lord responds to such people, "Surely your turning of things upside down shall be esteemed as the potter's clay: for shall the work say of him that made it, He made me not? or shall the thing framed say of him that framed it, He had no understanding?" (Isa. 29:16). The irony and ultimate futility of the creation's impudence towards its Creator is one of Isaiah's favorite themes. In Isaiah 45:9 there is a similar image: "Woe unto him that striveth with his Maker! Let the potsherds strive with the potsherds of the earth. Shall the clay say to him that fashioneth it, What makest thou? or thy work, He hath no hands?" And in Isaiah 10:15 the Lord says, "Shall the axe boast itself against him that heweth therewith? Or shall the saw magnify itself against him that shaketh it?" In its context, Isaiah 29:15–24 is directed against those who would resist, based on the wisdom of men, God's marvelous work and wonder.

(David Rolph Seely, *Studies in Scripture, Vol. 4*, ed. Kent P. Jackson [Salt Lake City: Deseret Book Co., 1993], 124.)

The prophets, both ancient and modern, have clearly taught that God knows everything. Psalm 147:5 reads: "Great is our Lord, and of great power: his understanding is infinite." In Doctrine and Covenants 38:1–2, Jesus Christ introduces himself in these words: "Thus saith the Lord your God, even Jesus Christ, the Great I AM . . . The same which knoweth all things." (See also Alma 26:35.) The Prophet Joseph Smith also clearly taught this doctrine, as is indicated in his "Lectures of Faith" which appeared in the early editions of the Doctrine and Covenants:

> . . . God is the only supreme governor and independent being in whom all fulness and perfection dwell; who *is* omnipotent [all-powerful], omnipresent [everywhere present] and omniscient [all knowing]; without beginning of days or end of life; and that in him every good gift and every good principle dwell. . . .

> . . . Without the knowledge of all things, God would not be able to save any portion of his creatures; for it is by reason of the knowledge which he has of all things, from the beginning to the end, that enables him to give the understanding to his creatures by which they are made partakers of eternal life; and if it were not for the idea existing in the minds of men that God had all knowledge it would be impossible for them to exercise faith in him. ("Lectures on Faith," Lecture 2, paragraph 2; Lecture 4, paragraph 11.)

Joseph Fielding Smith quotes his grandfather, Hyrum Smith, as having said: "I would not serve a God that had not all wisdom and all power." Then Joseph Fielding Smith continues, "Do we believe that God has all 'wisdom'? If so, in that, he is absolute. If there is something he does not know, then he is not absolute in 'wisdom,' and to think such a thing is absurd." (*Doctrines of Salvation*, 1:5.) President Smith indicates possible areas in which God is progressing (glory, honor, etc.), and then concludes, "Do you not see that it is in this manner that our Eternal Father is progressing? Not by seeking knowledge which he does not have, for such a thought cannot be maintained in the light of scripture. It is not through ignorance and learning hidden truth that he progresses, for if there are truths which he does not know, then these things are greater than he, and this cannot be" (*Doctrines of Salvation*, 1:7).

(Daniel H. Ludlow, *A Companion to Your Study of The Book of Mormon*
[Salt Lake City: Deseret Book Co., 1976], 138–39.)

2 Ne. 27:28   LEBANON
(Isa. 29:17; Deut. 1:6–7; Josh. 11:1–4)

Lebanon was the northernmost portion of Palestine. It was part of the land promised to the Israelites when they crossed into Canaan. . . . Isaiah's prophecy has been interpreted to include the entire land of Canaan. President Joseph Fielding Smith wrote of the "deplorable condition" of this land prior to its redemption in recent years, which redemption was in fulfillment of prophecy.

Elder Orson Pratt noted that this changed condition would occur only following the publication of the book which Isaiah saw; at which time Lebanon and all the land of Canaan is again to be blessed, while the fruitful field occupied by the nations of the Gentiles, "will be esteemed as a forest:" the multitude of the nations of the Gentiles are to perish, and their lands which are now like a fruitful field, are to be left desolate of inhabitants and become as Lebanon has been for many generations past: while Lebanon shall again be occupied by Israel, and be turned into a fruitful field. These great events could not take place until the Lord should first bring forth a book out of the ground" (*OPW*, 276–77).

(Hoyt W. Brewster, Jr., *Isaiah Plain and Simple*
[Salt Lake City: Deseret Book Co., 1995], 171–72.)

Lebanon/fruitful field. These terms may refer to the reforestation and the agricultural development of Lebanon, or Palestine, at the time of the coming forth of the Book of Mormon. . . . This verse also has symbolic meaning—the forest represents the people of God, and the fruitful field represents their works.

(Donald W. Parry, Jay A. Parry, and Tina M. Peterson,
Understanding Isaiah [Salt lake City: Deseret Book Co., 1998], 272.)

Palestine had been a desolate and arid place for centuries. In 1917, during World War I, it was taken from Turkey by a British army under General Allenby. A short time later came the Balfour Declaraction, and the United States and Great Britain sponsored the establishment of a homeland for the Jews.

As is well known, the nation of Israel has developed a vast reclamation project in the Holy Land. The Jews not only opened up large areas to agriculture with an irrigation system involving both the Jordan River and the Sea of Galilee, but they planted literally millions of trees throughout the valleys, and on the mountains as well.

Palestine is now a "fruitful field" as the scripture foresaw, and this has all evolved since 1917. But the book [Book of Mormon] which Isaiah saw was destined to come forth before that happened; that is, before 1917! . . .

The farms of Palestine are fruitful, the mountains are covered with forests, and the nation is exporting large volumes of fresh produce with its own fleet of merchant marine."

(Mark E. Peterson, *This Is Life Eternal* [Salt Lake City: Bookcraft, 1982], 78.)

2 Ne. 27:29   **DEAF HEAR AND BLIND SEE**
(Isa. 29:18)

Now that the Book of Mormon has been published in Braille it is interesting to note that in 2nd Nephi, 27th Chapter and 29th verse, the following appears: "And in that day shall the deaf hear the words of the book and the eyes of the blind shall see out of obscurity and out of darkness."

While there are not many blind people in our own communities it is estimated that there are more than 125,000 in America.

(George Albert Smith, *Sharing the Gospel with Others*, comp. Preston Nibley [Salt Lake City: Deseret Book Co., 1948], 102.)

2 Ne. 27:32 **AN OFFENDER FOR A WORD; LAY A SNARE . . . TURN ASIDE THE JUST**
(Isa. 29:21; Philip. 2:3; D&C 121:16–17; 2 Ne. 28:16; refer in *Latter-day Commentary on the Book of Mormon,* Bassett, to Hel. 16:2; Eth. 13:13–15, 20–22)

By one means or another, the swiftest method of rejection of the holy prophets has been to find a pretext, however false or absurd, to dismiss the man so that his message could also be dismissed.

(Spencer W. Kimball, *Ensign*, May 1978, 77.)

We refer you to Isaiah, who considers those who make a man an offender for a word, and lay a snare for him that reproveth in the gate. We believe that the old Prophet verily told the truth: and we have no retraction to make. We have reproved in the gate, and men have laid snares for us. We have spoken words, and men have made us offenders. And notwithstanding all this, our minds are not yet darkened, but feel strong in the Lord.

(Joseph Smith, *Teachings of the Prophet Joseph Smith*, comp. Joseph Fielding Smith [Salt Lake City: Deseret Book Co., 1976], 124.)

Some few within the Church, openly or perhaps far worse, in the darkness of anonymity, reproach their leaders in the wards and stakes and in the Church, seeking to make them "an offender for a word," as Isaiah said. To them the Lord said: "Cursed are all those that shall lift up the heel against mine anointed, saith the Lord, and cry they have sinned when they have not sinned . . . but have done that which was meet in mine eyes, and which I commanded them.

"But those who cry transgression do it because they are the servants of sin, and are the children of disobedience themselves. . . .

". . . because they have offended my little ones they shall be severed from the ordinances of mine house.

"Their basket shall not be full, their houses and their barns shall perish, and they themselves shall be despised by those that flattered them.

"They shall not have right to the priesthood, nor their posterity after them from generation to generation" (D&C 121:16–17, 19–21).

That terrible penalty will not apply to those who try as best they can to live the gospel and sustain their leaders. Nor need it apply to those who in the past have been guilty of indifference or even opposition, if they will repent, confess their transgressions, and forsake them.

(Boyd K. Packer, *Ensign*, Nov. 1996, 7.)

Divine doctrine of the Church is the prime target of attack by the spiritually contentious. Well do I remember a friend who would routinely sow seeds of contention in Church classes. His assaults would invariably be preceded by this predictable comment: "Let me play the role of devil's advocate." Recently he passed away. One day he will stand before the Lord in judgment. Then, I wonder, will my friend's predictable comment again be repeated? . . .

Dissecting doctrine in a controversial way in order to draw attention to oneself is not pleasing to the Lord. . . . Show compassionate concern for others. Control the tongue, the pen, and the word processor. Whenever tempted to dispute, remember this proverb: "He that is void of wisdom despiseth his neighbour: but a man of understanding holdeth his peace" (Prov. 11:12; see also 17:28).

Bridle the passion to speak or write contentiously. . . . Let us respectfully disagree without being disagreeable.

(Russell M. Nelson, *Ensign*, May 1989, 70–71.)

2 Ne. 27:33   JACOB . . . WAX PALE
(Isa. 29:22; D&C 123:12)

The house of Jacob has been made ashamed, and his face has waxed pale, ever since he was driven away from Lebanon or Canaan, but the Lord has now brought forth out of the ground a book which shall, accompanied by His power, restore the tribes of Jacob from the four quarters of the globe, and establish them in the land of Palestine and Lebanon forever.

(Orson Pratt, *Orson Pratt's Works: The Light of Understanding*
[Salt Lake City: The Deseret News Press, 1945], 278.)

2 Ne. 27:35   ERRED IN SPIRIT . . . LEARN THE DOCTRINE
(Isa. 29:35)

Oh, How precious must be the contents of a book which shall deliver us from all the errors taught by the precepts of uninspired men! Oh, how gratifying to poor, ignorant, erring mortals who have murmured because of the multiplicity of contradictory doctrines that have perplexed and distracted their minds, to read the plain, pure and most precious word of God, revealed in the Book of Mormon! It is like bread to the hungry—like the cool refreshing fountain to him that is ready to perish with thirst. . . . Let all that have murmured because of the uncertainty of the precepts of men, read the words of the book, and they "shall learn doctrine."

(Orson Pratt, *Orson Pratt's Works: The Light of Understanding*
[salt Lake City: The Deseret News Press, 1945], 278–79.)

Do not be surprised when non-doers scoff. . . . When Jesus focused His hearers on doctrines, "they were astonished at his doctrine" (Matt. 22:33). The only cure for the doctrinal illiteracy of those who murmur will be to learn doctrine.

(Neal A. Maxwell, *Ensign*, May 1986, 36.)

In the Apocryphon of James, Jesus reportedly told an afflicted Peter and James, "If you consider how long the world existed before you, and how long it will exist after you, you will find that your life is one single day and your sufferings one single hour.". . . How like what the Lord told suffering Joseph in jail: "My son, . . . thine adversity and thine afflictions shall be but a small moment" (D&C 121:7).

One's life, therefore, is brevity compared to eternity—like being dropped off by a parent for a day at school. But what a day! . . .

If we blend "longsuffering and doctrine" (2 Tim. 4:2), some who "murmur" about the human predicament "shall learn doctrine" (Isa. 29:24; 2 Ne. 27:35). . . .

One-dimensional man with only a one-dimensional view of the world will surely focus upon the cares of the world, yielding to the things of the moment. . . .

Premortality is not a relaxing doctrine. . . . Just because we were chosen "there and then," surely does not mean we can be indifferent "here and now." . . . Those called and prepared must also prove "chosen, and faithful." (See Rev.17:14; D&C 121:34–36.)

(Neal A. Maxwell, *Ensign*, Nov. 1985, 17.)

Some of us are too content with what we may already be doing. We stand back in the "eat, drink, and be merry" mode when opportunities for growth and development abound. We miss opportunities to build up the kingdom of God because we have the passive notion that someone else will take care of it. The Lord tells us that He will give more to those who are willing. They will be magnified in their efforts. . . . But to those who say, "We have enough, from them shall be taken away even that which they have." . . .

Church history includes incidents of priesthood holders of great capacity. A few were brilliant but also erratic and unreliable and so lost the spiritual gifts and talents with which the Lord had so richly endowed them. I would like to tell you about one such.

Samuel Brannan led some Saints around Cape Horn on the ship *Brooklyn*. They made a brief stop in Hawaii before docking at San Francisco Bay. He became convinced that the main body of the Saints should not settle in the Rocky Mountains but should go on to California. So he traveled east and encountered the first party of emigrants under the leadership of Brigham Young in Green River, Wyoming. He used all of his persuasive powers trying to convince Brigham Young to take advantage of the opportunities which he felt California offered. Brigham Young responded, "Let us go to California, and we cannot stay there over five years; but let us stay in the mountains, and we can raise our own potatoes, and eat them; and I calculate to stay here." Brannan stayed with the main body of the Saints for a few days, but then, because he was headstrong and self-centered, in August of 1847 he headed back to California. . . .

Sam Brannan was not focused on building up the kingdom of God. Instead he was directed toward business and making money. He became the first millionaire in California, with numerous business ventures and extensive land holdings. Because he had been the leader of that group of Saints, President Young asked him to account for the tithing that he had collected from the members of the Church in California, including those involved in the gold rush, but he did not do so. Nor did he use those funds to establish the Church or to help the members there.

For a time and a season, Brannan was very successful in establishing enterprises and acquiring land for his own benefit, but eventually he fell on hard times. His family did not stay together. When he died he was alone, broken physically, spiritually, and financially. For 16 months no one claimed his body. Eventually it was placed in San Diego's Mount Hope Cemetery. Sam Brannan accomplished much in his life, but in the end he paid a terrible price for not honoring his priesthood stewardship and having failed to follow the prophet of God.

(James E. Faust, *Ensign*, Nov. 2002, 50–51.)

2 Ne. 28:9

(Isa. 29:15; refer in this text to 2 Ne. 27:27)

2 Ne. 28:14

(Isa. 29:13; refer in this text to 2 Ne. 27:25)

2 Ne. 28:16

(Isa. 29:21; refer in this text to 2 Ne. 27:32)

2 Ne. 28:30   **LINE UPON LINE**
(Isa. 28:10, 13; refer in this text to 2 Ne. 27:6–11)

The Lord gives us revelation; as we accept and live by that revelation, we are given more revelation, but if we do not accept what is revealed, we lose the knowledge we have already gained.

(Monte S. Nyman, *Great Are the Words of Isaiah* [Salt Lake City: Bookcraft, 1980], 102.)

Some people get impatient because the Lord hasn't revealed more than He has—unmindful of the fact that He already has revealed more than we are able to digest, in most cases.

(Harold B. Lee, *The Teachings of Harold B. Lee*, ed. Clyde J. Williams [Salt Lake City: Bookcraft, 1996], 424.)

How many have read the *Book of Mormon* through? How many have made themselves familiar with the things revealed to us in the *Doctrine and Covenants* regarding what the Lord has said of our duties as members of the Church and what he has said regarding our salvation and exaltation and how it may be obtained? Until we are prepared to receive the things already given. I fear the Lord will hold from us those other things which one time will be revealed. (D&C 59:4; 101:32–34.) . . .

When we, the members of the Church, reach the point that we are willing to live by all that the Lord has revealed, *he will give us more that can be placed in the Doctrine and Covenants. The Lord is withholding from us great and mighty truths because of the hardness of our hearts.* Why should we clamor for more when we will not abide in what we already have? We are led by revelation today just as much as they were anciently.

(Joseph Fielding Smith, *Doctrines of Salvation: Sermons and Writings of Joseph Fielding Smith,*
ed. Bruce R. McConkie, 3 vols. [Salt Lake City: Bookcraft, 1954–1956], 3:202.)

2 Ne. 28:32

(Isa. 9:12–13)

2 Ne. 29:1

(Isa. 29:14; 11:11; refer in this text to 2 Ne. 21:10–12 & 2 Ne. 27:26)

2 Ne. 30:9, 12–15

(Isa. 11:4–9; refer in this text to 2 Ne. 21:4 & 2 Ne. 21:6–9)

Jacob 4:15–18   A STONE
(Isa. 28:16; 1 Pet. 2:6; Rom. 9:33)

The prophecy that the stone would be rejected by the Jews is also found in Psalms 118:22 and is quoted by the Savior in the New Testament (see Matt. 21:42). In the Book of Mormon, Jacob quoted the allegory of Zenos to show how the rejected stone would become the head of the corner (see Jacob 4:15–18).

(Monte S. Nyman, *Great Are the Words of Isaiah* [Salt Lake City: Bookcraft, 1980], 104.)

Mos. 12:20–24;   **HOW BEAUTIFUL UPON THE MOUNTAINS**
15:11–18   (Isa. 52:7–10; Mosiah 27:35–37; refer in this text to 3 Ne. 20:40)

One cannot help but wonder as to the motivation behind the question. Did the high priest actually desire understanding of the verses? [21–24] Or, rather, was he essentially saying: "I thought that the prophet Isaiah had said that blessed are those who declare *good* tidings and bring *peaceful* salutations. Why is your message so negative, so pessimistic, and why are you so prone to such gloomy prophecy?"

Abinadi nevertheless treated the questioner with enough respect as to suggest a direct answer; the answer would, however, not be given at the moment (see Mosiah 15:11–18).

(Robert L. Millet, *A Symposium on the Book of Mormon*
[Salt Lake City: The Church of Jesus Christ of Latter-day Saints, 1986], 98.)

I had great joy yesterday in hearing of the call of Elder Helio da Rocha Camargo, our companion and fellow member of the Church. Brother Camargo and his wife were stalwart, faithful people before they joined the Church. They had been brought up in the nurture and admonition of the Lord. Brother Camargo was a graduate of the military academy of Brazil. Later, still a young man, he became a Methodist minister. . . . One evening two young men called at his home. He said that the first thing he noticed was the huge feet of one of the young men. He looked upward from the feet until he found the face of the tallest North American he had ever met. He was not at first impressed with the beauty of either the feet or the face. However, he invited the young men in, and in the process of their presentation they left him a copy of the Book of Mormon.

On a subsequent visit they inquired if he had read the book. He explained that he had read considerable, making notes of the things with which he did not agree. The elder then suggested that it was not in keeping with a book of scripture to read it to see what was wrong with it, but that it should be read as Moroni says, "with a sincere heart" and "real intent," having "faith in Christ" and desiring to know the truth of the book. (See Moro. 10:4.)

Brother Camargo said he found it necessary to read the book again. In the process the Spirit witnessed to him that it was the true word of God, and he joined the Church with his family. He sometimes refers to the scripture in Isaiah 52:7 which says, "How beautiful upon the mountains are the feet [those huge missionary feet] of him that bringeth good tidings, that publisheth peace; . . . that sayeth unto Zion, Thy God reigneth!" The truth he has found has brought similar beauty to the feet of three of his sons as they have served as missionaries.

(William Grant Bangerter, *Ensign*, May 1985, 64–65.)

Not long ago, President Gordon B. Hinckley, in a commencement address at BYU—Hawaii, admonished graduates to "stop seeking out the storms and enjoy more fully the sunlight" (*Church News*, 3 July 1983, 10.) He pointed out that we can be negative and look for the ugly in life and the faults and failings of those around us, or we can develop positive attitudes and see the beautiful in life and the good, the strong, the decent, and the virtuous in people, which brings joy and happiness. It is a matter of attitude. . . .

The Lord has told us that we can be beautiful, even like a temple. In 1 Corinthians he said, "Know ye not that ye are the temple of God, and that the Spirit of God dwelleth in you?" (1 Cor. 3:16) . . .

As we live righteous and unselfish lives, the Spirit of the Lord enters our souls and then radiates from us. We become beautiful, even as a holy temple is beautiful.

(Keith W. Wilcox, *Ensign,* May 1985, 27.)

The imagery embodied in the poetry of Isaiah 52:7–10 is that of watchmen on a city wall who witness the approach and arrival of a messenger who travels on foot. Walled cities were commonplace in ancient Israel and throughout the ancient Near East, and watchmen, or lookouts, were regularly posted above city gates. The job security and probably the life of a watchman depended on his ability to remain alert to anyone or anything approaching his city, especially things appearing suspicious in nature. . . .

What is fascinating about Isaiah's use of imagery here is that not only does he mention a messenger or herald, but he also focuses on the messenger's feet with the notation that they are "beautiful." Feet are not generally considered among the more attractive body parts; they are functional, yes, but not beautiful. What did Isaiah intend by this description?

Interestingly, the word rendered "beautiful" in verse 7 is the Hebrew term *na'wu* (from the rarely attested verbal root *N'H*), the word from which Joseph Smith coined the city name "Nauvoo." This particular form is used only here and in Song of Solomon 1:10, where it is rendered "comely" in the KJV.

Since walking on dirt roads with sandal-shod feet was the major form of transportation for most people in ancient Israel, feet were not only quite visible but required daily washing and attention. The cleansing and care of a guest's feet was long considered a basic act of hospitality. However, despite the importance of foot care in ancient Israel, when Isaiah described the messenger's feet on the mountains as "beautiful," he was probably not suggesting that the arriving herald had remarkably clean and well-manicured feet!

It is not the condition of the feet but their observable activity, their *progress,* that is being emphasized by the description "beautiful." . . . The focus of the passage is on the delivery of the message as well as on the arrival of the messenger.

(Dana M. Pike, *Isaiah in the Book of Mormon,* ed. Donald W. Parry and John W. Welch,
[Provo, Utah: Foundation for Ancient Research and Mormon Studies, 1998], 254, 258.)

Abinadi recited and interpreted Isaiah 53 because his accusers, the priests of Noah, had challenged him to explain the meaning of Isaiah 52:7–10. What was the thrust of their challenge? It appears that the priests intended, by their direct examination of Abinadi, to catch him in conflict with that scripture and thereby convict him of false prophecy—a capital offense under the law of Moses (see Deut. 18:20).

In essence, they were apparently asking Abinadi why he bore tidings of doom and destruction when Isaiah had declared that the beautiful and true prophet brings good tidings and publishes peace: "How beautiful upon the mountains are the feet of him that bringeth *good* tidings" (Mosiah 12:20–22, emphasis added). Isaiah gave cause for great joy: "They shall see eye to eye when the Lord shall bring again Zion; break forth into joy" (Mosiah 12:22–24), and yet Abinadi had brought nothing but bad tidings of destruction.

Abinadi's rebuttal was an extensive and brilliant explanation of the true essence of redemption and how it brings good tidings to those who accept Christ (see Mosiah 12:29–37 and chapters 13–16).

(John W. Welch, *Isaiah in the Book of Mormon,* ed. Donald W. Parry and John W. Welch,
[Provo, Utah: Foundation for Ancient Research and Mormon Studies, 1998], 294.)

The cause to which I speak is of missionary work as couples. . . . There has never been a greater need than now for an army of mature couples to go out into every far corner of this earth and retain the fruit of the harvest. . . .

I think we will not be tested in the way the pioneers were tested. They were called to leave all worldly possessions, homes, even family and loved ones to cross the prairies to dry and desolate, forbidding lands. They buried their babies, children, and companions on the Great Plains in shallow, unmarked graves. Physically, they suffered beyond belief, nor can tongue tell the sad, pitiful story. . . .

There is a need—*not* to leave homes forever, but for a time—then return and reap the rich harvest of the faithful labor. Your children and grandchildren will be blessed. . . . "How beautiful upon the mountains are the feet of him that bringeth good tidings; that publisheth peace" (Mosiah 12:21).

(Vaughn J. Featherstone, *Ensign,* May 1992, 42.)

Mos. 14   **ISAIAH'S TESTIMONY OF THE COMING MESSIAH**
                      (Isa. 53; Acts 8:26–35; Matt. 8:17; 1 Pet. 2:24–25;
                      Rom. 4:25; 10:13–17; John 12:37–41.)

ABINADI'S COMMENTARY ON ISAIAH IS FOUND IN MOSIAH 15

(This grid shows the verses in chapter 15 which give commentary to the verses shown in chapter 14.)

Isaiah 53	Abinadi's Commentary
Mosiah 14:2	Mosiah 15:2–4
Mosiah 14:3	Mosiah 15:5
Mosiah 14:4–6	Mosiah 15:9
Mosiah 14:7	Mosiah 15:6
Mosiah 14:8	Mosiah 15:10,12–13
Mosiah 14:10	Mosiah 15:11–12, 23

It should be noted that the entire chapter of Isaiah 53 in Mosiah 14 is a poem in four stanzas of three verses each (vv. 1–3, 4–6, 7–9, 10–12), constructed with well-known Hebrew parallelism. . . . Jews read Isaiah 53 as a prophecy directed to the Suffering Servant as the house of Israel. While it is clear the whole of chapter 53 is about the mortal ministry of the Messiah, . . . Abinadi's interpretation of Isaiah 53 precedes the coming of Christ by almost 150 years and yet remains the most clear and full interpretation of this prophetic chapter anywhere in the scripture.

(David Rolph Seely, *The Book of Mormon: The Foundation of Our Faith,*
The 28th Annual Sidney B. Sperry Symposium [Salt Lake City: Deseret Book Co., 1999], 204–205.)

Now *Bible* commentators will tell you that this [Isa. 53] has nothing to do with the life of Jesus Christ. To them this story is one concerning suffering Israel. I want to tell you that it is a story, a synopsis of the life of our Redeemer, revealed to Isaiah 700 years before the Lord was born.

(Joseph Fielding Smith, *Doctrines of Salvation: Sermons and Writings of Joseph Fielding Smith,*
ed. Bruce R. McConkie, 3 vols. [Salt Lake City: Bookcraft, 1954–1956], 1:23.)

Abinadi was, of course, a prefiguration, a type and shadow of the Savior, a fact that makes his moving tribute to Christ even more powerful and poignant (if that is possible) than when Isaiah wrote it.

(Jeffrey R. Holland, *Christ and the New Covenant* [Salt Lake City: Deseret Book Co., 1997], 89.)

Mos. 14:1   WHO HATH BELIEVED . . . TO WHOM IS REVEALED
(Isa. 53:1)

The opening lines of this chapter pose two questions: Who will believe what will be recounted here? And To whom is the "arm of the Lord" revealed? The sense of the first question can be taken in several different ways. Most obviously it appears to be a rhetorical question—expecting a negative answer—that no one has or will believe this incredible report of God coming to earth as a mortal. On the other hand, it may be an invitation to all who hear the report to consider it and to accept and believe it.

(David Rolph Seely, *The Book of Mormon: The Foundation of Our Faith,*
The 28th Annual Sidney B. Sperry Symposium [Salt Lake City: Deseret Book Co., 1999], 206.)

When John's disciples questioned whether he was or was not the One to come, he asked them simply to follow him around. And then he said: Tell John what things ye have seen and heard

(Luke 7:23). On another occasion, he said: I told you [that is, gave you the report] and ye believed not: the works that I do in my Father's name, they bear witness of me [that is, reveal the Father]. But ye believe not (John 10:25–26; see also 10:5–7; Matt. 12:24). Why do ye not understand my speech? Even because ye cannot hear my word (John 8:43). When they refused to see God revealed by his words and works, Jesus called them blind and deaf. Thus John could say: Though he had done so many miracles before them, yet they believed not on him: That the saying of Esaias [Isaiah] the prophet might be fulfilled, which he spake, Lord, who hath believed our report? and to whom hath the arm of the Lord been revealed?" (John 12:37–38).

(Keith H. Meservy, *A Witness of Jesus Christ: The 1989 Sperry Symposium on the Old Testament,*
ed. Richard D. Draper, [Salt Lake City: Deseret Book Co., 1990], 157.)

That is, To whom has God revealed his priesthood, his gospel, those things wherein is found the power of God unto salvation?

(Joseph Fielding McConkie and Robert L. Millet,
Doctrinal Commentary on the Book of Mormon, 4 vols. [Salt Lake City: Bookcraft, 1987–1992], 2:221.)

Now, as Isaiah expressed it, "Who hath believed our report? And to whom is the arm of the Lord revealed?" (Isa. 53:1).

If you believe the words of Joseph Smith, you would have believed what Jesus and the ancients said.

If you reject Joseph Smith and his message, you would have rejected Peter and Paul and their message. . . . We invite all . . . to ponder. . . . Do I have the moral courage to learn whether Joseph Smith was called of God? . . . Am I willing to pay the price of investigation and gain a personal revelation that tells me what I must do to gain peace in this world and be an inheritor of eternal life in the world to come?

(Bruce R. McConkie, *Ensign,* Nov. 1981,
[Salt Lake City: Published by The Church of Jesus Christ of Latter-day Saints, 1981], 48.)

"Who hath believed our report, and to whom is the arm of the Lord revealed?" (Mosiah 14:1). Surely he was delivering a report. This query might be a common cry from every prophet who ever revealed to his people the coming of the Messiah. In this instance it is both Isaiah's and Abinadi's cries that may echo Christ's own lament when he used Isaiah's words to describe the people's rejection of him even though he had done so many miracles in their sight (see John 12:37–38).

(Ann Madsen, "What Meaneth the Words That Are Written?", *Journal of Book of Mormon Studies,* vol. 10, no. 1:9.)

Mos. 14:2   **TENDER, DRY GROUND—NO BEAUTY THAT WE SHOULD DESIRE HIM**
(Isa. 53:2; Luke 2:40; refer in *Latter-day Commentary on the New Testament,* Pinegar–Bassett–Earl, 31–36)

Under the watchful eye of his Heavenly Father, he was "tender" in at least two ways–he was young, pure, innocent, and particularly vulnerable to the pain of sin all around him, and he was caring, thoughtful, sensitive, and kind—in short, tender.

(Jeffrey R. Holland, *Christ and the New Covenant* [Salt Lake City: Deseret Book Co., 1997], 90.)

In a garden setting, plants do not normally take root and grow up in dry ground. The tender plant is symbolic of Christ; the dry ground is apostate Judaism. . . . If the religion of the day did not nourish Jesus, what was his source of spiritual growth and sustenance? His Father in Heaven was the source. Jesus would grow up before his Heavenly Father as a tender plant and would be nourished and strengthened by the true source of strength, not the dried-up religion of the times.

(S. Brent Farley, *A Symposium on the Old Testament*
[Salt Lake City: The Church of Jesus Christ of Latter-day Saints, 1983], 65.)

Isaiah uses two plant metaphors to portray the young mortal Jesus: "tender plant" and "root." Jesus was like a tender plant, untouched by corruption and sin. . . .
Jesus came forth not in fertile land, but in "dry ground," both temporally and spiritually. . . . The dry ground represents the spiritual barrenness of apostate Judaism.

(Donald W. Parry, *Visualizing Isaiah*
[Provo, Utah: The Foundation for Ancient Research and Mormon Studies, 2001], 89.)

We have no reason to believe that Christ was unattractive physically, but this verse may suggest that he was plain—as in "plain and precious." In any case we know that his power was an inner, spiritual gift, and that as the son of a mortal mother, he did not stand out in any distinctive physical way, leading his surprised and offended contemporaries of the day to say of him and his messianic announcement, "Is not this Joseph's son?" He certainly did not come to them in a way that filled the people's traditional hopes and views of a Messiah who would be striking in visage or powerful in politics.

(Jeffrey R. Holland, *Christ and the New Covenant* [Salt Lake City: Deseret Book Co., 1997], 90–91.)

In appearance he was like men; and so it is expressed here by the prophet that he had no form or comeliness, that is, he was not so distinctive, so different from others that people would recognize him as the Son of God. He appeared as a mortal man.

(Joseph Fielding Smith, *Doctrines of Salvation: Sermons and Writings of Joseph Fielding Smith*, ed. Bruce R. McConkie, 3 vols. [Salt Lake City: Bookcraft, 1954–1956], 1:23.)

"He shall grow up . . . as a tender plant, and as a root out of a dry ground"—"not like a stately tree, but like a lowly plant, struggling in arid soil. So the human life of the Messiah was one of obscurity and humility." (*Dummelow*, p. 446.) Or: "Messiah grew silently and insensibly, as a sucker from an ancient stock, seemingly dead (*viz.*, the house of David, then in a decayed state)." (*Jamieson*, p. 490.) Or: Perhaps better still, he grew up as a choice and favored plant whose strength and achievement did not come because of the arid social culture in which he dwelt; it was not poured into him by the erudition of Rabbinical teachers; but it came from the divine Source whence he sprang, for as the Inspired Version has it, "He spake not as other men, neither could he be taught; for he needed not that any man should teach him" (JST, Matt. 3:25).

There is no mystique, no dynamic appearance, no halo around his head, thunders do not roll and lightnings do not flash at his appearance. He is the Son of the Highest, but he walks and appears as the offspring of the lowest. He is a man among men, appearing, speaking, dressing seeming in all outward respects as they are.

(Bruce R. McConkie, *The Promised Messiah* [Salt Lake City: Deseret Book Co., 1978], 477–78.)

This verse describes the early childhood or upbringing of Jesus. Scholars agree that this does not describe his physical appearance, but rather teaches that people would misjudge him because they were expecting their Messiah to come in a more glorious or supernatural way. His growing up would be watched over by the Father, just as a gardener cares for a tender plant. Luke records that "the child grew, and waxed strong in spirit, filled with wisdom: and the grace of God was upon him" (Luke 2:40). Jesus' declaration to his mother when he was only twelve years of age is ample evidence that he had been nurtured and prepared by his Father in Heaven during his years in Nazareth (see Luke 2:41–49).

(Monte S. Nyman, *Great Are the Words of Isaiah* [Salt Lake City: Bookcraft, 1980], 207.)

"Is not this the carpenter's son?" they asked. "Is not his Mother called Mary? And his brethren, James, and Joses, and Simon, and Judas? And his sisters, are they not all with us? When then hath this man all these things?" (Matt. 13:55–56.)

Even within the immediate family of Jesus there was unbelief. Mary knew his identity, for the angel had declared it unto her. And Joseph, her husband, had been similarly informed. But Mary evidently did not broadcast her knowledge; she "kept all these things, and pondered them in her heart." (Luke 2:19.)

Her other sons, born to her by Joseph, did not believe, at least not at first. They had grown up with Jesus. He was their older brother. They had become so accustomed to him as they all grew up together that they saw nothing unusual about him, certainly nothing divine. Jesus was so much like other men that not even his own blood brothers recognized his true status.

This was revealed in the scripture telling of their visit to Jerusalem for the Passover. The brothers planned to attend and wondered if Jesus would go also. It is not indicated whether they invited him to accompany them to Jerusalem. They knew of his reported miracles, but seemed to doubt them. They knew he had been persecuted and hence had shunned the crowds in Jerusalem.

They said to him, "Depart hence, and go into Judea that thy disciples also may see the works that thou doest. For there is no man that doeth any thing in secret, and he himself seeketh to be known openly."

Then they daringly added, "If thou do these things, shew thyself to the world." Note that "if." How much did they really doubt him? It seems that they even taunted him, "For neither did his brethren believe in him" (John 7:1–5).

(Mark E. Petersen, *Isaiah for Today* [Salt Lake City: Deseret Book Co., 1981], 45–46.)

Jesus of Nazareth, though the literal son of God and thus possessor of the very powers of immortality, was to undergo the throes of mortality, including the tender and helpless years of infancy and childhood characteristic of all children. He would grow as a root in the arid and parched ground of apostate Judaism. This root-stock or "stem of Jesse" would develop in a sterile and barren religious soil, in the midst of great learning but gross spiritual darkness. . . .

The Son of God was not to be known or recognized by any outward beauty; rather, those with an eye of faith would know by the witness of the Spirit who it was that ministered among them.

(Robert L. Millet, *A Symposium on the Book of Mormon*
[Salt Lake City: The Church of Jesus Christ of Latter-day Saints, 1986], 99.)

Mos. 14:3   **A MAN OF SORROWS . . . ACQUAINTED WITH GRIEF**
(Isa. 53:3; Alma 36:27; refer in *Latter-day Commentary on the Book of Mormon, Bassett,* to Alma 7:11–12)

We will all have some adversity in our lives. . . . Some of it may even strain our faith in a loving God who has the power to administer relief in our behalf.

To those anxieties I think the Father of us all would say, "Why are ye so fearful? how is it that ye have no faith?" . . .

Jesus was not spared grief and pain and anguish and buffeting. No tongue can speak the unutterable burden he carried, nor have we the wisdom to understand the prophet Isaiah's description of him as "a man of sorrows" (Isa. 53:3). His ship was tossed most of his life, and at least to mortal eyes, it crashed fatally on the rocky coast of Calvary. . . .

Peace was on the lips and in the heart of the Savior no matter how fiercely the tempest was raging. May it so be with us . . . We should not expect to get through life individually or collectively without some opposition.

(Howard W. Hunter, *Ensign*, Nov. 1984, 43.)

President Brigham Young spoke of what evoked the "why" from Jesus, saying that during the axis of agony which was Gethsemane and Calvary, the Father at some point withdrew both His presence and His Spirit from Jesus (see *Journal of Discourses*, 3:205–6). Thereby Jesus' personal triumph was complete and His empathy perfected. Having "descended below all things," He comprehends, perfectly and personally, the full range of human suffering! (see D&C 88:6; 122:8). A spiritual sung in yesteryear has an especially moving and insightful line: "Nobody knows the troubles I've seen; nobody knows but Jesus" (see also Alma 7:11–12). Truly, Jesus was exquisitely "acquainted with grief," as no one else (Isa. 53:3).

(Neal A. Maxwell, *Ensign*, Nov. 1997, 23.)

There are those who feel that if we follow the Savior, our lives will be free from worry, pain, and fear. This is not so! The Savior Himself was described as a man of sorrows. Those early disciples who followed the Christ experienced great persecution and trials. The Prophet Joseph Smith was no exception. Nor were the other early Saints of this last dispensation. And it is no different today. . . .

I have had the opportunity to speak with a woman who heard the call of the Savior when she was 18. Her father, who was a high official in another church, became angry with her and forbade her from being baptized. He let her know that if she became a member of The Church of Jesus Christ of Latter-day Saints, she would be ostracized from the family.

Even though the sacrifice was great, this young woman heeded the call of the Savior and entered the waters of baptism.

Her father could not accept her decision, however, and tried to force her into abandoning her new faith. He and his wife reviled her for her decision to become a member of the Church and demanded that she recant and forsake her new religion.

Even through the rage, the bitterness, and the indignity, her faith remained strong. She endured the verbal and emotional abuse, knowing she had heard the call of the Savior and she would follow Him, whatever the consequence.

Eventually this young woman managed to find a safe haven, a place of refuge with a kind member family far away from the threats and unkindness of her father.

She met a faithful young man, and the two of them were married in the temple, receiving the choice blessings that accompany a temple marriage.

Today she stands among the multitude of those who have sacrificed so much to follow the call of the Savior.

Yes, I do not suggest that the road will be easy. But I will give you my witness that those who, in faith, leave their nets and follow the Savior will experience happiness beyond their ability to comprehend.

(Joseph B. Wirthlin, *Ensign*, May 2002, 17.)

I know some of you do truly feel at sea, in the most frightening sense of that term. . . . I testify of God's love and the Savior's power to calm the storm . . . in that biblical story that He was out there on the water. . . . Only one who has fought against those ominous waves is justified in telling *us—as well as the sea*—to "be still" (Mark 4:39). Only one who has taken the full brunt of such adversity could ever be justified in telling us in such times to "be of good cheer" (John 16:33). Such counsel is not a jaunty pep talk about the power of positive thinking, though positive thinking is much needed in the world. No, Christ knows better than all others that the trials of life can be very deep, and we are not shallow people if we struggle with them. . . . Surely His ears heard every cry of distress, every sound of want and despair. To a degree far more than we will ever understand, He was "a man of sorrows, and acquainted with grief" (Isa. 53:3).

(Jeffrey R. Holland, *Ensign*, Nov. 1999, 14.)

On some days we will have cause to remember the unkind treatment. . . . We can remember that Christ was also troubled on every side, but not distressed; perplexed, but not in despair; persecuted, but not forsaken; cast down, but not destroyed (see 2 Cor. 4:8–9).

When those difficult times come to us, we can remember that Jesus . . . suffered pains and afflictions and temptations of every kind that he might be filled with mercy and know how to succor His people in their infirmities (see D&C 88:6; Alma 7:11–12). . . .

However dim our days may seem they have been darker for the Savior of the world.

In fact, in a resurrected, otherwise perfected body, our Lord of this sacrament table has chosen to retain for the benefit of his disciples the wounds in his hands and his feet and his side— . . . signs, if you will, that pain in this world is *not* evidence that God doesn't love you. It is the *wounded* Christ who is the captain of our soul—he who yet bears the scars of sacrifice, the lesions of love and humility and forgiveness. . . .

All this we could remember when we are invited by a kneeling young priest to remember Christ always.

(Jeffrey R. Holland, *Ensign*, Nov. 1995, 69.)

With these words, Isaiah draws every human being into his account. We all are part of the eternal congregation who must choose to accept or reject this Savior. "He was despised, and *we* esteemed him not" (Mosiah 14:3; emphasis added). This rhetorical device is often used in Isaiah's writing and in many Jewish texts. One can hear in the Passover seder this same self-inclusive notion: "Were *we* not strangers in the land of Egypt . . .?" Through this language we are participants, joined with those who were there. We are with them.

(Ann Madsen, "What Meaneth the Words That Are Written?",
Journal of Book of Mormon Studies, vol. 10, no. 1:9–10.)

Mos. 14:4; 15:9   BORNE OUR GRIEF AND CARRIED OUR SORROW
(Isa. 53:4; Matt. 8:14–17; Heb. 4:15; refer in *Latter-day Commentary on the Book of Mormon,* Bassett, to Alma 7:11–12)

When his body was taken from the cross and hastily placed in a borrowed tomb, he, the sinless Son of God, had already taken upon him not only the sins and temptations of every human soul who will repent, but all of our sickness and grief and pain of every kind. He suffered these afflictions as we suffer them, according to the flesh. He suffered them all. He did this to perfect his mercy and his ability to lift us above every earthly trial.

(Howard W. Hunter, *Ensign,* May 1988, 16–17.)

Interestingly, the word *forgive* does not appear in this chapter of Isaiah, though the Hebrew root *nasa,* from which the word *forgive* is usually translated, does appear twice, as "borne" in verse 4, and "bare" in verse 12. . . . Christ "bore" or carried our sins so that we do not have to carry their burden (John 1:29; see 1 Pet. 1:18–20). Or, as we say, "He has *forgiven* us," meaning he "gave" the price "before."

(Victor L. Ludlow, *Isaiah: Prophet, Seer, and Poet* [Salt Lake City: Deseret Book Co., 1982], 452.)

Certainly as he bore the sins and sadness, the heartbreak and hurt of every man, woman, and child from Adam to the end of the world, it is an understatement to say he was "a man of sorrows, and acquainted with grief." . . . Many thought that if there is suffering, there surely must be guilt. Indeed, there was plenty of guilt here—a whole world of it—but it fell upon the only utterly sinless and totally innocent man who had ever lived.

(Jeffrey R. Holland, *Christ and the New Covenant* [Salt Lake City: Deseret Book Co., 1997], 91.)

When the unimaginable burden began to weigh upon Christ, it confirmed His long-held and intellectually clear understanding as to what He must now do. . . . In Gethsemane, the suffering Jesus began to be "sore amazed" (Mark 14:33), or, in the Greek, "awestruck" and "astonished."

Imagine, Jehovah, the Creator of this and other worlds, "astonished"! Jesus knew cognitively what He must do, but not experientially. He had never personally known the exquisite and exacting process of an atonement before. Thus, when the agony came in its fulness, it was so much, much worse than even He with his unique intellect had ever imagined! No wonder an angel appeared to strengthen him! (See Luke 22:43.)

The cumulative weight of all mortal sins—past, present, and future—pressed upon that perfect, sinless, and sensitive Soul! All our infirmities and sicknesses were somehow, too, a part of the awful arithmetic of the Atonement. (See Alma 7:11–12, Isa. 53:3–5, Matt. 8:17.) . . .

His suffering—as it were, *enormity* multiplied by *infinity*—evoked His later soul-cry on the cross, and it was a cry of forsakeness. (See Matt. 27:46.)

(Neal A. Maxwell, Ensign, May 1985, 72–73.)

Mos. 14:4   **SMITTEN OF GOD**
(Isa. 53:4; refer in *Latter-day Commentary on the Book of Mormon*, Bassett, to Mosiah 3:7)

Was He "smitten of God"? Not in the sense that His Father was meting out some kind of punishment. Yet the great Elohim knew the agony to which His Only Begotten would be subjected as He fulfilled His foreordained assignment. Of necessity, the Father of us all had to deny or to turn a deaf ear to the agonizing plea, "O my Father, if it be possible, let this cup pass from me."

(Hoyt W. Brewster, Jr., Isaiah Plain and Simple [Salt Lake City: Deseret Book Co., 1995], 251.)

Mos. 14:4   **STRICKEN**
(Isa. 53:4; refer in this text to Mosiah 14:8)

This particular verb is used sixty times in Leviticus 13 and 14, always with the same meaning—that of suffering the emotional pain of having leprosy. The Servant will be viewed with the same disdain as the Jews viewed a leper.

(Donald W. Parry, Jay A. Parry, and Tina M. Peterson,
Understanding Isaiah [Salt lake City: Deseret Book Co., 1998], 474.)

Mos. 14:5   **WOUNDED FOR OUR TRANSGRESSIONS**
(Isa. 53:5; refer in *Latter-day Commentary on the New Testament*, Pinegar–Bassett–Earl, 362–65.)

Verse 5 speaks concerning Christ's atoning sacrifice. The expression "he was wounded for our transgressions" may better be translated from the Hebrew as "he was pierced for our transgressions."

Jesus Christ was pierced for the transgressions of all mankind while on the cross. The Psalmist prophesied: "They pierced my hands and my feet" (Psalm 22:16). In April 1829, Joseph Smith received this revelation from the Lord: "Behold the wounds which pierced my side, and also the prints of the nails in my hands and feet" (D&C 6:37).

(Donald W. Parry, *Visualizing Isaiah*
[Provo, Utah: The Foundation for Ancient Research and Mormon Studies, 2001], 90.)

On the night Jesus was betrayed, He took three of the Twelve and went into the place called Gethsemane. There He suffered the pains of all men. He suffered as only God could suffer, bearing our griefs, carrying our sorrows, being wounded for our transgressions, voluntarily submitting Himself to the iniquity of us all, just as Isaiah prophesied. . . .

It was in Gethsemane that Jesus took on Himself the sins of the world, in Gethsemane that His pain was equivalent to the cumulative burden of all men, in Gethsemane that He descended below all things so that all could repent and come to Him. The mortal mind fails to fathom, the tongue cannot express, the pen of man cannot describe the breadth, the depth, the height of the suffering of our Lord—nor His infinite love for us.

(Ezra Taft Benson, *The Teachings of Ezra Taft Benson* [Salt Lake City: Bookcraft, 1988], 14.)

Mos. 14:5   BRUISED FOR OUR INIQUITIES
(Isa. 53:5)

The phrase "he was bruised for our iniquities" is more correctly rendered "he was crushed (Hebrew *daka*) for our iniquities." Jesus Christ was crushed in the Garden of Gethsemane. The word Gethsemane (Hebrew *Gath Shemen*) itself signifies "oil press." Just as olives are crushed at an olive press to render pure olive oil, so the Anointed One was crushed to sanctify mankind. He suffered so mightily in the Garden of Gethsemane that he bled from every pore (Luke 22:44; Mosiah 3:7; D&C 19:18).

(Donald W. Parry, *Visualizing Isaiah*,
[Provo, Utah: The Foundation for Ancient Research and Mormon Studies, 2001], 91.)

Mos. 14:6   SHEEP GONE ASTRAY
(Isa. 53:6)

It is very important that sheep should not be allowed to stray away from the flock, because when by themselves they are utterly helpless. In such a condition, they become bewildered, for they have no sense at all of locality. And if they do stray away, they must be brought back. The Psalmist prayed the prayer: "I have gone astray like a lost sheep; seek thy servant" (Ps. 119:176). The prophet Isaiah compared man's waywardness to that of sheep: "All we like sheep have gone astray" (Isa. 53:6). David sang of his divine Shepherd: "He restoreth my soul" (Ps. 23:3).

(Fred H. Wight, *Manners and Customs of Bible Lands* [Chicago: Moody Press, 1953], 158.)

Mos. 14:7   **OPPRESSED AND AFFLICTED**
(Isa. 53:7; refer to Latter-day Commentary on
The New Testament, Pinegar - Bassett - Earl, 366–79)

We may understand from these words that He was trampled down by abuse of power and authority vested in the Jewish Hierarch. Seventy-one of its elders and wise men formed a council known as the *Sanhedrin* which, under their Roman conquerors, had complete jurisdiction over the religious, civil, and criminal affairs of the people. They sought to crush Him, and scatter His followers.

He was afflicted. This same *Sanhedrin* which oppressed Him, not only permitted Him to be abused, (–their duty was to protect Him–) but also, its members joined in the cries against Him, and suffered Him to be wounded. They heaped sorrows (pains) upon Him that amounted to physical calumny. . . .

Dr. Adam Clarke in his *Commentary on the Old Testament* . . . , gives one example of the many customs to which Jesus had an appeal, but of it He had not benefit. Dr. Clarke says:

A learned friend has communicated to me the following passages from the *Mishna*, and the Gemara of Babylon, as leading to a satisfactory explication of this difficult place. It is said in the former, that before anyone was punished for a capital crime, proclamation was made before the prisoner by the public crier, in these words: "Whosoever knows any thing of this man's innocence, let him come and declare it." . . . On which passage the Gemara of Babylon adds, that before the death of Jesus this proclamation was made for forty days; but no defence could be found." On which words Lardner observes: "It is truly surprising to see such falsities, contrary to well-known facts." . . . The report is certainly false; but this false report is founded on the supposition that there was such a custom, and so far confirms the account given from the *Mishna*. The *Mishna* was composed in the middle of the second century according to Prideaux; Lardner ascribes it to the year of Christ 180.

Casaubon has a quotation from Maimonides which further confirms this account: . . . "It was customary when sentence of death was passed upon a criminal, and he was led out from the seat of judgment to the place of punishment, a crier went before, and spoke as follows:–'This man is going to suffer death by _____ because he has transgressed by _____ such a transgression, in such a place, in such a time; and the witnesses against him are _____ He who may know any thing relative to his innocence, let him come and speak in his behalf." . . . No proclamation was made for any person to bear witness to the innocence and character of Jesus; nor did any one voluntarily step forth to give this attestation to it.

(George Reynolds and Janne M. Sjodahl, *Commentary on the Book of Mormon*,
ed. Philip C. Reynolds, 7 vols. [Salt Lake City: Deseret Book Co., 1955–1961], 2:161–62.)

Mos. 14:7   **OPENED NOT HIS MOUTH**
                   (Isa. 53:7)

Herod began to question the Prisoner; but Jesus remained silent. The chief priests and scribes vehemently voiced their accusations; but not a word was uttered by the Lord. Herod is the only character in history to whom Jesus is known to have applied a personal epithet of contempt. "Go ye and tell that fox" He once said to certain Pharisees . . . As far as we know, Herod is further distinguished as the only being who saw Christ face to face and spoke to Him, yet never heard His voice. . . . Christ had words—of comfort or instruction, of warning or rebuke, of protest or denunciation—yet for Herod the fox He had but disdainful and kingly silence.

(James E. Talmage *Jesus the Christ: A Study of the Messiah and His Mission According to Holy Scriptures both Ancient and Modern* [Salt Lake City: The Church of Jesus Christ of Latter-day Saints, 1981], 636.)

Here the image of wayward sheep in verse 6 (the human family) is shifted in verse 7 to that of an innocent sheep (Christ), who goes to the slaughter without utterance. When confronted by the high priest Caiaphas, Jesus "held his peace." Later Herod questioned with him in many words; but he answered him nothing. Finally with Pilate, the one man who could have spared his life, Jesus "gave him no answer." He was the Lamb of God prepared from before the foundation of the world for this ultimate and infinite sacrifice. In his sacrifice he was giving millennia of meaning to the untold number of lambs that had been offered on an untold number of altars in anticipation and similitude of this final blood offering of God's Firstborn."

(Jeffrey R. Holland, *Christ and the New Covenant* [Salt Lake City: Deseret Book Co., 1997], 92–93.)

The vivid image of Christ's suffering in silence is symbolized by a sheep, which makes no sound as it is being sheared. Even though all our iniquities have been laid on him, "yet he opened not his mouth." We, the straying sheep for whom he paid the debt, can hardly understand such restraint. We cry out at the slightest hurt. He conserved his power for Gethsemane and the cross.

(Ann Madsen, "What Meaneth the Words That Are Written?", *Journal of Book of Mormon Studies,* vol. 10, no. 1:10.)

Mos. 14:7   **LAMB – SHEEP**
                   (Isa. 53:7; refer to *Latter-day Commentary
                   on the New Testament,* Pinegar–Bassett–Earl, 47–48.)

Isaiah uses two similes to describe Jesus Christ's atoning sacrifice: "as a lamb" and "as a sheep." Not only is Christ the Good Shepherd (John 10:14), but he is also the sacrificial lamb, who went without protest or resistance to his death. This contrasts with mankind, the sheep that willfully went astray (Isa. 53:6). The sacrifice of an unblemished lamb under the law of Moses prefigured the atoning sacrifice of Christ (Gen. 22:7–8; Ex. 12:3). The Atonement fulfills the symbolism of the lamb.

(Donald W. Parry, *Visualizing Isaiah*
[Provo, Utah: The Foundation for Ancient Research and Mormon Studies, 2001], 93.)

Mos. 14:8   **STRICKEN**
(Isa. 53:8; refer in this text to Mosiah 14:4, under STRICKEN)

Ancient translators add to these words and render them, "He was smitten to death." (The Septuagint reads *lemaveth*, which, in the Greek into which the Old Testament was translated, means "to death.")

(George Reynolds and Janne M. Sjodahl, *Commentary on the Book of Mormon*,
ed. Philip C. Reynolds, 7 vols. [Salt Lake City: Deseret Book Co., 1955–1961], 2:162.)

Mos. 14:8–9   **PRISON, JUDGEMENT, GENERATION, GRAVE, NO EVIL**
(Isa. 53:8–9)

I think that the first clause means that our Lord was taken away (from life) by oppression and by a miscarriage of justice. The second clause, "and who shall declare his generation," is often taken to mean "and among his contemporaries who was concerned?" I think that "generation" here means "posterity," but in a very special sense. It has reference to the "seed" or "believers" of Jesus in the sense explained by the prophet Abinadi in Mosiah 15:10–13, or by the Savior to the brother of Jared when he said, "In me shall all mankind have light, and that eternally, even they who shall believe on my name; and they shall become my sons and my daughters [i.e., *my seed* or *my generation*] (Ether 3:14).

(Sidney B. Sperry, *Book of Mormon Compendium* [Salt Lake City: Bookcraft, 1968], 304.)

And who shall declare his generation? This has been interpreted, "And his manner of life who would declare?" Although we quote concerning the meaning stated of the question that is asked, we prefer to believe that it refers to the growth of the numbers of Christ's followers. "Of the increase of his government and peace there shall be no end" (Isa. 9:7). "And he shall reign over the house of Jacob for ever; and of his kingdom there shall be no end" (Luke 1:33).

(George Reynolds and Janne M. Sjodahl, *Commentary on the Book of Mormon*,
ed. Philip C. Reynolds, 7 vols. [Salt Lake City: Deseret Book Co., 1955–1961], 2:162.)

Christ was taken prisoner by soldiers who entered the garden of Gethsemane expressly to seize him, and he spent the rest of his remaining hours in bondage and judgment at the hands of Pilate. He died with the wicked, crucified between two thieves, and found a burial place at the hand of the wealthy Joseph of Arimathea. Christ was the embodiment of truth, with no deceit of any kind ever having passed his lips. Nor would he do evil (even in word) in his time of greatest injustice, praying in the last hours of his life that his Father would forgive those involved, "for they know not what they do."

(Jeffrey R. Holland, *Christ and the New Covenant* [Salt Lake City: Deseret Book Co., 1997], 93.)

We gain an even stronger appreciation for the remarkable detail of the prophecy of Isaiah quoted by Abinadi. Jesus was indeed put to death "with the wicked," literally crucified between two thieves (see Luke 23:32). At the same time, he was buried "with the rich," in the sense that he was placed in a tomb owned by a wealthy man, Joseph of Arimathea (see John 19:38–42).

(Robert L. Millet, *Symposium on theBook of Mormon*
[Salt Lake City: The Church of Jesus Christ of Latter-day Saints, 1986], 100.)

Jewish tradition is heavy with the idea that a son must somehow speak for his father after his death. There is a formal ceremony at the grave one year after the father's death in which the son speaks a formulaic prayer in his father's behalf, thus "declaring his generation" and the continuance of "his seed."

(Ann Madsen, "What Meaneth the Words That Are Written?" *Journal of Book of Mormon Studies,* vol. 10, no. 1:11.)

**Mos. 14:10;   PLEASED THE LORD TO BRUISE HIM . . . SEE HIS SEED
15:10   PROLONG HIS DAYS AND THE PLEASURE OF THE LORD**
                   (Isa. 53:10)

Certainly it did not "please" the Father to bruise his Son, as we currently understand and use that word. Modern translations of Isaiah render these opening lines "it was the will of the Lord" rather than "it pleased the Lord." That gives a clearer meaning of what was meant by the word *pleased* when Joseph Smith translated this passage early in the nineteenth century. Furthermore, acknowledging Christ's submission to the will of the Father in Mosiah 14 is consistent with and sets the stage for the very teaching Abinadi was about to give to King Noah and his people in Mosiah 15. Indeed, Abinadi would give a succinct definition of those who are Christ's seed. They are those whose sins he has borne and for whom he has died. His soul truly was "an offering for sin," bringing the joy of a glorious heavenly reunion with "his seed," a reunion nowhere more movingly described than in President Joseph F. Smith's vision of the righteous dead. All of this is, indeed, a pleasure to the Lord.

(Jeffrey R. Holland, *Christ and the New Covenant* [Salt Lake City: Deseret Book Co., 1997], 93–94.)

If this prophecy was meant to be fulfilled during his mortal sojourn on earth, we would list it as having failed. He did not prolong his days; a voluntary death overtook him in the prime of life. . . . It is only in the resurrection that the pleasure of the Lord is perfected, for it is only when "spirit and element" are "inseparably connected" that either God or man can "receive a fulness of joy" (D&C 93:33). Thus, having made his soul an offering for sin; having seen his seed—all the righteous dead from the days of Adam to that moment—as they assembled to greet and worship him in the paradise of their Lord; and having thereafter risen in glorious immortality to live and reign forever, our Messiah truly fulfilled the prophetic utterance, for then his days were prolonged forever and the pleasure in his hand was infinite.

(Bruce R. McConkie, *The Promised Messiah* [Salt Lake City: Deseret Book Co., 1978], 362.)

"It pleased the Lord to bruise him" is a declaration that Christ's sacrifice was a freewill offering, on the part of both the Father and the Son. In John 3:16–17, Jesus declared that the Father had sent his Son to be sacrificed because of his love for the world. In Doctrine and Covenants 34:3, Jesus declared that he voluntarily gave his life because of his own love for the world."

(Monte S. Nyman, *Great Are the Words of Isaiah* [Salt Lake City: Bookcraft, 1980], 210.)

This is a verse which requires careful consideration. God our Eternal Father loved his Only Begotten and, like any parent, surely anguished with the pain of his child. And yet, as infinitely painful as it must have been for Elohim, the hours of agony were necessary—they were a part of that plan of the Father of which Jehovah had been the chief advocate and proponent in premortality. Indeed it was needful that the "Lamb slain from the foundation of the world" be slain, in order that life and immortality might be brought to light. And thus "it pleased the Lord [the Father] to bruise him," in the sense that Jesus carried out to the fullest the will of the Father, in spite of the pain associated with the implementation of the terms and conditions of that will. "Oh," Elder Melvin J. Ballard said, "in that moment when He might have saved His Son, I thank Him and praise Him that He did not fail us, for He had not only the love of His Son in mind, but He also had love for us. I rejoice that He did not interfere, and that His love for us made it possible for Him to endure to look upon the sufferings of His Son and give Him finally to us, our Saviour and our Redeemer. Without Him, without His sacrifice, we would have remained, and would never have come glorified into His presence. And so this is what it cost, in part, for our Father in heaven to give the gift of His Son unto men" (Melvin J. Ballard—*Crusader for Righteousness* [Salt Lake City: Bookcraft, 1966], 137).

(Robert L. Millet, *Symposium on the Book of Mormon*
[Salt Lake City: The Church of Jesus Christ of Latter-day Saints, 1986], 100.)

Isaiah's prophecy and Abinadi's interpretation speak only of those who have been and not of those who shall yet believe. . . . Let us note the time and circumstances under which he will see them.

Abinadi's rendition of Isaiah's inspired utterance says: "When his soul has been made an offering for sin he shall see his seed." In other words, he shall see his seed after he has worked out the infinite and eternal atonement. . . . (Luke 23:40–43.) . . .

(1 Pet. 3:18–20; 4:6.) In his glorious vision of the redemption of the dead, President Joseph F. Smith saw what transpired when the Messiah visited the departed dead. "The eyes of my understanding were opened, and the Spirit of the Lord rested upon me," he said, "and I saw the hosts of the dead, both small and great. And there were gathered together in one place an innumerable company of the spirits of the just, who had been faithful in the testimony of Jesus while they lived in mortality. . . . All these had departed the mortal life, firm in the hope of a glorious resurrection, through the grace of God the Father and his Only Begotten Son, Jesus Christ." (JFS–V 11–14.) . . .

If this prophecy [Isa. 53:10] was meant to be fulfilled during his mortal sojourn on earth, we would list it as having failed. He did not prolong his days; a voluntary death overtook him in the prime of life. . . . It is only in the resurrection that the pleasure of the Lord is perfected. . . . Thus, having made his soul an offering for sin; having seen his seed—all the righteous dead from the days of Adam to that moment . . . our Messiah truly fulfilled the prophetic utterance, for then his days were prolonged forever and the pleasure in his hand was infinite.

(Bruce R. McConkie, *The Promised Messiah* [Salt Lake City: Deseret Book Co., 1978], 360–62.)

Mos. 14:11–12   TRAVAIL OF HIS SOUL
(Isa. 53:11–12)

Christ certainly did know and feel the "travail of his soul," an anguish commencing in the garden of Gethsemane, where he "began to be sorrowful and very heavy . . . even unto death." He prayed so earnestly through the depths of that agony that his sweat became "as it were great drops of blood falling down to the ground." Later he would describe the experience of that suffering: "[It] caused myself, even God, the greatest of all, to tremble because of pain, and to bleed at every pore, and to suffer both body and spirit–and would that I might not drink the bitter cup, and shrink."

But he was faithful to the end, "satisfied" in its most literal, legal sense, having made reparation and restitution sufficient to appease the demands of justice. Because he "poured out his soul unto death" bearing the "sin of many," he received the inheritance of the great, sitting on the right hand of God, where all that the Father has was given him. True to his nature and true to his covenant, Christ will share that divine inheritance with all others who will be strong in keeping the commandments, thus making them "heirs of the kingdom of God" in precisely the way Abinadi declared this doctrine to King Noah.

For such merciful protection and glorious promises we must never again "hide our faces from him and esteem him not."

(Jeffrey R. Holland, *Christ and the New Covenant* [Salt Lake City: Deseret Book Co., 1997], 94.)

His soul was made an offering for the sins of *many* whom he would one day see and own. The *many* would be those who had chosen to seek and know him and give away their sins to become like him. The day would come when he, as heir, would divide all he had been given with those who had willingly taken upon them his name.

(Ann Madsen, "What Meaneth the Words that Are Written?" *Journal of Book of Mormon Studies,* vol. 10, no. 1:10.)

Mos. 14:12   **POURED OUT HIS SOUL UNTO DEATH**
                      (Isa. 53:12)

Redeeming Jesus also "poured out his soul unto death" (Mosiah 14:12; see also Isa. 53:12; D&C 38:4). As we on occasion "pour" out our souls in personal pleadings, we are thus emptied, making room for more joy!

(Neal A. Maxwell, *Ensign,* May 2001, 60.)

Mos. 15:29–31   **WATCHMEN LIFT UP THEIR VOICE . . . EYE TO EYE**
3 Ne. 16:18–20
3 Ne. 20:32–35
                    (Isa. 52:8–10; refer in this text to 3 Ne. 20:32–35)

I received, by a heavenly vision, a commandment in June following, to take my journey to the western boundaries of the State of Missouri, and there designate the very spot which was to be the central place for the commencement of the gathering together of those who embrace the fullness of the everlasting Gospel. Accordingly I undertook the journey, with certain ones of my brethren, and after a long and tedious journey, suffering many privations and hardships, arrived in Jackson County, Missouri, and after viewing the country, seeking diligently at the hand of God, He manifested Himself unto us, and designated, to me and others, the very spot upon which he designed to commence the work of the gathering, and the upbuilding of an "holy city," which should be called Zion—Zion, because it is a place of righteousness, and all who build thereon are to worship the true and living God, and all believe in one doctrine, even the doctrine of our Lord and Savior Jesus Christ. "Thy watchmen shall lift up the voice; with the voice together shall they sing: for they shall see eye to eye, when the Lord shall bring again Zion."

(Joseph Smith, *Teachings of the Prophet Joseph Smith,*
comp. Joseph Fielding Smith [Salt Lake City: Deseret Book Co., 1976], 79–80.)

The Savior quoted all three verses twice to the Nephites and said they would be fulfilled through both the Nephites and the Jews. This again shows the dual nature of Isaiah's prophecies. The Savior first quoted this passage following his declaration that the land of America was to be given to Lehi's descendants after the Gentiles reject the fulness of the gospel and are "trodden under foot" by the house of Israel; he said this would fulfill the words of the prophet Isaiah (see 3 Ne. 16:10–20). He later quoted the passage while instructing the Nephites concerning the restoration of the Jews. He changed the wording from "thy watchmen" to "their watchmen," as he was referring to Jerusalem's watchmen in this case rather than those of Zion (see 3 Ne. 20:29–35). Abinadi also recognized the universal application of this passage in teaching that "the salvation of the Lord shall be declared to every nation, kindred, tongue, and people" and quoting these three verses as evidence (see Mosiah 15:28–31). Joseph Smith designated Jackson County, Missouri, as the Zion spoken of in verse 8 (see *TPJS*, 79–80). The "watchmen" are those who preach the gospel, as indicated in verse 7. The song to be sung in Zion will be a new song, sung when all will know Christ (i.e., during the Millennium). The words of the song, which will include parts of verse 8, are recorded in Doctrine and Covenants 84:99–102.

The Lord will "make bare his holy arm in the eyes of all the nations" at his second coming (see D&C 133:2–3). Doctrine and Covenants 133:4 admonishes the members of the Church to sanctify themselves in preparation for that day.

(Monte S. Nyman, *Great Are The Words of Isaiah* [Salt Lake City: Bookcraft, 1980], 199–200.)

Eye to eye. This metaphor represents being united in purpose and understanding (Mosiah 16:1; Alma 36:26; D&C 84:98). Unity is one of the key characteristics of Zion, as Moses recorded: "The Lord called his people Zion, because they were of one heart and one mind" (Moses 7:18). . . .

Lord hath made bare his holy arm. In ancient times, men prepared for battle by throwing their cloak away from the shoulder of their fighting arm (Ps. 74:11). At the second coming of Christ, God will make bare his arm when he shows forth his power for all to see (D&C 133:2–3). . . .

Ends of the earth shall see the salvation. Every part of the earth will see and know the power of the Lord; all will see how he delivers those who turn to him. Joseph Smith promised the suffering Saints: "The days of tribulation are fast approaching, and the time to test the fidelity of the Saints has come. . . . but in these times of sore trial, let the Saints be patient and see the salvation of God. Those who cannot endure persecution, and stand in the day of affliction, cannot stand in the day when the Son of God shall burst the veil, and appear in all the glory of His Father, with all the holy angels" (*History of the Church*, 1:468).

(Donald W. Parry, Jay A. Parry, and Tina M. Peterson,
Understanding Isaiah, [Salt Lake City: Deseret Book Co., 1998], 465–66.)

These prophetic words, from Isaiah 52:8–10, will be fulfilled after the Lord Jesus appears in glory, cleanses the earth, gathers his people from the four quarters of the earth, and establishes Zion, a society of the pure in heart. Then all shall see the salvation of God, meaning the victory of our Lord over the forces of evil and corruption. And then the earth shall rest (see Moses 7:60–64).

(Joseph Fielding McConkie, Robert L. Millet, and Brent L. Top,
Doctrinal Commentary on the Book of Mormon, 4 vols., [Salt Lake City: Bookcraft, 1987–1992], 112.)

In the full and true sense, Israel shall triumph over her foes only when the Millennium is ushered in, only when her Messiah comes to deliver them from the aliens, only when the wicked are destroyed and the Lord reigns gloriously among his saints.

It is in this setting—a millennial setting; a day of millennial glory; the day when peace prevails because the wicked have been destroyed—it is in this setting that Jesus says: "Then"—in the day of which we speak—"the words of the prophet Isaiah shall be fulfilled." These are the words: "Thy watchmen shall lift up the voice; with the voice together shall they sing, for they shall see eye to eye when the Lord shall bring again Zion." We are establishing Zion now, but our Zion is only the foundation for that which is to be. We are laying a foundation; the promises relative to the glorious Zion of God which shall yet stand upon the earth shall be fulfilled after the Lord comes. "Break forth into joy, sing together, ye waste places of Jerusalem," Isaiah continues, "for the Lord hath comforted his people, he hath redeemed Jerusalem." The true and full redemption of Jerusalem must await the day of the Lord's return. "The Lord hath made bare his holy arm in the eye of all the nations; and all the ends of the earth shall see the salvation of God." (3 Ne. 16:4–20.)

(Bruce R. McConkie, *The Millennial Messiah* [Salt Lake City: Deseret Book Co., 1982], 242.)

3 Ne. 20:32–45   OFTEN QUOTED ISAIAH 52
(Rev. 18:4; 2 Cor. 6:17; 1 Ne. 22:10–11; 2 Ne. 8:24–25; Mosiah 12:21–24; 15:14–18; Moro. 10:31; 3 Ne. 16, 18–20; D&C 38:42; 82:14; 84:98–99)

3 Ne. 20:32–35   WATCHMEN LIFT UP THEIR VOICE
(Isa. 52:8–10; 2 Sam. 18:19, 23–25, 27; Ezek. 33:1–9; refer in this text to Mosiah 15:29–31.)

When the day of the Gentile has been fulfilled, that is, when the gospel will be taken from them because of their iniquities, the Savior will remember the covenant he made with those of Judah to return them to their ancient covenant land. Of this yet future day, he said, "The fulness of my gospel shall be preached unto them; and they shall believe in me, that I am Jesus Christ, the Son of God, and shall pray unto the Father in my name." After their conversion to Christ, after that time when their "watchmen" come to see "eye to eye" with their Savior, "then will the Father gather them together again, and give unto them Jerusalem for the land of their inheritance" (3 Ne. 20:29–33). It will be in this future setting, the Savior explained, that the prophecies of Isaiah relative to Zion putting on her strength (the authority of the priesthood), and loosing herself from the bands of her neck (returning to the Lord and receiving revelation) shall be fulfilled. (See Isa. 52:1–2; D&C 113:7–10.)

(Joseph F. McConkie, *Studies in Scripture, Vol. 8*, ed. Kent P. Jackson, [Salt Lake City: Deseret Book Co., 1988], 189–90.)

As all the world knows, many Jews are now gathering to Palestine, where they have their own nation and way of worship, all without reference to a belief in Christ or an acceptance of the laws and ordinances of his everlasting gospel. Is this the latter-day gathering of the Jews of which the scriptures speak? No! It is not. . . . It does not fulfill the ancient promises. Those who have thus assembled have not gathered into the true Church and fold of their ancient Messiah. They have not received again the saving truths. . . .

This gathering of the unconverted to Palestine—shall we not call it a political gathering . . . or shall we not call it a preliminary gathering brought to pass in the wisdom of him who once was their God? —this gathering, of those whose eyes are yet dimmed by scales of darkness and who have not yet become the delightsome people it is their destiny to be, is nonetheless part of the divine plan.

(Bruce R. McConkie, *The Millennial Messiah* [Salt Lake City: Deseret Book Co., 1982], 229.)

3 Ne. 20:35   MADE BARE HIS ARM
(Isa. 52:10; 53:1; Mosiah 14:1)

To "make bare the arm" is a metaphorical expression denoting preparation for active work, especially for war. The beauty of the figure is seen, not only in the fact that the arm is an appropriate emblem of power, but also in the additional fact that the Oriental costume permits the arm to be bared in an instant. Jowett says: "The loose sleeve of the Arab shirt, as well as of the outer garment, leaves the arm so completely free, that in an instant the left hand, passing up the right arm, makes it bare; and this is done when a person, a soldier, for example, about to strike with his sword, intends to give the arm full play."

(James M. Freeman, *Manners and Customs of the Bible* [Plainfield, New Jersey: Logos International, 1972], 274.)

3 Ne. 20:36–38   PUT ON THY STRENGTH, O ZION
(Isa. 52:1–3; Joel 3:17; refer in this text to 2 Ne. 8:24–25)

The first half of the verse is addressed to the Saints of the latter days who will be gathering to America. What does the Lord mean when he says to "put on thy strength"? Joseph Smith said: "He [the Lord] had reference to those whom God should call in the last days, who should hold the power of priesthood to bring again Zion, and the redemption of Israel; and to put on her strength is TO PUT ON THE AUTHORITY OF THE PRIESTHOOD, which she, Zion, has a right to by lineage; also to return to that power which she had lost" (D&C 113:8; emphasis added).

The Lord also instructs Jerusalem to put on her "beautiful garments." This no doubt refers to the rebuilding of Jerusalem and the beautifying of all her suburbs. At the present time the fulfillment of this prediction has almost become an obsession with the Jews. Even though they have been in a state of virtual war or siege ever since Israel became a nation in 1948, the Jews have spent great sums of money and tremendous energy rebuilding Jerusalem. The buildings are constructed out of "Jerusalem stone," which is white limestone with a pink or beige hue. It is becoming one of the most beautiful cities in the world. However, in this verse the Lord is referring to a yet future time when it will have become sanctified following the great battle of Armageddon and after the sudden appearance of the Savior. It is in that day that it will indeed be a "holy city," and the Lord declares that "henceforth there shall no more come into thee the uncircumcised and the unclean." Those sublime circumstances are far from the situation today. There are many people now treading the streets of that famous city (including Jews, Arabs, and Christians) who live unclean lives and violate the commandments of God continually. These are the uncircumcised of heart whom the Lord has declared he will one day cleanse from the city of Jerusalem in order that it might be prepared for the coming Messiah, who will no longer permit the uncircumcised to pollute its sacred precincts.

(W. Cleon Skousen, *Isaiah Speaks to Modern Times* [Salt Lake City: Ensign Publishing Co., 1984], 643–644.)

3 Ne. 20:37   SHAKE THYSELF FROM THE DUST; ARISE, AND SIT DOWN
(Isa. 52:2)

The . . . Orientals sitting on the ground with their feet drawn under them, gradually gathering dust on their garments, and rising occasionally to shake it off, and then resuming their seats. This, however, is only a partial explanation of the allusions of the text. The "dust" referred to may be either that in which Jerusalem had been sitting, or that which she had put upon her head. In either case the idea of mourning would be represented. The mourner is exhorted to arise from the dust and take a higher position; not to sit down again in the dust. The language seems to embrace the idea of a throne, a high seat.

(James M. Freeman, *Manners and Customs of the Bible* [Plainfield, New Jersey: Logos International, 1972], 273–74.)

3 Ne. 20:40   BEAUTIFUL UPON THE MOUNTAIN . . . HIM THAT PUBLISHETH PEACE
(Isa. 52:7; refer in this text to Mosiah 12:20–24)

Ultimately it is Christ who is beautiful upon the mountain. And it is His merciful promise of "peace in this world." . . .

The search for peace is one of the ultimate quests of the human soul. We all have highs and lows, but such times come and they usually always go. Kind neighbors assist. Beautiful sunshine brings encouragement. A good night's sleep usually works wonders. But there are times in all of our lives when deep sorrow or suffering or fear or loneliness make us cry out for the peace which only God Himself can bring. These are times of piercing spiritual hunger when even the dearest friends cannot fully come to our aid.

Perhaps you know . . . courageous people who are carrying heavy burdens and feeling private pain, who are walking through the dark valleys of this world's tribulation. Some may be desperately worried about a husband or a wife or a child, worried about their health or their happiness or their faithfulness in keeping the commandments. Some are living with physical pain, or emotional pain, or disabilities that come with age. Some are troubled as to how to make ends meet financially—and some ache with the private loneliness of an empty house or an empty room or simply empty arms. . . .

They are tired in brain and body and heart, they wonder if they can get through another week or another day or sometimes just another hour. . . . We declare to all the world that for real and abiding peace to come, we must strive to be more like that exemplary Son of God. . . .

In seeking true peace some of us need to improve what has to be improved, confess what needs to be confessed, forgive what has to be forgiven, and forget what should be forgotten in order that serenity can come to us. . . .

If one of you has made a mistake, even a serious mistake, but you have done all you can according to the teachings of the Lord and the governance of the Church to confess it and feel sorrow for it and set it as right as can be, then trust in God, walk into His light, and leave those ashes behind you. . . .

Closely related to our own obligation to repent is the generosity of letting others do the same—we are to forgive even as we are forgiven. In this we participate in the very essence of the Atonement of Jesus Christ. Surely the most majestic moment of that fateful Friday, when nature convulsed and the veil of the temple was rent, was that unspeakably merciful moment when Christ said, "Father, forgive them; for they know not what they do" (Luke 23:34). As our advocate with the Father, He is still making that same plea today—in your behalf and in mine. . . .

It is one of those ironies of godhood that in order to find peace, the offended as well as the offender must engage the principle of forgiveness. . . . Life has its moments when uninterrupted peace may seem to elude us for a season. We may wonder why there are such times in life, particularly when we may be trying harder than we have ever tried to live worthy of God's blessings and obtain His help. When problems or sorrows or sadness come and they *don't* seem to be our fault, what are we to make of their unwelcome appearance?

With time and perspective we recognize that such problems in life do come for a purpose, if only to allow the one who faces such despair to be convinced that he really does need divine strength beyond himself, that she really does need the offer of heaven's hand. . . .

Praying for peace, pleading for peace, seeking peace in any way that would not compromise union, Abraham Lincoln said in those dark, dark days of his First Inaugural, "Though passion may have strained, it must not break our bonds of affection. The mystic chords of memory," he said, "will yet swell . . . when again touched, as surely they will be, by the better angels of our nature."

The better angels of our nature. That is much of what the Church and general conference and the gospel of Jesus Christ are about. The appeal today and tomorrow and forever . . . to seek peace and always be believing.

(Jeffrey R. Holland, *Ensign*, Nov. 1996, 82–84.)

In Hebrew, "how beautiful" is *mah na wu*. From this phrase the Prophet Joseph Smith derived the name *Nauvoo*, which he interpreted as "place of rest" or "beauty."

(Joseph Smith, *Teachings of the Prophet Joseph Smith*, comp. Joseph Fielding Smith [Salt Lake City: Deseret Book Co., 1976], 182.)

I am satisfied that a man cannot do well in his work unless there is peace in his home. You recall that when the Prophet Joseph was translating the Book of Mormon, he quarreled with his wife and discovered that "the gift and power of God" left him. Brethren, be true to your wives. Wives, keep faith with your husbands. Parents, admire and respect your children. Without peace and mutual respect in your homes, there will be neither peace nor proficiency in your labors.

(Gordon B. Hinckley, *Teachings of Gordon B. Hinckley* [Salt Lake City: Deseret Book Co., 1997], 424.)

The word *peace* appears frequently in scripture and has many meanings. In classical Greek the word refers to cessation, discontinuance, or absence of hostilities between rival forces. This definition is the antithesis of war and strife. The New Testament, however, has given a far wider range of meaning. This is partly due to the influence of the Hebrew word for peace, which is far more comprehensive of meaning. It was commonly used as a form of greeting when persons met or parted: "May peace be with you" (see Mark 5:34 and John 20:19–21) . . .

The peace for which the world longs is a time of suspended hostilities; but men do not realize that peace is a state of existence that comes to man only upon the terms and conditions set by God, and in no other way. . . .

Peace can come to an individual only by an unconditional surrender—surrender to him who is the Prince of Peace. . . . One may live in beautiful and peaceful surroundings but, because of inner dissension and discord, be in a state of constant turmoil. On the other hand, one may be in the midst of utter destruction and the bloodshed of war and yet have the serenity of unspeakable peace. . . .

This peace shelters us from the worldly turmoil. The knowledge that God lives, that we are his children, and that he loves us soothes the troubled heart.

(Howard W. Hunter, *The Teachings of Howard W. Hunter*, ed. Clyde J. Williams
[Salt Lake City: Bookcraft, 2002], 171–72.)

3 Ne. 20:41   **BE YE CLEAN THAT BEAR THE VESSELS OF THE LORD**
(Isa. 52:11; D&C 109:20; 38:42; 133:5; Alma 11:37; 3 Ne. 27:19; refer in
Latter-day Commentary on the Book of Mormon, Bassett, to Alma 39:4–6)

Let me tell you what that phrase "bear the vessels of the Lord" means. Anciently it had at least two meanings, both related to the work of the priesthood.

The first refers to the recovery and return to Jerusalem of various temple implements that had been carried into Babylon by King Nebuchadnezzar. In physically handling the return of these items, the Lord reminded those early brethren of the sanctity of anything related to the temple. Therefore as they carried back to their homeland these various bowls, basins, cups, and other vessels, they themselves were to be as clean as the ceremonial instruments they bore.

The second meaning is related to the first. Similar bowls and implements were used for ritual purification in the home. The Apostle Paul, writing to his young friend Timothy, said of these, "In a great house there are . . . vessels of gold and . . . silver, . . . of wood and of earth"—these means of washing and cleansing were common in the time of the Savior. But Paul goes on to say, "If a man . . . purge himself [of unworthiness], *he* shall *be* a vessel . . . sanctified, and meet for the master's use, and prepared unto every good work." Therefore, Paul says, "Flee . . . youthful lusts: . . . follow righteousness, . . . call on the Lord out of a pure heart."

In both of these biblical accounts the message is that as priesthood bearers, not only are we to *handle* sacred vessels and emblems of God's power—think of preparing, blessing, and passing the sacrament, for example—but we are also to *be* a sanctified instrument. Partly because of what we are to *do* but more importantly because of what we are to *be*, the prophets and apostles tell us to "flee . . . youthful lusts" and "call on the Lord out of a pure heart." They tell us to be clean.

(Jeffrey R. Holland, *Ensign*, October 2000, 39.)

While the power *of* the priesthood is unlimited, our individual power *in* the priesthood is limited by our degree of righteousness or purity.

Just as clean wires, properly connected, are required to carry electrical power, so clean hands and pure hearts are required to carry priesthood power. Filth and grime slow or prevent the flow of electrical power. Unclean thoughts and actions interfere with individual priesthood power. When we are humble, clean, and pure of hand, heart, and mind, nothing righteous is impossible. An ancient Oriental saying declares, "If a man lives a pure life, nothing can destroy him." . . .

There is no individual power in the priesthood outside of individual purity. . . Since there is nothing Satan can do about the power *of* the priesthood, he concentrates his energy on trying to limit our individual power *in* the priesthood by attempting to dirty our hands, hearts, and minds through abuse, anger, neglect, pornography, selfishness, or any other evil he can entice us to think or do. He knows if he can sufficiently soil us individually, he can, to that degree, keep us from the purity needed to properly exercise the priesthood and thus bring more light, life, and love to this earth and all the inhabitants thereof—past, present, and future.

(John H. Groberg, *Ensign*, May 2001, 43–44.)

Young men of the Aaronic Priesthood, remember the scriptural injunction "Be ye clean who bear the vessels of the Lord" (3 Ne. 20:41; D&C 38:42; see also Isa. 52:11). Remember the story of Joseph in Egypt, who hearkened not to the wife of Potiphar and maintained his purity and virtue (see Gen. 39:6–20).

Consider carefully the words of the prophet Alma to his errant son, Corianton, "Forsake your sins, and go no more after the lusts of your eyes" (Alma 39:9). "The lusts of your eyes"—in our day what does that expression mean? Movies, television programs, and video recordings that are both suggestive and lewd. Magazines and books that are obscene and pornographic.

We counsel you, young men, not to pollute your minds with such degrading matter, for the mind through which this filth passes is never the same afterwards. Don't see R-rated movies or vulgar videos or participate in any entertainment that is immoral, suggestive, or pornographic. Don't listen to music that is degrading.

(Ezra Taft Benson, *The Teachings of Ezra Taft Benson* [Salt Lake City: Bookcraft, 1988], 222.)

According to a 1997 nationwide survey, divorce is 32 percent more likely among those who engaged in premarital sex than it is among the general population. And almost three times as many separated or divorced Americans have committed adultery, compared to the general population. Further, 82 percent of adults who rate their marriage as "very strong" (9 or 10 on a 10-point scale) did not engage in premarital sex. This should not surprise us. Immorality is a breach of integrity of the highest order. On the other hand, those who have demonstrated sexual purity are also likely to have cultivated other moral virtues that contribute to the success of any relationship, particularly marriage. . . .

Both experience and divine wisdom dictate that moral virtue and cleanliness pave the way that leads to strength of character, peace of mind and heart, and happiness in life. There is no question that the way of safety and the road to a sense of genuine fulfillment lie in sexual abstinence before marriage and fidelity following marriage.

It has been my privilege on various occasions to converse with five presidents of the United States. At the conclusion of each such occasion, I have reflected on the rewarding experience of standing with confidence in the presence of the acknowledged leader of the free world. And then I have thought, what a wonderful thing, what a marvelous thing it would be to stand with confidence—unafraid and unashamed and unembarrassed—in the presence of God. This is the promise held out to every virtuous man and woman. . . .

Personal virtue is worth more than any salary, any bonus, any position or degree of prominence.

(Gordon B. Hinckley, *Standing For Something* [New York: Random House, Inc., 2000], 31, 34, 43–44.)

We want morally clean young men in the mission field. . . . We want the morally clean life to be your way of life.

Yes, one can repent of moral transgression. The miracle of forgiveness is real, and true repentance is accepted of the Lord. But it is not pleasing to the Lord prior to a mission, or at any time, to sow one's wild oats, to engage in sexual transgression of any nature, and then to expect that planned confession and quick repentance will satisfy the Lord. . . .

One of our fine stake presidents shared with us the following experience:

"I remember a girl that I had gone to high school with. She was from a good LDS family, but when she was a junior in high school, she began to compromise her standards and principles.

"I remember how stunned I was one afternoon as a group of us were in the back of the bus riding home from school. We were talking about the consequences of sin or transgression, and she flatly announced that she wasn't worried about committing any sin because her bishop had told her she could easily repent and could be quickly forgiven.

"Well, I was shocked with this flippant attitude that didn't reflect any understanding of repentance or appreciation of the miracle of forgiveness. I was also sure that she had grossly misunderstood the instruction and counsel of her bishop." . . .

Young men of the Aaronic Priesthood, remember the scriptural injunction "Be ye clean who bear the vessels of the Lord" (3 Ne. 20:41; D&C 38:42; see also Isa. 52:11).

(Ezra Taft Benson, *Ensign*, May 1986, 57–58.)

Consequently, if we are "raising the bar" for your sons to serve as missionaries, that means we are also "raising the bar" for you. If we expect more of them, that means we expect more of you and your wife as well. Remember, Helaman's 2,000 stripling warriors were faithful because "they had been taught to keep the commandments of God and to walk uprightly before him" (Alma 53:21) and that instruction came in their homes.

Some fathers don't think they have the right to ask worthiness questions of their children. They think that is the purview of the bishop alone. Fathers, not only do you have the right to know the worthiness of your children, you have the responsibility. It is your duty to know how your children are doing with regards to their spiritual well-being and progression. You need to monitor carefully the issues and concerns they share with you. Ask specific questions of your children regarding their worthiness, and refuse to settle for anything less than specific answers.

Too often our bishops have to instruct youth to talk to their parents about problems they are having. That procedure should actually flow the other direction. Parents should be so intimately aware of what is going on in their children's lives that they know about the problems before the bishop does. They should be counseling with their children and going with them to their bishops if that becomes necessary for complete repentance. As divinely appointed judges in Israel, the bishop and the stake president determine worthiness and resolve concerns on behalf of the Church; but, fathers, you have an eternal responsibility for the spiritual welfare of your children. Please assume your rightful place as counselor, adviser, and priesthood leader, in preparing your sons to bear the Melchizedek Priesthood and to serve as missionaries.

(Russell M. Ballard, *Ensign*, Nov. 2002, 48.)

It is a divine commandment. If you believe in Christ, touch not the unclean thing!

Lust and covetousness are completely destructive. Sex sin is deadly. Intoxication is vicious. Greed is of the devil. So is selfishness, as it leads to all forms of dishonesty. They contaminate and demoralize our very souls. They are completely opposite to the Christlike life.

(Mark E. Petersen, *Ensign*, Nov. 1982, 17.)

Because sexual intimacy is so sacred, the Lord requires self-control and purity before marriage, as well as full fidelity after marriage. In dating, treat your date with respect, and expect your date to show that same respect for you. Tears inevitably follow transgression. Men, take care not to make women weep, for God counts their tears.

(Thomas S. Monson, *Ensign*, Nov. 1990, 47.)

3 Ne. 20:42; 21:29   WILL GO BEFORE YOU—WILL BE YOUR REARWARD
(Isa. 52:12)

The Eastern shepherd never drives his sheep as does the Western shepherd. He always leads them, often going before them. . . . This does *not* mean that the shepherd is *always* in front of his sheep. Although he may be usually in that position when traveling, he often walks by their side, and sometimes follows behind, especially if the flock is headed for the fold in the evening. From the rear he can gather any stragglers, and protect such from a sly attack from a wild animal. If the flock is a large one, the shepherd will be in front, and a helper will follow behind. Isaiah speaks of the onmipresent Lord in a double relationship to His people: "For ye shall not go out with haste, nor go by flight: for the Lord will go before you; and the God of Israel will be your rearward [rear guard]" (Isa. 52:12). [refer in *Latter-day Commentary on the New Testament*, Pinegar–Bassett–Earl, 241–46.]

(Fred H. Wight, *Manners and Customs of Bible Lands* [Chicago: Moody Press, 1953], 157.)

When Israel left Egypt, she did so in *haste* and in *flight* (Ex. 12:39; Deut. 16:3). When her people now go forth in the gathering to Zion, leaving Babylon, they will do so in peace and safety, with neither haste nor flight (D&C 133:14–5). . . .

God will lead those who return to Zion and will also protect them in the rear. The Hebrew makes it clear that Jehovah will lead them and the Father will come behind (Isa. 58:8; D&C 49:27).

(Donald W. Parry, Jay A. Parry, and Tina M. Peterson,
Understanding Isaiah [Salt Lake City: Deseret Book Co., 1998], 467.)

3 Ne. 20:43–45; 21:8–10   MY SERVANT
(Isa. 52:13–15; D&C 10:43; JS–H 1:33)

While these verses are almost universally accepted as a prophecy of Christ, the Book of Mormon and Doctrine and Covenants definitely show it to be a future event. When the Savior visited the Nephites in A.D. 34 after his ministry and resurrection, he quoted these verses along with others as being fulfilled when the covenant of the father with the house of Israel was to be fulfilled. If they had already been fulfilled, there would have been no reason for him to quote them. He then spoke of the sign which was to be given to the Lamanites when these things were about to take place. The overall sign was the Book of Mormon coming forth from the Gentiles to the Lamanites in America (3 Ne. 21:1–9). He speaks of the servant who will bring forth this work:

> "But behold, the life of my servant shall be in my hands; therefore they shall not hurt him, although he shall be marred because of them. Yet I will heal him, for I will show unto them that my wisdom is greater than the cunning of the devil" (3 Nephi 21:10).

The Savior's comments will be recognized as a paraphrase of Isaiah 52:13–14. The marring of this servant spoken of by Isaiah is shown in the Doctrine and Covenants to be the loss of the first 116 pages of manuscript of the translation of the Book of Mormon. After revealing to Joseph Smith the designs of those wicked men who had obtained the 116 pages he tells the Prophet to translate what we know today as the Small Plates of Nephi. This will confound those who had altered the first 116 pages. He then states: "I will not suffer that they shall destroy my work; yea, I will show unto them that my wisdom is greater than the cunning of the devil" (D&C 10:43). You will note that these are the exact words of 3 Nephi 21:10 spoken by the Savior to the Nephites in A.D. 34 after his resurrection when he was talking about the great and marvelous work (the Book of Mormon) to come forth. Therefore, the Savior himself, who had already been marred while on earth, identifies the servant spoken of in Isaiah 52:13–15 as a man to bring forth the Book of Mormon in the latter days. This can be none other than Joseph Smith. This interpretation is not to deny that Christ did fulfill this prophecy, but we must acknowledge that this prophecy is dual. It foretells the marring of Joseph Smith as well as his role in bringing forth the Book of Mormon.

(Monte S. Nyman, *Isaiah: Prophecies of the Restoration* [Salt Lake City: Millennial Press, 1998], 18–19.)

Some scholars read the passage in Isaiah 52:13–15 about the servant whose "visage" was to be "marred" together with Isaiah 53, referring to the same suffering servant. The Book of Mormon never places it in this context; rather, the resurrected Jesus appears to have read this passage as referring to a servant who was yet to come (3 Ne. 20:43–45). He explained the passage in the context of the latter days, referring to a future servant who will be marred but healed (3 Ne. 21:9–10). Some have seen this as a prophecy referring to the coming of the Savior himself, who has been marred but preserved through the resurrection. Others see it as a reference to Joseph Smith or some other latter-day servant.

(Keith A Meservy, *Studies in Scripture, Vol. 4*, ed. Kent P. Jackson [Salt Lake City: Deseret Book Co., 1993], 151.)

Many people assume that the servant promised in the last three verses of Isaiah 52 is the same servant described throughout Isaiah 53. If so, these verses describe Christ, his great works, and the persecutions and suffering he endured. (See Mosiah 14; compare D&C 19:10–13.) However, in the Book of Mormon adaptations of Isaiah 52 and 53, neither Abinadi nor Christ combine Isaiah 52:13–15 with chapter 53. In fact, Christ includes this prophecy of a servant with other promises of the last days. . . .

Unless the Savior is speaking about himself in the last days, he must have had another person in mind as the servant of the last days. Particularly as the Savior comments upon these verses later in 3 Nephi 21:7–11, it appears obvious that he is not talking about himself, but about his servant. This servant will take God's word to the Gentiles, and those who will not accept the word will be separated from God's covenant people (3 Ne. 21:11). Although some people will attempt to harm this servant, Jesus promises that he will heal the servant and show that Christ's power is greater than "the cunning of the devil" (3 Ne. 21:10).

There are several reasons to consider Joseph Smith as this promised servant. This whole series of verses, as quoted by Christ in 3 Nephi, refers to the restoration of the gospel, the revelations of the Lord through his prophets, and the gathering of Israel. It would be natural to mention the servant whom the Lord would employ to carry out this great work. When Moroni visited Joseph Smith, he told him that the Lord had a great work for him to do and that Joseph's name would be known for good and ill among all nations. (JS–H 1:33.) Indeed, no one except Jesus Christ has been more important in bringing about the eternal purposes of the Lord here on earth than the Prophet Joseph Smith. (D&C 135:3.) The work of Joseph Smith demonstrates that he fulfilled that which the Lord required of him. As prophesied in Isaiah 52:13, on the one hand he has been extolled by the Saints, yet on the other hand, hardly any man has been maligned and misrepresented as much as Joseph Smith. Among other things, he has been called a money-digger, a dreamer, a liar, an imposter, and a lunatic. During his lifetime he hardly knew a period without persecution. . . . Through the work of Joseph Smith, the nations of the earth have been "sprinkled" or blessed with many missionaries and messengers of salvation. Many people, including the great ones of this earth, have heard or will hear the message of the gospel. This "new" or restored gospel is one that the people of the earth have not earlier considered, heard, nor seen. Joseph Smith was the man who made it possible for the Lord to fulfill his commitment to call, restore, and gather the house of Israel in the last days, and thus might easily be the servant promised in Isaiah 52:13–15.

Another modern prophet might be this promised servant. As Christ comments on Isaiah's words, he says that when the latter-day Lamanites begin to grow in their knowledge of the restored gospel, they will know that the Father's work is being fulfilled with the house of Israel. (3 Ne. 21:7.) When that day comes, he continues, kings will be speechless (3 Ne. 21:8; compare Isa. 52:15) at the great work declared by a man to the people (3 Ne. 21:9; compare Isa. 52:13). Christ describes his servant of the last days as one who will be marred, yet healed by the Lord (3 Ne. 21:10; cf. Isa. 52:14).

This description can easily be applied to President Spencer W. Kimball. Evaluating President Kimball's inspired leadership, one notes a very dramatic increase in missionary work, especially among the Lamanites. He has no equal in bringing Christ's word to the Gentiles and Abraham's posterity. Indeed, the gospel *is* being "sprinkled" among many new nations as more countries open their doors and as kings and rulers see and hear things that have not been told them or considered by them earlier. (See Isa. 52:15.) President Kimball has helped "*gather* many nations" (JST v. 15, italics added), as people throughout the world are joining covenant Israel.

It is well known that President Kimball has probably suffered more physical ailments than any other latter-day seer. Yet, in spite of a larynx marred by cancer, boils and sores, and numerous heart attacks, he has always made remarkable recoveries. "Yet I will heal him," says the Lord. (3 Ne. 21:10). God has healed President Kimball many times so that he can visit the many nations of the earth and deliver his message to hundreds of thousands. . . .

In short, the final three verses of Isaiah 52 prophesy of the Lord's servant in the last days. But one need not feel constrained to identify this servant only with Israel, Christ, Joseph Smith, or Spencer W. Kimball, since Isaiah could be describing any or all of these people. If this prophecy deals with one particular person, the servant might not yet have fulfilled his role. Some future prophet might be the servant who will perform this great work.

(Victor L. Ludlow, *Isaiah: Prophet, Seer, and Poet* [Salt Lake City: Deseret Book Co., 1982], 439–41.)

3 Ne. 21:29

(Isa.52:12; refer in this text to 3 Ne. 20:42)

3 Ne. 22

(Isa. 54)

The fulfillment of this beautiful poem—Isaiah 54 is all poetry—is to be found in this dispensation. Part of it has probably already been fulfilled since the restoration of the gospel; the remainder will be in a time yet future.

(Sidney B. Sperry, *Book of Mormon Compendium* [Salt Lake City: Bookcraft, 1968], 412.)

The children are those who have gathered to the family of Christ as members of the Church. . . . In 3 Nephi 20–21 Jesus told the Nephites some of the things that would transpire before the events recorded in Isaiah 54. Among them were the following: the gospel would go forth to the Gentiles (20:27–28; 21:2), the Jews (20:29–31), the Lamanites (21:4–7), and the dispersed of Israel (20:13; 21:26–28); the remnants of Israel would gather to Zion (21:1); and the covenant people of the Lord would be restored to the lands of their inheritance (20:14, 22, 29, 33, 46; 21:26–28).

(Donald W. Parry, Jay A. Parry, and Tina M. Peterson,
Understanding Isaiah [Salt Lake City: Deseret Book Co., 1998], 479–80.)

This chapter shows the Lord's promise and devotion to Zion in the last days. As such, it is a natural continuation of the prophetic, covenantal promises Christ was giving the Nephites, promises that would be fulfilled as a result of the restoration of the gospel and the gathering of Israel that would flow from that. . . .

Verses	*Husband Provides Wife*	*Jehovah Provides Israel*
1–3	Children	Gathering and Great Growth
4–8	Love	Mercy and Redemption
9–10	Commitment	Unbreakable Covenant
11–12	Material Comfort	Splendor in a New Jerusalem
13–17	Protection for the Family	Peace, Freedom from Fear and Oppression for Zion.

(Jeffrey R. Holland, *Christ and the New Covenant* [Salt Lake City: Deseret Book Co., 1997], 289, 291.)

In 3 Nephi 22, Jesus uses a poetic text from Isaiah to address the more righteous part of the Nephites and an audience of Book of Mormon readers in the latter days. The Lord promises to redeem Zion and reestablish her reputation of righteousness:

1. He sings a song of redeeming love (*?ir yedidot*) to Zion.
2. He compares her to faithful covenant women, such as Sarah and Hannah.
3. He trusts her to become a mother to children in the house of Israel.
4. He calls her to suffer as he suffered in the atonement.
5. He supports and protects her like a husband.
6. He compares her to Noah, a just and perfect man who walked with God (Genesis 6:9).
7. He extends temple blessings to Zion and her children.
8. He counts Zion among his servants.

The Lord redeems Zion through his covenant of peace and perfect love. Zion responds by singing a song of redeeming love and by bringing her children into the new and everlasting covenant.

(Cynthia L. Hallen, "Redeeming the Desolate Woman," *Journal of Book of Mormon Studies*, vol. 7, no. 1:47.)

3 Ne. 22:1   SING, CRY ALOUD
(Isa. 54:1)

In Jewish culture, childbirth is associated with singing, rejoicing, and reciting psalms. A woman sings when she first discovers that she will have a baby, as Mary does after Gabriel's annunciation that she would bear the Christ child: "My soul doth magnify the Lord, And my spirit hath rejoiced in

God my Saviour" (Luke 1:46–47). A woman also sings when her baby is safely delivered, as Hannah does after the birth of Samuel: "My heart rejoiceth in the Lord, mine horn is exalted in the Lord: my mouth is enlarged over mine enemies; because I rejoice in my salvation" (1 Sam. 2:1). Even today, an orthodox Jewish mother will use the words of a psalm to give thanks for the birth of her firstborn child: "Sing aloud unto God our strength: make a joyful noise unto the God of Jacob" (Ps. 81:1). Singing is a token of the covenant that promises that barren women will have posterity, that the Lord will have children in Zion, and that the Lord's people will have children in their homes. The singing of angels heralded the birth of Jesus, who will redeem the whole earth with a covenant of peace and goodwill (see Luke 2:13–14).

Cry aloud means "shout," especially to make a joyful noise as in singing (see Ps. 55:17; Isa. 24:14). The Lord tells the barren woman to cry aloud with joyful singing because she will soon cry aloud with paradoxical pain as she breaks forth into the joys of childbirth.

(Cyntia L. Hallen, *Isaiah In The Book of Mormon,* ed. Donald W. Parry and John W. Welch
[Provo, Utah: Foundation for Ancient Research and Mormon Studies, 1998], 315–16.)

The Hebrew name for the poetic form the Lord uses in 3 Nephi 22 is *?ir yedidot,* a "song of loves" or wedding song. The text reads like an *epithalamium,* a wedding poem from classical Greece that celebrates the joy of a bride and her groom. Singing is a symbol of the vibrant love that is possible between a man, a woman, and their children when they follow the Lord's way.

In Bible lands, childbirth is often associated with rejoicing, singing, or chanting poetry in the form of psalms. A woman sings when she first discovers that she will have a baby. Mary sang after Noah appeared as the angel Gabriel to announce that she would bear the Christ child: "My soul doth magnify the Lord, and my spirit hath rejoiced in God my Savior" (Luke 1:46–47). A woman also sings when her baby is safely delivered, as Hannah did after the birth of Samuel: "My heart rejoiceth in the Lord . . . I rejoice in my salvation" (1 Sam. 2:1). Nursing professor Lynn Callister reports that even today an orthodox Jewish mother will recite the words of a psalm to give thanks for the birth of her firstborn child: "Sing aloud unto God our strength: make a joyful noise unto the God of Jacob" (Ps. 81:1). Singing is a token of the promise that the Lord's covenant people will have children in their homes.

Paradoxically, Zion will cry aloud with pain as well as joy as she experiences the miracle and labor of bearing children, literally or figuratively. The cry of a woman enduring labor pains as she gives birth to a child mirrors the anguished prayers of Christ as he suffered agony to give new life to us through his atoning sacrifice (see Luke 22:44).

(Cynthia L. Hallen, "Redeeming the Desolate Woman," *Journal of Book of Mormon Studies,* vol. 7, no. 1:46.)

3 Ne. 22:1 MORE ARE THE CHILDREN OF THE DESOLATE
(Isa. 54:1)

Isaiah now commences chapter 54 by returning to the earlier theme concerning the restoration of Israel in the latter days. It is interesting that this chapter was quoted in its entirety by the Savior when he appeared among the Nephites following his resurrection (see 3 Ne., chapter 22). However, before quoting it the Savior outlined what would precede it (3 Ne. chapter 21). There would be a free nation raised up in America where the Gospel would be restored among the Gentiles. The Lord's servant who restored the Gospel would be "marred because of them," but the Lord would heal him (3 Ne. 21:10; see also Isa. 52:14). Eventually there would be a cleansing of the land, leaving many of the Gentile cities in America "desolate." Then the Lord would prepare to destroy the wicked in other parts of the earth. However, before doing so, he would gather out all the members of the Church and as many Gentiles as would repent. This is the great final gathering spoken of by Jesus when he said:

"Yea, the work shall commence among ALL THE DISPERSED OF MY PEOPLE, with the Father, to prepare the way whereby they may come unto me. . . .

"Yea, and then shall the work commence, with the Father among all nations in preparing the way whereby his people may be gathered home to the land of their inheritance.

"And they shall GO OUT FROM ALL NATIONS; and they shall not go out in haste, nor go by flight, for I will go before them, saith the Father, and I will be their rearward." (3 Ne. 21:27–29; emphasis added.)

Jesus then introduces Isaiah chapter 54 by saying, "AND THEN SHALL THAT WHICH IS WRITTEN COME TO PASS" (3 Ne. 22:1; emphasis added).

(W. Cleon Skousen, *Isaiah Speaks to Modern Times* [Salt Lake City: Ensign Publishing Co., 1984], 667–68.)

"More are the children of the desolate than the children of the married wife, saith the Lord." That is, greater are the numbers of Israel born outside of the covenant than those born within it.

(Joseph F. McConkie, *Studies in Scripture, Vol. 8*, ed. Kent P. Jackson,
[Salt Lake City: Deseret Book Co., 1988], 192–93.)

The comparison of Zion to a childless woman evokes the stories of Eve, Sarah, Rebekah, Rachel, Hannah, Elizabeth, and other female ancestors in Israel who received the blessings of posterity after a trial of their faith. Children are the greatest blessing that the Lord can bestow, so to be barren is a great affliction. In Near Eastern societies of the Bible, barren women were among the most vulnerable people, often subject to disgrace. . . .

Zion will receive so many children that she will not know where they came from, just as Saints in the latter-days marvel when missionaries throughout the world bring nearly 1000 persons per day into the new life of the gospel.

(Cynthia L. Hallen, "Redeeming the Desolate Woman," *Journal of Book of Mormon Studies*, vol. 7, no. 1:43.)

3 Ne. 22:2   **LENGTHEN THY CORDS—STRENGTHEN THY STAKES**
(Isa. 54:1–2; 40:21–22; Ps. 104:1–5; D&C 101:21; 109:59;
133:9; refer in this text to Moroni 10:31)

The tent . . . represents the gospel of Christ. [Isaiah] states that in the last days the cords of the tent would be stretched across the earth and stakes would be planted in every land. We literally are seeing that fulfilled today.

(Merrill J. Bateman, *Ensign*, May 1994, 65.)

We are not suggesting in the "lengthening of our stride" that we try to move faster than we are able, or than would be wise. . . . The idea of "lengthening our stride" or "stretching our muscles" or "reaching our highest" has an interesting scripture base. The second verse in the fifty-fourth chapter of Isaiah proclaims: "Enlarge the place of thy tent, and then stretch forth the curtains of thine habitations: spare not, lengthen thy cords, and strengthen thy stakes."

(Spencer W. Kimball, *The Teachings of Spencer W. Kimball,* ed. Edward L. Kimball
[Salt Lake City: Bookcraft, 1982], 175.)

New tents are very seldom made among the Bedouins. About the only time this happens is when a young groom and bride set up housekeeping for themselves in a different location from that of the groom's parents, and this rarely happens. The usual procedure is to accumulate the goat clippings of a year or so, and with these make a new strip with which to repair the old tent. The women do this work. The section of the tent roof that is most worn is ripped out, and a new piece of the cloth replaces it. The old piece is then used for a side curtain. Each year new strips of cloth replace old ones and the "house of hair" is handed down from father to son without its being completely new or completely old at any one time.

As the tent-dweller's family grows larger, or as he becomes richer and wishes to enlarge his tent, he does so by simply adding another section to his old tent, very much like the Occidental would build another room on to his house; but there is this difference: instead of building a new tent they just continue patching. Isaiah had this process in mind when he compared the prophetic prosperity of Israel to a Bedouin tent. "Enlarge the place of thy tent, and let them stretch forth the curtains of thine habitations: spare not, lengthen thy cords, and strengthen thy stakes" (Isa. 54:2).

(Fred H. Wight, *Manners and Customs of Bible Lands* [Chicago: Moody Press, 1953], 17–18.)

The term *stake* is a symbolic expression.

Picture in your mind a great tent held up by cords extended to many stakes that are firmly secured in the ground.

The prophets likened latter-day Zion to a great tent encompassing the earth. That tent was supported by cords fastened to stakes. Those stakes, of course, are various geographical organizations spread out over the earth. Presently, Israel is being gathered to the various stakes of Zion . . . (D&C 68:25–26).

Here we see one of the major purposes of stakes. They are organized to assist parents who have "children in Zion" to teach them the gospel of Jesus Christ and administer the ordinances of salvation. Stakes are formed to perfect the Saints, and that development begins in the home with effective gospel instruction. . . .

Stakes of Zion are to be "for a defense, and for a refuge from the storm, and from wrath when it shall be poured out without mixture upon the whole earth" (D&C 115:5–6). Stakes are a defense for the Saints from enemies both seen and unseen. The defense is direction provided through priesthood channels that strengthens testimony and promotes family solidarity and individual righteousness. . . .

The Lord also states . . . that He "shall have power over his saints, and shall reign in their midst" (D&C 1:36).

He does this as He works through His anointed servants and stake and ward authorities.

The Book of Mormon prophet Nephi foresaw the day when the Saints would be scattered in stakes all over the world. He saw the time when the Lord would extend His protection to them when menaced by a storm of destruction that threatened their existence. Nephi prophesied:

> "And it came to pass that I, Nephi, beheld the power of the Lamb of God, that it descended upon the saints of the church of the Lamb, and upon the covenant people of the Lord, who were scattered upon all the face of the earth; and they were armed with righteousness and with the power of God in great glory" (1 Ne. 14:14).

From the revelations, we can see that a stake has at least four purposes:

> 1. Each stake, presided over by three high priests and supported by twelve men known as a high council, becomes a miniature Church to the Saints in a specific geographic area. The purpose is to unify and perfect the members who live in those boundaries by extending to them the Church programs, the ordinances, and gospel instruction.
>
> 2. Members of stakes are to be models, or standards, of righteousness.
>
> 3. Stakes are to be a defense. They do this as stake members unify under their local priesthood officers and consecrate themselves to do their duty and keep their covenants. Those covenants, if kept, become a protection from error, evil, or calamity.
>
> We only build temples in stakes. The blessings and ordinances of the temple prepare one for exaltation. . . .
>
> 4. Stakes are a refuge from the storm to be poured out over the earth.

(Ezra Taft Benson, *Ensign*, January 1991, 2–5.)

The tent figuratively represents the priesthood organization of the church in Zion. The images of enlarging and stretching suggest the preparations in a woman's body for the birth of a child. The lengthened and strengthened cords and stakes represent the growth of the church. Furthermore, the Lord transforms the portable tent of Zion into a permanent temple, just as he transforms the temporal tabernacle of our mortal bodies into perfect temples of immortal glory in the resurrection. Zion's tent in the wilderness becomes the House of the Lord in the New Jerusalem, a new home for all the families of the earth. The tent is thus a metaphor for the Lord's covenant with Enoch, Noah, Abraham, Isaac, and Jacob. Children from all nations, kindreds, tongues, and peoples will eventually have the opportunity to dwell in the haven of gospel covenants in the latter days.

(Cynthia L. Hallen, "Redeeming the Desolate Woman," *Journal of Book of Mormon Studies*, vol. 7, no. 1:42–43.)

3 Ne. 22:3   BREAK FORTH ON THE RIGHT . . . AND . . . LEFT
(Isa. 54:3)

Sometimes by choice and sometimes by circumstance, Israel has been a barren, childless woman who had not borne fruit or lived up to her promises, potential, and covenants. Nevertheless, desolate Israel can—and will—be fruitful, even in the times and places of her scattering and dispersion.

The large movement of Israel's conversion, gathering, and return to the lands of her inheritance will require strong, enlarged stakes in Zion. Growth will be "on the right hand and on the left," with Gentile cities (probably left desolate by the wrath "poured out without mixture upon the whole earth" (D&C 115:6) inhabited by the children of the covenant. It is from this imagery of Israel's wilderness tent/tabernacle with its cords, curtains, borders, and stakes that The Church of Jesus Christ of Latter-day Saints draws its use of the word *stake* for the name of its basic ecclesiastical unit.

(Jeffrey R. Holland, *Christ and the New Covenant* [Salt Lake City: Deseret Book Co., 1997], 289–90.)

In the day of their final gathering, the Saints will break forth on the right hand and on the left. The Israelites will not only occupy the mountains, valleys, desert, and plains, but they will invade the "desolate" and abandoned cities of the Gentiles. This would suggest that a certain amount of domestic warfare will have cleansed the land of Gentile wickedness. After each of the world wars ended, it was amazing how the people were able to clean up the rubble and erect magnificent modern cities in a relatively short time. The gathering Saints will do the same in America. They will take over the desolate cities of the Gentiles and cause them to be inhabited.

(W. Cleon Skousen, *Isaiah Speaks to Modern Times* [Salt Lake City: Ensign Publishing Co., 1984], 670.)

While the Church was in its infancy, the Lord pointed to a time when those earlier gathering places would not have room for all who would be gathered for reasons for which he declared that his church should be united.

(Harold B. Lee, *Ensign*, May 1973, 3.)

3 Ne. 22:4–6 THOU SHALT NOT BE ASHAMED
(Isa. 54:4–6; refer in this text to 2 Ne. 7:1–2)

The word "adultery" and the word "idolatry" were originally one, that is, they sprang from the same root, and mean essentially the condition of being false to a solemn covenant.
The Lord compared himself—though in terms of rebuke—to the Israelites of old, as their husband.

(James E. Talmage, *Conference Report*, Oct. 1930, 71.)

Even though there has been barrenness and sometimes unfaithfulness, yet will the husband (Christ) reclaim and redeem his bride (Israel). The imagery of Jehovah as bridegroom and Israel as bride is among the most commonly used metaphors in scripture, being used by the Lord and his prophets to describe the relationship between Deity and the children of the covenant.

(Jeffrey R. Holland, *Christ and the New Covenant* [Salt Lake City: Deseret Book Co., 1997], 290.)

Like people who are widowed, divorced, or never married, Zion is alone for a season, but not forever. The Savior of the whole earth is her husband. The etymology of the English word *husband* is a compound of *house* and *prepare*; thus, a husband is "one who prepares or builds a house." The Lord is Zion's husband or "house builder" because he makes the earth as a home for all creatures, he creates bodies as temples for spirit children, he builds temples as places of worship, and he prepares heavenly mansions for his children.

(Cynthia L. Hallen, "Redeeming the Desolate Woman," *Journal of Book of Mormon Studies*, vol. 7, no. 1: 44.)

3 Ne. 22:7–10 NEITHER SHALL THE COVENANT OF MY PEACE BE REMOVED
(Isa. 54:7–10)

Christ has, on occasion, been rightfully angry with backsliding Israel, but that has always been brief and temporary— "a small moment." Compassion and mercy always return and prevail in a most reassuring way. The mountains and the hills may disappear. The water of the great seas may dry up. The least likely things in the world may happen, but the Lord's kindness and peace will never be taken from his covenant people. He has sworn with a heavenly oath that he will not be wroth with them forever.

(Jeffrey R. Holland, *Christ and the New Covenant* [Salt Lake City: Deseret Book Co., 1997], 290.)

3 Ne. 22:8   **WRATH**
                    (Isa. 54:8)

A distinction should be made between the appropriate anger of God, which is a righteous application of the law of justice, and the unbridled anger of a fallible mortal. The Lord has consistently counseled his children against anger (Matt. 5:21–22; 3 Ne. 11:21–22); furthermore, we have been instructed that the devil "is the father of contention . . ." (3 Ne. 11:29). One who is angry loses the Spirit and his love of his fellowman (Moro. 9:3–5). In contrast, properly understood, God's anger is a divine display of his love. It is a manifestation of truth (see 2 Ne. 1:24–27).

(Hoyt W. Brewster, Jr., *Doctrine & Covenents Encyclopedia* [Salt Lake City: Bookcraft, 1988], 18.)

3 Ne. 22:8   **EVERLASTING KINDNESS**
                    (Isa. 54:8; D&C 133:52–53, 56)

God's love is complete and without limit for you and for all mankind. . . . He is perfectly kind and understands your circumstances and condition. He knows you better than you know yourself. Because your Heavenly Father is perfect, you can have complete faith in Him. You can trust Him.

(Joseph B. Wirthlin, *Ensign*, Nov. 1999, 38.)

The relationship between the Savior and Zion is one of "everlasting kindness." The Hebrew word for kindness is *hesed*, which has connotations of mercy, courtship, favors, loyalty, cherishing, marital duty, and constant attention. The mercy of the Lord is linked with the intimacy of kindness within the family. The earliest known source for the English word *kindness* is the reconstructed Indo-European root *gen-*, meaning "to give birth, beget; with derivatives referring to . . . procreation and to familial and tribal groups." Several other terms come from the same root as kindness: kin, king, kindred, and kinder (the German word for "children"), gentile, gentle, generation, genealogy, genesis, progenitor, pregnant, natal, nation, nativity. Such terms of kindness and relationship are woven throughout the scriptures as a testimony of the Savior.

(Cynthia L. Hallen, "Redeeming the Desolate Woman," *Journal of Book of Mormon Studies*, vol. 7, no. 1:45.)

3 Ne. 22:8   I HID MY FACE
(Isa. 54:8)

Among orthodox Jews, a husband is not allowed to watch his wife going through the labor of childbirth. He sits in the corner of the delivery room with his back turned so that she will not feel embarrassed or immodest in her unavoidable hour of agony. He does not abandon her, although she may feel very much alone. The woman recites or sings psalms as she endures contractions. When the pain becomes too great for her to continue singing, the husband takes over, reciting psalms for her. Although Zion cannot see the Lord in the time of her probation, when she weeps, he weeps with her; when she sings, he rejoices with her.

(Cynthia L. Hallen, "Redeeming the Desolate Woman," *Journal of Book of Mormon Studies*, vol. 7, no. 1: 46.)

3 Ne. 22:9–10   WATERS OF NOAH
(Isa. 54:9)

After God cleansed the earth with a flood, he promised Noah that he would never again destroy the earth in that manner. (Gen. 9:13–17.) Here Isaiah impresses upon Israel that the promise God made to gather and redeem her is as valid as his promise to Noah.

As part of his promise, the Lord says that he will never again rebuke Israel (v. 9). The Lord cannot lie, and since he has sworn not to be angry with Israel nor to rebuke her, and since he has also promised that he will "chasten" or rebuke those whom he loves if they are wicked (D&C 95:1), Isaiah's prophecy means that a time will come when Israel will become righteous enough that she will need no chastisement from the Lord.

When all Israel and the earth as a whole is righteous, the Lord's millennial reign will be established.

(Victor L. Ludlow, *Isaiah: Prophet, Seer, and Poet* [Salt Lake City: Deseret Book Co., 1982], 461.)

The destiny of latter-day Zion is parallel to the pattern of Noah. . . . Both Noah and Zion strive to remain faithful to their covenants in darkening days of abomination and desolation. They each witness a cleansing of the earth, first by flood and later by fire. Their lives are spared, but they mourn for those who are lost. Zion feels homeless and tempest-tossed, like Noah and his family must have felt during the stormy days in the ark (see Gen. 7:6–20). Zion longs for a place to rest just as Noah looked hopefully for the birds to bring signs of land. The Lord redeems Zion by renewing the covenant of peace that he made with Noah, whose name in Hebrew means "comfort" or "rest."

The new covenant is an unconditional "Royal Grant" of land and blessings, typically given by a king to his faithful servants in the ancient Near East.

Like a rainbow after a storm, the promise moves from the waters of Noah to the shining beauty of the temple in the city of Zion. When the Lord redeems Zion, she and her children will receive all the blessings of the temple.

(Cynthia L. Hallen, "Redeeming the Desolate Woman," *Journal of Book of Mormon Studies*, vol. 7, no. 1: 43–44.)

3 Ne. 22:11   LAY THE FOUNDATIONS WITH SAPPHIRES
(Isa. 54:11; Ex. 24:10; 28:18; 39:11; Job 28:6, 16;
Lam. 4:7; Ezek 1:26; 10:10; 28:13; Rev. 21:19)

In the midst of a troubling world, the foundations I rely on come by my covenants with the Lord. They are indeed like sapphires and are treasures beyond price. . . . They are the restored principles and ordinances of the gospel of Jesus Christ which are available to righteous women and men alike through the power of the holy priesthood of God. They include baptism, the gift of the Holy Ghost, the sacrament, and temple covenants."

(Aileen H. Clyde, *Ensign*, May 1995, 28.)

Even in the midst and aftermath of great affliction, the Lord will shower material and spiritual blessings on Israel, including those jewels and precious metals that will be used to build the New Jerusalem.

(Jeffrey R. Holland, *Christ and the New Covenant* [Salt Lake City: Deseret Book Co., 1997], 291.)

Sapphires, like rubies, belong to the corundum or aluminum oxide family, with a hardness next to diamond.

(*The New Compact Bible Dictionary*, ed. T. Alton Bryant
[Grand Rapids, Michigan: Zondervan Publishing House, 1967], 366.)

3 Ne. 22:13–14   GREAT SHALL BE THE PEACE OF THY CHILDREN
(Isa. 54:13–14; D&C 45:58; refer in this text to 3 Ne. 20:40)

Surely every good parent would like this peace for his offspring. It comes from the simple life of the true Latter-day Saint as he makes his home and family supreme.

(Spencer W. Kimball, *Ensign*, July 1973, 16.)

[Sister Wirthlin quoted 3 Ne. 22:7,10,13, and then said] These words of the Savior are the theme for Primary . . . to teach children the gospel of Jesus Christ and help them learn to live it. As we witness the unfolding events of the last days, we cannot doubt that in this scripture the Lord is speaking directly to us. We are Israel of the latter days. . . . Peace that endures is not dependent upon outside forces that are beyond our control. . . . The Lord's words . . . give comfort to righteous parents who teach their children of Him. They speak to us at a time when peace in the hearts of children can seem but an elusive dream. But the Savior has assured us that it can be a reality if we teach our children. Primary supports parents in this important responsibility.

(Anne G. Wirthlin, *Ensign*, May 1998, 9.)

This is a favorite and oft-quoted scripture noting the peace and freedom from fear that will come to those in Zion, including—and especially—to the children of those who have made and kept their covenants.

(Jeffrey R. Holland, *Christ and the New Covenant* [Salt Lake City: Deseret Book Co., 1997], 291.)

Seven-year-old Jamie loved her mother dearly. The family had known for nearly a year that their wife and mother was dying of cancer. The father and seven children fasted and prayed; they pled with the Lord to heal her. Everything possible was done for their mother, yet at the end of three painfully difficult months, she passed from this life.

In the first hours following her death, the father brought the grieving family together. After prayer, the children went to their own rooms to prepare for bed. Jamie, who had spent many hours with her mother and was devoted to her, knelt at her own bedside. "Heavenly Father," she prayed through her tears, "we thank thee for the great mom you gave us. We thank thee for helping us try to make her well. Help us to be good so we can live with her again." Without a hint of bitterness, this little seven-year-old girl continued for several minutes in a sweet attitude of peaceful prayer, reflecting her understanding and acceptance of her mother's death.

Jamie was a child at peace. How did she come to that peace? She had been prepared by parents with spiritual understanding. Such preparation brings peace. . . .

Our Heavenly Father has promised peace to his children. "All thy children shall be taught of the Lord; and great shall be the peace of thy children" (3 Ne. 22:13). Peace in the Lord can give them freedom from self-doubt, freedom from fear, freedom from the confinement of their environment, freedom from enslaving habits. His peace can free them to unfold from the tender buds they are to the mature and fruitful adults they can be."

(Michaelene P. Grassli, *Ensign*, Nov. 1988, 90.)

3 Ne. 22:17   **NO WEAPON FORMED AGAINST THEE SHALL PROSPER . . . THIS IS THE HERITAGE OF THE SERVANTS OF THE LORD**
(Isa. 54:17; 1 Ne. 14:3; D&C 71:7–10; 109:24–25;
refer in *Latter-day Commentary on the Book of Mormon,* Bassett,
to 1 Ne. 22:16–17; Hel. 5:20–52)

The word *this* in "this is the heritage of the servants of the Lord" refers back to all of the ways in which the Lord will redeem the desolate woman in 3 Nephi 22. He will protect Zion from harm;

he will build a House for her that cannot be moved; he will bless her with children in the House of the Lord. The most important feature of Zion's redemption is the gift of life, the endowment of having children: "Lo, children are an heritage of the Lord: and the fruit of the womb is his reward" (Ps. 127:3).

(Cynthia L. Hallen, "Redeeming the Desolate Woman," *Journal of Book of Mormon Studies*, vol. 7, no. 1:47.)

Now, I think we all understand that this great latter-day kingdom has been set up for the last time, never again to be destroyed, and that never again will the necessity arise for another and future restoration. . . . But there is one great thing about this dispensation which differs from all the dispensations of the past. It is that this time, with the opening of the heavens and the revealing of the gospel in our day, there came the positive, unqualified assurance that the gospel was to remain on earth; that the kingdom was to be secure; that the Church of Jesus Christ of Latter-day Saints was to remain among men to prepare a people for the second coming of the Son of man.

(Bruce R. McConkie, *Conference Report*, Oct. 1958, 114–15.)

[A portion of the dedicatory prayer of the Kirtland Temple] "We ask thee, Holy Father, to establish the people that shall worship, and honorably hold a name and standing in this thy house, to all generations and for eternity; That no weapon formed against them shall prosper; that he who diggeth a pit for them shall fall into the same himself."

(Joseph Smith, as quoted in Hoyt W. Brewster, Jr., *Isaiah Plain and Simple*
[Salt Lake City: Deseret Book Co., 1995], 271.)

No unhallowed hand can stop the work from progressing; persecutions may rage, mobs may combine, armies may assemble, calumny may defame, but the truth of God will go forth boldly, nobly, and independently, till it has penetrated every continent, visted every clime, swept every country, and sounded in every ear, till the purposes of God shall be accomplished, and the Great Jehovah shall say the work is done.

(Joseph Smith, *History of the Church*, 4:540.)

We are constantly fed a steady and sour diet of pessimism, faultfinding, second-guessing, and evil speaking one of another. . . . Surely this is the age and place of the gifted pickle sucker!

A sustained diet of a negative point of view has serious repercussions. . . . This spirit of negativism grows and begins to hang as a cloud over the land . . . reaching down to the individual man and woman and influencing attitudes, outlook, and even values. . . .

There is too much fruitless carping and criticism of America. What might become of this land if we spoke less of its weaknesses and more of its goodness and strength, its capacity and potential? Without doubt, we shall have days of trial. . . . But if we will turn our time and talents away from vituperative criticism, away from constantly looking for evil, and will emphasize instead the greater good, America will continue to go forward with the blessing of the Almighty and stand as an ensign of strength and peace and generosity to all the world. This is a great land, a choice land, a chosen land.

I am an optimist! . . . With that frame of reference, my plea is that we stop seeking out the storms and enjoy more fully the sunlight. . . . I am not suggesting that our conversation be all sweetness and honey. . . . What I am suggesting is that we have had missing from our society a buoyant spirit of optimism. What I am asking is that we turn from the negativism that so permeates our culture and look for the remarkable good in the land and times in which we live . . . that optimism replace pessimism; that uncertainty and worry be pushed aside by an enduring feeling of hope. . . .

We are creatures of our thinking. We can talk ourselves into defeat, or we can talk ourselves into victory. . . .

We all tend to worry about the future. And yes, there may be lean days ahead for many of us. . . . But we must not despair or give up. We must look for the sunlight through the clouds. . . .

Criticism and pessimism . . . spread a shroud of gloom over entire nations. We must resist partaking of the spirit of our times. We need rather to look for the good all about us. . . . To the extent we cultivate this virtue of optimism, we will bless all the world's peoples.

(Gordon B. Hinckley, *Standing For Something* [New York: Random House, Inc., 2000], 103, 106–107.)

But bear in mind that the Lord is directing this world. We are frequently reminded that conditions have been so developed in the powers of warfare that an accident or a rash move could set in operation those powers which might destroy our civilization. But let us bear in mind that this world is in the hands of God. All these things will happen only so far as they are in accordance with his plans and his purposes. And *let us not waste our time and our energy and get into a nervous condition about what is going to happen to the world.* . . . The Lord will take care of that. It remains for us to be devoted to the upbuilding of his kingdom and facing whatever conditions may come to us.

(George Q. Morris, *Conference Report*, April 1959, 102; italics added.)

The day is not far distant when this nation will be shaken from centre to circumference. And now, you may write it down, any of you, and I will prophesy it in the name of God. And then will be fulfilled that prediction to be found in one of the revelations given through the Prophet Joseph Smith. Those who will not take up their sword to fight against their neighbor must needs flee to Zion for safety. And they will come, saying, we do not know anything of the principles of your religion, but we preceive that you are an honest community; you administer justice and righteousness, and we want to live with you and receive the protection of your laws, but as for your religion we will talk about that some other time. Will we protect such people? Yes, all honorable men. When the people shall have torn to shreds the Constitution of the United States, the Elders of Israel will be found holding it up to the nations of the earth and proclaiming liberty and equal rights to all men, and extending the hand of fellowship to the oppressed of all nations.

(John Taylor, *Journal of Discourses*, 21:8.)

Neither this nation nor any other nation can do anything more than God permits. He sets up one nation, and puts down another, according to the counsels of his own will. . . . All men are but human; their breath is in their nostrils, and they have no power but that which God gives them. Anything beyond this they are powerless to do; and why, then, should His people fear? We certainly have a work to perform on the earth, and God our Father has selected us for that purpose.

(John Taylor, *Journal of Discourses*, 23:333.)

Men may fail in this country, earthquakes may come, seas may heave beyond their bounds, there may be great drought, disaster, and hardship, but this nation, founded on principles laid down by men whom God raised up, will never fail. . . . Yes, I repeat, men may fail, but this nation won't fail. . . .

I plead with you not to preach pessimism. . . . It is the nation that will stand despite whatever trials or crises it may yet have to pass through.

(Harold B. Lee, *Ye Are The Light of the World* [Salt Lake City: Deseret Book Co., 1974], 350–51.)

Yes, it was here under a free government and a strong nation that protection was provided for his restored Church. Now God will not permit his base of operations—America—to be destroyed. He has promised protection to this land if we will but serve the God of the land. He has also promised protection to the righteous even, if necessary, to send fire from heaven to destroy their enemies (Ether 2:12; 1 Ne. 22:17).

No, God's base of operations will not be destroyed. But it may be weakened and made less effective.

(Ezra Taft Benson, *Conference Report*, Apr. 1962, 104.)

Can you tell me where the people are who will be shielded and protected from these great calamities and judgments which are even now at our door? I'll tell you. The priesthood of God who honor their priesthood, and who are worthy of their blessings are the only ones who shall have this safety and protection. . . . They are at our very doors; not even this people will escape them entirely. . . . If you do your duty, and I do my duty, we'll have protection, and shall pass through the afflictions in peace and in safety.

> (Wilford Woodruff, *The Discourses of Wilford Woodruff*, ed. G. Homer Durham
> [Salt Lake City: Bookcraft, 1946], 230.)

We are fast approaching that moment prophesied by Joseph Smith when he said:

> "Even this nation will be on the very verge of crumbling to pieces and tumbling to the ground, and when the Constitution is upon the brink of ruin, this people will be the staff upon which the nation shall lean, and they shall bear the Constitution away from the very verge of destruction. . . ."

The sentiments of John Adams were these:

> "But whatever may be our fate, be assured that this [Constitution] will stand. . . . It may . . . cost us blood before we are through. It is my conviction, however, that when the Lord comes, the Stars and Stripes will be floating on the breeze over this people.

> (Ezra Taft Benson, *The Constitution, a Heavenly Banner* [Salt lake City: Deseret Book Co., 1987], 28, 32–33.)

Opposition has always existed whenever and wherever the gospel has been taught, but God has set bounds and limits to its influence, and everyone that shall revile against the truth will stand condemned and ultimately fall.

By chapter's end, the relationship between the Lord and his children of covenant is seen fully and poetically.

> (Jeffrey R. Holland, *Christ and the New Covenant* [Salt Lake City: Deseret Book Co., 1997], 291.)

Opposition is not new to the Church. We have had opposition in the past, and we shall continue to have opposition in the future. Do not become discouraged by what others say or do. Stay on the strait and narrow path. You do this by holding fast to the iron rod—the words of God as contained in the scriptures and as given by His living servants on this earth.

I carry with me a statement of the Lord from the Book of Mormon, which my brethren of the Twelve have heard me quote. The passage reads as follows: . . . (3 Ne. 22:17).

> (Ezra Taft Benson, *Ensign*, May 1984, 8.)

"These are perilous times—times of great international turmoil. . . .

We are confronted with economic problems, we are confronted with great faces of evil which wash over us like a flood. . . . I would just like to say that whatever happens in the world . . . that God will be with us. He will watch over us. He will protect us. He will see that we are provided for. And we shall endure under His watchful care if we will be true and faithful and obedient and harken to His word."

President Hinckley told Church members they may be inconvenienced, they may suffer a curtailment of some of their liberties, they may find themselves in more economic difficulties.

"But," he promised, "the peace of the Lord will be with us sustain us and help us go forward if we will be faithful and true unto the Lord."

(Gordon B. Hinckley, *Church News*, Feb. 22, 2003, 3.)

"If we will do our part, and if we will fulfill our destiny we will achieve exactly what the Lord has for us, and we will be protected in doing it. . . . You do not need to fear about anybody. Just serve the Lord and keep his commandments and build the Kingdom, and as you do so you will be protected in these last days. God will have his hand over you, and you can plan your lives in confidence"

(Mark E. Peterson, *CR*, Oct. 1960, 81–83).

3 Ne. 23:1–3 GREAT ARE THE WORDS OF ISAIAH
(3 Ne.16:17–20; 20:11–12; Morm. 8:23)

Isaiah spoke to scattered Israel and the Gentiles throughout many centuries, not just to the Israelites of his time (3 Ne. 23:2). Thus, any one group of people (such as Latter-day Saints) in a particular time might not easily understand how his message would apply directly to them. Many of his prophecies had double or even triple fulfillment in later generations.

(Victor L. Ludlow, *Unlocking the Old Testament* [Salt Lake City: Deseret Book Co., 1981], 151.)

The Savior's exhortation to "search" Isaiah's writings "diligently" is instructive. His choice of words suggests that more than a casual reading of the text is required to best comprehend and be blessed by the prophet's message. Rather than a quick and superficial "frisk" of text, the Lord is asking for a thorough and careful investigation, looking for clues, insights, and evidences that will edify and enhance our understanding.

(Terry Ball, *Thy People Shall Be My People and Thy God My God:*
The 22nd Annual Sidney B. Sperry Symposium [Salt Lake City: Deseret Book Co., 1994], 17.)

When the Savior commands us to read Isaiah, we should respond. But to understand it, we must read the Book of Mormon along with it, for that volume opens our eyes to the genuine meaning in his words. And further, we must look to the teachings of the Prophet Joseph Smith, who also provides valuable background for those ancient prophecies.

It is sad indeed to read the efforts of both Jewish and Gentile scholars as they try to interpret some of Isaiah's words. . . .

Isaiah is definitely for today. His dealings with the ancient kings of Judah and his confrontations with them over the attacks of the Assyrians and the Babylonians are all in the past. Reference to them is strictly historical and has little relevance for us.

But his writings concerning Christ, the restoration of the gospel, the gathering of the Twelve Tribes, and the second coming of the Lord are all relevant—very much so. In them he writes both *about* us and *to* us who live right now. He not only tells much about the restoration of the gospel that has already taken place, such as the coming forth of the Book of Mormon, but he also foretells the signs of the coming of Christ. The signs of the times are now all about us. Shall we not give heed to them?

(Mark E. Petersen, *Isaiah for Today* [Salt Lake City: Deseret Book Co., 1981], 6–8.)

Not only are Isaiah's writings distinctive but the man himself seems to stand out as an anomaly when compared with other prophets of his dispensation. When we think of an Old Testament prophet, we may picture a humble, simple man, one living in the wilderness and being fed by ravens like Elijah the Tishbite (1 Kgs. 17:3–4), or perhaps a gatherer of sycamore fruit and a herdsman like Amos (Amos 7:14). Isaiah seems to have been a man of relatively high social station who could find audience with kings (see, for example, Isa. 37:1–73; 38:1). Josephus proposes that King Hezekiah was actually Isaiah's son-in-law. Moreover, the complexity and beauty of his writings, complete with all the poetic elements of metaphor, parallelism, and elevated language, reflect his station as a well-educated man. Furthermore, Isaiah enjoyed exceptional longevity as an Old Testament prophet, serving half a century from about 740 B.C. to about 690 B.C. under four different kings of Judah: Uzziah, Jotham, Ahaz, and Hezekiah (Isa. 1:1). . . .

A pseudepigraphic work known as the Martyrdom and Ascension of Isaiah records that Isaiah's life ended when he was sawn in half by King Hezekiah's wicked son Manasseh, a claim supported by Josephus. See "Martyrdom and Ascension of Isaiah," in *The Old Testament Pseudepigrapha*, ed. James H. Charlesworth (Garden City, N.Y.: Doubleday, 1985), 163. See also Ginsberg, *Legends of the Jews*, 4:279. The circumstances surrounding the martyrdom are different in the Josephus account, but both accounts identify Manasseh as the one responsible for Isaiah's tragic death.

(Terry B. Ball, *Voices of Old Testament Prophets:*
The 26th Annual Sidney B. Sperry Symposium, [Salt Lake City: Deseret Book Co., 1997], 47, 57–58.)

Isaiah, when facing a difficult teaching situation, did not use the parable as a tool; instead, he veiled his message in clouds of symbolism, poetry, and complex terminology. In other words, instead of speaking at a simple level and letting his listeners build upon that foundation, Isaiah spoke at a high intellectual and spiritual level, thus challenging or even forcing his listeners to attain that level before they could begin to understand his words. Isaiah was not only difficult, he was deliberately difficult. We must study his words, wrestle with them, and ponder them at great length before his powerful, sublime teachings begin to emerge and inspire us. Because of this, it is easy to become discouraged and give up before we begin to understand his message. However, through serious and prayerful study, when we finally grasp the language and ideas of a particular chapter until they not only make sense, but enlighten and inspire as well, we realize that we have arrived at a profound level of understanding.

(Victor L. Ludlow, *Isaiah: Prophet, Seer, and Poet* [Salt Lake City: Deseret Book Co., 1982], 134–35)

Moroni 10:31   **BEAUTIFUL GARMENTS, DAUGHTER OF ZION**
(Isa. 52:1–2; 54:2; refer in this text to 3 Ne. 20:36 & 3 Ne. 22:2)

This is a season for strength. I conclude with these stirring words of Moroni, written as he sealed his record to come forth in the dispensation of the fulness of times: . . . (Moro. 10:31–32).

Put on thy beautiful garments, O daughters of Zion. Live up to the great and magnificent inheritance which the Lord God, your Father in Heaven, has provided for you. Rise above the dust of the world. Know that you are daughters of God, children with a divine birthright. Walk in the sun with your heads high, knowing that you are loved and honored, that you are a part of his kingdom, and that there is for you a great work to be done which cannot be left to others.

God be thanked for the wonderful women of this Church. May he plant in your hearts a sense of pride in your capacities and a conviction of truth which shall be a rudder to keep you safe through every storm.

(Gordon B. Hinckley, *Ensign*, Oct. 1983, 84.)

About the Author

K. Douglas Bassett is a graduate of Brigham Young University and received his doctoral degree from the University of New Mexico. He has taught seminary, religion classes at BYU, and is currently an instructor at the Orem Institute of Religion. Brother Bassett and his family enjoy a variety of activities, including basketball, racquetball, weightlifting, motorcycling, and horseback riding. He and his wife, the former Arlene Chapman, live in Mona, Utah, and are the parents of eight children.